WOMEN, DEVELOPMENT AND SURVIVAL IN THE THIRD WORLD

WOMEN, DEVELOPMENT AND SURVIVAL IN THE THIRD WORLD

Haleh Afshar

LONGMAN
London and New York

Longman Group UK Limited,
Longman House, Burnt Mill, Harlow,
Essex CM20 2JE, England
and Associated Companies throughout the world.

*Published in the United States of America
by Longman Inc., New York*

© Longman Group UK Limited 1991

First published 1991

British Library Cataloguing in Publication Data
Afshar, Haleh, 1944 –
    Women. development and survival in the Third World.
    1. Developing countries. Economic developments. Role of women. Social
    aspects
    I. Title
    330.91724

ISBN 0-582-03492-2 CSD
ISBN 0-582-03494-9 PPR

Library of Congress Cataloging–in–Publication Data
    Afshar, Haleh, 1944–
        Women, development, and survival in the Third World / by Haleh Afshar.
            p. cm.
        Includes bibliographical references.
        ISBN 0–582–03492–2 : £17.00 (est.). — ISBN 0–582–03494–9 (pbk.) :
    £8.95 (est.)
        1. Women in development—Developing countries.   2. Women–
    –Employment—Developing countries.   3. Rural development—Developing
    countries.   I. Title.
    HQ1240.5.D44A37   1991
    307.1'412'091724—dc20

                                                        89–13825
                                                        CIP

Set in 10/11 Times

Produced by Longman Singapore Publishers (Pte) Ltd.
Printed in Singapore

CONTENTS

ACKNOWLEDGEMENTS

I would like to thank the University of York's Open Lecture Series Committee as well as the Centre for Women's Studies and the Department of Politics and the Development Studies Association for funding and facilitating the meetings where the chapters of this book were presented and discussed. I should also like to thank each and evey one of our contributors, who agreed to participate in this project from various universities, government department and even a State prison. Many travelled to York from the four corners of the world to pull together the strands that form the arguments of this book. Their courage, pervasive good humour and prompt responses were sisterly and invaluable.

I would also like to thank Maurice Dodson, without whose constant help, support and encouragement this book would not have been completed.

Haleh Afshar

We are grateful to the International Labour Office for giving permission to reprint 'Agricultural mechanisation and the labour use: a disaggregated approach' by Bina Agarwal, which appeared in the International Labour Review, 120(1), January-February 1981: 115–27, and to Sage Publication, New Delhi for giving permission to reprint 'Institutional credit as a strategy towards self-reliance for petty commodity producers in India: a critical review' by Jana Everett and Mira Savara, which appeared in *Invisible Hands: Women in Home Based Production*, 1987, pp. 178–228.

Part One

DEVELOPMENT AND SURVIVAL STRATEGIES

Chapter One

WOMEN AND DEVELOPMENT:
MYTHS AND REALITIES;
SOME INTRODUCTORY NOTES

The process of development in the Third World has, by and large, marginalised women and deprived them of their control over resources and authority within the household, without lightening the heavy burden of their 'traditional duties'. A group from the Centre for Women's Studies at the University of York, in collaboration with colleagues in the field, addressed this aspect of subordination of women in an open lecture series which formed the basis of this book.

The group was all too aware that women's position is structured by a double set of determinants arising from relations of gender and relations derived from the economic organisation of society and that it is necessary to understand the dynamics of capitalism and imperialism to grasp the complexities of the structures that shape the subordination of women. To do so the contributors have adopted a wide interdisciplinary approach to analyse the historical context as well as the socio-economic dimensions of the experience of women and underdevelopment.

We begin by outlining the strategies that women have adopted in the contexts of differing historical and political experiences which permit different and specific solutions.[1] In all cases, however, there is an expectation that the process of development and economic prosperity would benefit women. A historical overview of Iranian women embattled against the veil provides a clear example of such hopes. But, as demonstrated by the Chinese development policies, prosperity can only benefit women if their interest is specifically noted by policy-makers – a provision that is not easily available to countries fighting against poverty, oppression, imperialism and, as in Nicaragua, experiencing economic underdevelopment as a result. Nevertheless women need to and do create alternative strategies of survival either by explicitly seeing their 'careers' in terms of provision of livelihood for their dependants, as is the case in Nigeria, or by engaging directly in food production. Thus the reality of economic need breaks through the barriers of historical misconceptions. Yet at

1

the same time historical perceptions of women as dependants have led to development policies that marginalise women and tend to confine them to the subsistence, rural sector. The studies of the rural sector help to highlight the difficulties faced by women cultivators, who do much of the work and have little formal entitlement to the lands they cultivate. But if and when they manage to acquire control over the cultivation, as was the case in Vietnam, women are unlikely to abandon such rights willingly.

Despite the specificities of women's experience, there is a general agreement that the process of development could benefit women only if and when it addresses the double burdens of production and reproduction carried by women. The case studies from India help to highlight the dilemmas of women workers and development planners. The fragmentation of development projects and separation of rural and urban concerns work on the whole to the detriment of recipients of governmental assistance as a whole and female recipients in particular. It is only if and when policies are integrated that there can be any realistic expectation of success. Even then those who are employed on the margins of urban economies remain constrained by absence of resources and opportunities. Once they move into the formal sector and negotiate protective legislations which permit them to carry their double burden, women become too costly and are marginalised by employers. Too often the solution appears to be home working with all the disadvantages of informal sector employment.

We offer no international solution, but each study provides a specific path for the women concerned to follow towards negotiating better terms and conditions. The process of development *per se* does not carry internally consistent liberating measures. But it does allow struggles against oppression to take place within a context of greater relative prosperity where there may be room for negotiation for better terms.

THE HISTORICAL PERSPECTIVE

What unites all women in developing nations is the remaining hope that organisation, education and resistance would in the long run provide many with a means of escaping from, or at the very least loosening the tight grip of, poverty and subordination. When times are hard and prospects grim, women turn to discover their own history to find room for such hopes and expectation. Taking the widest historical perspective thus enables those who are struggling against difficult odds to gain heart.

Haleh Afshar's chapter provides a more specific study of the interplay of myths and realities in shaping both the internal and the international views and politics concerning Iranian women. Burdened with the images of harem, veil and seclusion, Iranian women were in reality instrumental in helping in a constitutional monarchy, fuelling a constitutional revolution in 1906 and sustaining a fragile democracy by selling their own jewellery, setting up their own bank and launching international campaigns reaching out to Britain, Russia and elsewhere. The short-lived nature of their successes and their return to formal segregation in the 1980s also need much closer analysis and explanation than what has been on offer. Afshar places the historical process in a socio-economic context and analyses the roles of Islamic and modernisation ideologies in enforcing subjugation on Iranian women.

Although the process of modernisation with its emphasis on capital accumulation and the move away from artisan production is not of itself necessarily gender-specific, its effect has often been to deprive many poorer women of ready access to a reliable revenue based on subsistence production. This process has been reinforced by the male-orientated development projects and employment opportunities in the capitalist, waged sector which has reinforced the subordination of women. It is only if and when development policies are addressed directly to women and formulated for them that they may be able to alleviate their plight. Historically such attention to the cause of women is seen to have been paid more readily by revolutionary governments. Even then the location of women's experiences within more general frameworks, such as class analysis or efficiency requirement, may well prove detrimental to women.

WOMEN-CENTRED POLICIES

We were weary of the tendency to generalise about women; although in their biological and reproductive roles women experience a communality of functions and responsibilities, they are less cohesive in their experiences of domesticity and the extent to which the double burden of nurturing and productivity come into daily conflict. Wealthy Third and First World women are better described as 'home managers', often able to pass the domestic responsibilities to others. Nor do all Third World women share the denigrating radical views on motherhood and domesticity, often too readily transcribed from western literature by some members of the bourgeoisie. On the other hand it is essential not to underestimate the role of domestic violence and the interrelations of power and gender

3

within the marriage and household as they affect women and their participation in the process of development. Many feminists in the Third World and their counterparts in the First have developed specific feminist perspectives and theories according to the realities, complexities and particularities of each region, and appropriate strategies have been drawn up by women for women in order to initiate change.

In this we were all too aware of the different 'gender interests' that may operate within each society and the difficulty of formulating any policies that would find universal applicability even within societies.[2] In China, for example, as Delia Davin explains, it was necessary to separate out the oppression of women from their class oppression by the feudalists, and to recognise that gender discrimination operated across class and economic strata and was nourished by cultural practices such as patrilocal marriages. It is only through recognition of the detrimental effects of such practices, which render daughters a burden and sons an asset to households, that it is possible to liberate women. Sadly, economic parameters, which are gaining ground in China as elsewhere, mask these implications and identify women as 'natural' nurturers. The misconceptions which place the burden of domesticity on the shoulders of women alone make them too expensive to employ both in ideological and economic terms and pave the way for open discrimination against women.

By contrast, the long-running war in Nicaragua has made it necessary both economically and ideologically to employ women in previously all-male occupations. Yet 'the revolution did not demand the dissolution of women's *identities*, it did require the *subordination* of their *specific interest* to the broader [revolutionary] goals'.[3] Nevertheless it is women themselves who have highlighted the controversial issues of sexism. As Mary Stead's chapter shows, Nicaraguan women are all too aware of the experience of working women elsewhere, where wartime equality was reversed once the men returned from the war. As a result there has been a continuous attempt to legislate against sexual discrimination, in the knowledge that making a reality out of laws is in itself a major problem. But once men are at war, it is women who carry the exclusive burden of child-rearing, and need to earn a livelihood for the family. It is at this point of need for large numbers of women that political organisation and struggles come to the fore. Unlike Iran, whose large population has allowed the government to retain the gendered division of labour, Nicaraguans, of necessity have had to facilitate the participation of women in the labour market on terms and conditions that permit them to carry the double burden.

It is the responsibility of providing an economic livelihood for children that has created the need to facilitate female employment in Nicaragua. In the case of Yoruba women this need is perceived in terms of the concept of a career. As Carolyne Dennis's chapter demonstrates, the ability to generate successfully a reliable income reinforces the position of a woman in her husband's household and strengthens her ability to educate her children. Here it is not that the men are elsewhere, but the fact that the responsibility for raising the children, both physically and economically, rests with women.

However, whereas in Nicaragua the war has forced the government to recognise the contributions of women to the labour market, and adopt a 'political model of development', in Nigeria, the International Monetary Fund's restructralist policies have led to the opposite out-come. As households are forced back into subsistence as a result of these policies, so the basis of a career is lost to women. They lose their access to resources with which to generate an income and become unpaid household labour.

In many respects the economic policies of structural adjustment embody the classic misconceptions that planners have had about women, either not seeing them as economic agents at all, or merely labelling them as profligate consumers. Joanna de Groot looks at the social and economic responsibilities of women in the Third World, before and during the penetration of capitalism, to analyse how these roles were perceived by foreign observers and how these perceptions in the long run were translated into various myths and misconceptions concerning women. All too often such misconceptions were fundamental in the formulation of policies which served to undermine the social and economic position of women. By analysing the history of the assumptions and images imposed on the Third World and on women during the nineteenth and twentieth centuries, it will be possible to understand the neglect and misconception of Third World women's situation and interest which characterise the work of observers, scholars and development 'experts' both past and present.

THE RURAL EXPERIENCE

The analytical framework that posits nurturing and liberation as contradictory goals also views women in the rural sector in the Third World as 'not integrated' into the development process. The outcome of such analysis is either to reinforce the subordination of women and endorse such domesticity or to seek to liberate women from such chores and 'integrate' them into the modernisation process – this without realising that women are already part and parcel of the process, but have been integrated at the very lowest levels and into the unpaid or least well-paid occupations.

The process of situating women at the lowest levels of the economy is the concern of the second part of the book, which outlines the experience of rural women and the effect of differing political contexts in delineating their rights and obligations. Anne Akeroyd's chapter discusses the contradictory effects of the reality of women in southern Africa finding themselves located within small-scale subsistence rural production in the context of economistic assumptions about the non-productiveness of women and stagnation of subsistence sector. Anne Akeroyd looks at women cultivators in Zambia, Zimbabwe and Malawi in relation to their access to and control of resources such as land, labour, livestock, money and credit. What emerges is that, whereas women are responsible for 60–80 per cent of food production, they reap little benefit from their labour. Even where they have *de facto* responsibilities, as temporary heads of household, they lack *de jure* control over decision-making and the allocation of resources. The feminisation of poverty is increasing in the region, partly as a consequence of the high proportion of female-headed households; but the unfavourable lot of women and children in male-headed households on agricultural settlement schemes shows that these may offer no panacea.

The impoverishment of rural women is one of the many common experiences of Third World women participating in the development process. Bina Agarwal's chapter on agricultural mechanisation in South Asia looks at the kinds of mechanisations which undermine the participation of women in cultivation and the effect of the introduction of high-yielding varieties of wheat on the use of female labour. Agarwal argues for a gendered disaggregation of agricultural labour. This would highlight the reality shown by Akeroyd – that, for example, in Sub-Saharan Africa the term 'farmer', far from being of the male gender, should denote a female cultivator. In the case of the Indian sub-continent such disaggregation would allow observers to distinguish between the impact of mechanisation on labour displacement and its positive impacts through tube well, and so on, and note the sexual division of the beneficiaries and those who have not been favoured by the process.

This disaggregated analysis is taken further by Cecilia Ng's detailed study of the diffusion of modernisation practices on female labour utilisation. Advanced mechanisation of rice production has very specific impacts on the gender division of labour. In Malaysia, it has led to a reduction in both intensity and variety of work performed by women and a consequent loss of skill and knowledge about rice on their part. The reduction of the importance of female labour in rice production in turn undermines the traditional recognition of women's entitlement to jointly cultivated land. Once rice production becomes more of a male preserve, wives lose their entitlement to joint land on divorce. Cecilia Ng argues that this is in part the result of the ideological separation of women and work which leads to specifically male-orientated modernisation policies of the government.

This provides a clear contrast to the experience of Vietnamese women. Once more, as in China and Nicaragua, a revolutionary process finds it necessary to adopt explicitly women-centred policies. Le Thi Nham Tuyet's chapter highlights the triple revolution that took place in the spheres of production, ideology and culture and science and technology. In the rural sector this led to the participation of women and their families in the movement for agricultural collectivisation. One immediate result was a dramatic increase in the numbers of women participating in cultivation, a rise from 5 per cent of the total female population in 1954 to 46 per cent in 1980. Once more, the need for female labour led to the introduction of measures to curtail rooted discriminatory ideologies and their influences in subordinating women in the rural areas. This was assisted by the changing patterns of household and familial relations. Working women sought and obtained more education, got married later in life and bore fewer children. Formal participation in the productive sector made it necessary for them to gain more knowledge and skill and made child-rearing relatively expensive in terms of opportunity costs.

What all these studies show is the pivotal role of familial obligations in shaping women's lives the world over. On the other hand, governmental policies and development projects can, if formulated with women in mind, facilitate the liberation of women and at the same time lighten their burden of child-bearing and domesticity.

RESOURCES, SKILL AND WAGED EMPLOYMENT: THE INDIAN EXPERIENCE

Aware of the need to analyse specificities, the contributors decided to concentrate on the Indian sub-continent as a case study of problems and possibilities of embarking on women-centred development policies. It is all too obvious that to have such policies is only the first step on a difficult and uncertain path. In the past decades India has been relatively free of long-running imperialist wars, revolutions and IMF restructuring orders. Indian women with their long tradition of unionised formal employment and political activism have carved new and imaginative paths towards organising the informal sector and formulating integrated, women-centred development policies. Their historic struggles are beginning to bear fruit and provide room for much optimism for other women in developing countries.

7

There is much to learn and little room for complacency, but what emerges is the clear indication that if and when women succeed in obtaining resources, then they may be able to embark on the path to survival. But, as Leena Mehendale's case study indicates, the struggle is located both against ideolo/gical misconceptions and against bureaucratic divisions. What women need is an integrated developmental approach; what governments offer are segmented administrative units with differing responsibilities, and little interest in collaboration in the interest of women. If and when the rural urban administrative divide is bridged, as it was in this case, then government-funded training provisions can be linked with government-backed marketing facilities. What is needed is for different parts of the administration to recognise destitute women not as a burden on the nation but an asset for economic development. Once the alternatives to begging and prostitution as a means of gaining a livelihood are in place, then women, even those who had been traditionally offered to beg for the Gods, can reasonably be expected to choose to abandon their degrading lot and fight for successful economic survival.

What the Indian studies show is the need to break down ideological misconceptions about poorer women, particularly the misconceptions that define destitute women as a burden that should be discarded and label them as unemployable. It is essential for those who are fighting for improvement in the lot of impoverished women to obliterate these negative misconceptions. To do so they need to obtain resources, assets and, in particular, money and educational facilities to enable them to move them from the fringe to the centres of economic production. In this process access to institutional credit is a vital strategy for facilitating self-reliance for slum-dwelling, home-based producers. Jana Everett and Mira Savara's study shows the problems that arise even when government policies permit the emergence of women-centred projects. The government agreed to provide low-interest-bearing loans for particular groups of borrowers. These proved to be largely women. But as the existing financial structures are predominantly male-orientated, the organisations staffed by men and the intermediaries between recipients and loans of the traditional views, it was none too easy to provide cheaper loans to destitute women. Furthermore, there was a confusion of goals for bank workers, who saw the measures as suitable for social workers and not bankers. The reluctance of what Jana Everett and Mira Savara call 'street bureaucrats' to deal directly with the women led to the emergence of intermediaries who in turn set up patron–client relations of dependence with the recipients. It was only when women's organisations stepped in and provided not only credit but also organisational support for self-reliance that the subsidised loans began to have a positive impact on the lives of the recipients. The authors conclude that, though necessary, credit alone is not sufficient for breaking down social and economic constraints on women workers in the informal sector.

Nevertheless, as Rohini's study shows, organisation and participation in the formal labour market are not of themselves necessarily a panacea for success. The chapter follows through the experience of working in the modern industrial sector for Indian women and highlights both the problems and the possibilities in terms of creating effective forms of resistance. If women's waged employment does not reduce their responsibility for unwaged domestic work, then not only are they condemned to carrying the double burden, but also they remain perceived as supplementary income-earners and therefore in need of lower pay. The refusal to accommodate reproductive roles as a social duty incumbent on all workers regardless of their gender makes women workers into low-status, high-cost workers. Thus child-caring facilities, maternity leave and protective legislations come to be seen as applicable to women alone, and in the case of textile industries in India led to a fall in the number of women employed.

In the end the recognition of women as the bastion of domesticity tends to move them out of the formal sector and confine them to home-based production. Management comes to prefer to contract out short-term piece-work and abdicate from the provision of social and welfare facilities.

Many of the problems are rooted in the misconceptions about women and their productive role. This is not confined to imposition of stereotypes and inattention by male observers alone. Many women share the common language that denies the existence of women's work as such and carry an ideal image of non-working, home-based, child-rearing women. Such ideals are more likely to ossify into mythologies and beliefs for immigrant women who, while compelled by economic necessity to work in the west, carry the illusion of having non-working antecedents back home. Sallie Westwood's study takes as its starting point the powerful myth that Indian women do not work outside the home. In order to explore this, the final chapter looks at the politics of production in a hosiery factory employing large numbers of South Asian women in the UK and argues that these policies are heavily gendered. Specific areas such as union relations and forms of resistance are analysed in relation to both the formal and informal sectors of employment in India. The chapter concentrates on Gujarat and Bombay, where the textile mills have been an important source of waged work for women. Sallie Westwood argues that gender and class have their material expression in the labour processes through the forms of division of labour and subordination that they produce. What is important is to recognise these and organise to erode those that are detrimental to women. Discussing both Rohini's P. H. and Jana Everett and Mira Savara's studies, this chapter concludes that the Indian experience provides much room for optimism both in terms of increased employment opportunities in the formal sectors for women and the vitality of the informal sector. Falling opportunities in textiles are more than compensated by better prospects in the modern industries; difficulties of formal institutional credit provision have been combated with the women's organisations' own alternative loans.

Despite the many obstacles and problems that Third World women face, there is much scope for optimism, based on the very activities and life experiences of those who choose to fight for the cause and succeed. In their different ways, the chapters of this book address the issues of development, the historical context of underdevelopment and the methods chosen by Third World women to embark on struggles which, though long and hard, are likely to succeed in the long run.

NOTES AND REFERENCES

1   For an analytical discussion, see Deniz Kandiyoti, 'Bargaining with patriarchy'. *Gender and Society*, 2 (3) (Sept. 1988): 274–90.
2   For a detailed discussion, see Maxine Molyneux, 'Mobilization without emancipation? Women's interests: the state and revolution in Nicaragua'. *Feminist Studies*, 11 (2) (Summer 1985): 227–54.
3   Molyneux, 'Mobilization without emancipation?', 229.

Chapter Two

THE EMANCIPATION STRUGGLES IN IRAN: PAST EXPERIENCES AND FUTURE HOPES

Haleh Afshar

There are times in the life of any women's movement when a brief survey of the past may prove of greatest value in providing guidelines for appropriate strategies and hope at moments of desperation. It may be argued that Iranian women are now at such a juncture. In a matter of three or four years they have lost the hard-gained ground fought for for over a century or more, and there are times when the future seems even bleaker than the past. At such times it is salutary to unravel the myths and realities of the past and observe the process by which our predecessors, fighting under much harder conditions, created their own, and not an imported and what is now labelled 'imperialist', form of liberation.

Much of the writings of historians of Iran in the eighteenth and nineteenth centuries tended to concentrate on the lives and deeds of men. Conveniently, Iranian women were hidden under their heavy veils and were confined firmly to the sphere of domesticity. That women were covered is known; they all wore a black veil, the *chador*. In more recent times women wore a short white mask, the *pichet*, and the older generation a long face cover called the *rouband* and a loose pair of trousers held close to the ankles, called a *cahqchur*. The more modern women

> sometimes wore lovely dresses which they allowed to show from under their *chador* and were so clever that they managed to show that part of their face which was the prettiest.[1]

> These clever and fragile people have found a solution for every problem and have coped with the issue of *hejab* extremely well and in public promenades and gardens and religious plays and mournings men and women are well able to see one another almost quite clearly.[2]

Such views of women's 'cleverness' may have been instrumental in the formulation of the laws that stated that 'During late afternoon and evenings in busy streets in Tehran . . . men should walk on one side and women on the other. It was illegal for them to walk on the

11

same side after 4 p.m.' Similarly, 'men and women were forbidden to ride together on the same *doroshkeh* [horse-drawn cabs], this applied even to husbands and wives and to fathers and daughters'.[3] Then as now the imposition of social segregation and public invisibility under the veil was justified in the name of the God of Islam.

Thus what writing there was concentrated on their mysterious apparel and their sexually desirable behaviour within the harems. The little that there is refers in passing to the beautiful harem girls, the luscious life style of the Qajar kings in their harems and the silent, black-clad women of Iran gliding past on separate pavements and travelling in separate carriages and living out their lives in seclusion, darkness and ignorance. A typical example is a report by Ahmad Mirza writing about Fath Ali Shah's wives:

> Those women who were on night duty, two slept in the bed so that whichever side His Majesty rested on, the one who was behind him would hold his head and shoulders and the other would wait for His Majesty in case he wished to turn over and rest his head and shoulders in her arms. Two others took it in turn to rub the Shah's feet. Another would recount tales and entertain His Majesty and another was there to fetch and carry according to the Shah's wishes . . . There were three story tellers, six women for rubbing the Shah's feet and three for rendering any necessary services . . . all in attendance in the royal bed chamber.[4]

Like all myths, there is of course some truth and much imagination. Though there was segregation, and illiteracy was widespread, Iranian women were not ignorant, either about their own fate or about the wider international perspectives. In Iran as elsewhere women, particularly among the middle and upper classes, were beginning to embark on the long and hard struggle for liberation. Though there were harems, women there were not necessarily powerless. By the mid-nineteenth century, during the reign of Nasseredin Shah, many of the harem women were beginning to play an important role in the political activities of the country, not only as individuals, but also as a cohesive group. Perhaps the best-known example of such resistance is the decision of Nasseredin Shah's wives to go against the royal will.

In 1891 the Shah granted a tobacco monopoly to a British company to control this industry from the point of production to consumption. At the time, the smoking of water pipes was common among men and women and the handing over of such a lucrative industry to foreigners caused intense opposition amongst the merchants and their close ally the religious establishment, as well as the general populace. As a result the most eminent Shiite, Haj Mirza Hasan Shirazi, issued a *fetva* (religious order) banning the use of tobacco. The entire nation, including the thousand women of the Shah's harem, obeyed the order and broke their water pipes.

When the Shah smoked a *qalyan* [water pipe] in the presence of his favourite wives and ordered them to follow his example; forthwith, they replied: 'Your Majesty, alcoholic drink is forbidden by Islam and we do not let it pass our lips. Right now tobacco has been forbidden by the senior clergy of the religion. It cannot be made licit for us by the monarch's command'.[5]

In addition to general influence exercised by the harem as a whole, which played its part in the subsequent cancellation of the monopoly in 1892, there were individual women of great political importance in the harem. Not least amongst these was the Shah's mother, Mahde Alia, who was instrumental in securing the throne for her son in 1848 and continued to intervene in national politics, much to the dismay of the Prime Minister, Amir Kabir. Morteza Ravandi, in his *History of Iran*, notes that this lady caused much grief to Amir Kabir and that 'Amir Kabir frequently protested that her interventions prevented him from getting on with the job of government'.[6] The same source also reports that 'There is a suspicion that his lady may have played a part in the troubles that befell Nasseredin Shah's brother Mirza Nayeb and Amir Kabir'.[7] Both of them met with untimely deaths.

In addition to his powerful mother, two of the Shah's wives, Amineh Qods and Anisedoleh, also played significant parts in the government of the country. Amineh Qods held the key to the kingdom's treasury and played a key role in decisions concerning its disbursements. Anisedoleh, who was originally a *siqeh*, temporary wife, was a miller's daughter who, according to Lord Curzon, charmed the Shah by lifting her veil to the Shah when he was out riding. 'She fascinated the monarch so that she was removed next day to the royal harem.'[8] Although she bore no children, her influence over the Shah increased over time. Not only was she elevated to the status of formal wife, of whom she was the third (and there could only be four), but also she secured lucrative appointments for many of her friends and relations and when necessary intervened to retain their posts:

Nasseredin Shah had given the post of Governor General of Fars to his brother Muhammad Taqi Mirza Roknedoleh but after two or three months he decided to give it to someone else. When Roknedoleh learned about this he wrote a brief note to Nasseredin Shah's favourite wife, Fatemeh Khanoum Anisedoleh, asking her to help in the case and stop his dismissal. Anisedoleh then wrote a letter to Nasseredin Shah in these terms: 'I would sacrifice my life for you, it is worth less than the blessed dust under your feet. Not long ago Roknedoleh went to Fars; why do you wish to dismiss him now? If a bigger repayment is needed, he will pay it. If he is dismissed, your majesty's subjects will be dismayed. They will ask why a governor who has scarcely arrived has to be sent back so soon. Please let the eunuch bring back your reply!' Nasseredin Shah wrote at the foot of Anisedoleh's letter: 'To Anisedoleh. Roknedoleh will remain in Fars. Nobody is going to replace him. No repayment is needed'.[9]

Anisedoleh learned French from Madame Golsazeh Farangi, a Frenchwoman married to the painter Abas Shirazi, who had met her in Paris and brought her back to Iran in the 1860s. Speaking a foreign language enabled the Shah's favourite wife to be responsible for receiving foreign female guests, conversing with them and acting as an intermediary between the current western ideas of the time and the Iranian ladies of the harem.

Anisedoleh was one of the royal women who accompanied the Shah on his first trip to Europe in 1872. But in Moscow the monarch decided to send all the accompanying women back to Tehran. Anisedoleh saw this as a serious slight to herself and set about engineering the subsequent downfall of the Prime Minister, Mirza Hossein Khan Sepahsalar, whom she thought responsible for her 'disgrace'.[10]

However, perhaps the most remarkable women of this period were the famous Baha'i philosopher Qoratol Ayn and two of Nasseredin Shah's daughters, Tajelsaltaneh and Malekeyeh Iran. All of them, in their different ways, showed intense awareness of the plight of their sisters, and embarked on learned, well-argued discourses to secure their emancipation.

Qoratol Ayn, whose name was Zarin Taj but who like most noblewomen of her time was best known by her title, has been described by the historian Morteza Ravandi as 'a poet and a freedom fighter' and as 'the first woman to fight for emancipation and die for the cause'.[11] Born in 1817, she was the daughter of one of the leading *ulama* of Qazvin, Haji Mulla Muhammad Saleh Baraqani. Ravandi reports that Quoratol Ayn was a renowned beauty, and Nasseredin Shah sought her hand in marriage but she refused and sent him the following poem:

> Yours is the crown and the reign of the land
> Mine is the path of the wandering dervish
> If the one is high and worthy then it is your due
> If this is bad then it's all I deserve.[12]

She was married off to her paternal cousin and bore him two sons and a daughter. In the meantime, however, she continued her education, which had begun in her father's house, and she became acquainted with the works of the religious leader Sheikh Ahmad Ahsayi, the founder of the Sheikhi school of Shiism. Qoratol Ayn was one of his first disciples and at the age of twenty-nine she decided to abandon her spouse and children and move to classes in Karbala to work and study with Sheikh Ahmad's successor, Siyyid Kazim Rashti. In the event she arrived after his death and set up discussion classes of her own and took to addressing the devout from behind a curtain.

Finally she returned to Iran to work with Seyedeh Babi. Babi, who has been denounced by orthodox Shiias as a heretic, advocated a more enlightened version of Islam which allowed women a higher status and was of the view that Islam, like all faiths, must evolve and should not stagnate at the point left by the Prophet. This 'revisionist' view has earned Babi the ardent hatred of the Muslim orthodoxy in general and the Shiias in particular. It has been said that the enmity between Babis and Shiias resulted in Qoratol Ayn's father and her husband being killed by the Babis in Iran.[13]

Qoratol Ayn continued her struggles, and in 1846 she caused a scandal by appearing unveiled before a Babi meeting at Behdasht in the north-eastern province of Khorasan. Afterwards, in a general round-up of Baha'is, she was put under house arrest in the house of the mayor of Tehran. Five years later she was killed. Sources differ in their explanation; either she died by Nasseredin Shah's order,[14] or because it was feared that she might influence him. In any case she remains one of the renowned heroines of Iranian feminism. At the time her activities were well known beyond the confines of Iran, and the *Asiatic Magazine* reported in 1866:

> How is it possible that a woman, a weak creature in Iran, and then in Qazvin, a place with many famous and influential *ulama*, has been able to attract the government's attention, to stage an uprising and to organise support in such an unfavourable environment? This point has even baffled Iranian historians.[15]

Another unlikely rebel of the time was Tajelsaltaneh, a favourite daughter of Nasseredin Shah. She was engaged to Hassan Khan Shoja Saltaneh at the age of 9 and married to him at 13 and bore him two daughters. But Tajelsaltaneh, who had been educated in the harem and had learned French literature and history, found her marriage intolerable and divorced her husband. But not even her royal birth could prevent him from taking her daughters away to his next wife. In her recently discovered memoirs, Tajelsaltaneh deplores the situation of Iranian women:

> who have been separated from the mass of humanity and treated like beasts, living without hope from morning till night in a prison . . . in houses with walls 3–5 *zar* [metres] high, creatures with bound heads and tied hands, some naked, some weeping and apprehensive day and night . . . held in bondage in the chains of slavery.
>
> Iranian women's lives are either black or white. Either they must wear the black veil and appear in the hideous guise of mourning or don the white shroud and leave this world . . . . I am one of these unfortunate women and prefer the white shroud to the hideous mourning wear, and always abhor that clothing and cover. As compared to this dark, bleak life, death is the harbinger of the brightest day of our lives.[16]

Though confined to the harem, Tajelsaltaneh was familiar with the suffragettes' campaign:

> The suffragettes in Europe defend their rights and pursue their quest at all costs and demand the right to choose, the right to vote for Parliament, the right to participate in political affairs of their country, and they have succeeded . . . . How I wish that I could travel and tell these women, 'When will you who are full of happiness and integrity and are defending your rights and achieving success, throw a glance at this corner of Iran?'[17]

> I regret that Iranian women have been kept apart from the advanced world and have not sought their equal rights.[18]

> It breaks my heart to see those of my gender, to see that women in Iran are unaware of their rights and are not actively seeking their human rights, that they should be sitting wasted and uninformed and useless in the corners of their houses . . . they ought to be aware that they are the mothers of future generations.[19]

In seeking solutions, Tajelsaltaneh did not only refer to the western experience, but also she was well aware that there were women in her own country who enjoyed relative freedom. She was convinced that the ability to participate on an equal footing with men was not only essential to economic development, but that also it would bring improved social and moral conditions:

> If the two thirds of the population who are women worked with the other third of course the country would progress twice as fast . . . . As it is, one male worker earning 2 *qeran* [about 2p] a day supports a household including mother, wife, sister, niece and daughter. But if these five women were educated and able to work in schools, offices, shops or coffee houses, then they would not be a burden on that man, but a support to him.[20]

> One of the results of the general position of women is that since the salaries of this gentleman or that saltaneh, doleh or malek [honorary titles equivalent to duke, knight or marquis] are not enough to meet their perceived needs, they are obliged to steal, to degrade themselves and the people, to sell the country, to destroy their own motherland . . . . Now if women were freed from the veil like all civilised people . . . then life would improve for the country as a whole . . . . This lack of progress is caused by confining women behind the veil.
> We can see that by observing peasant women who along with the men work in the fields . . . there is not a single woman prostitute in the villages since men and women do not marry until each is sufficiently wealthy and since they can see each other's faces they are able to choose their own spouses.[21]

Of course, at that time, peasant women were not constrained, but they were no more free than their urban counterpart. Whereas in towns, women were enclosed in the home and protected and those who were wealthy were confined to idleness, rural women were enslaved and obliged to work from day-break to dusk on the fields and from dusk to dawn in their home. The double burden was eternal and the demands were unending. So although they may not have been imprisoned, the royal view of their existence was far too romantic and created a myth of rural liberation. Nevertheless, such observations naturally led Tajelsaltaneh to support the constitutional movement, which aimed at severely curtailing the powers of her father and even to come to the conclusion that 'today we do not have a more open and extensive school of thought than that of social-ism'.[22] Her support for the constitution was firm and unequivocal:

> Constitutionalism is to fulfil the condition of freedom and progress for a nation without ulterior motives and treachery. Each and every progress-ive nation must shoulder the obligation to achieve such rights.
>
> Since the government of nations rooted in a constitution has a correct foundation on basic rules which facilitate a legal structure and empower the nation to succeed, laws can only be effective when the system of autocracy has been dismantled.[23]

Like her sister Malekeyeh Iran, Tajelsaltaneh began by initiating secret societies to secure a constitutional revolution and subse-quently was one of the founders of the Women's Freedom Society, *Anjomaneh Azadi Zanan*, which held twice-monthly meetings outside Tehran city boundaries and admitted men accompanying their wives or mothers. The princess was convinced that women would make much better politicians than men:

> Surely they would not seek success in terms of ministerial office and high officialdom; they would not ride rough-shod over the populace and their rights; they would not steel the wealth of the Muslim people and sell their country down the river. We would choose the right path and lay a firm foundation for progress. We would not squander the people's wealth to buy splendid palaces, parks and carriages . . . . We would work hard to serve the people . . . . You may laugh and tell me that the men of this land did not find another road to success, how can you, who are an uninformed woman, find a legitimate and appropriate way to progress? But my tutor, is the mind not free? . . I would neither seek to oppress the people nor pursue personal profit, but would seek to secure the success of humanity. I would extend commerce, set up factories . . . factories that would meet the internal demands and make us independent of foreigners and their goods. God has given us plenty of resources; there are oil fields in Bakhtiar that make a fortune of profits; well-used, not handed over to the British, it would lay the foundation for developing our agriculture . . . . We could build roads, organise better distribution of foodstuffs. Like California we could hand over the uncultivated lands to our people and help them to dig water channels, *ganats*, and cultivate the land. We could plant forests, redirect the Karaj river towards Tehran and free people from chronic water shortages and infected water supply. Without thieving and selling our

country to foreigners we could free our own people and progress as a nation.[24]

It is worth noting that all these measures finally found their way on to the political agenda in the course of the next eighty years.

Like her sister, the Princess Malekeyeh Iran was an active constitutionalist and feminist as well as belonging to a dervish order. Married to the famous constitutionalist Zahiredoleh, who led the secret society of the Ekhvan (brethren), Malekeyeh Iran used to attend and address their meetings unveiled. She even had her photograph taken, along with those of their daughters Foruq-ol-molk and Malek-ol-molk, all three wearing the traditional dervish garment and no veil. She was a noted revolutionary, and in 1908, when her brother Muhammad Ali Mirza decided to bombard the Majlis, he also ordered the wrecking and pillage of Malekeyeh Iran's house.[25]

PUBLIC DEMONSTRATIONS

Dressed as they were it was not easy to recognise women, and traditionally it had not been customary to assault them in public. In Iran as elsewhere the very appearance of women on public protest was taken as a sign of the gravity of the situation: 'They have a saying in Tehran that when the women take part in a [riot] . . . the situation becomes serious.'[26] Before the constitutional revolution, women's uprisings almost invariably led to a change of policy, so that, for example, early in Nasseredin Shah's reign, when the inflationary price of copper imported from Britain began to cripple the artisans of the bazaar, the wives of the guildsmen in Isfahan mobilised themselves and took to the streets in public demonstrations; they attacked the British consulate in Isfahan. The consulate reported the event to the British ambassador, who ordered that the price of copper should be halved.[27]

At the time, women protested not only for economic improvements, but also for better standards of morality on the part of the monarch. Thus, for example, some women attacked the royal procession and complained to the Shah that instead of looking after his people both in the city and in the countryside he was wasting his time chasing women and murdering virtuous men.[28]

However, it was during the constitutional revolution that Iranian women came into their own and played a highly visible part in the struggles that ensued. The influential historian Ahmad Kasravi reported:

One of the new features of this revolutionary movement is the disturbances amongst women. These covered-up creatures of the harem who should not have been even heard by outsiders, have now come forth to the battlefields. We see them participating, and effectively so, in the public demonstrations . . . . They grapple with the soldiers . . . take food and water to those who are besieged in the mosques. They have been so successful that Eiynehdoleh has ordered the armed forces to prevent them from taking to the streets and demonstrating.[29]

Similarly, Shuster notes:

It is not too much to say that without the powerful moral force of the so-called chattels of the oriental lords of creation . . . the revolutionary movement, however well conducted by Persian men, would have early paled into a mere disorganised protest. The women did much to keep the spirit of liberty alive.[30]

Initially, in 1906, as in 1979, it was the influence of the religious establishment that brought out the Iranian women on mass demonstrations in Tehran. During both of these periods, the Muslim preachers were the most effective means of communication; honoured as the earthly interpreters of the will of God, they were followed by all in the early years of the century and untroubled by the censors who cut back other forms of public communication in the 1970s. In 1906, as in 1979, it was the disrespect shown by the government to the religious establishment that was used by the latter to orchestrate resistance and bring out the women. The arrest of a number of religious leaders in 1906 was viewed as an unforgivable sin by many women, a group of whom intercepted the royal carriage and stopped the procession!

Yelling and screaming and crying they said: we want our masters and religious leaders! we are Muslims and owe absolute obedience to their commands! They have ratified our marriage contracts, they are the ones who act on our behalves to rent out our houses. In short all our worldly and other-worldly affairs are in the hands of these gentlemen. How could we allow anyone to banish or exile our *ulama*? O Shah of the Muslims, respect the leaders of Islam. O Shah of Muslims, do not denigrate or undermine the leaders of Islam! O Shah of Islam, should Russia or England come to you these leaders could order sixty thousand Iranians to fight a *jehad*, holy war, against them.[31]

The close alliance of the religious establishment and the bazaar merchants and guilds provided believing Muslim women with a justifiable perception of their religious duty to support the constitutional revolution while also giving them the backing of the most conservative social group, that of the petty bourgeoisie. At the same time, the women of the aristocracy and upper middle classes joined forces with the revolutionaries in the hope of obtaining equal opportunities and breaking out of the constraints of the veil. Where, as in Iran at the turn of the century, the elite group is small and the intelligentsia even smaller, discrimination against women may well be superseded by class interest; the paucity of numbers makes every middle class person, male or female, a potential ally. It was certainly the case that amongst the first committees of the constitutionalists, women were both well represented and active. So that, for example, the first revolutionary committee had twenty women in its total of fifty-four members.[32] Frequently these women were the daughters of enlightened *ulama* who had allowed their daughters to be educated, or were related to the old aristocracy or the new upper-class professionals.[33] But the clergy–merchant alliance was instrumental in preventing Iranian women from obtaining equal rights under the first constitution of Iran.

Although undoubtedly women had been effective – and historians such as Kasravi often reported their many successes – the initial decision by the constitutionalists to offer universal suffrage to all was thwarted by the conservative elements. So that although the Fundamental Law of 30 December 1906 and the Supplementary Fundamental Law of 30 September 1907 adopted the principle of universal suffrage, by 1909 (when the first election laws were passed), women, along with imbeciles and minors, were denied the right to vote. This may explain Kasravi's curious comments that

> Women were not very effective during the constitutional movement. But how could they be expected to be – women were ignorant of the meaning of 'country', who did not know what a revolution should be? The freedom fighters had hoped that women would participate, but not much help could be hoped for from veiled women who were separated from the rest of the population.[34]

That is to say, within a very short period the actual sacrifices and activities of women were forgotten and the false myths and perceptions returned. In this respect too we find great similarities between the experiences of Iranian women in the first and eighth decades of this century.

Although Iranian women now have the vote they experience the same discriminatory attitudes when it comes to the veil and employment. Kasravi himself is an eloquent supporter of the view of a segregated labour market, arguing that

> God created women for certain jobs and men for others [others being politics, commerce and the army, which are] very demanding of foresight, being able to keep secrets, patience and fortitude, and these qualities are weak in women . . . . The further they're kept from the domain of politics the better it is.[35]

That Kasravi and others were blatantly wrong can be shown in the bravery of individual women and the success with which groups of Iranian women ran their secret societies. One unnamed woman was reported to have carried a gun under her veil and shot a preacher who was giving a sermon degrading women and the nationalists.[36]

Another woman drew a pistol to shoot at a crowd who had murdered a constitutionalist and were tearing him apart:'She used up all the bullets without hitting anybody. This brave deed infuriated the murderers. All at once they pounced on her and tore her to pieces with daggers and swords and did atrocious things to her.'[37]

Another memorable woman of the period, Qezi, is mentioned by the historian Nazem al Islam Kermani:

> There has been much praise for a woman named Qezi, daughter of Said Mahdi Khan and head of the Sagvand tribe. Much has been said about her beauty and wisdom and bravery and other honourable characteristics. Once, she alone on a horse chased a hundred men on horseback who had been sent to catch her husband, a man named Qassem. She chased these riders for about a *farsakh* (a mile), killed eight and chased the rest away. In short this woman is of such beauty and such virtue that are rarely seen in womankind, and in bravery she is counted among the men of this world and there is none as honourable and respected as this lady.[38]

During the revolutionary uprising she wrote a letter to Modir al Islam to congratulate him on the success of the constitutionalists, warn him against oppressing the peasants in general and the Bakhtiaris in particular and warn him against the closure of the Majlis, Parliament:

> Even if you took an army with all the usual equipment to fight us, it would be useless . . . we have proved this with Eqbal al Doleh and it's unnecessary to repeat it . . . . Eqbal al Doleh with two hundred *foj* (foot soldiers) and three to five hundred cavalry and many guns and much ammunition . . . was unable to fight against a handful of Bakhtiaris, of whom there were never more than ten or fifteen on the battle ground and in this historical dishonour was defeated and ran away . . . .
>
> Now it is time to leave off old prejudices and obey the laws of God and the prescriptions of the *ulama* [who supported the constitutionalists] so that we can get on with a clear mind and pursue our own affairs. God did not create us to amuse and entertain your whims, but created you to serve us and create our peace and comfort for us.
>
> The lamb is not for the shepherd; it is the shepherd who serves the lamb . . . .
>
> If you think of the Indian maharajas, the Egyptian kings, the rulers of Bulgaria and Romania, the lords of Bokhara, the Queen of Madagascar, the Sultan of Burma and elsewhere you will observe that they all respect the peasants in their task and continue to serve their countries and countrymen . . . . .
>
> The people are of the view that you must reinstate a separate administrative power to serve the constitution and remedy past short-comings.

The lady concludes her thoughtful letter by assuring the central authorities that should the government act according to her advice and not interfere with the lives of her tribe 'in such a way as to make it unnecessary to correspond and complain to your

21

highness, we will then secure total calm and will completely set your mind at rest about the affairs of the State in areas south of the capital'.[39]

SECRET SOCIETIES

Little is known about the secret societies formed to fight for equality. We are indebted to Shuster, amongst a few others, for the few details that there are about these societies. In the first instance they grew out of the traditional women's gathering, the *doreh*, that took place on a more or less regular basis amongst family groups. Some remained anonymous but effective, where Morgan Shuster says 'all sorts of moves were being made to thwart the intrigues of traitors to the country; and one of the societies' actions was to gather information about me because I was a pro-Iranian foreign adviser'.[40]

Other societies, such as the Anjomaneh Azadiyeh Zanan (women's freedom society), are better known and held their meetings on a more formal basis outside Tehran city boundaries.[41] All showed great evidence of foresight, patience, fortitude and such success at secrecy that to this day historians have difficulty in untangling the details of their activities. In general these societies demanded independence from Russian intervention and freedom for women. So, for example, in September 1908 the *Comiteyeh Zananeh Iran*, Iran's women's committee, appealed to General Edward Grey to help them in their battles against Russian interference in Iran.[42]

The effectiveness of women's organisations were seen publicly in the massive demonstrations that they organised in December 1911, when, led by a royal Qajar lady, they gathered outside the Majlis, mounted on rostra, and made rousing speeches denouncing the parliamentarians' cowardice before the imperialist demands of Russia (Russia had sent an ultimatum demanding among other things that Shuster should be removed from Iran). On subsequent days they moved to the telegram officer and sent a telegram out to the Majlis protesting against its ineffectiveness. They also appealed to the women's suffragist committee in London: 'The Russian government by an ultimatum demands us to surrender to her our independence; the ears of men in Europe are deaf to our cries; could you women not come to our help?'[43]

The suffragettes responded: 'Unhappily, we cannot make the British government give political freedom even to us, their country-women. We are equally powerless to influence their action towards Persia'[44]

In Iran response came not from the deputies but from the Russian delegation that pointed out that Iranian women had in no way benefited from the constitutional revolution and had no interest in supporting it. The women responded by saying: 'We hope that our position will be improved through the enactment of the code of equality, because human worth and dignity are secured by the improvement and extension of laws and no other way.'[45]

According to the historian Abdolah Razi, the women were so incensed by the Russian intervention that they threatened to murder the parliamentarians:

> Three hundred veiled women carrying guns arrived at the Majlis, threw aside their face covers and threatened the representatives that if they failed to protect the national dignity and honour they, the women, would murder their men folks and then commit suicide.[46]

The Majlis refused to comply with the Russian ultimatum and the cabinet closed the Majlis. But despite the high profile of women and their activities during the early turbulent years of constitutionalism in Iran, subsequent attempts at obtaining the vote were equally unsuccessful. Thus when in 1911 the representative for Hamadan Haj Vakeel Rooyi made an impassioned speech demanding female enfranchisement, the Speaker 'asked the official reporters to make no records in the journals of the House of this unfortunate incident'.[47] A formal explanation offered subsequently was as follows:

> The reason for excluding women is that God has not given them the capacity needed for taking part in politics and electing representatives of the nation. They are the weaker sex, and have not the same power of judgement as men have.[48]

EDUCATION AND PUBLICATIONS

On the whole Iranian women were far more successful in their educational activities than their political ones. If we are to learn anything from the past we must look closely at the publications and the activities of the more or less clandestine groups and women's journals and newspapers and the setting up of formal schooling for girls.

The first girls' school in Iran was set up by American missionaries in 1874, but like its counterpart in the small village of Chilas near Kerman, it admitted only Christian girls. The first Iranian, Touba Azmudeh, to open such a school, (in 1907) belonged typically to the upper middle classes and was the daughter of an army officer, and was married to another. But her example was followed by two remarkable women related to religious leaders. One, Safiyeh Yazdi, was married to a leading *mojtahed* (a religious leader), and the other, Mehresoltan Amir Sehhi, was the daughter of a merchant and the wife of a religious leader – one of the rare occasions when the alliance of the bazaar and the clergy benefited women. These schools were the butt of much opposition and their founders were attacked for opening such dens of 'iniquity'. Despite considerable hostility, the education of women continued, and finally in 1918 the government capitulated and opened ten state schools for girls as well as a women's training college.

These activities were complemented by the publication of journals by various women's groups and societies. The first of these, *Danesh*, was published in 1910, followed by *Shokoufeh*, in 1913. These publications, which had begun with educative intentions, became increasingly more militant, so that by the end of the decade they had adopted an openly liberal position advocating not only education, but also enfranchisement of women and the removal of the veil. These radical journals included *Zabaneh Zanan*, published in 1919, *Nameyeh Banovan* and *Alameh Nesavn*, in 1920 and *Jahaneh Zanan*, in 1921. The political stance of these publications, which came out in Esfahan, Tehran and Mashahd, resulted in the persecution of their editors whose homes were pillaged and who were exiled from their towns and denounced for being anti-Islamic and sources of corruption.

What mattered was the firm perseverance of these women, which played an important part in the eventual removal of the veil in 1936. But central as they remain to the emancipation of women in Iran, the changing international and particularly national climate played a decisive role in paving the way to freedom. With the departure of the Qajar and the coup by Reza Shah in 1922 the country moved to a new phase of modernisation, which included a demand for the paid labour of women in the newly installed textile industries and provided a place for educators to staff the rising numbers of state-funded girls' schools and training institutions. Three decades of political and educational struggles were finally bearing result.

The early days of removal of the veil and admission to the newly opened Tehran University marked the first peak of success. The Faculty of Arts opened with its chairs of European and Russian literature occupied by a woman, Fatemeh Sayah, who had obtained her Ph.D. at Moscow University where, by 1936, she had already been teaching for four years. In the same year Dr Sayah was sent to the seventeenth meeting of the UN in Geneva and became the only Iranian woman to represent her country on a foreign political mission; a distinction that remained unique for the two decades that followed.

With the espousal of the cause of women by the Shah, most independent women's organisations gradually accepted the royal leadership and opted for centrally directed progress. On the whole during the reign of the Pahlavis, the women's cause benefited from the royal patronage and although progress was extremely slow, it did come. The result was enfranchisement in 1963, the introduction of Family Protection laws in 1967 and 1975 which curtailed polygamy and the automatic paternal rights of custody of children on divorce and provided for payment of alimony and legalisation of abortion in 1978. At the same time conditions of women's employment were considerably improved, and crèches and nurseries were made compulsory for all firms employing more than ten mothers of babies or young children. Although many of these legal provisions merely adorned the statute books and lacked the necessary enforcement agencies, undoubtedly the years 1960 to 1970 marked the apex of the success of the Iranian women's movement.

THE POST-REVOLUTIONARY STRATEGIES

The Islamic revolution of 1979 was strongly supported by women, who took part in massive numbers in the street demonstrations and who played their part in the Islamic resistance movements that preceded the revolution. Although some of the intelligentsia and many middle-class women became rapidly disillusioned and began mobilising against the Islamification process, there are still many women who support the post-revolutionary government despite its oppressive measures.

In Iran, as in Pakistan and other Islamifying countries, the success of the grip of ideology is most clearly seen by the apparel and demeanour of women. Islam's firm hold is demonstrated through the elimination of women from the public domain and by attempts at making women physically invisible by wrapping them in the Islamic *hejab* (cover). Once more, Iranian women are expected to don the black and white wraps so despised by Tajelsaltaneh. It is, however, the similarities of the ideologies of oppression and some of the social conditions imposed on women that makes the experience of the past so valuable.

Furthermore, Iranian women now have the experience of some thirty years of compulsory, free, primary education. Although, like most legal provisions, those dealing with literacy fell far short of their aims, nevertheless a large percentage of urban women in Iran are literate and all still retain the memory of a more open labour market and a past when paid employment, at least in the informal sector, was a feasible alternative to destitution. Whereas the memoirs of Tajelsaltaneh are among the few contemporary protests against the oppression of women at the turn of the century which have yet been discovered, current women's magazines in Iran regularly print a constant stream of protest not against the veil, which is the official emblem of Islam and as such unassailable in the media, but against the injustices of polygamy, of easy divorce, of absence of rights to matrimonial property and the unresolvable problems of destitution that befall 'unprotected' divorced women, problems which are severely exacerbated by the state's policies of exclusion of women from all but a few professions. Thus whereas in the early years of the twentieth century resistance to the veil and demand for education were voiced largely if not exclusively by the privileged middle classes, currently in Iran many of the poorer women are lending their support to the battles for the removal of discriminatory practices against women in the public domain and at work places.

Within two years of its inception, the Islamic Republic had marginalised women in all domains. They have been excluded from large areas of education, particularly law, sciences, engineering and agriculture, the only exceptions being medicine, midwifery and nursing. Large numbers have been moved out of the civil service, and the Qassas laws of 1981 deprived them of the right to give uncorroborated evidence before any court, corroboration being required from a male witness, and apportioning rights of retribution for men against women, but making women's rights and blood money considerably less than those of men. Ousted from the public domain, denied the right of equality before the laws, women have been admonished to return to their domestic role, and to facilitate this the legal age of marriage has been brought down from 18 to 13 years for girls. Polygamy and temporary marriages have been reinstated, as has the unquestioned right of custody which has been returned to fathers and paternal ancestors and taken away from mothers. Thus once more Iranian women have to embark on the long struggle for freedom.

Now, as at the turn of the century, it is the unholy alliance of the *ulama* and the bazaar that poses the severest threat to liberation of women. The religious establishment in particular has become the bastion of reactionary attitudes to women, and the merchants and petty bourgeoisie are willing participants in the oppression of their wives, mothers and daughters. Furthermore, the nine long years of war and the state policy of exclusion of women from the formal labour market has left many with the honourable but unpaid titles of 'mothers of martyrs' which brings little earthly reward. Now that the war has ended and the men begin returning from the front, what little marginal female employment that had been permitted is disappearing and the situation of women is likely to get worse before it gets better. This is particularly problematic since, unlike the USA and the UK during the world wars, and Iraq during the Gulf war, the rate of female employment in Iran has been falling rather than rising during the war years.[49]

Nevertheless, active groups are fighting for improved conditions. Some have returned to forming secret societies, others, particularly those working with the left-wing Fadayan and the Islamic Mojahedin, have agreed to relegate the women's question to a future time. All rely on journals, handouts, secret meetings and public broadcasts to voice their views, and all claim differing degrees of support amongst different groups of women. But perhaps the most effective groups in action are women working in factories who have simply refused to give up their jobs, despite repeated requests from the factories' Islamic Councils.[50] Whereas the early feminists in Iran were largely members of the middle and upper classes, there is now a cross-class interest that unites the affluent and the poor in their battles against the establishment. The awareness of the successes in the past, when the struggle was conducted against greater odds and with fewer resources, makes for much optimism amongst women fighting what may otherwise seem like a lost cause.

NOTES

1   Morteza Ravandi, *Takhireh Ejtemayieh Iran*, vol 3, 2nd edn (Amir Kabir Publications, Tehran, 2536), p. 729.
2   Ibid., p. 721.
3   Badrelmoluk Bamdad, (ed. and trans. by R.R.C. Bagley) *From Darkness to Light*, (Exposition Press, New York, 1977), pp. 16 and 17.
4   *Tarikheh Azodi*, p. 3–17, quoted by Ravandi, *Takhireh Ejtemayieh Iran*, p. 717.
5   Bamdad, *From Darkness to Light*, p. 9.
6   Ravandi, *Takhireh Ejtemayieh Iran*, p. 719.
7   Ibid.
8   G.N. Curzon, *Persia and the Persian Question* (London, 1966), p. 408, quoted by Mongol Bayat-Phillip, in 'Women and Revolution in Iran', in Lois Beck, and Nikkie Keddie, *Women in the Muslim World* (Cambridge, MA, Harvard University Press, 1978), p. 297.
9   Anisdedoleh's letter and Nasseredin Shah's replies are reproduced in facsimile in Mokhberodoleh's book *Khaterateh va Khaterat* (Tehran, 1950), quoted by Bamdad, *From Darkness to Light*, p. 50.
10   Ibid.
11   Ravandi, *Takhirek Ejtemayieh Iran*, p. 721.
12   Ibid.
13   Hoda Mahmoudian, 'Tahira: an Early Feminist', in A. Fathi (ed.), *Women and the Family in Iran* (E.J. Brill, Leiden, 1985), p. 83.
14   Ibid.
15   *Asiatic Journal* 7, (1866) p. 474, quoted in *Nimeh Digar*, 1, year 1 (Spring 1984), p. 99.
16   Khaterateh Tajolsaltaneh, in Fereydoun Adamiat and Homa Nateq

(eds), *Afkareh Ejtemayi va Sia va Eqtesadi as Assareh Montasher Nashodeh Deoeyeh Qajar*, p. 157.

17 Ibid.
18 Ibid.
19 Ibid.
20 Ibid., p. 158.
21 Ibid.
22 Ibid., p. 159.
23 Ibid., p. 260.
24 Ibid., p. 163.
25 Ibid., p. 163–4
26 Bamdad, *From Darkness to Light*, p. 32.
27 Ravandi, *Takhireh Ejtemayieh Iran*, p. 729.
28 Ibid., p. 721.
29 Ahmad Kasravi, *Khaharan va Dokhtaraneh Ma* (Tehran, 1944), pp. 17–19, quoted by Carol Regan, in 'Kasravi's Views on the Role of Women', in A. Fathi, (ed.), *Women and the Family in Iran* (E.J. Brill, Leiden, 1985), p. 63.
30 Morgan Shuster, *The Strangling of Persia* (New York, 1968), p. 195.
31 Ahmad Kasravi, *Qanouneh Mashroutiat*, quoted in *Donya*, the journal of the Tudeh Party (Dey, 1358) (10 November, 1979), p. 77.
32 Nazemol Eslam Kermani, *Tarikheh Bidariyeh Iranian* (Bonyadeh Farhangeh Iran, Tehran, 1972), vol. 1, p. 121.
33 Roshanak Mansouri, 'Chehreyeh zan dar jarayedeh mashroutiat', in *Nimeh Digar*, 1, Year 1 (Spring 1984), p. 14.
34 Kasravi, *Khaharan va Dokhtaraneh Ma*, pp. 18–20.
35 Ibid.
36 Mansouri, 'Chehreyeh zan dar jarayedeh mashroutiat', p. 26.
37 From *Secrets of the Iranian Struggles for Constitutional Government*, quoted by Bamdad, *From Darkness to Light*, p. 41.
38 Nezamolsaltaneh Kermani, *Tarikheh Bidariyeh Iranian*, vol 1, pp. 306–9.
39 Ibid.
40 Morgan Shuster, *The Strangling of Persia* (New York 1968) p. 195.
41 Shuster, *The Strangling of Persia*, quoted by Bamdad, *From Darkness to Light*, p. 28.
42 For more details, see Shuster, *The Strangling of Persia*; Bamdad, *From Darkness to Light*; and Sansarian, 1982.
43 Mansouri, 'Chehreyeh zan dar jarayedeh mashroutiat', p. 25, and Bayat-Philip, 'Women and revolution in Iran', p. 299.
44 *The Times*, Dec. 1911, quoted by Mansouri, 'Chehreyeh zan dar jarayedeh mashroutiat', and Bayat-Phillip, 'Women and Revolution in Iran'.
45 Ibid.
46 Quoted by Bamdad, *From Darkness to Light*, p. 39.
47 Abdolah Razi, *Takhireh Kameleh Iran* (Eqbal Publications, Tehran), pp. 564–5.
48 *The Times*, 22 Aug. 1911, quoted by Bayat-Phillip, 'Women and Revolution in Iran', p. 301.

49 For further discussion see Haleh Afshar 'Ideology not structural adjustment in Iran' in H. Afshar and Carolyne Dennis (eds) *Structural Adjustment and Women in the Third World,* (Macmillan, London, 1991), and Val Moghadam 'Women, work and ideology in the Islamic Republic of Iran', *International Journal of the Middle East Studies,* May 1988 pp. 221–43 and *Nimeyeh Digar* No. 10 Winter 1368 pp. 16–51.

50 Haleh Afshar 'Women in the Work and Poverty Trap in Iran' in Haleh Afshar and Bina Agarwal (eds) *Women, Poverty and Ideology in Asia,* (Macmillan, London, 1989) pp. 17–24.

REFERENCES

Adamiat, Fereydoun and Nateq, Homa (eds), *Afkareh Ejtemayi va Siasi va Eqtesadi as Assareh Montasher Nashodeh Deoeyeh Qajar*; 'Khaterah Tajolsaltaneh'.
Asiatic Journal, 7, 1866.
Bamdad, Badrelmoluk, *From Darkness to Light* (ed. and trans. by F.R.C. Bagley, (Exposition Press, New York, 1977).
Bastani, Parizi, *Takhireh Azadi: Mohiteh Siasi va Zendeganieh Moshi-rodeloeh Pirnya,* (Tehran, 1969).
Bayat-Phillip, Mongol, 'Women and Revolution in Iran', in Lois Beck and Nikkie Keddie (eds), *Women in the Muslin World,* (Cambridge, MA, Harvard University Press, 1978).
Curzon, G.N., *Persia and the Persian Question* (London, 1966).
Donya, the journal of the Tudeh Party.
Kasravi, Ahmad, *Khaharan va Dokhtaraneh Ma* (Tehran, 1944).
— *Qanouneh Mashroutiat.*
Kermani, Nazem al Islam, *Tarikheh Bidariyeh Iranian* (Bonyadeh Farhangeh Iran, Tehran, 1972).
Mansouri, Roshanak, 'Chehreyeh zan dar jarayedeh mashroutiat', in *Nimeh Digar,* 1, Year 1 (Spring 1984).
Mokhberodoleh *Khaterat va Khaterat*eh (Tehran, 1950).
Nimeh Digar
Ravandi, Morteza, *Takhireh Ejtemayieh Iran,* vol. 3, 2nd edn (Amir Kabir Publications, Tehran 2536).
Razi, Abdolah, *Takhireh Kameleh Iran* (Eqbal Publications, Tehran).
Regan, Carol, 'Kasravi's Views on the Role of Women', in A. Fathi (ed.), *Women and the Family in Iran* (E.J. Brill, Leiden, 1985).
Shuster, Morgan, *The Strangling of Persia* (New York, 1968).
The Times (London).

Chapter Three

CHINESE MODELS OF DEVELOPMENT AND THEIR IMPLICATIONS FOR WOMEN

Delia Davin

Since the establishment of the People's Republic in 1949, China has been struggling for 'development'. However, great changes have taken place in the way that development is conceived of and worked for. Until the death of Mao Zedong in 1976, the development model used was basically a political one, whereas since the late 1970s it has been primarily economic. This is a simple way of summing up the transformation which has affected almost every area of Chinese social and economic policy and the everyday lives of China's enormous population. In this chapter I discuss the implications of these changes for women in an attempt to see what benefits and drawbacks the two models have had for women.

From its inception, women were on the Chinese Communsit Party's agenda for the revolution. It was for women both a strength and a weakness of the Communist Party's analysis that it saw women's oppression as an integral part of feudal and bourgeois class oppression and women's liberation as a necessary and inevitable part of socialist revolution. It was a strength because it meant that the Party was committed to liberating women, but a weakness because, in locating women's oppression in the class system, this analysis failed to explain, or even to recognise, major elements of that oppression. After 1949, discriminatory attitudes, actions and behaviour towards women tended to be dismissed as mere 'feudal remnants', a soothing explanation which implied that they would gradually disappear. Unfortunately this has not been the case.

The Party was committed to bringing about women's emancipation through involving them in productive work outside the home, and through legal reforms designed to produce sexual equality in the family, and equal political and economic rights. A programme of this sort was evolved in the first areas to be administered by the Communist Party, the Chinese soviets of the late 1920s and the early 1930s, and it continued to be developed and refined through to the establishment of the People's Republic in 1949.[1] Both before and after 1949, laws intended to improve the position of women were widely publicised. Recognising that considerable effort would have to be expended in order to make paper reforms effective, the authorities launched implementation campaigns in which millions of government cadres and members of the Women's Federation took part. It was made quite clear that a change in the status of women was one of the political goals of the Communist Party. The application of negative political vocabulary, such as 'feudal', 'backward' and 'male chauvinist', to family customs and attitudes of which the Party disapproved, and of positive terms, such as 'progressive' and 'socialist', to the new ones which it was trying to introduce, helped to politicise the whole area of family relations and to make it difficult to argue that they were a private matter.

Policy towards women and the family underwent various changes of emphasis both before and after the establishment of the People's Republic. The tension between the ideal of sexual equality and the disruption threatened by attempts to achieve it was ever-present, and often produced modifications of policy or great caution in implementing it, especially in sensitive areas like marriage and divorce.[2] None the less, equality for women, like other political goals, remained an explicitly acknowledged part of the vision of China's future promoted by the state. Economic growth, industrialisation, a strong China and even raised living standards were also included in that vision, but overall, the model could be characterised as political. Economic goals were to be achieved within a clearly defined political context by methods which were revolutionary and mobilisational. Challenges to the dominant ideal were sometimes made by Party leaders who felt that economic goals were being sacrificed to political ones, but in the first decades of the People's Republic such challenges met with limited success. On the whole, to borrow a Maoist slogan, it was a case of 'politics in command'.

After the death of Mao in 1976, the challengers slowly gained the upper hand. The great turning point was the third plenum of the 11th Central Committee to the Chinese Communist Party in 1978. Reforms approved at this meeting transformed the whole framework within which China's future is officially envisaged. Change is still the order of the day, but economic goals are now primary. Pragmatism has replaced idealism. Deng Xiao-ping's famous dictum, 'It doesn't matter whether the cat is black or white so long as it catches mice', reflects the most pressing requirement of policy: it should work. (And for mice we should read economic growth.)

The vision of China's future which is now offered to the people is of a strong, modernised, prosperous country. Priority goals are a steadily rising gross national product per capita and regularly improving living standards. In this model of development social goals are secondary to economic ones and often derive from them. Thus, for example, a stringent and comprehensive population policy has been introduced because China's economic development is thought to be under threat from rapid population growth. The recommendation (or requirement) that couples limit themselves to one child has produced a greater concern with child health, with styles of parenting and with the care of the aged. Policy in these areas, and in many others important to the lives of women, is now determined less by social ideals than by the logic of the model of economic development being followed.

THE POSITION OF WOMEN UNDER THE POLITICAL DEVELOPMENT MODEL

China's tradition of extreme subordination of women was attacked in the early years of the People's Republic and its worst abuses were brought to an end. The practice of foot-binding, which had already died out in all but the most backward areas by the 1940s, was finally eliminated. Women and girls were no longer openly sold, as they had been in the past, to be child daughters-in-law, concubines, bondmaids or prostitutes. Marriage legislation prohibited polygamy and interference with free-choice marriage, and proclaimed the equality of husband and wife in the family and in society.[3] The much-publicised new concepts of family life encouraged women to assert themselves more within the family. The ideal of female seclusion which had severely restricted the activities of women of the better-off classes was discredited, enabling women to take on new roles outside the family.

In the cities, particularly, a greater range of activity opened up to women and it became an established norm for women of all classes to work both before and after marriage. The working week was standardised at forty-eight hours, a big improvement over the longer hours previously worked. The introduction of eight weeks' maternity leave and a range of child-care facilities made life a little easier for working mothers.

The individual was still dominated by the family. Even in the cities, independence of the family was unattainable, and indeed undesired, by most people, whether male or female. Single people who lived away from their parents had to make do with dormitory accommodation; 'a home of one's own' only became a possibility on marriage, or in many cases long after it. Within the urban family, however, the position of women was strengthened by their increased access to education, their earnings and their experience outside the home.

Similar changes occurred in the countryside although they were more limited. Under collectivisation the family lost some of its importance as an economic unit while retaining considerable importance in the lives of its members. Control over the means of production and the deployment of the family labour force passed to the collective. Work was measured in work-points on the basis of piece-rates or time-rates. Work-points totalled at the end of the year determined the share of the collective income to which each individual was entitled. Individuals did not control their own earnings; they were received, mostly in kind, by the head of household in accordance with the Chinese custom of income-pooling within the household, but the system did ensure that work done by women for the collective passed through a public measuring process, instead of remaining invisible as it was on a family farm.[4]

The new regime weakened the old family hierarchy based on sex and age, but many provisions of the marriage law – free-choice marriage, the right of widows to remarry if they so wished, and the possibility of divorce for ill-matched or unhappy couples – proved extremely difficult to realise in rural areas.[5] The family remained the basis of social life in the village. On marriage a woman became a member of her husband's family and was lost to her natal family. A wedding thus involved a transfer of labour as well as the considerable expenditure. It closely concerned not only the two principals, but family interests on both sides. Consequently arranged marriage tended to survive, but in a modified form, with the prospective bride and groom at least gaining the chance to meet and get to know each other before marriage. Free-choice marriage in the sense of the couple selecting each other remained unusual for peasants, but young people did sometimes veto their parents' first choice, a practice unheard-of in the past.

In both the cities and the countryside reality still fell far short of the ideals expressed in slogans such as 'women hold up half the sky' or 'what men can do, women can do too'. Women who broke the male monopoly on jobs such as train-driving, oil-drilling and steel-smelting were fêted as models, but sex segregation in the labour market remained general. Men dominated heavy industry, most skilled trades, management and secondary teaching, while women were most numerous in areas such as light industry, textiles, the service sector and kindergarten teaching.[6] Being clustered in the lower-paid occupations, women tended to earn less than men despite the principle of equal pay for equal work. In collective agriculture women also tended to be allocated to the lower-paid jobs, but where men and women did perform the same tasks they were not usually on the same work-point rates.[7]

Patrilocal marriage remained the norm, especially in the country-side. Indeed, the marriage reform campaigns did not target this custom; it ceased to be universal in the cities only because the severity of the accommodation shortage drove young couples to live wherever they could find the space. Yet patrilocal marriage was profoundly damaging to women's interests.[8] It gave a rational economic basis to son preference. The parents of a boy could expect to rely on him and his wife for support in their old age, while the parents of a girl knew that they would lose her. The fact that girls were expected to marry out made both families and collective units understandably reluctant to invest in education and training for them. Women's rights to property or inheritance were hard to enforce. In their natal families they were seen as temporary members whose rights ceased on marriage. A wife was dependent on her husband for access to property and inheritance.[9] A woman who left the family into which she had married, either through divorce, or as a widow, through remarriage, normally went with nothing, although through her labour she had contributed to the income and savings of the family.[10]

Despite calls for men to 'help' with housework and childcare, re-sponsibility for both continued to fall more heavily on women whose 'double burden' limited their leisure and affected their prospects for training and promotion.[11] Motherhood was a particular handicap. Provision of nurseries and kindergartens in cities was impressive but still failed to satisfy demand. In the countryside there were fewer successful attempts to provide communal childcare and mothers fre-quently dropped out of the workforce or worked only in the busy seasons of the agricultural year. When they did, they most often relied on female relatives for childcare.

In the 1950s and early 1960s the Women's Federation campaigned vigorously, if on limited fronts, for women's interests. However, its potential was limited by its official status. It could influence the formulation of state policy, but once beyond that stage it could only follow. Thus the Federation actually colluded with a short-lived attempt to pull married women out of the workforce in 1955–6, and accepted an almost complete veto on the discussion of gender issues in the mid-1970s. Prior to this, at the height of the Cultural Revo-lution, the Women's Federation, like other Party-led organisations, had virtually ceased to function.[12]

In assessing the record of the period of the political development model, some western feminist commentators have been very critical of the gap between the rhetoric of liberation for women in China and the realities of their position. Others have argued that we cannot dis-count the more optimistic perceptions of Chinese women themselves and that we need to focus on the distance travelled as well as on that still to go.[13]

THE IMPACT OF THE ECONOMIC MODEL OF DEVELOPMENT ON WOMEN

THE RURAL REFORMS

In the programme of economic, political and organisational reform carried out after 1978 the rural reforms were implemented comparatively early and have had profound effects.[14] The rural reforms were intended to favour agriculture by raising the prices paid for agricultural products, to improve incentives to the peasant producer by linking effort more closely to reward, and to encourage the rational use of resources by allowing peasants greater freedom to choose what crops to produce. At least in the early years, the reforms had the desired effect. Production and land yields registered remarkable increases, peasant incomes rose and a mood of great optimism prevailed. Unfortunately, this growth seems not to have been sustained in the latter half of the 1980s.[15] It appears that the rural reforms did indeed result in more efficient resource allocation, but if the growth generated by these changes is now exhausted, additional measures may be necessary to produce new growth.

In relation to social change, the most important of the rural reforms was the introduction of household responsibility or contract systems which superseded the collective system evolved in the 1950s and 1960s. Under these systems the household is allocated land, livestock and equipment. In return, it contracts to supply the state with fixed quotas of specified crops calculated according to the expected yield of the land. Any surplus is retained by the household for its own consumption or sold either in the free market or to the state at above-quota prices. The peasant household is responsible for crop management from planting to harvesting, for production costs and for investment decisions. Originally there was an attempt to divide the land on an equitable basis. Each family received some poor- and some good-quality land and the amount was determined on a per capita or a per labour-power basis. The intention at first appears to have been to redistribute 'responsibility land' every few years. However, it was quickly recognised that lack of secure land tenure was inhibiting proper land management. Not knowing how long they would cultivate it, peasants were tempted to work the heart out of their land rather than investing in its fertility. Tenure of responsibility land was therefore raised to at least fifteen years.

Another important change in the rural areas was in policy towards 'household side-line production', a term used to cover production on private plots, domestic pig- and poultry-raising, cottage handicrafts and other small-scale, income-generating activities.[16] Even before the introduction of responsibility systems, the household was the basic unit of production in this sector which supplied most of the non-staple foods consumed by peasants and an important part of their cash income. However, under the collective system, attitudes to household side-lines were ambivalent. At the height of the Cultural Revolution such ventures were often suppressed. Later, they were tolerated but not encouraged. State purchasing agencies offered low prices for their products, while prohibitions on private trading made it impossible for peasants to obtain better prices elsewhere. Since the late 1970s, policy has been reversed. Peasant households can now raise loans to invest in side-line enterprises, and raw materials and advice are easier to obtain. The state offers more realistic prices for produce but it can also be disposed of in the flourishing free markets.

For some households this type of production has ceased to be a side-line. These are the so-called 'specialised households' (zhuanye hu) which concentrate effort and resources in the production of a particular commodity or service. A household is categorised as 'specialised' if more than 50 per cent of its total income is generated from some specialised activity.[17] Such households are not bound to contract for arable land; indeed, as part of the promotion of specialisation they are encouraged to move out of ordinary fieldwork. Households with responsibility land may sub-contract it to other families in order to devote themselves to their specialised enterprise.

When the rural reforms were first introduced, there was an enormous amount of debate about their implications. Critics regarded them as a threat to the interests of socialism and the collective. Those who supported them admitted that they might initially increase inequality but argued that 'some had to get rich first', that socialism should not mean 'everyone sharing the same poverty', and that the reforms would produce a general rise in the standard of living. There has been less interest, at least in China, in the repercussions of the rural reforms on relations within the household and in their implications for the sexual division of labour and women's roles. The omission is significant because it reflects a tendency to ignore or compartmentalise such issues typical of the economic model of development. Prior to 1976, by contrast, whenever the case for collectivisation was being made, its supposed benefits for women were enumerated.

So what were these benefits and how has decollectivisation affected them? The authority and importance of the peasant household have been greatly increased by the responsibility systems. Both farming and non-farming economic activities are now based in the household. Production decisions, field management and the deployment of labour, all formerly the province of the production-team leader, are now in the hands of the household head. These are negative developments for women because, despite the earlier attempts at family reform, the peasant household remains a patriarchal institution normally headed by a man. The idea that a household needs a head has hardly been challenged; indeed, both the state and the collective re-inforced the institution by following the tradition of holding the head responsible for family members and by dealing with him alone in matters such as the census, civil registration and work-point income. The same assumptions are followed under the contract system. The head of household agrees to and signs the contract on behalf of the household and is thus the final decision-maker for his family members.

In the collective period, women had regular contact with peasants from other families through work in the collective fields or enterprises, whether in women's work teams or in mixed ones. Under the household responsibility systems they are more likely to work only with members of their own family. Work is supervised by senior family members. Young women have therefore lost a chance to communicate at work with their own peer group, with cadres and with people outside the family generally. This limitation is unfortunate in the context of Chinese village society. As women marry away from their own localities, they are cut off from the people they were brought up with or got to know at school or work before marriage. When they came as strangers to their husbands' communities, work gave them an important chance to make friendships beyond the family circle. The double burden ensures that young wives enjoy little leisure for social activity and few other ways to form bonds. A lack of relationships outside the family makes it difficult for a young woman to establish even a minimum of personal identity and autonomy. Within the village she will tend to be known as the daughter or daughter-in-law of a certain family instead of being identified by her own qualities or skills. An unmarried girl will be less likely to make the acquaintance of a young man independently of introductions, and will find it harder to call on cadres for support in the event of a family conflict over the marriage to be arranged for her.

The sexual division of labour appears to have been affected in contrasting ways by the rural reforms. There have been many reports in the Chinese press of women thankfully abandoning fieldwork for cleaner, lighter and more flexible tasks in side-line production.[18] On the other hand, in some areas men have been drawn away from agriculture into construction work, forestry, transport, trading or other activities, leaving farmwork to be taken over by women.[19]

The development of side-lines is certainly desirable in that it raises production and rural incomes. Moreover, since the peasant household normally provides the capital, it does so at minimal cost to the state, a great advantage in a poor country. In exceptional cases side-line work has generated peasant fortunes. Women engaged in pursuits such as the production of cultivated pearls, minks or angora wool have apparently sometimes become the main income-earners in their households.[20] However, these spectacular examples, though widely publicised, are of course the exception. Monotony, isolation and low productivity characterise most side-line production, which is inevitably therefore poorly remunerated.

Where men move out into non-agricultural activities and agriculture becomes feminised, then women should at least gain recognition as the producers of food. Moreover, in some such situations where men are absent from the villages for long periods, large numbers of households are managed and headed by women. The implications of these developments for female status are not necessarily straightforward. It has been observed from development experience elsewhere that female-headed households are all too often correlated with low status and low income.[21] Where agriculture is left to women it is because better-paid, more prestigious work is available elsewhere. Hence women are being relegated to unpopular work in the least remunerative sector of the economy. In this situation household investment decisions are unlikely to favour agriculture, and the gap in productivity between male and female activities is therefore likely to widen with time.

THE CONTROL OF HOUSEHOLD PROPERTY, RESOURCES AND INCOME

Legally women and men have equal rights to own, control and inherit property in the People's Republic.[22] The *de facto* situation in rural China is somewhat different. Personal property is hardly recognised in village tradition, the ownership of all major property being vested in the household and available for the use of all the members of the household.[23] When household division (fenjia) takes place, perhaps on the death of the household head or the marriage of one of his sons, property is divided between the males of the family. The most that a daughter expects to obtain is some personal items for her dowry. Household property comprises all that is necessary for its members' survival: housing, household goods, furniture, livestock and tools and equipment. If challenged, inheritance discrimination against daughters is justified on the grounds that they will have access to such necessities through their husbands, and that it would be unfair and inconvenient to share this sort of property with a woman who married into another village. Inheritance is also viewed in a sense as a reward to adult sons for their support of their parents. Hence the son who undertakes the major support is entitled to an extra share, while daughters who have remitted money for their parents' support do sometimes successfully claim a share of the patrimony.

The principle of the equal rights of husband and wife to conjugal property is actually put to the test only in cases of divorce or of the remarriage of widows, both rather rare events in the countryside. As we have seen, neither the divorcee nor the widow is likely to leave her husband's home with any more than the personal possessions from her dowry. In effect, this means that she will have gained nothing but her keep from the labour she has put into that household.

Women suffered from this lack of control over property in the collective era and, despite the Inheritance Law of 1985 which reiterated their legal rights, there is no evidence that the situation has improved in recent years. The injustice is more blatant and more damaging in decollectivised rural society. Households are now permitted to own as private property assets which formerly belonged to the collective. Rising incomes mean better housing, but income is also increasingly being invested in important means of production for agriculture and side-lines. Peasants can buy vehicles, agricultural machinery, electric pumps, sewing machines and so on. Although land cannot be purchased, the long-term control of land is now available to the household through the contract system. So a peasant woman's access to the means of income-generation, whether in the form of land or in the form of machinery, equipment and stock now depends on her relationship to a man.[24] This contrasts sharply with the collective era, when membership of the collective conferred use rights to the means of production.

As it was customary under the collective system to pay over to the household head everything that had been earned by his household members, it might seem that the return to family farming has changed control over income little. The household head controlled the pooled earnings of the household in the past and does so still. However, as I have argued elsewhere, even where women do not directly control the income they have earned, their contribution to family income, if clearly perceived, may at least enhance their status and influence within the family. The work-point system operated by the communes discriminated against women in various ways, but did at least measure their work outside the home and give it a clear value. Except where women take the major role, there is a danger that their work contribution to family farming will become 'invisible' and no more capable of conferring status than is their household labour.

The income from household side-lines provides a significant part of total peasant income; 38 per cent of the total in 1982. Where a side-line is a major part of household activity, or in a specialised household where it is effectively the family business, income from it will be pooled and women's labour contribution may be no more visible than on the family farm. The income from craftwork which is done only by women with no major input of family resources will be differently perceived. In this case women's contribution is impossible to ignore, and they may even be able to retain a little of the cash for personal spending. This is still more likely to be the case if women are responsible for selling the produce themselves in the free markets. In a society quite close to subsistence with people still producing the bulk of what they consume, even small amounts of spending money are very precious. They enable people to please or placate others by the purchase of small gifts such as special food or medicines for older people, a scarf for a woman, cigarettes for men and so on. Women may also make small purchases for the household which are important to them, a light plastic bucket for carrying water, for example, or detergent to ease the burden of washing clothes.

RURAL EDUCATION AND HEALTH

Even in China, where the tendency has been to discuss only the beneficial effects of the rural reforms, some disquiet has been expressed about their implications for rural education, health and welfare facilities. In the past these were largely financed by the collective. When the responsibility systems were first introduced there were many reports of kindergartens, schools and clinics being closed for lack of funds. Village committees have now taken over many of the former functions of the collective, and welfare and educational facilities have partially recovered.[25] Their finance, however, is more precarious than in the past.

Education has suffered as children are kept back to help on responsibility land or with side-lines. Primary school attendance was never compulsory, free or universal, but there have been many reports of falls in the percentage of children enrolled in school since the introduction of the rural reforms, and those who do attend are more often absent. The revelation from 1982 census data that 70 per cent of China's 200 million illiterates were female reflected the fact that in the past parents allowed their sons more schooling than their daughters.[26] Education for boys is still more likely to be perceived by parents as a worthwhile investment for the future. Moreover, there is a widespread belief in China that small girls are more obedient and useful than their brothers. It therefore comes as no surprise that female enrolment, even at primary school level, is far less complete than male.[27] The loss of even the basic education offered by a rural primary school will inevitably have deleterious effects on the future status and employment prospects of these girls.

URBAN WOMEN AND THE POST-MAO REFORMS

Economic reform in the cities since 1978 has been less far-reaching than agricultural reform. Yet life in the cities has changed greatly and in very visible ways. Consumerism is rife. Small businesses, shops and free markets have proliferated. People are proud to show off what they own and now dress for show. Politics plays a far less important part in daily life. Advertising slogans have largely replaced political ones. Freed from the burden of endless meetings, people have more leisure. There is more to watch on television and at the cinema. The quantity and variety of books and periodicals on sale have multiplied many times. Television programmes and films are purchased from abroad, and magazines run articles and features about other countries. All this feeds a tendency to idealise the world outside China and a rather uncritical desire to imitate it. Foreign influence is reinforced by the presence of an increased number of foreigners in China, by the operations of foreign businesses and by the availability and advertising of foreign products. These developments are too diffuse and complex to be adequately discussed here. In the following discussion I will focus on only a few of them, trying to select those which most closely affect women and which have a clear relationship with the economic reforms introduced by the post-Mao leadership.

EMPLOYMENT AND WORK

The equivalent of the specialised household in the countryside is the individual household (getihu) in the city. These are households which run small family businesses producing goods, meals or services and usually selling direct to the public. Such small family businesses were suppressed or pushed into co-operatives in the 1950s. The reformers, seeing this sector as a potential source of badly needed employment and economic growth, reversed this policy and actively promote small businesses. There are probably more women running such concerns on their own account in the cities than in the countryside, though many others, like their village sisters, work as part of a family labour force. Individual households excite considerable envy among other city people who tend to imagine that they are making fortunes. In fact the majority scrape a living. Even when they do well, unlike workers in state enterprises, they have to risk capital, lack security and enjoy no fringe benefits.

The post-Mao decade has seen considerable questioning of women's place in the urban workforce. There has been an explicit rejection of the attacks on the sexual division of labour which were part of policy on women under the political model of development. These peaked during the Cultural Revolution when many young women were encouraged to take on heavy jobs formerly done only by men. In the early 1980s, partly as a result of official directives, partly in response to the mood of the times, many young women were transferred out of such jobs usually into lower-waged activity. Female train-drivers became clerical workers in the Railway Bureau, construction workers were sent to work in light industry and others simply lost their jobs.[28] Once it had been considered feudal to argue that women could not do 'men's jobs'; now, under the cover of stressing women's different capabilities and the need to protect their health, it became commonplace. The new line was neatly summarised in the *Tianjin Daily*, 'We absolutely must not ignore women's biological nature and the limitations of their physical strength and blindly persist in the principle that "what men can do women comrades can certainly do too."'[29]

There also appears to be an increasing unwillingness on the part of employers to employ women at all. It is open to question whether this is a completely new phenomenon. The new political climate makes it easier for employers to admit to such unwillingness and for the media to air debates on the issue. But it does seem to be generally believed in China that employment discrimination is far more serious than in the past, and it is possible to see reasons why this might be the case. One result of the post-Mao reforms is that enterprises are now responsible for their own profits and losses. The pressure to cut costs is far greater than before and managers have to be selective about their labour force. High unemployment means that they can pick and choose. Managers seem to regard female labour as expensive. At first sight, this has some economic justification: paid maternity leave, earlier retirement age and the childcare facilities which enterprises with large numbers of female employees are supposed to provide all add to the costs of employing women. On the other hand, in most cases it is the husband's work unit, not the wife's, which supplies the accommodation in which the couple lives, a factor which must at least balance out the costs.[30]

It seems that fundamentally the reluctance to employ women must spring from profound beliefs about the differences between male and female capacities. While women are seen as conscientious and good at rote-learning, a quality which is actually held against them when it is used to explain and discount their higher examination grades, men are thought to be more intelligent and better at practical work.[31] They are also considered (and in Chinese society are brought up to be) more assertive, competitive and self-confident. In the sort of society which China is now trying to build, these qualities are prized. In the new, more open climate these beliefs about the relative efficiency and ability of men and women can be freely expressed. What perhaps needs explanation is that years of counter-propaganda apparently failed to destroy them. Here perhaps the influence of the Cultural Revolution is relevant again; it did nothing for the credibility of assertions of women's competence that these were made so strongly in what is now perceived as a disastrous chapter in China's history. Finally employers may regard women as less efficient than men because women are still expected to carry the main responsibility for childcare and housework. Whether justified or not, the resulting assumption is that women will be less able to give all their efforts to the job.[32]

Whatever the reason for discrimination, it has been highly visible in recent years. Factories and other enterprises either demand higher examination scores from female secondary school graduates who apply for employment or turn them down outright. Technical and vocational schools which take secondary school leavers also discriminate against females, except for recruitment to training courses in traditional female skills such as nursing, office work and kindergarten teaching. Even university graduates suffer from the prejudice against employing women. Only just over a quarter of students in higher education are female and China is desperately short of graduates, and yet the officials in charge of job assignment report not only that many work units prefer male graduates but that some reject all women or accept only a tiny number.[33] There have been cases where men with poor marks have been preferred over women with excellent ones, and a notorious one where members of a laser institute made every effort to recruit a student on the strength of a brilliant graduation thesis, only to change their minds when they discovered her sex. State-owned enterprises, government offices and even educational institutions have all been guilty of this sort of behaviour. Perhaps most distressing of all, the Women's Federation asked the Beijing Foreign Studies University to allocate it two interpreters from the 1989 English language class and specified that they should be men.[34] The problem of allocating female graduates is so serious that some universities have considered reducing the number of female students they will accept.

The government has urged an end to discrimination, but has taken no steps to make it a punishable offence, nor to intervene directly, even where its own departments are concerned. There has been considerable public protest from the Women's Federation as well as from the victims and their families. The Women's Federation has given the issue wide publicity, both in its own periodicals, and in the press, and has entered into negotiation with labour bureaux in order to reduce the degree of discrimination.

Perhaps the fiercest battle has been waged over women's right to work at all. In 1980 some economists suggested that China's acute unemployment problem might be solved if women, or at least married women, withdrew from the labour force to devote themselves to domesticity, and the idea was raised again in the press on several occasions. The Women's Federation came strongly to the defence of women's right to work. It sent letters to the Central Committee and to the press pointing out that the basis of their whole strategy to liberate women had been to get them into the labour force.[35] More pragmatically, it argued that the unemployed would not necessarily be suited to the jobs which women would vacate, and that most families needed the wife's earnings. The Federation also conducted public-opinion surveys which seem to indicate wide acceptance of the idea that women need to work for more than mere economic reasons. Out of 200 employed women interviewed, 76 per cent indicated that they would want to work even if their families did not need their earnings. A more surprising finding came from the interviews with men. Forty-four out of fifty interviewed said that no matter what increase was made to their own wages, they would not want their wives to stay at home as housewives.[36]

CHINA'S FEMININE MYSTIQUE

Other important changes for urban women have been associated with a cluster of factors which can be summarised as femininity, consumerism and domesticity. These are depicted in the media as belonging peculiarly to a woman's sphere and as being the proper concerns of a modern woman.

Ostentation in dress and excessive attention to personal appearance used to be frowned on in the People's Republic. This reached ridiculous extremes in the Cultural Revolution when people were harassed and even assaulted on the streets for wearing anything unusual, and when Red Guards forbade hairdressers to offer anything but a standard bob.[37] A few unfortunates whose hair was naturally curly even had it straightened to avoid accusations of a bourgeois perm.

The extremes of the Cultural Revolution are not surprisingly condemned, but women seem to have differed in their reactions to the simplicity and frugality which was encouraged in dress in less fanatical times: some found it a convenience and others argue that it was a denial of their femininity. The pendulum has certainly swung the other way with a vengeance. Fashionable attire for young women is now all too often impractical, uncomfortable and fussy. Beauty parlours and hairdressing salons have proliferated, and more sordid establishments offering operations to produce rounded (Caucasian-looking) eyes or to expand bustlines have also made an appearance.

It is difficult to assess how Chinese women themselves feel about these developments. No doubt many get great pleasure from their new power to experiment with and make decisions about their appearance. But it is obvious too that the change has introduced new anxieties and pressures. As wives and girlfriends, but also in their work roles, women have to worry about the attractiveness and appropriateness of their clothes and appearance to a far greater extent than in the past.

The new consumerism also bears a certain ambiguity for women in relation to the home. Obviously, better-off urban women have benefited immensely from the new availability of appliances like fridges and washers, which ease the heavy burden of domestic work. On the other hand, both advertising and magazines directed towards domestic or family affairs constantly depict women as the exclusive users of such appliances, as homemakers and as the guardians of domestic tranquillity. Not only does this reinforce the conservative images of women which, as we have seen, tend to hamper them in the world of work; it may also produce a further sense of failure. Urban homes in China tend to be very over-crowded – two or three generations normally share one, two or three rooms – and the uncluttered elegance of these ideal homes is quite beyond the reach of ordinary people.

The most pressing problem for many urban women at present is that of the domestic budget. This relates to two aspects of the economic reforms: changes in job security and price rises. After 1949 the Communist government offered a job for life, commonly known as the 'iron ricebowl', to state employees. In fact this was not as absolute as is sometimes claimed; down-turns in the economy did sometimes produce drastic cutbacks in the workforce, but the majority enjoyed a high degree of job security. From the mid-1950s until the 1980s, again with some exceptions, urban people benefited from very stable prices, especially for basic foodstuffs. Heavily subsidised rents also contributed to a low and steady cost of living. These factors were important to popular support in the towns for the Communist government.

In the post-Mao decade it was argued that the 'iron ricebowl' had a negative impact on both incentive and efficiency and that subsidised food prices were enormously costly. Both policies have been officially condemned, though moves to change practice progressed rather more slowly. Enough had been done by the mid-1980s to shatter the old sense of security among the urban population, but complaints were still quite muted as wage rises and bonuses were adequate to ensure most people a steadily rising standard of living. More recently, however, China has suffered from accelerating inflation. Government decisions about changes in fixed prices are not the main cause of this round of inflation, which has clearly gone out of control. Urban families on low or fixed wages are the main victims in this situation, and women who buy the food and manage the household budget carry the heaviest burden of anxiety.

POPULATION POLICY: THE IMPLICATIONS FOR RURAL AND URBAN WOMEN

A stringent population policy has been one of the most striking features of China's economic model of development. In fact, the desire

45

to control population growth also characterised the last years of the political model; in the 1970s couples were urged to limit their families to two well-spaced children and the decade saw an impressive drop in the birth-rate. Unfortunately, however, the age structure of the population by the end of the 1970s made some demographic growth inevitable, and it was calculated that China's population would double to nearly 2 billion by the 2020s if couples had just three children each.[38] Given China's poor ratio of land and other resources to population, this was an alarming scenario threatening not only the deceleration of economic growth but ultimately, the spectre of famine. The government's response was to make the demand that each couple limit themselves to one child. Compliance was to be rewarded with allowances, longer maternity leave and privileged access to education, health and housing; defiance brought fines, demotion and disgrace.[39]

Since the mid-1980s, the policy has been modified, mainly by allowing an increase in the exemptions granted to the one-child rule. The most important exemption, because it will affect the largest number of people, is for peasant couples whose first child is a girl. Out of consideration for their concern about their support in old age they are now allowed to have a second child, though it must be well spaced.[40] Currently the policy seems to have been largely successful in the cities, where very few children under 10 now have a sibling. Compliance has been much less general in the countryside. Some peasants, especially those whose first child is a son, have taken the one-child pledge. Others have gone ahead with a second birth either after obtaining an exemption or in defiance of the policy. Successful provinces boast that they have very few third or higher-order births, but in a few backward provinces these still make up 20 per cent of total births.[41]

I have written elsewhere on the consequences of this policy for women, and the broad outlines will suffice here.[42] Son preference is still very strong in China for various reasons, but most importantly because a boy is the best source of support in old age. This is especially the case in the countryside, where cases of female infanticide were reported in the early years of the policy. Indeed, this factor seems to have influenced the decision to make rural policy more flexible. The one-child policy meant that the birth of a girl, if she survived, ended the family's hopes of having a son. The disappointment experienced was often taken out on the mother. There were many reports of women who had given birth to girls being scolded or beaten by irate husbands and in-laws. Anxiety about the sex of the foetus makes pregnancy in China today a period of great tension.

The most-used contraceptive method in China is the IUD, and this is followed by the pill. Female sterilisations far outnumber male ones. The abortion rate has risen since the introduction of strict population pole, and most abortions today are performed on married couples who, although they have consented to the sterilisation, are in many cases, like another ... perform ... when there appear the heavy physiological and psychological ... the role

In the course of trying to implement the one-child policy the authorities have been forced to recognise how strong a preference there still is. This has promoted greater care about the amount of discrimination China must still ... against women in allocating a second child only to peasant couples whose ... It is a thought, the government in ... this ... risk of appearing to ... the notion that a daughter is worth less than a son.

I do not wish to argue that the policy is unduly negative for women ... that the policy has deprived Chinese women of control over their fertility ... is not the case. In the absence of modern contraception ... given their subordination within the family, they accept ... control. This policy even has some advantages for women. Having only one children will certainly lighten the labours of ... mother. If then women ... then the one-child ... enjoy a ... more maternity ... In the long ... fond having fewer children it should reduce the dangers of childbirth, and ... health it should reduce the dangers of ... Finally, those parents who have only daughters will ... much ... value, love and care in her. Should ... their daughters ... so that she should have a significant effect on the attitudes ... by women in the next generation. Of course, they will ... their ... bounds and problems scarcely change. At ... but parents ... the future are entirely focused on their own ... by ... be subjected ... light this bride of ...

Delivery Room.

I want a boy.

要男生 – We want male students.

Student recruitment.

要男工

We want men.

Taking on workers.

要 ...... I want ......

At the Marriage Bureau.

What they want.

CONCLUSION

It is not possible to draw up an account of what the differing approaches to development in China since 1949 have achieved for women or to weigh one against the other. The approaches are related too closely ... as much as they are ... from one another ... I have made between the two approaches ... a distinction which I have ... device. Many features of the lives of women and of Chinese attitudes to women are common to both periods. Moreover, the second period was in very important ways ... by the first ... the worst abuses of women had been dealt with in the 1950s, the reformers were free to search for ways to eliminate them in the 1980s. The difference then of

47

policy, and most abortions today are performed on married women who, although they have consented to the operation, would in many cases like another child if it were permitted. Women therefore bear the heavy physiological and psychological costs of the policy.

In the course of trying to implement the one-child policy the authorities have been forced to recognise just how strong son preference still is. This has promoted greater honesty about the amount of discrimination Chinese women still face. However, in allowing a second child only to peasant couples whose first is a daughter, the government runs the risk of appearing to validate the notion that a daughter is worth less than a son.

I do not wish to argue that the policy is entirely negative for women. It is sometimes implied that the policy has deprived Chinese women of control over their fertility. This is not the case. In the absence of modern contraception, and given their subordination within the family, they never had such control. The policy even has some advantages for women. Having only one or two children will certainly lighten the burdens of parenthood, which tend to fall mainly on the mother. Urban women who take out the one-child certificate enjoy a six-month maternity leave with pay. In the cities at least having fewer children may enable some women to achieve more in their careers, but at very least it should reduce the drudgery of their lives. Finally, those parents who have an only daughter will invest all their resources, love and care in her. Statistically there will be many only daughters, so that this should have a significant effect on what is achieved by women in the next generation. Of course they will encounter discrimination as their mothers' generation did, but parents whose aspirations for the future are entirely focused on their own daughter may be expected to fight this harder than parents who also have a son.

CONCLUSION

It is not possible to draw up account sheets of what the different approaches to development in China's post-1949 history have achieved for women or to develop an argument that one is superior to the other. The approaches started from different base-lines and encountered different problems. Even the distinction which I have made between the two periods is in some ways artificial, an analytic device. Many features of the lives of women and of Chinese attitudes to women are common to both periods. Moreover, the second period was in very important ways shaped by the first. As the worst abuses of women had been dealt with in the 1950s, the reformers did not have to search for ways to eliminate them in the 1980s. The ultra-leftism of the Cultural Revolution became associated with a strong (if somewhat rhetorical) commitment to breaking down discrimination against women. This seems to have provoked a backlash and to have made it more difficult to argue for equal employment rights for women in China today.

In both periods the Chinese population experienced vast improvements in the standard of living, education, health and the expectation of life. Women shared in these benefits of development with men, even if they did not always get a fair share.

Perhaps the most discouraging aspect of both periods was the failure to address the problem of the continuing subordination of women in any satisfactory way. Common to the official literature of both periods is the insistence that as China is a socialist country, it could only be a matter of time before the remnants of the oppression of women disappeared. Nothing in this analysis could explain the survival of the subordination of women through China's far-reaching social transformations, or its regular appearance in new forms. Here the 1980s do offer some comfort. The possibility of expressing a greater range of opinions has enabled some 'feminist voices'[43] to be heard. These come from women who are determined to seek new explanations of women's inferior status. But, for the moment at least, they come only from a small number of intellectuals. It is difficult to see how they can move from challenge, debate and protest in a limited arena to effective action in society. The Women's Federation which, as a Party-led organisation, can exploit a certain prestige can, as we have seen, sometimes intervene successfully to help women with specific problems. But its very origins and official status preclude the Federation from evolving or approving an analysis of women's oppression which puts gender on an equal plane with class. The need for women's action is obvious but it is not clear how this need can be satisfied.

NOTES AND REFERENCES

1   See Delia Davin, *Woman-work: Women and the Party in Revolutionary China* (Clarendon Press, Oxford, 1976).

2   This tension is especially strongly emphasised by Judith Stacey, *Patriarchy and Socialist Revolution in China* (Berkeley, University of California Press, 1983) and by Kay-Ann Johnson, *Women, the Family and Peasant Revolution in China* (University of Chicago Press, Chicago, 1983).

3   For the details of the law, see M.J. Meijer, *Marriage Law and Policy in the Chinese People's Republic* (Hong Kong University Press, 1971);

and for the implementation campaign see Johnson, *Women, the Family and Peasant Revolution in China*, chs 9 and 10. On choice of partner and negotiation, see Elisabeth Croll, *The Politics of Marriage in Contemporary China* (Cambridge University Press, Cambridge, 1981).

4　See Davin, *Woman-work*, ch. 4, and Elisabeth Croll, *Women in Rural Development: the People's Republic of China* (International Labour Office, Geneva, 1979).

5　Davin, *Woman-work*.

6　For a discussion of women in the urban labour force and the discriminatory division of labour, see Margery Wolf, *Revolution Postponed: Women in Contemporary China* (Stanford University Press, Stanford, CA, 1985), ch. 4.

7　Discrimination in work-point rates is dealt with in Davin, *Woman-work*, pp. 143–6.

8　The best exploration of its consequences for women is in Norma Diamond, 'Collectivisation, Kinship and the Status of Women in Rural China', *Bulletin of Concerned Asian Scholars* (Jan–March 1975), pp. 25–32; and in Rayna Reiter (ed.), *Towards an Anthropology of Women*, Monthly Review Press, New York and London, 1975.

9　See Delia Davin, 'China: the New Inheritance Law and the Peasant Household', *The Journal of Communist Studies*, 3(4) (Dec. 1987): 50–63.

10　William L. Parish and Martin King Whyte, *Village and Family in Contemporary China* (Chicago University Press, Chicago, 1978), p. 195.

11　See Margery Wolf, *Revolution Postponed*, ch. 3, and Phyllis Andors, *The Unfinished Liberation of Chinese Women* (Wheatsheaf, Brighton, 1983), pp. 80–9.

12　Davin, *Woman-work: Women and the Party in Revolutionary China*, Clarendon Press, Oxford, 1976, ch. 2

13　Among the most critical approaches are those of Johnson, *Women, the Family and Peasant Revolution in China*; Stacey, *Patriarchy and Socialist Revolution in China*; and Wolf, *Revolution Postponed*. Approaches which, though critical, are prepared to make more allowances for the difficulties, come from Elisabeth Croll, *Feminism and Socialism in China* (Routledge & Kegan Paul, London, 1978); Davin, *Woman-work*; and Marilyn Young, 'Chicken Little in China: some Reflections on Women', in Sonia Kruks, Rapp and Marilyn B. Young (eds), *Promissory Notes: Women in the Transition to Socialism* (Monthly Review Press, New York, 1989).

14　There are now many preliminary studies of the rural reforms. For a good general study, see Peter Nolan and Suzanne Paine, 'Towards an Appraisal of the Impact of Rural Reforms in China, 1978–85', in Ashwani Saith (ed.), *The Re-emergence of the Chinese Peasantry* (Croom Helm, London, 1987).

15　For a discussion of the underlying reasons, see Reeitsu Kojima, 'Agricultural Organization; New Forms, New Contradictions', in *China Quarterly*, 116 (Dec. 1988); 729.

16　Elisabeth Croll, 'The Promotion of Domestic Sideline Production in Rural China since 1978', in Jack Gray and Gordon White (eds), *China's New Development Strategy* (Academic Press, London, 1982).

17   'Anhui Regulations on Specialised Households', translated in *BBC Summary of World Broadcasts: Far East*, 28 April 1984.

18   See, for example, Hong Ying, 'Women in China Making Headway to Full Equality', *China Daily*, Beijing, 6 March 1982.

19   A woman in this position is Ling Qiao in the documentary film *Small Happiness*, directed by Carma Hinton and Richard Gordon.

20   See, for example, Wu Naitao, 'Rural Women and New Economic Policies', *Beijing Review*, 7 March, 1983. See also the account of a peasant woman who made a fortune raising minks, in Zhang Xinxin and Sang Ye, *Chinese Lives: an Oral History of Contemporary China*, trans. and ed. by W.J.F. Jenner and Delia Davin (Macmillan, London, 1988; Penguin, Harmondsworth, 1989).

21   See Barbara Rogers, *The Domestification of Women* (Tavistock, London, 1980).

22   This is asserted in the 1950 and 1980 *Marriage Laws of the People's Republic of China* (Foreign Languages Press, Beijing, 1950 and 1981). It is spelt out in detail in the *Inheritance Law of the People's Republic of China*, adopted April 1985 (Shanghai People's Publishing House, 1986) (in Chinese).

23   For a discussion of traditional inheritance, see Shuzo Shiga, 'Family Property and the Law of Inheritance in Traditional China', in David C. Buxbaum (ed.), *Chinese Family Law and Social Change* (University of Washington Press, Seattle, 1978).

24   For a more detailed treatment of peasant women and property under the rural reforms, see Davin, 'China: the New Inheritance Law'; and Davin, 'Woman, Work and Property in China in the 1980s', in Diane Elson, *Male Bias in the Development Process* (Manchester University Press, Manchester, forthcoming).

25   For a discussion of the decline in rural health facilities in the early 1980s, see Judith Banister, *China's Changing Population* (Stanford University Press, Stanford, CA, 1987), pp. 73–4; for education, see Pauline Keating, 'Middle Level Education in Contemporary China', in Neville Maxwell and Bruce McFarlane (eds), *China's Changed Road to Development* (Pergamon Press, Oxford, 1984).

26   Report of the Preliminary Meeting of the Fifth National Women's Congress, *Beijing Review*, 19 Sept. 1983.

27   See State Statistical Bureau, ed., *Statistical Handbook of China* (Statistical Publishing House, Beijing, 1984) (in Chinese), p. 490. This source puts females at 43.7 per cent of enrolled primary school pupils in 1983.

28   Here I draw on an interview with the chairperson of the Women's Committee of the All-China Federation of Trade Unions, Beijing, March 1981, and on discussions with officials of the Women's Federation in Beijing in September 1987.

29   *Tianjin Daily*, 15 Oct. 1980, quoted in Emily Honig and Gail Hershatter, *Personal Voices: Chinese Women in the 1980s*, (Stanford University Press, Stanford CH, 1988). I am very much in debt to the authors of this fine book for both data and ideas on urban women in China in the 1980s.

30   There have been complaints in China that the system for allocating

accommodation is in itself sexist, as it forces women rather than men to commute. A minority of work units do supply accommodation to female employees.

31   This paragraph is based on many years of argument with Chinese friends but also on more systematic interviewing of parents and teachers in Beijing, Shenyang and Chengdu in September 1987. See also Honig and Hershatter, *Personal Voices*, pp. 17–19.

32   For discussion of the double burden and the sexual division of housework in China, see Martin King Whyte and William L. Parish, *Urban Life in Contemporary China* (University of Chicago Press, Chicago, 1984), and Honig and Hershatter, *Personal Voices*, pp. 255–63.

33   Honig and Hershatter, *Personal Voices*, p. 249. Pages 248–50 contain an extremely useful discussion of the whole problem of women graduates.

34   Private information from a teacher at the University. Officials of the National Women's Federation were vehement in their condemnation of discrimination against women graduates in discussion in 1987.

35   National Women's Federation, Letter of 15 Aug. from the Secretariat to comrades Wan Li and Peng Chong. In National Women's Federation (ed.), *Selected Women's Movement Documents from the Period of the Four Modernisations 1981–1983* (Chinese Women's Press, Beijing, 1983) (in Chinese). For a discussion of the initial exchange, see Davin, 'Engels and the making of Chinese family policy', pp. 146–8 in Janet Sayers, Mary Evans and Nanneke Redclift (eds), *Engels Revisited: New Feminist Essays* (Tavistock, London, 1987). For a detailed update, see Honig and Hershatter, *Personal Voices*, pp. 250–5.

36   Ibid., p. 252.

37   For Red Guard memories of such activities, see 'Diploma', in Zhang Xinxin and Sang Ye, *Chinese Lives*, pp. 55–61. For a hairdresser's comments on politics and changing hairstyles, see 'Vieux Paris', in ibid., pp. 171–4.

38   Charles C. Chen and Carl W. Tyler, 'Demographic implications and Family Size Alternatives in the People's Republic of China', *China Quarterly* (March 1982): 67.

39   For a detailed discussion, see Delia Davin, 'The Single-Child Policy in the Countryside', and Penny Kane, 'The Single-Child Policy in the Cities', in Elisabeth Croll, Delia Davin and Penny Kane (eds), *China's One-Child Family Policy* (Macmillan, London, 1985).

40   Interview with Mme Peng Peiyun, Minister in Charge of the State Family Planning Commission, in *People: International Planned Parenthood Federation Review of Population and Development*, 16(1) (1989): 11–13.

41   Peng Xizhe, 'Regional Patterns of China's Fertility Transition', *People*, 16(1): 18.

42   Delia Davin, 'Gender and Population in the People's Republic of China', in Haleh Afshar (ed.), *Women, State and Ideology: Studies from Africa and Asia* (Macmillan, London, 1987).

43   The best account of these is in Honig and Hershatter, *Personal Voices*, pp. 308–37.

Chapter Four

WOMEN, WAR AND UNDERDEVELOPMENT IN NICARAGUA

Mary Stead

[As a result of the elections in February 1990, a new government took over in Nicaragua in April 1990. The Sandinistas are still by far the largest single party, but a coalition of eleven parties, under the presidency of Violeta Chamorro, took power. Among their election promises was the restoration of the traditional Nicaraguan family, and it is feared that they will attempt to reverse the gains made by women under the eleven years of Sandinista government Women in Nicaragua now have to defend the successes of the past decade, and work in a far more hostile political climate to achieve progress for themselves. Nicaraguan women worked for two decades to overthrow the dictator Somoza, in 1979, and made up 30 per cent of the forces fighting the well-equipped army.[1]]

> Women participated in all the social and political struggles of our people in this century . . . despite the adverse historical and cultural conditions (politics were precisely one of the arenas reserved for men); women of all ages broke taboos, left their homes, rebelling against their families or companions, and left to take their positions in battle . . . they were members of the FSLN, collaborators, messengers, organizers of safe houses, underground fighters, guerrillas in the mountains . . . political leaders and military commanders . . . mothers of political prisoners, mothers of the disappeared, mothers of those tortured, . . . also victims of the repression.
>
> (FSLN Proclamation March 1987)

The image of Nicaraguan women, in their own eyes, and those of other people, was irrevocably transformed by this activity.[2]

Since the early 1980s the USA has been funding a counter-revolutionary war, keeping contra forces supplied with money, uniforms, equipment and, when Congress permits, weapons and training. The war reached its most destructive phase in the mid-1980s, affecting the north, the mountainous centre and the southern border, and also the culturally distinct Atlantic Coast area. All men aged 18 to 25 were conscripted for two years, with up to three months annual reserve duty thereafter. Beginning in 1983 this seriously affected production in a country devastated by the effects of the 1972 Managua earthquake, and the decade of fighting against Somoza. Women lost male relatives in the contra war, adding to those already lost in the anti-Somoza struggle; over 50 per cent of the national budget was diverted to the war effort, cutting spending on health, childcare and education. Conversely, the absence of so many men gave women employment and training opportunities beyond their reach in peacetime. US trade restrictions, culminating in a complete embargo from May 1985, and US interference in international agencies approached for loans by Nicaragua, have resulted in the deliberate 'underdevelopment' of Nicaragua's economy, bringing it near collapse by 1989. Contra attacks have also made the infrastructure a target, so as to incite the people to rebel against the government elected in 1984, with a 66 per cent vote for the FSLN (Sandinista National Liberation Front).

Close economic ties inherited from the Somoza era made the break with US trade even more damaging. Sources of spare parts for second-hand machinery were lost, as were markets for agro-industrial products (sugar, bananas, tobacco, cigars, meat, cotton, coffee and timber). Falling world prices for exports and rising prices for essential imports, including oil and industrial raw materials, have widened the trade gap, and resulted in serious shortages of foreign exchange and control-defying inflation. One solution, currency reform, has had little success, and state efforts to control the black market are controversial. The rationalisation or 'compactation' of state employees has caused much suffering among teachers, childcare workers and office workers, many of them women. If this process results in some stemming of migration to the towns, and encourages the development of the countryside and the rural economy on which the country depends for its survival, it will have achieved a long-term goal, but in the meantime, many of the early gains of the revolution appear to be being lost in the process.

The contras have not succeeded, whether by armed action, sabotage or undermining the economy, but the cost of the war, and the difficulty of maintaining rural production, have created a situation so serious that the survival of the present government is under threat. Despite US training in the manipulation of public opinion, contra credibility has not been established. Large amounts of public and private US funding have not been able to erase the horror remaining in memories from the Somoza era, and this has so far prevented discontent from manifesting itself as support for any contra political project. But the present government, despite all its concessions since the various Central American peace initiatives, still remains under internal and external pressure which threatens its well-established base of popular support. It is in this context that the situation of Nicaraguan women must be considered.

THE SITUATION OF NICARAGUAN WOMEN AT THE END OF THE 1980s

Any analysis of the present situation of Nicaraguan women must focus on certain key areas, in which change has been attempted during the past decade. These include legislation, ideology, organisation, work, health, education, housing and defence. It is not easy to separate the lives of Nicaraguan women into convenient categories without considerable overlap; for example, legal change may affect both the family life and work of women. Class and gender also need to be considered as interacting. Thus the 1987 FSLN proclamation summarises the situation which women faced in 1979:

> Nicaraguan women were . . . victims of other forms of exploitation and oppression due to their subordinate position in society as workers. In fact women, particularly working-class women, bore a double burden of social discrimination that oppressed them even more . . . women were treated and educated as second-class citizens.[3]

Nicaraguan women have been investigating their own situation, and doing well-documented research,[4] while the war itself has done more for the status of Nicaraguan women than years of campaigning to redefine their official role in Nicaraguan society. Again, the FSLN proclamation summarises the situation:

> The war and the necessities it imposes have forced an accelerated abandonment of some prejudices, and women have had the opportunity of taking, under equal conditions, jobs previously reserved for men. Because of this there is a growing participation of women in the workforce in the countryside and in the cities which, even though imposed by the objective situation the country faces, produces deep ideological and social changes.
>
> For the FSLN, this means fighting discriminatory laws and policies, the subordinate position of women in society and the family, paternal irresponsibility, physical and moral abuse, and machismo. All of these obstacles and attitudes must be overcome by men and women.

This resulted from years of debate within the party. At the same time the national women's organisation, the Association of Nicaraguan Women Luisa Amanda Espinosa (AMNLAE) announced a change in its style of leadership and organisation, and research initiated by the ATC (Rural Workers' Union) in 1985 was published.[5] The government Women's Office, renamed the Institute of Nicaraguan Women, and the AMNLAE Legal Office put women on the public agenda, resulting in a wealth of information on women, recognising their importance in the economy and in society, as the mainstay of the family. Contra attempts to establish an internal front among disaffected women had to be frustrated by a more serious consideration of women's real problems and priorities.

Early fears that women would return to the home (in so far as they had ever been confined to a domestic existence) proved groundless, since a temporary rise in the already high birth-rate and the worsening economic situation forced women out into the economy to ensure the survival of their children. There has been a decline in political activity in AMNLAE, some unions and the CDS (Sandinista Defence Committees, a community organisation), blamed on physical exhaustion as much as disillusionment or war-weariness, and measures to restructure such organisations to facilitate women's participation are under discussion.[6]

I was fortunate to live in Esteli, in northern Nicaragua, for six months in 1985, staying with families and researching the situation of women tobacco-workers, to try to assess the impact of the revolution on their lives, and to examine the constraints on them, and the official and unofficial strategies for overcoming these constraints. Hours of conversation, formal and informal interviews and much help from Nicaraguan and foreign women living and working in Nicaragua resulted in some insight into the realities of their lives. This left me sceptical of some of the over-simplified official pronouncements about women, but full of admiration for the women I met, and for the ways in which they were working to change and improve their situation. Some very impressive work is being done by women committed to fulfilling the short-term and long-term needs of Nicaraguan women. The most notable expectations raised by the 1979 revolution were in the fields of education, health care, housing, equality at work, equality before the law, attention to the practical needs, such as childcare, and reconstruction of social relations to eliminate tension and discrimination between women and men, adults and children.

Many Nicaraguan women are well informed about women's experience elsewhere, and of the universal nature of women's problems and possibilities. Feminist perspectives are a controversial area of debate, and Nicaraguan women are also aware of the problems faced in Europe and the USA by women, whose brief wartime equality was reversed when men returned from the two major wars of this century. Thus in an article by the ATC published in 1987, the following point is made:[7] 'How are fighting men valuing women's work? What will happen when they return from the war? Are they ready to take in the change which has taken place in their women? Does hero = man in their minds?'

Nicaraguan women express interest in any strategies which can be used to maintain the position which they are in the process of achieving as a result of the war.[8] Their work to redefine their identity and role can be paralleled in other parts of the world, and any informed critique of their situation can also provide a useful commentary on our own. An appreciation of cultural and practical differences must prevent comments which are at best irrelevant, and at worst, patronising and totally inappropriate. In a country under extreme external pressure, solutions are developed to ensure national survival, but could also be applied where the debate on women is less developed, and where governments are not committed to advancing the cause of women. In Nicaragua the pro-government media can be used to disseminate the results of research and to stimulate discussion aimed at increasing public awareness and self-criticism, as a means of bringing about change from below, not imposing it from above. There is in Nicaragua a great fear of controversial issues dividing the country in a time of war and economic hardship, but there is also the political will to find solutions to problems, and to make them work. Such potentially divisive issues, which have been faced, include: sexist attitudes at work and in the unions, the role of the national women's organisation, childcare policy, abortion, divorce, violence against women and the need for sex-education and contraception. Opposition has come from traditionalist sections of the Catholic Church, and from the new fundamentalist churches, from some trade unionists, employers, a few FSLN members, some defenders of the traditional middle-class family and its gender-roles, and even from some women schooled in cultural and economic subordination.

There are no easy answers, and the timidity of some women in the early years of the revolution is understandable. Of the FSLN members 38 per cent are women, and in the 1987 proclamation it was said that they occupy 31.4 per cent of leadership positions in the government, 26.8 per cent of membership of the regional FSLN committees, 43 per cent of the literacy brigade members (in 1980), and between 55 and 70 per cent of the volunteers for people's health days, as well as 40 per cent of agricultural union membership, and 15 per cent of local leadership positions, and 67 per cent of membership of the CDS. They are 45 per cent of the seasonal workforce. Thirteen FSLN women were elected to the National Assembly in 1984.[9] Women are not in agreement over what should be done to improve women's situation, but they have gone far beyond simplistic Marxist analysis, based on the work of Engels or Trotsky, as have many male FSLN members. The interaction of class and gender dominated early discussions (measures designed to benefit the poorest would by definition benefit women, over-represented in this category), but this has largely been replaced by a more specific focus on women, their situation and demands.[10] Practical and ideological change, attempted simultaneously, reinforce each other.

WOMEN AND IDEOLOGICAL CHANGE

In 1979 there was a commitment by the FSLN to implement the six policies on women first drawn up ten years before. They aimed to abolish discrimination and establish full equality between men and women, supporting mothers and protecting children, not discriminating between 'legitimate' and 'illegitimate' children. The elimination of prostitution, the right to maternity leave and the increased economic and political participation of women were among other aims. Integration of women into political and economic life was seen as the means to emancipate them, demonstrating full formal equality. They were to become productive workers, while maintaining their reproductive role. Some ex-*comandantes* from the anti-Somoza struggle were women, and were given ministerial responsibility for such traditionally feminine areas as health, education and social services. The post-1979 exodus of trained people put educated and trained women in positions of responsibility at regional and local level, but the male political leadership of the FSLN took some time to move beyond their limited vision of women as ex-comrades restricted to 'caring' roles in public and private. Until the contra war began to dominate national life, the emphasis was on reconstruction, and on healing the social and political divisions left in 1979, so potentially difficult issues which went beyond a narrow definition of women's rights were avoided or evaded. Nevertheless, women's concerns were never completely downgraded, or postponed until other goals had been achieved, contrary to experience after radical changes of government elsewhere. The war has made it necessary for the FSLN to try to justify its position:

> The Sandinista People's Revolution will abolish the odious discrimination that women have been subjected to compared with men: it will establish economic, political and cultural equality between women and men.
> (a) It will pay special attention to the mother and child.
> (b) It will eliminate prostitution and other social scourges, through which the dignity of women will be raised.
> (c) It will put an end to the system of servitude women are subjected to, which is reflected in the tragedy of the abandoned working mother.
> (d) It will establish for children born out of wedlock the right to equal protection by the revolutionary institutions.
> (e) It will establish a two-month maternity leave before and after birth for women who work.

(f) It will raise women's political, cultural and vocational levels through their participation in the revolutionary process.
(FSLN programme formulated during the 1960s, quoted in the 1987 Proclamation)

There has been an ongoing debate about feminism and its relevance to Nicaragua. It is criticised because it has a gendered, individualised perspective, not a class analysis, and it is also seen as a means of ghettoising women, leaving them alone to resolve problems which are the responsibility of the whole of society.[11]

We reject tendencies which propose the emancipation of women as a result of a struggle against men, and as an action exclusively by women, since this type of position divides and distracts the people from their fundamental tasks.

(FSLN proclamation)

Lea Guido, in 1987 leader of AMNLAE, said:

AMNLAE is an organization which struggles to integrate women, enabling them to develop as human beings, and to see which obstacles there are in the way of their participation, within the broad concept of integrating everything into the revolution . . . it is an organization which raises women's issues, but we cannot take women out of their context, because this is a mistake which has been made elsewhere. Also, sometimes they ask me if I am a feminist, and I say I have a revolutionary focus on women's oppression. If this is called feminism, it must be a coincidence, because we are confronting women's problems.[12]

Some early feminist critics of Nicaragua unintentionally fuelled this debate, with their ethnocentric, ill-informed questions and conclusions. However, it is of great interest that some of the issues once dismissed as 'bourgeois' or 'western feminist' have now appeared on the Nicaraguan agenda. Nicaraguan women generally avoid the label 'feminist', but the information they are producing on women's situation and concerns, and the recognition of the strength of the forces opposing women's liberation, would be recognised by any western feminist as common to their own perspective.

A recent example is abortion. Once a taboo subject, the stock response to any question about it was either reference to Somoza's extremely unpopular population control policies, or to the country's need for more workers and farmers. A call for more sex education used to be the most positive reply until a study in the main women's hospital revealed that botched abortions were the main cause of female death and sterility. This changed attitudes, and from 1985 abortion has been openly debated in the press, and discussed in the mass organisations.[13] Now, although anti-abortion legislation remains on the statute book, being little modified by the ambiguous 1987 Constitution, women seeking an abortion are not prosecuted if caught. Doris Tijerino, ex-*comandante*, said when she was head of the police: 'I am in favour of legalising abortion, not only as a woman, but also as Chief of Police' (quoted in *Barricada*, 9 December 1985). She gave as her reason that it would facilitate the prosecution of exploitative back-street abortionists, and would provide women with a safe alternative. Lea Guido, when questioned about it in 1987, raised a practical difficulty, the shortage of hospital beds, even for births, let alone abortions.[14] However, the need for sex-education and reliable contraception is seen as the long-term answer to this widespread problem, even if it offends some Nicaraguans.

Discrimination, as the cause of women's subordinate position in society, is recognised, and measures to combat it are discussed:

> Historically Nicaraguan women have been subjected to social discrimination which has placed them in a subordinate position in society. In addition to this discrimination, the majority of them also suffer discrimination as part of the exploited and oppressed classes of the people.
>
> (FSLN Proclamation)

The role of AMNLAE as a defender of women's rights was doubted for several years in the early 1980s, until a crisis meeting in September 1985, where the problem was made public. Its three phases (reconstruction 1979–82, defence, especially support for mothers 1983–5, and its more combative role since 1985) reflect the development of thinking about women in Nicaragua. It maintained its credibility by including in its agenda some of the most pressing concerns of Nicaraguan women: discrimination at work, sexual abuse and domestic violence, the need for sex education and an end to the culture of machismo, especially its result – 'irresponsible fatherhood'.[15] The FSLN included these in its 1987 proclamation, especially the criticism of machismo. Despite its silences on controversial issues like abortion, this proclamation marked a significant step forward and changed the nature of the debate. Machismo, identified in other earlier publications by, for example, the ATC,[16] was roundly condemned by the FSLN as 'a backward ideological survival, unacceptable to revolutionaries'. The proclamation defined the approach to the difficulties faced by women as follows:

> All bodies and members of the FSLN, all the social, union and mass organizations are obligated to promote the massive incorporation of women into the different tasks of the revolution, responding to their specific interests and struggling against all forms of oppression and discrimination . . . the defence of the revolution will be strengthened with new categories of fighters, workers, teachers, professionals, to the degree to which we are able to go on eliminating the obstacles which impede the integration of women and keep them in a discriminatory position.

Women are seen as protagonists in achieving their own liberation.

The FSLN proclamation was directed towards convincing the less-progressive men that the emancipation of women would benefit the whole of society, and would not become a disruptive force. It seeks their co-operation in resolving the problems which they and women face, through communal solutions, such as collective childcare, rather than solely at an individual level. The stress on the need to share the domestic workload, socialising it where possible, is a clear example of this dual approach. In 1987 the FSLN proclamation was given favourable publicity in the two pro-government newspapers, *Barricada* and *Nuevo Diario*, and widely discussed, with favourable responses from women activists,[17] while since 1987 leading members of the FSLN and AMNLAE have elaborated on the thinking which led up to it, and which has resulted from it. Perhaps the essence of it was caught by a headline in *Barricada* (19–20 March 1987): 'The enemy is not men, the enemy is the system.' AMNLAE leaders and Nicaraguan researchers and journalists also elaborated on the same theme.[18] The ATC, for example, explained its approach to the concerns raised by its women members:

> The ATC has taken care not to fall into feminist positions, which enlarge the gap the system has opened between men and women. Reactionaries use this for their objective of dividing the working class . . . . When we meet with union leaders to discuss issues, some feminists say this is the union's business, not women's . . . . We have of course noticed that in any discussion of women's rights, put this way it is easier to make the men listening more aware.[19]

The most important advance since the 1987 proclamation is that, given the official backing for their demands, women can now ask why they are not getting their rights, rather than needing to argue for such rights. They are in a stronger position to discuss issues which were formerly mentioned only in private, for fear of being seen as a distraction from revolutionary priorities. While it would be naïve to suggest that a statement of intent changes attitudes overnight, this declaration of political will marks the first stage in a long process.[20] Thus the purpose of the proclamation is described as consolidating since 1979 'the discussion and enactment of laws to abolish discrimination against women and generate new relations within the family, ones based on equality, respect and solidarity'.

WOMEN AND LEGISLATIVE CHANGE

Between 1979 and 1984 there were various well-documented legislative changes affecting women,[21] including the ban on use of women's bodies in advertisements, a commitment to legal equality, reiterated in the new Constitution, and the beginning of an attack on the very unfair divorce and custody legislation, '*patria potestad*', which reinforced the power of men over women and children. An example is the different grounds for divorce: adultery for a woman, but open concubinage for a man. Other controversial measures included legal change in a woman's favour to attempt to increase male participation in household tasks, payment for children fathered and the two 'family' laws. One, so-called 'Rights and Responsibilities of Mothers, Fathers and Children' and the other, 'Provision Law', were proposed by AMNLAE, and hotly debated in the National Assembly, the main legislative body. Although passed, they were neither published nor implemented, giving rise to widespread dissatisfaction. The strength of opposition from those who feared any infringement of the 'traditional family' (never a reality for generations of working-class Nicaraguans) or diminution of the power and status of men was demonstrated. The FSLN, despite its large parliamentary majority, did not feel that it could carry enough others with it to make the legislation a reality.

The question of divorce must take into account the Nicaraguan reality: less than half of couples are married, consensual unions being the most common, so divorce legislation affects a minority only. In fact since 1979 women have expressed the need to cement relationships so as to avoid the abandonment which leaves them as the sole household head, with full economic responsibility for any children. In theory men can be required to pay up to 50 per cent of their salary to maintain children, without regard to the legal status of the relationship with the mother, but it is reported that less than a third of women in fact receive such support.[22] Even when they do, half of a very small wage is insufficient, especially if this is shared by several other women and their children. Since 1979, official propaganda has favoured the nuclear family and castigated paternal irresponsibility. But some women complained that this is an attempt to impose middle-class family structure on the extended woman-headed families common in Central America and the Caribbean, where men are merely passing visitors. In Nicaragua this structure has been blamed on the migrant labour pattern required by an export economy, where all the cash crops were harvested within a four-month period. This left men with the option of establishing relationships in several different locations.[23] The culture of machismo, older than the export economy, stressed virility, proved by children, often by several different women at the same time. This subject and the role of the traditional Catholic Church in creating the virgin/whore antithesis, imposed on women in the culture of machismo, has been debated endlessly. Whatever the cause, the result is a predominance of woman-headed households, paradoxically characterised by child-bearing, forcing women into economic activity in order to maintain their children. For this reason, some Nicaraguan women aspire to escape into, rather than from, domesticity.

The 1987 Constitution attempted to redefine the family, in line with Nicaraguan reality, recognising the present responsibilities of women. It also tries to instil in men some sense of responsibility for the children they have fathered, in the interests of the children as much as their mother. It has yet to be seen if this changes social attitudes, but it expresses a commitment to change at least:

> Family relations rest on respect, solidarity and absolute equality of rights and responsibilities between men and women. Parents must work together to maintain the home, and provide for the integral development of their children, with equal rights and responsibilities.
>
> (Article 73)

This echoes the commitment expressed in the FSLN proclamation:

> The family is the basic unit of society, and guarantees social reproduction, not only from a biological point of view, but also of the principles and values of society. Women have been the fundamental pillar of Nicaraguan society . . . we are going to continue investing efforts and resources in supporting the family in the care of children . . . so that women can fulfil their maternal function and family responsibilities in even better conditions, without those responsibilities becoming insuperable obstacles to their own development and personal fulfilment . . . . We are going to continue struggling against irresponsible fatherhood and the physical and moral abuse of women and children . . . . We are going to promote real solidarity between couples, with respect to domestic tasks and family responsibilities.

Some early legislation had been passed with far less controversy, giving women equal rights to adopt, a necessity with so many war-orphans, and legislation giving all over the age of 14 equal pay for equal work, ending payment by family unit during the coffee harvest, so that women were registered as workers, not family helpers. Women's rights to social security (for the few permanent employees where subscriptions were paid) and to union membership were passed, as were provisions for maternity leave and time off during working hours to breast-feed. Non-compliance by both public and private-sector employers has become an issue with working women, who now have the law in their favour.[24]

Confusion over the divorce laws has led to cases being delayed while judges seek to resolve contradictions between legislation on equality and surviving pre-1979 laws on divorce. AMNLAE's Women's Legal Office has tried since 1983 to resolve some conflicts, examine existing and proposed legislation, and to advise women on their rights. Regional offices have been opened, and records kept on cases and enquiries, with a result that divorce and domestic violence have emerged as major preoccupations.[25]

After a stormy national meeting of women workers in 1983,[26] about the non-implementation of existing legislation on equal pay, and equal access to land in co-operatives, the ATC took steps to gather information on the realities of the lives of rural Nicaraguan women, to provide evidence in support of the complaints.[27] It appeared that men were still being paid for the work of the whole family, that women and children were not being registered separately, even when over 14 and entitled to equal pay. Furthermore few agricultural co-operatives would include women as members, except some widows who appeared to have inherited their husband's rights. Women were not getting their right to three months' maternity leave, with pay, and were being dismissed for pregnancy. They were not getting time off for breast-feeding, even when this was practicable, and were not being given lighter work for the same wage during late pregnancy. They were generally treated as second-class workers, expensive to employ, and shunned by both private and state contractors.[28]

In industry, similar non-compliance with equal-pay legislation was revealed. Women were kept on tasks rated as less-skilled, and penalised when they found it hard to work night-shifts because of family opposition.[29] In both industry and agriculture there has been much discussion about women's ability to achieve the same norms of production as men, but any suggestion of reduced norms, in recognition of household responsibilities, was rejected by the women themselves. The ATC has campaigned for women to have time off, with pay, to care for sick children. The law on equal pay cannot take into account women's double day, which leaves them too short of time and energy, and too worried about childcare and domestic work, to fulfil the same norms as men. If they are politically active, they may have a triple day, making their situation even more difficult. The struggle to make equal pay legislation a reality, and to make sure that women have equal access to land, training, promotion and co-operative membership, and work in safe conditions, still continues.

Heliette Ehlers, representing the ATC on the AMNLAE executive, wrote in the union journal *El Machete* (August 1987, page 8):

> Taking into account the importance of female labour, it is essential that they take responsibility for productivity. For that, men must value and respect their identity as women in union life, and not fear that they are only concerned with their own problems. This will enable us to strengthen working-class unity.

Finally, the need to educate men and many women about their rights to achieve public equality is acknowledged, and educational work through the media and mass organisations is seen as essential. Most cases brought to the AMNLAE Legal Office concern family matters (divorce, maintenance, domestic violence).[30] They are likely to reflect only the needs of a small number of urban women, being too far from women in remote rural areas, who are unlikely to seek their help. Employers, male and female workers, union officials, supervisors, judges and some sections of the press still have to be convinced that women are equal citizens in Nicaragua.

A further example is provided by the question of prostitution. Formerly a major economic activity, outlawed in 1979, it has survived in clandestinity.[31] Official opposition is limited to occasional raids on premises used by prostitutes, and only the women, not their clients, were subject to legal penalties. The problem was tackled by various schemes to train women in other skills. AMNLAE and some church groups took the lead, but many women continued to find this a lucrative way to earn a living, especially as inflation undermined wages in other work. This embarrassed the government, dedicated to the eradication of prostitution. Recently an article in the pro-government press suggested that the police should take prostitutes to check on their health card, to make sure that they were receiving regular examinations, but not to prosecute them.[32] It may be that the war offers alternative employment possibilities for some of the women, and literacy and access to education may have widened their options. But low salaries in the formal sector are a problem which various schemes to provide cheap consumer goods and foods to productive workers have not been able to overcome.

Since 1979 the INSSBI (the Social Welfare Institute) has operated departments of family protection, and for the protection of working minors, especially street-children, to try to prevent abuse, and to ensure that they are receiving their rights, especially to education. Recent cutbacks have severely affected this work. Legislation which aims to protect children can only take effect when their contribution to household survival is not crucial. A child may go to school on a shift-basis, but be too tired from working to be able to benefit. The need to buy books and writing equipment, formerly free, may also act as a deterrent. Thus the economic crisis is preventing the implementation of some of the most enlightened and well-intentioned legislation.[33]

WOMEN AND POLITICAL PARTICIPATION

The frequently heard phrase 'children, women and adults' gives some idea of the extent of women's subordination before 1979, nevertheless, many women were active in anti-Somoza demonstrations and armed actions. This illustrates the paradox that a woman can do as a mother what would be unthinkable for her as a woman. Many women recount tales of such activities and of their motivation to act in a way totally out of keeping with female submissiveness required at that time. The death of family members was the most common motive, and remains as an impetus to their continuing participation. This experience, which has affected many Nicaraguan families, is one of the problems the contras have been unable to overcome. The further deaths and disablement resulting from the contra war have kept the issue fresh in people's minds, reminding them of the continuity of the present struggle with the anti-Somoza struggle. It has been pointed out that the form of struggle against Somoza meant that the main location of the activity was in the reproductive, not the productive, sphere, giving a neighbourhood, rather than a workplace, location, which also influenced the early development of the women's organisations AMPRONAC, later AMNLAE, and the CDS structure.[34] This made it easier for women to become involved, working in their own neighbourhoods and homes, and may account for their unusually high participation rate. The CDS committees developed from the CDCs (anti-Somoza civil defence committees, defending areas against the security forces).

The FSLN's commitment to maintaining women's active participation is fundamental to the survival of existing society, and to plans to bring about lasting change within it, and cannot be dismissed as a cynical attempt to channel and control women's energies. Low representation of women in leadership positions, despite some notable exceptions, and sexist assumptions held and expressed by some Party members in the early years after 1979, have to some extent been counteracted by the 1987 proclamation, outlawing such attitudes as unacceptable.

The FSLN had first promoted the participation of women through the Patriotic Alliance of Nicaraguan Women, during the 1960s, then through AMPRONAC from 1977, the Association of Nicaraguan Women Confronting the National Problem (namely, Somoza) which later became AMNLAE. This women's organisation began life with male leaders and spokesmen, but this soon changed. AMNLAE has been through various changes in orientation and structure, beginning as a mass movement, then developing a more tightly organised structure, and now moving back towards the concept of a mass movement including all women, not just the feminine wing of the FSLN. Its priorities have changed in line with the changing situation in the country, from reconstruction, to support for the war effort, and now on behalf of women's expressed needs and demands.

AMNLAE experienced much criticism, from within and outside its ranks, during the early 1980s. It focused on conventionally defined 'women's work' which was seen as reinforcing traditional feminine roles, and it had a too-exclusive concentration on women as mothers, ignoring their role as workers and heads of household. Unwillingness to touch controversial issues like domestic violence, abortion and sex education weakened its reputation as a defender of women's interests. However, by 1985 these matters were included in the AMNLAE discussion document used to focus workplace discussions during the preparation for the September anniversary celebrations.[35]

In 1986 and 1987 AMNLAE was further restructured, and in 1987 a new secretariat, including well-known women from most sectors of economic and social life, was elected, to ensure the widest possible representation of women's interests and maximum relevance to the needs of Nicaraguan women. The intention was to set up a structure enabling AMNLAE to speak with authority when trying to change laws and attitudes, so as to become a movement of women and not duplicate the work of existing organisations such as unions. The aim was to be able to appeal to women outside the FSLN and mass organisations in support of the revolution.[36] How far this can be achieved, especially incorporating women from other non-FSLN political groups, will have to be seen in practice.

One consequence of AMNLAE's failings in the early 1980s was the growth of women's work in other organisations – initially the ATC, then the small rural producers' union, UNAG, and belatedly in the CST (Sandinista Workers' Union), the main umbrella organisation for urban workers. Other groupings of women exist in CONAPRO (a professional workers' union) and around the AMNLAE Legal Office. This now runs workshops to train AMNLAE members, health workers, army officers (male) and police (mixed) as well as Sandinista Youth (JS 29 Julio) on such topics as abuse, discrimination, machismo, sexuality, abortion and the Constitution. The government Women's Office, now the Institute of Nicaraguan Women, took a leading role. Unlike other government offices, it had its budget increased from its 1982 foundation, under the direct control of the Ministry of the Presidency, giving some idea of its national importance and the status of its work. So successful was the work of the other organisations that there was a serious debate about the continued need for AMNLAE.

It is difficult to assess AMNLAE's effectiveness. At a grassroots level, there was some doubt of its relevance, because most active women were in the CDS, or unions, rather than AMNLAE. Only a few women are politically active, because of lack of time and energy, and childcare constraints.[37] There were also tensions within AMNLAE between grassroots activists and Managua officials, seen by some working-class women as too remote from the lives of ordinary men and women. But a result of this tension has been the incorporation of more working-class women into regional and local leadership[38] along lines proposed in the 1987 proclamation. This may increase its influence as a movement rather than a mass organisation through its current campaigning. Its longer-established concerns continue: support for bereaved women and those with relatives mobilised, propaganda in favour of resource conservation, production of food plants and animals, and of medicinal plants, and the more efficient use of fuel, as well as ensuring women's access to health care, education and housing. The main change is the new focus on women as workers, rather than just as housewives, reflecting their new position in the economy.[39]

AMNLAE's influence may be out of all proportion to its membership, since so many of its activists are also FSLN members, and it exerts considerable influence over policy-making. It suggests legislative change to the National Assembly, and carries out educational campaigns designed to provide public support and understanding for these changes. Its early role, the prevention of women becoming a backward, conservative force, favouring the contras, has given way to a new focus on response to problems expressed by women both inside and outside AMNLAE. Sometimes it has been seen as too far in advance of public opinion, as in its campaign to have women included in conscription. This failed, but resulted in women being allowed to volunteer, but not be given combat duties (until 1986). This issue had recently received further publicity, and women were being urged to join the army in 1987, on an equal basis to men. But family opposition is still rendering female conscription too unpopular. This was a result of the continuing war, as was women's participation in the economy, leading to a greater consideration for their specific needs and demands, far beyond that achieved by years of campaigning by AMNLAE.

WOMEN AND WORK (RURAL AND URBAN)

The proportion of women among the economically active population has increased to 42 per cent by 1983, with a particularly high proportion (51 per cent) in commerce and textiles, and 35 per cent in agriculture. The concentration of women in typically female manufacturing jobs is notable. Women are usually in low-paid occupations, where little training is given, and the only recognised skill is manual dexterity and attention to detail. The greatest changes since 1979 have been in the agricultural sector, where many women now have permanent work.[40]

Up to 1983, the ATC had few women leaders and a low female participation in meetings. Women received scant respect from male comrades. This changed after the 1983 meeting of female agricultural workers led to calls for greater participation by women, and more attention to the constraints on them, and to injustices at work and at home. The ATC then carried out a major survey, with Centro de Investigaciones Economicas de la Reforma Agraria (CIERA) based on interviews and questionnaires by ATC members in their workplaces. The results illuminated the difficulty of rural women's lives, and provided much valuable data. Lack of childcare, sexual harassment at work, the family wage instead of equal wages, danger at work (from, for example, pesticides), male prejudice against women workers, and poor health (due to exhaustion, poor nutrition and frequent child-bearing) and low self-evaluation emerged as major problems. Women's importance in the export crop economy, and their role as household heads, contradicted the marginal image of female agricultural workers. In response, the ATC prepared a discussion booklet, in photo-story style, for use by women with a low level of literacy[41] in workplace discussion groups. Studies of hazardous industries were also initiated – for example, the study of Ocotal tobacco-workers, jointly with the Ministry of Health (MINSA) and the Ministry of Labour (MITRAB).[42] Pressure was put on employers and union officials and on male workers to secure the provision of workplace childcare, however rudimentary, and to make sure that women's rights to maternity leave, breast-feeding time and equal pay were respected, as well as a canteen providing cooked food for workers, transport to work, proper tools for the job, sensible allocation of tasks, an end to sexual harassment, supply centres in rural areas for scarce consumer goods, and communal maize mills and laundries. These were to reduce time and energy wasted at work, and to lighten the domestic workload. Technical training as tractor drivers, pest controllers, supervisors and in all the technical skills formerly reserved for better-paid male workers was requested. The enforcement of legislation on women's rights to full co-operative membership was also demanded.[43]

This very practical focus had been facilitated by the ATC's work with women, so that the demands came from the women themselves, not from union officials. It was important that the necessary changes were fully understood by all rural workers, male and female, to ensure that they were carried out.[44] By 1986 only a few of these changes had taken place, because of lack of resources: twenty-six child development centres (CDIs in urban areas), forty-two rural childcare centres (SIRs in rural areas), seventy children's canteens (in rural areas) and ten (in urban areas).[45] All of these are now under threat because of the economic situation and the need to make cuts in the national budget. The incorporation of women in tasks formerly defined as male may do much to change conventional ideas about 'men's work' and 'women's work'. An even more important change would be brought about by men's acceptance that they need to do some of the household tasks left at present to the females in the house.[46] A study made during the 1970s[47] revealed great disparities in male and female domestic work in rural Nicaragua. The ATC/CIERA research showed that little had changed a decade later, with politically active men likely to use their union or other work as an excuse for non-participation. The realities of housework with mud floors, walls which let in wind, rain and dust, roofs which harbour much small wildlife, water supplies from a well, stream or standpipe, and no electricity, need to be considered. Men in Nicaragua do some tasks, such as repairing the house, fetching firewood, caring for large animals, clearing land, and planting cash and food crops. But women care for children, small animals and poultry, tend gardens, make medicine, make and repair clothing, and do all the food-processing tasks, helped by the children, who also fetch water and care for younger siblings. Many rural women begin their day as early as 3 a.m. and continue until after dark, often fitting in an eight-hour paid working day as well.[48]

A similarly heavy workload, without agricultural tasks, was reported for urban women, despite their higher participation in paid work.[49] The increased importance of rural production in the Nicaraguan economy, and the need to make life in the countryside more attractive, to stem and even reverse the drift to the towns, has resulted in greater public attention to rural women and their heavy workload.[50] The attitude that men are for work, women for the house, still underlies many common assumptions about male and female capabilities, not least in the minds of rural women themselves.[51] But the problem is now seen as a social and ideological one for society, rather than for the individual.[52]

The need for women's labour in paid work has been the main agent bringing about more sympathetic attitudes to rural women. So indirectly the war has benefited these women as a group, while threatening their lives, homes and livelihood as individuals. The response of the ATC has been exemplary, and the widespread publicity given to the need to meet some of the practical demands of women members has been effective,[53] as has AMNLAE's work to spread the same information even more widely. But the other main rural organisation, UNAG, has been slower, although it has now published a training booklet on women's issues as well.[54]

In urban areas, there has been less positive action. The CST has been slow to acknowledge that its workers have a gender. Early efforts to organise among women were not successful. For example, the maids' union attracted mainly domestic workers who were cooks and cleaners in public workplaces, not the women working in private homes who were most at risk of exploitation. Legislation exists to ensure that they are paid a reasonable wage for a limited working day, with time off for study. But they still tend to be treated as one of the family, with all the duties but none of the rights that this implies, and this is even true in the homes of some women activists. Probably the most hopeful sign of improvement in their situation has been the difficulty in recruiting maids, demonstrating the availability of other opportunities in the formal and informal sectors of the economy.

Women in the informal sector in urban areas are usually engaged in some form of trade. During the early 1980s there was discussion of the policy of the Ministry of Commerce (MICOIN) to discourage such women in the hope that they would find work in the formal sector instead. There was no acknowledgement of the need these women had for flexible working hours, which could be combined with childcare, or access to a means of earning a living, as the sole household head, which would not be eroded by inflation. A study in 1985[55] provided data to change this perception of such women as unproductive and parasitic, likely recruits for the black market, and to recognise the valuable role they played in the distribution of the nation's food-supplies. The contrast between their motives and means of operation and those of the large-scale retailers had not been fully appreciated before.

In the formal sector, women worked in factories or in small work-shops in tasks seen as an extension of their domestic role. High turnover of staff was explained by poor working conditions and lack of opportunities for training and promotion. This was illustrated by a detailed study of the textile industry.[56] It focused on the constraints under which the women worked, the prejudice they faced from man-agers, supervisors and male workers, and the other difficulties they la-boured under, which made escape to the so-called 'unproductive' for-mal sector seem an attractive proposition to the women themselves. There is a need to involve more women in the urban workforce, not as sellers of soft drinks, tortillas and cakes, but as producers of the food, clothing, chemicals and consumer goods required to raise living standards and satisfy urgent needs in Nicaragua. This may result in urban women gaining similar consideration to that given to rural women, although at present this process is less advanced.

WOMEN AND HEALTH

There have been impressive improvements in health standards in Nicaragua, including the eradication of polio, and the reduction of malaria, diphtheria, whooping-cough, measles, tetanus and other infectious diseases through immunisation and control programmes. Tuberculosis treatment has been introduced, and oral rehydration for children suffering from infant diarrhoea has saved many lives.[57] A mother-and-child health programme involving pre- and post-natal check-ups has reduced maternal mortality to 3 per thousand.[58] There has been a major effort to provide free health care throughout the country, by a system of regional hospitals, clinics and health posts, in urban and rural areas. Most of this work has continued during the 1980s[59] but the war has inflicted heavy damage, since the medical programme has been one of the main targets for contra attacks. International aid, in the form of medicines, equipment, training and health personnel, has helped to offset this damage, and the United Nations had funded a health-education study. But contra attacks on health clinics and health posts, in rural areas and on health personnel, have left over 10 per cent of the country with no health care. This has had a serious effect on health campaigns, including immunisations, TB control and malaria control, reflected in a rise in infant mortality, and reports of poor health and malnutrition.[60] Inflation has eroded health workers' salaries, and part-payments in kind (for example, in food) have so far failed to remedy this. There was already a shortage of trained staff as a result of the 1979 exodus, and the slight improvement in life expectancy (64 years for women) has barely been maintained.[61] Much remains to be done to improve public health standards and nutritional knowledge, to provide the resources to put knowledge into practice, and to improve the attention given to women in public hospitals, providing adequate equipment and drugs.[62] Free treatment and prescriptions have become war casualties. Over a third of patients are expected to pay for the cost of drugs, although exemption is given to TB and malaria patients, and to mother-and-child health control patients.

The drain on health personnel has partly been offset by a more liberal attitude to private practice, recognising that in the present situation trained staff need to be encouraged to remain practising in Nicaragua, even if this fails to meet the reforming expectations of 1979. Health was seen as one of the key areas of the FSLN programme, and access to health care was one of the most prized post-1979 gains, which explains why the contras have made it a target. Staff working within the health sector, mainly women, have done their best to overcome the constraints within which they are forced to work. They reuse disposable gloves and syringes, use a variety of drugs and contraceptive supplies, and cope with the loss of all refrigerated supplies, especially vaccines and blood, during the frequent power-cuts. Water shortages and cuts make medical work and personal hygiene difficult, and the impact on child health is considerable – for example, storing water in houses provides breeding-grounds for mosquitoes, leading to outbreaks of malaria and dengue fever.[63]

Nevertheless, Nicaragua has continued pioneering work in mental health, dealing with war trauma and the rehabilitation of disabled people, especially war victims. Progress since 1979 gives some idea of what could be achieved in a country like Nicaragua without the special circumstances that were introduced.

Programmes which have a particular impact on women have been expanded into new areas: detection and control of cervical and breast cancer, and of sexually transmitted diseases; fertility control; and sex-education. MINSA and AMNLAE have worked together on some of these programmes,[64] even though in the whole country there are only about ten people trained to read a cervical smear. Family planning has obvious implications for women's health and well-being, and was identified as a priority area. One result is that now clinical sterilisation is available to women with five children, at their own request, and not only at the request of a husband or other relative.[65] Another example is the sex-education programmes in the media and through the mass organisations, but the birth-rate remains high, and women have, on average, six surviving children. The rural birth-rate is higher than the urban rate.[66]

There has also been some progress in women's occupational health, although the use of pesticides without protective clothing or proper equipment and training has continued. There is now information and awareness of the dangers, and certain pesticides, widely used before 1979, are now banned (DDT, 245T among them). Foreign exchange problems have limited the import of others, but there is experimental research to find pesticides made from natural products. In the tobacco industry the Ministries of Health and Labour have carried out research to assess the dangers and recommend alternatives to dangerous practices.[67] The progress made in public awareness has alerted some unions to the dangers their members face at work. But the needs and restrictions of the export economy curtail the implementation of necessary measures.

WOMEN AND EDUCATION

In the first year after the overthrow of Somoza the Literacy Crusade involved women, students and schoolchildren, who left home to work and live in rural communities for six months, teaching whole communities to read. Many women refer to this as the most formative experience of their lives, freeing them from family control, and showing them how the majority of Nicaraguans lived. The less well-publicised contribution of older, urban women, working in urban neighbourhoods, and with street children, is also important – as was the end result: literacy for the majority of women, who had formerly been illiterate. They can now read a newspaper, write to mobilised sons, or to children studying abroad, and the excuse of illiteracy can no longer be used to deny them training at work.

Literacy can be rapidly lost without practice, so an adult education campaign began in 1984, designed to bring adults up to the same level as children who had completed their school education. At higher levels, as a result of the absence of men on military service, women now make up the majority of university students. But they may face considerable family opposition, or criticism from their peer group if they become politically active – in the students' union, for example.[68] Older women may take university courses to improve their level of education; for example, many schoolteachers are trying to raise qualifications so as to teach at secondary level. Small grants are available to some students.

However, the war has had a destructive impact on education as well. The education budget was frozen when military spending exceeded 50 per cent of the national budget, and subsequent cutbacks have severely affected school building and maintenance, teachers' salaries (in a mainly female profession), and spending on textbooks and equipment. This has had a disproportionate impact on women and women students, since their relative disadvantage before 1979 meant that greater effort was needed to bring them up to male educational levels. The contras have burnt schools and books, kidnapped, raped, tortured and killed teachers, making volunteer adult education workers their special target in rural areas. Pioneering work in education continues despite these attacks,[69] but as with health, popular support for the government depends on its ability to deliver services of which the majority were deprived before 1979, a fact of which the contras are only too well aware. The statistics for women in education, as educators and educated, indicate their importance,[70] but there is still much to be achieved.[71] New requirements for children to buy their own books may limit access to education for the poorest, usually woman-headed, families.[72]

The government also uses the media for educative and propaganda purposes. Transmission problems, broadcasts by hostile radio and TV channels from neighbouring countries, and lack of electricity or batteries all restrict access to pro-government media, especially in remote areas and among the poorest rural and urban families. Access to education in its widest sense is guaranteed under the Constitution.[73] But there needs to be an awareness that not all sectors of the population are well informed about their rights or easy to reach by the main communication channels.

WOMEN AND HOUSING

Women give more importance to housing than men do, in any country, since so much of their lives will be determined by the conditions in which a large part of their daily work is carried out. Following the Somoza period, reconstruction was the main priority, and during the past decade great pressure has been put on existing resources to fulfil the demand for timber, bricks, cement and roofing materials (tiles, zinc or asbestos cement). Local authorities and the Ministry of Housing (MINVAH) are the main suppliers of materials for self-construction of housing, with MINVAH responsible for the allocation of plots not privately rented or sold, and for the construction of public housing. This is another sector badly affected by cutbacks.

The war has meant that scarce resources have been diverted to military building, to rehousing refugees and those moved from the conflict zone, and has limited the supply of materials like timber, affected by contra activity in the mountain forests. Private housing received lower priority, but house construction dominates the priorities and budgets of even relatively poor families. Home improvements, replacement of mud by a tiled floor, or the provision of water or electricity, reduce the domestic workload enormously. Rents to absentee landlords were frozen after 1979, and in many cases the property was 'intervened' by MINVAH, to which rents were paid. 'Intervened' is used here as a technical term for the state taking over private property on a temporary basis should the landlord prove to be inadequate in some way. In 1985 rents were an almost insignificant part of household budgets.

In Managua the situation was different. In middle-class areas, demand from local and foreign employees led to a parallel economy, with rents paid in dollars. This increased rent differentials as inflation progressed. Managua is a unique case. It still bears the obvious scars of the 1972 earthquake and the Somoza redevelopment strategy. It contains one-third of the national population, and deliberate underinvestment to discourage migration to it has exacerbated its housing, transport and infrastructure problems, and has had a serious impact on its inhabitants. However, for those living in other towns, or in rural areas, this is not significant.

One controversy aroused by MINVAH was about the allocation of the few new public-sector houses. Some were allocated through the mass organisations, including the unions, for productive workers, which did not usually include woman-headed families. The design of new housing areas rarely took into account the practical needs of a Nicaraguan family: space for growing food or keeping animals, for example.[74] MINVAH has now amalgamated with the Ministries of Transport and Construction. Nicaragua has a low population relative to its land area, though this population is growing rapidly, and is not urbanised, after the near complete destruction of the centre of the capital city in the earthquake and subsequent fighting to overthrow Somoza. If government policy succeeds, migration to the towns will be reversed, but this may have a gendered impact. Many women, especially when abandoned with children to support, seek work in urban areas and woman-headed households are a clear majority in Managua. Work opportunities in the formal and informal sectors are found in towns, especially those employing mainly women.

WOMEN AND DEFENCE

The work of AMNLAE to include women in the armed forces as conscripts has already been discussed, but women are also active in the voluntary defence force, the militia, which at times has had a female majority, and in volunteer vigilance, especially at night in housing areas, and at workplaces. Since 1979 women have also been highly visible as members of both the volunteer and professional police forces. Women carrying guns are commonplace in Nicaragua, much to the surprise of visitors, and this must have done much to change the image of Nicaraguan women themselves.

As with so many aspects of public life in Nicaragua, the active women are in a minority, and are likely to be doing guard-duty, working as fire-fighters and health or first-aid volunteers, as well as teaching voluntarily, and trying to work in the unions, and possibly also the CDS and AMNLAE. This is one of the main problems: the excessive burden which falls on the politically active and the non-involvement of other women. However, the level of participation in defence is related directly to the perceived threat. When the contras are active nearby it proves much easier to convince people of the value of defence. Civil defence is another factor; the relatively low level of casualties in the 1988 hurricane reflects the high level of organisation and public response. Following the 1987 and 1988 peace negotiations for regional peace agreements, and the scaling down of economic aid from the US administration, the danger of a co-ordinated attack has receded. But the contras remain a threat, with isolated bands living in the hills. Although the Atlantic Coast situation has improved, vehicles are still attacked, roads mined and co-operatives threatened, and some of the remoter rural areas are still risky. In these areas women are used to carrying guns about their daily work. But the threat in urban areas seems remote.

There is some continuity from the late 1970s, when many women and girls preferred to go and join the guerrillas in the hills, rather than risk imprisonment, torture, rape and death in the towns. Women who have braved physical hardship and sometimes social ostracism are often among present-day activists. However, a few have found the criticisms they faced on their return so devastating that they now refuse to speak of their time in the mountains, where they were completely challenging all assumptions about the sheltered lives expected of middle-class girls.

The role of the police and armed forces is defence against the contras, not oppression, nevertheless women often have non-combat, clerical and educational work, or do 'domestic' duties. Women themselves differ in their estimate of their strength and reliability relative to men, although the war has resulted in women doing many nontraditional tasks in the armed forces, as elsewhere in society. Many wish to be more than mothers of heroes and martyrs, and their presence in the armed forces offers an evident challenge to this traditional image, with which many Nicaraguan women would still identify.

CONCLUSION

The current situation of women in Nicaragua presents many contradictions. This is perceived by outsiders visiting the country, and by Nicaraguan women themselves. Attempts to present a new image of women, and to take on new roles while challenging old ones, have been given a greater chance of success, at least temporarily, by the contra war than by any number of good intentions. Nicaraguan women are well aware that they are in danger of losing these advances when the war ends and the men return. The progress made should not be underestimated, but even without the war Nicaragua would be a small country ravaged by inflation and the 1988 hurricane, with serious economic problems consequent on its low level of development. Much work remains to be done in the fields of law, ideology, health and education should circumstances permit, but at present the priority is national survival.

NOTES

1   *Envio*, 6:78 gives 20–40% women as an estimate.
2   In the early years after the revolution, photographers like Susan Meiselas, video-makers like Fiona Macintosh and Adriana Angel portrayed Nicaraguan women, and popular books on women were produced by Margaret Randall, Jane Deighton and others. More detailed theoretical analysis was done by Hermione Harris, Maxine Molyneux, Elisabeth Maier, Susan Ramirez-Horton and others. More recently, Molyneux has written a new chapter in Walker (1985), and

the Nicaragua Solidarity Campaign Women's Network was preparing a book which was due out in 1989.

3   See also *Envio*, 6:78 (Dec. 1987) on the interaction of class and gender in the analysis of women's situation.

4   During the past few years several valuable research reports have been published, including an assessment of the progress made during the UN Decade of Women, and a general overview by Lea Guido, former Minister of Health, now head of AMNLAE. An investigation into the obstacles in the way of the elimination of all forms of discrimination against women by Ileana Rodriguez, and a study of Nicaraguan women in the economy by Paola Perez Aleman and Ivonne Siu have added another valuable overview, supported by more detailed research to be mentioned later. The most significant factor lending respectability to studies of the situation of Nicaraguan women within the country itself is the need to encourage women into the economy. This has focused attention on the constraints under which they live and the factors which limit their participation.

5   'We are convinced of the need to break down the dichotomy between production and reproduction, between the class struggle and the struggle for women's liberation' (Rodriguez, 1987).

6   *Envio*, 6:78 refers to the time spent queueing for food.

7   In the ATC article 'Un estilo de trabajo . . .', in *Documentos sobre la Mujer* (Oct.–Dec. 1987) this point is made.

8   *Somos*, 29 (1986) raised similar issues and stressed the need to educate men to recognise women's work and share household tasks.

9   *Envio*, 6:78.

10   Ibid.

11   Beth Woronuik.

12   *Documentos sobre la Mujer* (Oct.–Dec. 1987).

13   Of maternal deaths, 27% resulted from botched abortions. The majority of women having abortions had been pregnant before, and only 23% of them were single, belying the stereotype of the young girl trying to avoid a scandal. Older women with several children, often abandoned by the man, were those most likely to seek abortions. This information emerged from a study by Aleman and Cardenas (1984) and Altamirano, Fuentes, Valle and Rodriguez (1985).

14   Lea Guido was quoted in *Documentos sobre la Mujer* (Oct.–Dec. 1987).

15   Orlando Nuñez in 'Moral y revolucion en la vida cotidiana', in *Cuadernos de sociologia*, 3 (Jan.–April 1987), discussed the need to reform attitudes in daily life, especially sexist assumptions.

16   This was discussed in several other publications – for example, the MIDINRA (Agrarian Reform Ministry) publication *Revolucion y Desarrollo*, 3 (1985), which has an article by Orlando Nuñez, 'Machismo y revolucion', pp. 44–8.

17   *Cuadernos de Sociologia*, 4–5, School of Sociology, UCA, Managua (May–Dec. 1987), especially 'Que es la practica del proclama del FSLN para nosotras?' by Milagros Barahona.

18   Lea Guido, at the time of publication general secretary of AMNLAE, elaborated on the proclamation, and Beth Woronuik added further

clarification, as do articles in *Envio*, 6:78, *Documentos sobre la Mujer*, published by AMNLAE (Oct.–Dec. 1987), *Cuadernos de Sociologia*, 4–5 (May–Dec. 1987), and *Barricada Internacional*, supplements on women in March 1987 and March 1988.

19 Report on the Third Meeting of Women Workers in the ATC, in *Documentos sobre la Mujer* (Oct.–Dec. 1987).

20 Perez Aleman and Siu (1986); Rodriguez (1987); Perez Aleman, Martinez and Windmaier (1987); and Perez and Diaz (1986).

21 Rodriguez (1987) and AMNLAE Legal Office publication *Los logros juridicos* (1985).

22 Interviews with female textile workers in Managua by Perez Aleman, Martinez and Windmaier (1987).

23 *Envio*, 6:78.

24 In the 1987 Constitution, replacing the 1974 Constitution, which had ten articles referring specifically to women's rights.

25 The Nicaragua Solidarity Campaign *Women's Network Newsletter*, 4, (1988) refers to the new divorce law passed in April 1988, which enables a marriage to be dissolved by either partner, even if the other partner opposes this divorce. Much anti-woman legislation is found in the 1904 Civil Code, according to *Envio*, 6:78. Article 72 of the new 1987 Constitution refers to the need to be able to dissolve marriages or common-law relationships by mutual agreement or the wish of one partner. AMNLAE Legal Office produced a pamphlet to explain the divorce situation in 1987.

26 After the first meeting of female agricultural workers in 1983 the ATC began campaigning, and in 1986 a second balance sheet was drawn up to assess how far progress had been made (Report to the Second National Assembly of Agricultural Workers in 1986, by the National Secretary for Women).

27 CIERA/ATC (1984) '*La mujer en las co-operativas agropecuarias en Nicaragua*', published by CIERA/MIDINRA, Managua, a case study analysis of women in agrarian co-operatives.

28 Article 74 of the Constitution confirms the right to paid maternity leave and employment protection for pregnant workers. Article 82 stresses that women have equal rights with men to earn equal wages, equal rights to promotion and social security, to work an eight-hour day and a six-day week, and to have good working conditions.

29 Perez Aleman, Martinez and Windmaier (1987); Castillo, Windmaier and Barone (1986).

30 According to the Legal Office, 51% of all cases concerned wife-beating and this occurred in all classes, although it was most likely when the woman was not working outside the home. Wife-beating is not yet specifically made illegal.

31 An INSSBI (Social Welfare Institute) study done in 1982, 'Estudio sobre la prostitucion en Nicaragua'.

32 *Barricada Internacional* (25 Aug. 1988).

33 Report of BRIN Women's Day-school, Managua (April 1987). Articles 75 and 76 stress that all children have equal rights, and Article 76 suggests that the state should create conditions conducive to their welfare. Article 121 of the Constitution is also relevant.

34   *Envio*, 6:78.

35   Discussion document 'Situacion de la mujer en Nicaragua', AMNLAE (Sept. 1985).

36   As a movement, its priorities were, according to Lea Guido, incorporation of women into the economy, to ensure the economic survival of the revolution, better childcare provision, and shared domestic tasks. The preservation of the dignity of women ending violence against them, and a sex-education programme were also priorities. This was discussed in *Envio*, 6:78. Articles 36–40 of the 1987 Constitution can also be used to defend women from abuse, and liberalise divorce laws, according to Milu Vargas, the National Assembly Legal Adviser. This was discussed in the Agencia Nueva Nicaragua publication, *Women in Central America* (March 1987).

37   Muhlberger and Brenner (1986) reported on a study done on the participation of women in the CDS.

38   AMNLAE must promote 'the incorporation of women into the tasks of the revolution; advance the struggle of women and all society against sexual discrimination through all institutions and organisations; educate about the gains and problems of Nicaraguan women; and represent them internationally . . . . AMNLAE should not try to become a mass organisation counterposed to or parallel to existing mass organisations . . . on the contrary, it should promote the incorporation of women into the unions, co-operatives, CDS, professional and student organisations, and so on . . . to promote action by society to win full equality' (FSLN proclamation); and in 1980 AMNLAE had stated its intention to become a mass movement rather than a mass organisation, as emphasised in *Envio*, 6:78.

39   Lea Guido, interviewed in *Barricada Internacional*, supplement on women (March 1988), said that during 1987, AMNLAE had lacked a programme of struggle, and admitted that the ideological battle would take time, but said that this year's campaigns would focus on abuse, sex-education, and increasing the number of women in positions of authority.

40   Perez Aleman and Siu (1986); Perez Aleman, Martinez and Windmaier (1987); Rodriguez (1987). Figures for women's participation in the economy are given, showing that the proportion of women in the EAP rose from 27% in 1950 to 42% in 1983, from 27% to 37% in manufacturing, from 36% to 65% in all types of commerce, and was a constant 51% in service activities. In industry, women workers were mainly in chemicals, pharmaceuticals, textiles and clothing, food, plastics and paper, and in small-scale manufacturing; for example, MIND (Ministry of Industry) gives 76% as the figure for small-scale clothing manufacture employees in Managua who are female. *Envio* suggests that 35% of the rural labour force were female, with female farmers in addition (6:78).

41   Ministerio de la Reforma Agraria (MIDINRA), in *Informaciones Agropecuarias* (March–April 1987), gave greater detail on women's participation, as relatively recent employees, in agriculture. The state sector employed most, with 74 per cent of the tobacco workers and 60 per cent of the coffee pickers being female, and 44 per cent of the

permanent labour force also female. Some regions had more women than others, especially Regions I and IV (opportunities, for example, in Region III gave women other choices, and most opted not to do low-paid agricultural work). The same article says that 80 per cent of the women working the land came from proletarian homes, and 58% of these were the sole support of their children; 22 per cent were the only member of their household in work, suggesting that the increased permanence of women's agricultural work was vital to family survival. It appeared that those seeking work were heads of households, whereas those only interested in temporary work were still living with their parents.

42 MITRAB (1983), study of tobacco workers in Ocotal.

43 Half of Nicaragua's co-operatives had women members (in 1983) but only 6 per cent of all co-operatives had women as full members (CIERA, 1984). By 1987 81 per cent of women farm workers were said to be in the ATC, especially if they worked in the state sector, with fewer in the private sector. Rodriguez (1987) says that from 1984 onwards more women had been given land titles in agrarian co-operatives, quoting a figure of 80 per cent of the beneficiaries of land reform since 1984 being women, redressing the former imbalance. This includes members of full co-operatives as well as of credit and service co-operatives, where the land is cultivated separately, not communally.

44 Ibid.

45 Bente Madsen's article, published by the government Women's Office.

46 *Somos*, 29 (1986) lists new tasks being done by women despite the belief that driving a tractor sterilises a woman or the better-founded theories that pesticides can provoke miscarriages.

47 Gillespie worked in Nicaragua in 1977, doing time-budget studies.

48 *Informaciones Agropecuarias* (March–April 1987) suggests that only 6 per cent of household tasks are undertaken by men. In an urban study where both of the partners were in paid employment, women devoted 56 per cent of their time to domestic labour, and men only 9 per cent of theirs, and in a rural area a woman may work a 16- or even an 18-hour day, according to the government Women's Office. Guerrero and Guerrero (1986) suggested in their study of Managuan households that women devoted 92 per cent of their time to tasks concerned with the survival of their household.

49 In urban Nicaragua, women made up 37 per cent of the textile labour force, and were concentrated in low-paid work. Of the commercial workforce 80 per cent were women, as were 65 per cent of those working in the informal sector, and of these, 50 per cent were heads of household (*Envio*, 6:78). A study by the School of Sociology at the University of Central America (UCA) of household survival strategies noted that the woman's working day was long because of all the reproductive tasks included in it, in addition to paid work – *Envio*, 5:66 (Dec. 1986).

50 In *Barricada* (31 July 1988) it was reported that the Sept. 1987 National Assembly of the ATC, the third one held, had discussed the

provision of childcare, the need for cheap supplies in the workplace, collective laundries, improved health care and food production, by and for families, as advances needed to facilitate women's inclusion in the agricultural workforce.

51 CIERA/CETRA/ATC, *La feminizacion de la fuerza de trabajo asalariado en el agro*, Managua (Oct. 1985). *Somos*, 29, described the attitude expected: the need to be silent and to know one's place in the presence of men.

52 *Informaciones Agropecuarias* (March–April, 1987) said that 87 per cent of female agricultural workers attended mass organisations and union meetings, and 36 per cent of them were active in more than one of these organisations. Of the problems identified as hindering participation, 80 per cent had to do with childcare and domestic work.

53 In 1986 the Second Assembly of Women Agricultural Workers run by the ATC passed resolutions later printed in the union journal '*El Machete*' and in booklet form as a discussion tool for use within the union membership structure. AMNLAE took the results into account in its campaigning, and *Somos*, 29 (1986), reports on a meeting of female farmworkers in Region III which took place in May 1986, where similar demands were raised to facilitate inclusion of women in the workforce.

54 Report of the Nicaragua Solidarity Campaign Women's Study Tour (1987), which suggested that when UNAG did give women responsibility, it was usually in 'feminine' areas like health and education.

55 MICOIN attacked small women street-traders and market-traders as parasites and speculators, apparently unaware of their importance in family survival and food distribution. A study by UCA researcher Aida Redondo: *El Sector informal: la mujer en el pequeño comercio.* Managua Asociación Nicaraguense de cientificos sociales (ANICS) (1985) revealed their real importance to the economy and the contrast between their scale of operation and their methods, and those of the black-market operators. See *Envio*, 5:66, for a translated summary.

56 The study by the Women's Office of women working in the textile industry in Managua stressed their high labour turnover, which could be reduced if they were not required to work on the night shift, especially when pregnant, and if they were given technical training. The problems they faced resulted from ignoring their real needs, and classifying them as weak, unreliable and unskilled workers, with high absenteeism and rapid turnover making it not worth putting them in positions of authority or giving them training or promotion.

57 Nicaragua Health Fund/Nicaragua Solidarity Campaign Newsletter 4 (Sept. 1987) and No. 8 (June 1988).

58 BRIN Day-school Report, 1987.

59 From 1982 to 1984 3,282 midwives were trained, giving many rural women access to trained help during childbirth for the first time, reducing the high neo-natal mortality rate, which used to result from ignorance and poor hygiene – *Servicio Holandes de Cooperacion Tecnica y Social*, SNV (1987).

60 Infant mortality is rising again and so is the incidence of malaria and mountain leprosy. Contra damage to health facilities totalled $70 million in 1985. Ten per cent of the country was without access to health care because of contra attacks. Twenty health workers had been killed, 25 raped and tortured, and at least 120 health centres destroyed, according to the 1987 briefing issued by the Nicaragua Health Fund.

61 Life expectancy remains low – 64 years compared with 57 years in 1975 – but 33 per cent of the females are under 9 years old, with another 50.6 per cent under 34 years old. 'La mujer en cifras' from *Documentos sobre la Mujer* (May–Nov. 1987).

62 Nicaragua Health Fund/Nicaragua Solidarity Campaign, *Bulletin 3* (1986).

63 Nicaragua Health Fund/Nicaragua Solidarity Campaign, *Bulletin 9* (1988).

64 MINSA and AMNLAE worked together on a Women's Integral Health Programme which included pre- and post-natal care, breast and cervical cancer screening and fertility control: *Nicaragua Health Fund Briefing*, 1987.

65 From 1987 safe clinical sterilisation was available for women who had five children, according to the *Barricada Internacional* supplement on women (March 1988).

66 Birth-rates remain high, averaging 6 per cent in 1983, rising to 7.1 per cent in rural areas, making this one of the highest birth-rates in Latin America, according to Perez Aleman and Diaz (1986).

67 For example, the training of pesticide operators to use protective clothing, according to the *Nicaragua Health Fund Briefing*, 1987. The MITRAB Ocotal tobacco workers study in 1985 considered the same issue.

68 *Barricada Internacional* (27 July 1987).

69 Current work includes the avoidance of sexist stereotypes in school texts, as women at the BRIN Day-school were told in April 1987.

70 In 1987, 28 per cent of the pre-school population were female, 52 per cent of the primary students, and 61 per cent of the middle-school students, with 49 per cent of those in adult education and 28 per cent of those receiving technical training: 'La mujer en cifras', from *Documentos sobre la mujer* (Oct.–Dec. 1987).

71 AMNLAE's training director informed the BRIN Day-school that 54 per cent of the women in urban areas had reached sixth grade in adult education, and 44 per cent of rural women had done the same. Among urban girls 52 per cent and among rural ones 46 per cent were in pre-school education. In 1986 secondary education included 60 and 70 per cent female participation, and higher education had 46 per cent female students in 1985. This had increased to 85 per cent in 1987, a dramatic increase. Of adult educators 50 per cent were women in 1987, according to the same source.

72 In 1987 the ratio of women to men in the poorest sectors of Managua was 354:100 (INEC data in Aleman, Martinez and Windmaier (1987).

73 Articles 121 and 122 of the new Constitution guarantee rights to basic and adult education.

74 See AMNLAE discussion document, Sept. 1985.

REFERENCES

Aleman Torres, D. and Cardenas, F. (1984) *Impacto del aborto provocado sobre la morbimortalidad maternal*. MINSA and UNAN, Managua.

Altamirano, L., Fuentes, C., Valle, A. and Rodriguez, M. (1985) *El aborto inducido ilegalmente: costos y consecuencias*. Hospital de la Mujer Bertha Calderon, Managua.

AMNLAE (1985) *Situacion de la mujer en Nicaragua* (17 Sept.), Managua.

AMNLAE Legal Office (1985) *Los logros juridicos de la mujer*. Managua.

— (1987) Pamphlet on divorce, 'El Divorcio'. Managua.

Angel, A. and Macintosh, F. (1987) *The Tiger's Milk: Women in Nicaragua*. Virago, London.

A.N.N. (1987) Monthly insert, Year 1:2 *Women in Central America* p. 4, 'New constitution secures women's rights', Agencia Nueva Nicaragua (A.N.N.), Managua.

ATC (Oct. 1986) 'II asamblea nacional de obreras agricolas', *El Machete (union journal)* pp. 7–8. ATC, Managua.

— (July 1987) 'En las grandes tareas de la revolucion', Article by Heliette Ehlers on Second Assembly of Agricultural Women Workers, *El Machete* p. 19. ATC, Managua.

— (Aug. 1987) 'No hay justificacion que valga'. Article by Heliette Ehlers on women, p. 8, *El Machete*, ATC, Managua.

— (1987) Report by the national secretary for women of the ATC to the Second National Assembly of agricultural workers (my translation).

— (1987) Resolutions of the Second Assembly of Agricultural workers (translated from booklet published by *El Machete*). ATC, managua.

Barahona, M. (1987) 'Que es la practica del proclama del FSLN para nosotros', *Cuadernos de Sociologia*, 4–5 (May–Dec. 1987): 137–40. UCA, Managua.

Barricada Internacional (Apr. 1984) Supplement on Women. Managua.

— (19–20 Mar. 1987) Interview with Lea Guido by Sofia Montenegro (my translation). Managua.

— (31 Jul. 1988) 'Muchas son destacadas pero pocas dirigentes' (my translation of article on women in unions). Managua.

— (Aug. 1987) Supplement on women, including articles on rural women (pp. 11–12), women at university (p. 12), urban women (p. 13). Managua.

— (Mar. 1988) Supplement on women, including interview with Lea Guido (pp. 2–3), divorce law (p. 4), abortion (p. 4), abuse (p. 5), workplace inequalities (p. 5), education (p. 6), construction (p. 7) and rural women (p. 8). Managua.

— (25 Aug. 1988) 'On the beat' (on police) (p. 6). Managua.

BRIN (1987) Report on day-school on women, held in Managua, with a women's group then known as Britons Resident in Nicaragua, now MIREN.

Broadbent, L. (1988) 'Women of the autonomous region', article on women on the Atlantic Coast. Printed on pp. 2–3 of *Sanity*, CND, London.

Castillo, V., Windmaier, C., and Barone, A. M. (1986) *Aportes por el analisis del maltrato de la mujer*, AMNLAE Legal Office, Managua.

CIERA (1984) *La mujer en las cooperativas agropecuarias en Nicaragua*. Centro de Investigaciones y Estudios de la Reforma Agraria, Managua.

CIERA/CETRA/ATC (1985) *La feminizacion de la fuerza de trabajo asalariada en el agro y sus implicaciones en en la produccion y organizacion sindical*. CIERA, Managua.

CIIR (1987) *Right to Survive – Human Rights in Nicaragua*. Catholic Institute for International Relations, London.

Collins, J. and Lappe, F. M. (1982) *What difference could a revolution make?* Institute for Food and Development Policies, San Francisco.

Deighton, J., Horsley, R., Stewart, S., and Cain, C. (1983) *Sweet Ramparts: Women in Revolutionary Nicaragua*. War on Want, London.

Documentos Sobre La Mujer (Oct.–Dec. 1987) Articles in this journal include 'Un estilo de trabajo que da pautas y ofrece logros' (pp. 8–10); 'Entrevista con Lea Guido' and 'El problema de la mujer no es un problema exclusiva de la mujer' (pp. 48–52). Managua.

Envio (July 1983; 3:25) 'Women in Nicaragua: a revolution within the revolution' (pp. 1c–9c) Managua.

— (Dec. 1986; 5:66; pp. 36–56) 'Managua's economic crisis: how do the poor survive?' Article based on 'Hipotesis sobre la estrategia de sobrevivencia de los clases populares en Managua, y el impacto del mensaje economico gubernamental', UCA Social Sciences Congress (9–12 Oct. 1986). Managua.

— (Dec. 1987; 6:78, p. 17–32) 'Becoming visible: women in Nicaragua'. Managua.

Flora, J.L., McFadden, J., and Warner, R. (1983) 'The growth of class struggle: the impact of the Nicaraguan Literacy Crusade on the political consciousness of young literacy workers.' *Latin American Perspectives*, 36 (X, I): 45–61.

La Gaceta (9 Jan. 1987; pp. 33–64) Published version of the new Constitution. Managua.

Gillespie, V. (1977) *Una metodologia modificada del presupuesto de tiempo para la accumulacion de datos basicos sobre el papel y las responsibilidades de las campesinas*. International Center for Research on Women. Washington, D.C.

— (1979) 'Rural women's time use' in *Studies in Family Planning*, 10:11/12 (Nov.–Dec. 1979): 383–4.

Guido, L. (1987) 'Apuntes sobre la situacion de la mujer en Nicaragua', *Cuadernos de Sociologia*, 4–5 (May–Dec.) School of Sociology, UCA, Managua.

Guerrero, L. and Guerrero, G. (1986) *Las relaciones familiares y el papel de la Mujer en la estrategia de sobrevivencia*. UCA, Managua.

Harris, H. (1983) 'War and reconstruction: women in Nicaragua', in *Latin American Women*, O. Harris (ed.), Minority Rights Group, London.

— (1983) *Nicaragua: Women's Participation in the Revolution: Problems and Prospects*. Paper presented at IDS, University of Sussex (June).

— (1984) 'Women in Struggle: Nicaragua', in *Third World Quarterly*, 5(4): 899–908.

Maier, E. (1985) *Las Sandinistas*. Editorial Cultura Popular, Mexico City.

Meiselas, S. (1981) *Nicaragua June 1978 – July 1979* (photos). Writers and Readers Publishing Co-operative, London.

MIDINRA (1985) 'Machismo y Revolucion', by Orlando Nuñez in *Revolucion y Desarrollo*, 3: 44–8. Managua.

— (1987) 'Ellas y los nuevos empleos en la produccion agricola', in *Informaciones Agropecuarias* (journal): 9–12, Managua.

The Militant (1 May 1987) 'Nicaraguan women hold national assembly', Report on Third National Assembly of AMNLAE (8 March), and comment of FSLN proclamation, p. 5. USA.

— (22 May 1987) 'Revolution opens door to women's equality', translation of FSLN proclamation. USA.

MITRAB/AMNLAE (1984) *Salud ocupacional de la mujer trabajadora* (Cartoon guide to safety at work).

MITRAB (DGHSO) (Duricción General de Higeine Sequridad del Qbrero) (1983) *Investigacion: relacion entre condiciones del trabajo y salud reproductiva en la mujer trabajadora del sector tobaco: caso Ocotal*. Managua.

Molyneux, M. (1981) 'Socialist societies old and new: towards women's emancipation', *Feminist Review*, 8: 1–34.

— (1984) 'Mobilization without emancipation: women's interests, state and revolution in Nicaragua', in *Critical Social Policy* (Summer): 59–75.

— (1986) 'Women', chapter in *Nicaragua: the First Five Years*, T. Walker (ed.), Praeger Publications, New York.

Muhlberger, V. and Brenner, E. (1986) *La participacion de la mujer en el proceso revolucionario*, University of Zurich, Switzerland.

Nicaragua Health Fund (1987) *Briefing Notes on Health in Nicaragua*, London.

Nicaragua Health Fund/Nicaragua Solidarity Campaign (1987) *Bulletin 2* (Feb.), 'No more angels' (article on midwives); *Bulletin 3* 'Women and Health', p. 8; *Bulletin 4* (Sept.), 'A good day's work' (article on vaccination), pp. 6–7; *Bulletin 5* (Nov.), 'Thought for food' (article on nutrition), pp. 4–5.

— (1988) *Bulletin 8* (June), 'Health reports from Nicaragua' p. 4–5; *Bulletin 9 (Sept.)*, 'Letter from Esteli' (article on problems in health service), pp. 4–5.

Nicaragua Solidarity Campaign (1987) *Women's Network Newsletter*, 2, including articles on women's Office, AMNLAE, AMNLAE Legal Office, and proposals for new Constitution. London.

— (1988) *Women's Network Newsletter*, 4. Article on the new divorce law, p. 1. London.

Nicaragua Solidarity Campaign (1987) Report on the Women's Study Tour 1987, including 'Visit to a State Farm' and 'Women's Section of the ATC', London.

Nuñez, O. (1987) 'Moral y revolucion en la vida cotidiana', *Cuadernos de Sociologia*, 3 (Jan.–Apr. 1987). UCA, Managua.

Perez Aleman, P. and Diaz P. (1986) *Informes: 10 anos de investigaciones sobre la mujer en Nicaragua, 1976–1986*. Ministry of the Presidency, Women's Office, Managua.

Perez Aleman, P. and Siu, I. (1986) *La mujer en la economic nicaraguense: cambios y desafios.* (paper presented to V Congress of Social Sciences, UCA, (9–12 Oct. 1986). Women's Office, Managua.

Women, war and underdevelopment in Nicaragua

Perez Aleman, P., Martinez, D., and Windmaier, C. (1987) *Fuerza laboral feminina en la rama textil-vestuario, segregacion, salarios y rotacion: avances de investigacion.* Women's Office, Managua.

Randall, M. (1981) *Sandino's Daughters.* Zed Press, London.

— (1984) *Risking a Somersault in the Air.* Solidarity Publications, San Francisco.

Ramirez-Horton, S. (1982) 'The role of women in the Nicaraguan Revolution', in *Nicaragua in Revolution.* T.W. Walker (ed.), Praeger Publications, New York.

Rodriguez, I. (1987) *Obstaculos a la promocion y aplicacion de las 'convenciones sobre la eliminacion de todas formas de discriminacion contra la mujer': caso de Nicaragua.* (UNESCO-funded sub-programme, 'Estudios y investigaciones sobre los derechos fundamentales de las mujeres'. Women's Office, Managua.

Rooper, A. (1987) *Fragile Victory: a Nicaraguan Community at War.* Weidenfeld & Nicolson, London.

Rosset, P. and Vandermeer, J. (1983) *The Nicaraguan Reader: Documents of a Revolution Under Fire.* Grove Press, New York.

Somos (1986) *Somos* 29 (AMNLAE journal) includes articles on rural women workers: 'Al principio sentimos temor', pp. 6–7; 'Obreras discuten y proponen', pp. 3–5; and 'Obreras agricolas: avances y dificultades', which reports the results of the CIERA/ATC survey on rural women. Managua.

UNAG (1987) *La participacion de la mujer campesina en la produccion* (study guide). Managua.

Walker, T.W. (ed.) (1985) *Nicaragua: the First Five Years.* Praeger Publications, New York.

—(1986) *Nicaragua: Land of Sandino.* (2nd edn, revised and updated), Westview Press, New York.

Women's Office, Ministry of the Presidency (1987) 'Fuerza laboral femenina en la rama textil-vestuario: segregacion, salarios y rotacion.' Summary of the study by Perez Aleman *et al.*, *Cuadernos de Sociologia*, 4–5 (May–Dec. 1987): 97–116. UCA, Managua.

Woronuik, B. (1987) *Women's Oppression and Revolution: the Nicaraguan Debate.* Occasional paper for CUSO Latin America Program (Dec. 1987). Distributed by Latin America Working Group, Toronto, or CUSO Americas Program, Ottawa.

Chapter Five

CONSTRUCTING A 'CAREER' UNDER CONDITIONS OF ECONOMIC CRISIS AND STRUCTURAL ADJUSTMENT: THE SURVIVAL STRATEGIES OF NIGERIAN WOMEN

Carolyne Dennis

For the past decade, many sub-Saharan African societies have experienced the results of economic policies categorised under the general heading 'Structural Adjustment', whether subject to IMF and World Bank conditionality or not. The manner in which these policies are experienced by women and the strategies by which they cope with them, depend upon the definition of women's responsibilities in different societies and the resources with which they are expected to meet them. This chapter will focus on the relationship between women's responsibilities and the strategies by which they attempt to ensure the survival of their families under the conditions of structural adjustment in one society, Nigeria and, especially in one part of that society, the Yoruba South-west. It is hoped that the particularly wide definition of women's household responsibilities in Yoruba society will provide a discussion of the impact of structural adjustment policies which will be helpful in developing an analysis of the impact of structural adjustment elsewhere in sub-Saharan Africa.[1]

In this chapter the major characteristics of the Nigerian economy in the past ten years and the impact upon it of the particular Structural Adjustment (SAP)[2] implemented by the Nigerian Federal military government will be explored. This will be followed by a brief examination of the manner in which the material responsibilities of Nigerian women towards their households is defined, especially in relation to Yoruba women. This will be used as the basis of an analysis of the way in which the SAP is affecting Nigerian women and the construction of gender relations in Nigeria.

THE NIGERIAN ECONOMY AND STRUCTURAL ADJUSTMENT

This discussion will focus on the characteristics of the Nigerian economy and its development which are most relevant to building an understanding of the particular characteristics of that economy under conditions of Structural Adjustment and its implications for Nigerian women as they seek to secure the survival of themselves and their families. It will thus begin with a brief discussion of the development of the Nigerian economy in the pre-colonial and colonial period, the rise of the 'petrol economy', the origins of the economic crisis, the character of the economic crisis in the 1980s and, finally, the development of the SAP which is intended to resolve that crisis. The manner in which women have been incorporated into these economic structures will be indicated as the basis of an analysis below of the household responsibilities of Yoruba women and the manner in which they have been affected by the SAP.

There was considerable variation in the economic structure of pre-colonial Nigerian societies. However, as in other West African societies, the majority of the population generated their subsistence from agriculture, carried out largely by the household labour of wives and children, supplemented by other sources of labour such as domestic labour and 'pawns' where available.[3] In societies with large centres of population and developed trading networks, large urban centres emerged, based on craft production and a sophisticated marketing and distribution system.[4] Early trading contacts with Europeans by coastal societies grew up within this context of short- and long-distance trading systems, closely related to the development of centralised states and their rise and fall.[5]

Pre-colonial West African societies appear to have been characterised by a scarcity of labour resources rather than of land.[6] Wealth derived from control of people which, in a system of lineage control of land, determined the size of farm an individual would be granted. The availability of household labour, largely consisting of women and children, was thus especially important. These societies were marked by the significant role played by women in agriculture. In those communities with large-scale craft production and established markets, there were manufacturing and marketing activities identified with women. This was especially true of large Yoruba communities in which women also had important religious and political functions.[7]

The imposition of colonial rule on Nigeria altered the political relationship between the territory and the United Kingdom and the structure of administration within Nigeria. It also intensified processes of economic change which had emerged in the period of trading contact with Europe. Colonial Nigeria was characterised by increasing

89

cash-crop production for external markets which deepened the monetisation of the economy. This was associated with and accompanied by the increasing penetration of the country by the European firms associated with the export of cash crops and the import of mass-produced consumer goods; notably the United Africa Company and John Holt.[8]

Women provided an important part of the labour force for the increased cash-crop production in this period but, as these were defined as 'male' crops, they were grown on land largely owned by men and men received the cash returns for them.[9] In societies in which women played an important part in craft production, women's production of cloth, pottery and mats was adversely affected by cheap imports. Women's access to the educational facilities and salaried employment created by colonial administrations and European companies depended upon the extent to which these facilities were created which differed between and within colonial possessions and the manner in which the appropriate female role was interpreted in changing circumstances.[10] Thus, in the Muslim North of Nigeria, girls were largely excluded from western education and also from salaried employment, whereas in the South they did have access to schools and employment although to a lesser extent than men.[11]

Thus, the manner in which women were incorporated into the colonial economy varied from one region to another. It depended upon the manner in which capitalist penetration and the imposition of colonial rule were experienced in the region concerned. It was also determined by the way in which existing dominant interpretations of appropriate social and economic roles for women were combined with ethnocentric European interpretations of the overwhelmingly private, domestic and unpaid role of women, in a situation of structural economic change.

In the 1960s, after independence, the Nigerian economy remained dependent on cash-crop production. The achievement of independence greatly increased the pressure for social expenditure, especially on education which was in turn dependent on the world prices for Nigerian cash crops, especially for cocoa.[12] The Nigerian economy was distinguished from others in West Africa by the expansion of the petroleum extraction sector in the late 1960s, but especially through the 1970s. The quadrupling of oil prices in 1973 acted as a watershed in the growth of this sector. The expansion of the oil sector, generating revenues which were concentrated in the hands of the Federal government and the manner in which those revenues were invested, created the characteristics of the Nigerian political economy in the 1970s. This in turn helped to determine the particular form taken by the economic crisis of the 1980s in Nigeria.

Exploration and extraction of petroleum was the responsibility of multi-national companies who paid royalties and taxes to the

Federal government. This altered the relationship between the Federal government and the State governments which had received the previously most significant source of public funds – Marketing Board surpluses. The Third National Development Plan provided an agenda for development based on the investment of these oil revenues. The priorities can be identified as the funding of large infrastructural projects, especially roads and dams, instituting the process of indigenising the industrial and service sectors and financing popular social infrastructure programmes, especially education.[13] The implementation of these planning objectives had a crucial impact on the Nigerian economy as government expenditure rose from N8.258 billion in 1975 to N13.291 billion in 1979 and N23.695 billion in 1980.[14]

The large construction projects placed great pressure on an under-developed construction industry in terms of supplies. They also created a demand for labour which was to affect the availability of labour for agricultural production and thus created the conditions for a fall in food-crop production in addition to the fall in cash-crop production.[15] The Indigenisation Decree was implemented at a time of considerable inward investment as the size and expansion of the Nigerian market made it increasingly attractive to manufacturers and assemblers of consumer goods such as textiles, food and drink and plastic goods, and led to characteristic patterns of ownership with partnerships between foreign investors and the Federal government, State governments and Nigerian businessmen.[16] The implementation of universal primary education and later expansion of secondary education had profound effects on labour markets in various sectors and on the occupational expectations of young Nigerians.

The manner in which the money derived from the petroleum sector was spent can only be understood fully within the context of the processes creating the Nigerian political economy. One characteristic of this structure, as in many other societies, is the process whereby political power or influence is converted into an economic resource. In Nigeria in the 1970s and 1980s the source of that political power varied between senior army officers, senior civil servants and politicians and the complex alliances between these groups. Two significant results of the availability of the oil revenues were the manner in which increased Federal government expenditure did not create but greatly increased the importance of the 'sole agent' who imported materials to be supplied to government organisations on contract, at a price to be settled by negotiation rather than by formal agreement. Secondly, the Indigenisation Decree led to the emergence of Nigerians who provided a name and facilitated administrative arrangements for foreign manufacturers. This relationship between the state bureaucracy and those with economic and political capital was made more complex by the process through which import licences were distributed under the Shagari regime. These developments need to be located within the context of a massive increase in imports, both of capital and raw materials and of consumer goods. The import of manufactured goods increased by 50 per cent in value from 1976 to 1978/9 and by nearly 100 per cent from then until 1981, reaching N2.6 billion.[17]

The 'mythical' explanation of the manner in which women were incorporated into the feverish Nigerian oil economy is that of the wife of a high-ranking army officer or civil servant who uses her husband's influence to obtain contracts with government departments or parastatals to supply them with imported goods. The significance of this 'myth' lay in its assumption that women will try to generate an income and that they will probably do it by trade, and in the way in which it foreshadowed the prevailing analysis of the economic crisis of the 1980s which focused on using women as scapegoats. It also indicates the manner in which the informal sector in Nigeria grew and became differentiated in the 1970s as the returns to those enterprises which were able to operate in the interstices of government expenditure and intervention became greater. The oil economy created in the 1970s led to new opportunities for particular groups of Nigerian women and a withdrawal of possibilities for others. It is necessary to disaggregate the experience of Nigerian women in this period in order to capture the range of the impact of the petroleum economy and its dissolution upon them.

The rapid expansion of government expenditure in the 1970s created a great deal of extra employment. Much of this was in the construction industry, which did not involve women except for those small-scale, labour-intensive construction enterprises in the informal sector which often employed women. But women did take up many of the teaching, nursing and clerical jobs created by the expansion in social infrastructure and benefited from the increase in educational opportunities and health facilities they provided. Women also took up a range of jobs within the expanding industrial sector, although these were usually both relatively low paid and insecure.[18]

Women further benefited from the expansion in the informal sector which took place as a result of the rise in public- and private-sector wage employment. However, the expansion of the informal sector in the 1970s took place as the capital requirements to enter the more profitable sub-sectors increased rapidly.[19] Women who did not possess the qualifications and experience to enter wage employment or the capital with which to generate a viable income from trade or craft manufacture were not able to participate in the benefits of economic expansion and, in addition, they were adversely affected by rising rates of inflation. This severely reduced their ability to provide materially for their families in a society in which this was expected of them.

The 1980s have been a period of economic crisis in many developing countries primarily as a result of over-borrowing in the 1970s, coupled with the rise in interest rates as payment became due. Nigeria benefited from the oil price rises in 1973 and the late 1970s which had such a devastating impact on other sub-Saharan economies, and pursued a development strategy which depended entirely upon the maintenance of a high oil price. This strategy, which involved large-scale borrowing by Federal and State governments, rapid increases in imports to finance import substitution industries and food imports to reduce urban living costs on the basis of an overvalued naira, contained the roots of the economic crisis.[20]

The economic crisis and the imposition of the SAP are perceived as coming to a head in 1984/5 but the immediate origin of the crisis can be located in 1978. The SAP contains much in common with earlier attempts to reduce Nigeria's international indebtedness. In 1978, General Obasanjo raised the price of Nigerian oil; sales fell, resulting in a balance-of-payments deficit of N1.3 billion; industrial production ceased to increase as fast as in the period prior to 1976, and public-sector debts increased. Deflationary measures were taken including an increase in tariffs, a ban on the import of some consumer items and a reduction in social expenditure by increasing hospital and school fees. The effect of the Iranian revolution on the international oil market assisted the apparent recovery of the Nigerian economy.

The Shagari government established an expansionary economic policy on the basis of the rise in oil prices. This regime intensified the fraud associated with imports referred to above. The fall in oil prices in late 1981 precipitated a more severe crisis than in 1978 and a collapse in Nigerian manufacturing industry as 50 per cent of factories closed. Essential commodities became scarce as imports fell, large numbers of workers were laid off and social services collapsed as salaries and recurrent expenditure were not met. These were the characteristics of the economic crisis experienced by the Nigerian population as the Shagari administration in April 1982 introduced the Economic Stabilisation Act which imposed a wide range of import restrictions, monetary controls and cuts in public expenditure. Negotiations were opened with the IMF. The economic crisis intensified as more companies collapsed, retrenchment of workers increased and the availability of basic commodities decreased. These conditions contributed to the coup which replaced the Shagari government by the Buhari military government at the end of 1983.

The Federal Military Government of General Buhari raised interest rates, imposed a wage freeze and established a licensing scheme to control imports. At the ideological level, the government instituted a War Against Indiscipline (WAI) to combat those sections of Nigerian society identified as being responsible for the crisis. Women were allocated a special place in this process.[21] Negotiations with the IMF were continued. In August 1985, General Babangida replaced

General Buhari in a coup and proceeded to reject the IMF loan and implement his own programme of Structural Adjustment. Thus by the time the SAP was introduced in 1986, the collapse of manufacturing industry and the subsequent loss of employment, the rapid rise in price and scarcity of essential commodities and the collapse of health and education services had been expanding and deepening for at least six years.[22]

The Nigerian SAP has been undertaken without IMF loans and conditionality but with the assistance of the World Bank. As has been discussed above, it was preceded by a series of measures designed to address the causes of the Nigerian economic crisis, but it is distinguished from them by its greater breadth, depth and the intended 'radical determination' of its implementation. The major objectives of the SAP are (1) to diversify the productive base of the dependence on oil and imports, (2) to achieve fiscal and balance-of-payments viability, (3) to lay the basis for minimal inflationary growth, and (4) to reduce unproductive public-sector investment, improve the efficiency of the public sector and intensify the growth of the private sector. The major policy for implementing these objectives has been the establishment of the Second-tier Foreign Exchange Market (SFEM), a foreign exchange bidding scheme supplemented by a series of measures to deregulate the economy, remove subsidies, encourage privatisation and to manage demand.[23]

Some elements of the SAP have been possible to implement more quickly than others; they include the SFEM, demand management through monetary and credit limits and an incomes freeze, reductions in government expenditure and subsequent retrenchment. Thus the characteristics of the economic crisis have in fact intensified under the SAP as capacity utilisation has fallen and unemployment has risen. Inflation has not been seriously monitored. The one area in which supply-side measures might be expected to operate is in agriculture with the establishment of the Directorate of Foods, Roads and Rural Infrastructure, but many of its activities are likely to be effective only in the medium and long term.[24]

The impact of the economic crisis and the SAP which followed it on Nigerian women will be discussed more fully below. One characteristic of the SAP has been the massive retrenchment of industrial and public-sector employment. The effect of this on industrial workers has been outlined by Bangura.[25] The effects of the crisis on urban industrial workers have been documented. It is much more difficult to evaluate the effects it has had on rural areas and the agricultural sector. The inflation and commodity shortages were probably felt most severely in rural areas. The problems of obtaining a food supply in the market meant that the crucial distinction was between those households which had access to a secure food supply and those which did not. Security of food supply required access to a very high cash income, influence with food suppliers or an ability to retreat into subsistence. Thus the geographical location and access to income and influence of households is crucial. But the choice of survival strategy and the manner in which the 'costs' of economic crisis and the SAP have been distributed depend on the structure and distribution of responsibilities within households – particularly the definition of the household responsibilities of women.

In societies in which the majority of the population live on very low incomes, the question as to whether a particular activity is a 'survival' strategy or an opportunity for income generation is perhaps of mainly semantic interest. However, in recent Nigerian history, there are two areas in which the survival strategies of particular groups of Nigerian women appear to be especially significant. In the period of rapid economic growth in the 1970s, women without substantial resources of capital and influence found it increasingly difficult to generate an income with which to fulfil their household responsibilities. In the 1980s, as the economy contracted, the situation facing Nigerian households, particularly in urban areas, became one not so much of accumulating the resources with which to take advantage of opportunities but of spreading risks in order to ensure survival in an increasingly unpredictable and hazardous world. In order to understand how this process has developed, it is necessary to examine the structure of households and the manner in which domestic responsibilities are defined in Nigerian society.

THE DIVISION OF RESPONSIBILITIES WITHIN NIGERIAN HOUSEHOLDS, WITH PARTICULAR REFERENCE TO YORUBALAND

In the section above on the pre-colonial economy, stress was placed upon the manner in which in Nigeria, as in many sub-Saharan societies, the reproductive and nurturing responsibilities of women were defined in the widest terms – as providing a significant proportion of the material provisions for the household and then managing their transformation into food and other products for consumption. For the majority of women, this meant being responsible for growing 'women's crops' and assisting with 'men's crops' and trading the surplus, if any, in local markets in order to obtain provisions which had to be bought: salt, soap, cloth. This pattern is also true for the majority of women in Yorubaland in the South-west of Nigeria, but, under particular historical circumstances, the domestic responsibilities of Yoruba women and their duty and opportunity to generate an income developed in a particular way.

Yoruba women play a much more important role in trade than is true for most sub-Saharan African societies, with the exception of southern Ghana.[26] It is difficult to reconstruct with certainty how this happened, but it appears to be related to the large size of Yoruba settlements which provided opportunities for specialisation in occupation and thus production and trade for the market. The long period of civil war with the consequent breakdown of safe travel in Yorubaland in the early nineteenth century appears to have led to a greater involvement of women in long-distance trade, in which they were likely to be safer than men. The opportunity for women to generate an income was greater for women living in such communities than for women involved in agriculture, the returns from which usually went to the male head of the household.[27] The need for such an independent income was intensified by the high rates of polygyny in Yoruba society, probably encouraged by the relatively low level of bridewealth.

Yoruba society covers a wide geographical area and has very varied manifestations. If it is possible to construct the most important constituents of a woman's material responsibilities, it might run something like this: in a polygynous marriage, the most significant unit is of mother and child. A woman has important duties to provide materially for her children, supplemented to a greater or lesser extent by her husband, and in order to do this she needs an independent, regular source of income. As her children grow up she has a duty to teach her daughter how to earn her own income, either by following her in craft production or, most likely, as a trader. This supplements the socially prescribed necessity of being responsible for the 'moral' training of her daughters, as their behaviour will reflect well or badly on her. As a woman grows up she should, therefore, be accumulating the necessary knowledge and contacts to generate her own income, although her ability to do this depends on where she lives, and in small rural communities it remains an ideal rather than an achievable objective. It is possible when she marries that her husband will provide her with the initial capital to trade or engage in petty commodity production, in which case she will be expected to contribute substantial resources to the household from the income she generates.

It has been argued elsewhere that this need to generate an income in order to fulfil responsibilities in the household and towards her children means that it is helpful to conceptualise the stages of a Yoruba woman's personal and working life as the attempted construction of a career in which advancement in one sphere can be used to support and reinforce efforts in another.[28] Thus the ability to generate a reliable income successfully reinforces the position of a woman in her husband's household and strengthens her ability to educate her children. It also enables her to establish an independent social position, which is important in a polygynous society. This means that if these mutually reinforcing elements of a career work in the optimum manner, a woman reaches old age with a recognised position within the household, an independent social position, and children who enhance her reputation and have the resources to support her in her old age. Without these advantages she is dependent upon the acceptance and approval of those around her without the resources to influence this process of granting or withholding approval. It is likely that the opportunities for constructing such a career have always been greatest in urban communities.

It has been stated above that there are special characteristics of the domestic responsibilities of Yoruba women which make it possible to conceptualise their family, income-generating and 'social' lives as coalescing into a personal career. This raises the question as to whether such a concept would be applicable to women in other Nigerian communities. In other Southern Nigerian communities such as the Igbo, women are under a similar, if less intense, pressure to generate an income, and they often play a more important role than Yoruba women in agriculture. In Muslim communities such as the Hausa, women's opportunities for income generation are obviously more restricted but it is striking how Hausa wives begin the process of building up their position within their husband's household, initiate some form of income generation and establish the practice of formal gift-giving with women within and outside their own household.[29]

In all personal biographies there are family, social and economic steps which are related and which together make up the life of the individual concerned. In industrial economies in which the majority of the economically active population are employed for wages, it appears to be possible to study the three – personal, social and economic – separately, and they may be perceived as separate worlds by individuals themselves, although it is likely that women are not able to make this separation. In societies in which men and women participate in domestic production or the informal sector, this separation is only possible at the conceptual level. In the lives of individuals, the different elements reinforce one another either positively or negatively. This relationship is clear in a society such as the Yoruba in which the necessity for women to generate an income and reinforce their position in a polygynous household is accepted. The nature of that relationship varies between societies; for example, for urban Hausa women for whom income-generation opportunities are limited, the use of resources to build up kinship and friendship networks to lessen the isolation of an enclosed marriage over time may be more important.

If individual women always construct a career with familial, social and income-generating elements, and if the constituents of that career and the emphasis placed on them vary from one society to another, this provides the basis for a discussion of the likely impact of such drastic economic shocks as the economic crisis of the late 1970s and early 1980s and of the SAP on them. The impact of such crises and policies will depend on the manner in which women's responsibilities are defined and how they define their preferred career.

THE IMPACT OF STRUCTURAL ADJUSTMENT

The history of the present economic crisis outlined above indicates that Nigerians experienced a crisis for household survival for at least six years before the imposition of the SAP. It is not easy to distinguish the effects of the two, although at present the SAP would appear to have intensified the effects of the crisis rather than resolved its underlying causes. The SAP has reduced formal-sector employment by direct retrenchment in government and parastatals and creating a lack of raw material supplies in industry. At the same time, the price of essential commodities has increased dramatically and their availability has decreased. Monitoring by Nigerian newspapers suggests that the prices of basic commodities rose by 75–150 per cent in the period February–October 1983.[30] Cuts in social expenditure have increased the cost and reduced the availability of health and educational facilities. The reform process has also led to an increase in farm gate prices.

The potential benefits of such restructuring are likely to occur only in the long term and, indeed, there are very few existing examples of the long-term benefits as yet. The costs, however, occur almost immediately. Rural households are likely to benefit from higher farm gate prices as producers and to suffer the impact of higher consumer prices and the unavailability of basic commodities in so far as they buy such commodities. The 'costs' of such programmes have been borne most intensely by the urban poor, who have been affected both by the loss of wage employment opportunities and the consequent loss in possibilities of informal-sector income generation, the rise in the price of food and basic commodities and the fall in health and educational provision. If it is poor urban households which are likely to bear the cost of such programmes, the manner in which those costs are distributed within households depends on the structure of responsibility and resources within households in particular societies.

A number of survival strategies have been identified as being possible for households confronting the decline in income-earning opportunities and rising prices characteristic of structural adjustment. These are: increasing the supply of labour to the economy and increasing self-production, labour exchange and selling assets. On the consumption side, purchasing patterns can be changed and thus may also change methods of food preparation, changes in overall consumption patterns and dietary patterns. There may also be changes in the intra-household division of food. There is evidence from many countries that these strategies are being adopted.[31]

The informal sector has had to absorb the labour 'released' from the formal sector at a time when there are limited possibilities for income generation within it. Thus, the increase in population in many African cities has slowed down as families have sent home appropriate members to villages to grow their own food and also to provide a surplus for urban-based members of their family.[32] Voluntary labour exchange is associated with famine conditions in rural areas and within kinship groups in urban areas.[33] Asset selling is associated with famine in agricultural areas with great inequality of land distribution and high levels of indebtedness perhaps more characteristic of South Asia than West Africa. Bangura suggests that male formal-sector workers in Ondo State 'retreated' into subsistence, a strategy possible in Yoruba towns with a strong link to agricultural hinterlands and having important implications for women.[34]

The survival techniques which depend on adapting consumption patterns would appear to be especially relevant to the West African and Nigerian context. It is not yet clear how much purchasing patterns have changed; this depends on monitoring the price and availability of food over time. The indications from other countries affected by structural adjustment are that these survival techniques do not prevent the non-survival of particular vulnerable groups. It is striking how the infant mortality rates of many sub-Saharan African countries have either not improved or have become worse over this period.[35] In the following paragraphs the emphasis will be on the possible impact of the SAP on the intra-household distribution of responsibilities to supplement the concern with the intra-household distribution of resources.

Analysis of mortality figures from previous situations in which food supplies to households have been at risk, notably famines, have shown mortality rates which reflect a significant inequality in distribution of food within households. In infant mortality statistics, the death-rates for female children have been higher than those for boys and the rates for women have been higher than those for men. The most detailed analyses have been made of the Indian famines, which may not be relevant to sub-Saharan Africa or to Nigeria in particular. On the other hand, there is qualitative evidence on the effect of famine on access to food supplies in Ghana during the 1970s famine which suggests that similar choices as to the distribution of food within households were being made.[36]

The distribution of food within households is a notoriously difficult subject to research. Where accurate mortality figures by sex are also not available, it is difficult to accumulate the necessary quantitative evidence. However, Bamisaiye's work, for example, provides an important indication of the likely effect of economic crisis and the SAP on Nigerian women.[37] This research suggests that the problems of living in Lagos under conditions of increasing insecurity of employment, food supplies, and health services are expressed in terms of increasing health problems for the mothers of children rather than being reflected in the declining health of their children, as expected.[37] This finding is similar to the research which has been undertaken as to the manner in which the 'costs' of famines are borne – an equivalent crisis in provisioning households.

It is impossible to analyse the effect of Structural Adjustment on the distribution of resources within households only in terms of investigating the proportionate division of material resources. The manner in which these resources are distributed depends upon the division of responsibilities within households on the basis of gender and the way in which they are redefined under conditions of crisis and threat to household survival. The way in which this redefinition takes place depends upon the character of gender relations in a particular society and the character of the crisis with which members of households are presented.

There are indications from other situations of crisis that women's responsibilities for 'managing' the household become translated into a responsibility for 'managing' the crisis at household level. So, for example, in the households of the British industrial working class, a wife's duty to manage her husband's wage packet is transformed, if he becomes unemployed, into a responsibility for managing without it, both by earning money and by assuming responsibility for keeping the household out of debt.[38]

Nigerian women have been confronted, as the economic crisis has developed and the SAP has been imposed, with declining opportunities for formal-sector employment for themselves and their male partners. Thus, for urban wage earners incomes have fallen. This process has been intensified by a corresponding decrease in opportunities within the informal sector. Meanwhile, prices of basic commodities have increased rapidly and their availability is often problematic. At the same time health and education facilities have declined. Apart from the decrease in educational facilities and their increased cost which primarily affect the long-term quality of human capital, and in the short-term ability of girls to compete for a declining stock of formal-sector jobs, the other effects have been experienced from the beginning of the crisis with cumulative intensity.[39]

Beginning from the manner in which the household responsibilities of Nigerian women are defined, in this crisis, initial observation suggests that this is likely to be translated into a special responsibility for women in relation to the reduced employment opportunities, rising prices, reduced availability of basic commodities and the rolling back of social services. Women have the responsibility for somehow managing households so that the effects of these interlocking problems are not evident, or at least minimally evident, to their families. At the same time, women, especially those attempting to earn a living outside the home, have been allocated a special place in the 'demonology' of the crisis since the War Against Indiscipline.[40]

The responsibility of Yoruba women to contribute materially to the household and to manage those resources in order to reproduce it from day to day and generation to generation suggests that the crisis of Structural Adjustment might affect them in a complex series of threats to household survival as they attempt to compensate for the effects of the SAP on the household. The situation created by indebtedness and the SAP affects the income-generating capacities of the urban poor and the prices and availability of essential commodities. For women, the crisis thus increases the necessity for them to bring an income into the household at a time when this is increasingly difficult in both the formal and the informal sector. It also makes the task of managing the resources of a household, particularly its access to food, much more difficult and increases the investment in time necessary to provision a household. The 'test' of the commitment of a wife and mother is the manner in which she manages a household, in order to make the fragility of access to income and essential commodities as little evident as possible to her children and especially her husband. It is this interpretation of women's responsibilities in especially difficult circumstances which explains the manner in which the health effects of the crisis appear to be reflected mainly in women's health status, as documented by Bamisaiye.

It means that the constituents of a 'career' outlined above become, under these conditions, the necessary constituents of a strategy for survival. If the household is forced back on to subsistence, it is likely that the basis for this career is lost as women lose their access to resources with which to generate an income and become household labour.

Structural Adjustment in Nigeria, as in other sub-Saharan African countries, has increased the problem of households obtaining sufficient resources for survival, especially for the urban poor. The generally accepted manner in which women's responsibilities are defined has meant that, within households, it is likely to be women who bear the major burden for maintaining the household under conditions of crisis. One inventory of the strains for Nigerian women under present conditions was constructed on the basis of the problems of women attending an outpatients' clinic in Ibadan, but appears to reflect generally articulated concerns. It is a striking combination of the problems of combining reproductive and productive roles in a customarily polygynous society in which the support of male partners

101

is either physically or emotionally absent, the pressure from families to support social occasions such as funerals is overwhelming, and household management is made more difficult by factors created or intensified by the crisis and the SAP, such as scarce and expensive food and basic commodities and erratic supplies of water, electricity and cooking fuel. Significantly, there is also an emphasis on the prevalence of death and disease in their immediate families.[41]

One way in which this stress and absorption of responsibility for managing the crisis is indicated is in the health status of women. There are also other indicators of the increased burden. In a society in which most personal and social explanations are constructed in religious terms, it is likely that the conditions of hardship and deprivation without a reasonable hope of any future improvement will be explained in religious terms. It is striking how the influence of fundamentalist Islam and Christianity have increased in Nigeria in the 1980s.[42] Pearce's work indicates that the number of women adherents of the *aladura*, or praying churches, in Yorubaland has greatly increased in the 1980s.[43] These churches give a greater social recognition to their women members than the missionary-based churches, and focus on the need to ask for effective supernatural help with the problems encountered in everyday life such as lack of money and health problems. It is likely that this upsurge in women's membership of these churches reflects a strategy of attempting to improve their own position and that of their households when money and health problems are especially urgent, supplementing inadequate material resources by supernatural assistance. It also reflects the search for some reassurance in a situation of constant strain and distress.

The discussion above indicates that our existing understanding of the impact of international indebtedness and Structural Adjustment on women in Nigeria suggests certain important areas for further investigation in any situation in which the impact of Structural Adjustment is being analysed. Firstly, the effect of the crisis on reproduction, production and consumption within the household will be a function of the particular character of the crisis and the existing gender division of labour and socially defined responsibilities of women. The impact of the crisis is likely to result in revised definitions of the appropriate responsibilities of women within and outside the household, and women will seek 'appropriate' assistance in coping with the widening and deepening of their responsibilities. This link between the availability of material resources and ideological definitions of women's responsibilities has important methodological implications. It cannot be investigated solely by the use of mechanistic social surveys. It requires both an attempt to construct the history of the situation and an attempt to present the various explanations offered of the crisis and its implications for men and women.

CONCLUSION

The economic crisis arising out of public- and private-sector indebtedness in particular developing countries and the stabilisation and Structural Adjustment Programmes which followed it are clearly having a significant impact on the population of those countries. Within those countries particular groups, such as the urban poor, have been most affected and have borne the costs of implementing these programmes. It is also clear that the costs of these programmes tend to be borne disproportionately by women, because of their household responsibilities which are intensified under conditions of crisis, an intensification which is justified by ideological redefinitions of 'women's role'. This chapter is intended to be a contribution to the beginning of the second stage of this debate, in which we construct an explanation of the manner in which the costs of Structural Adjustment are borne by women in different societies and the strategies for survival which they follow under conditions of potential crisis for household and personal survival.

NOTES AND REFERENCES

1   It is hoped that this chapter will take further the discussion opened out by Diane Elson in 'The impact of structural adjustment on women: concepts and issues', *DSA Annual Conference*, Manchester (1987).

2   The following terminology will be used in this chapter: the abbreviation commonly used in Nigeria for the Nigerian Structural Adjustment Policy – SAP – will be used to refer to the policy implemented by the Federal military government in Nigeria. Other policies with similar objectives will be called 'Structural Adjustment policies'.

3   See A. G. Hopkins, *An Economic History of West Africa* (Longman, London, 1973); C. Meillassoux, *The Development of Indigenous Trade and Markets in West Africa* (Oxford University Press, London, 1971).

4   Hopkins, *Economic History of West Africa*; J. D. Y. Peel, *Ijeshas and Nigerians: the Incorporation of a Yoruba Kingdom 1890s–1970s* (Cambridge University Press, 1987).

5   K. O. Dike, *Trade and Politics in the Niger Delta 1830–1885*, (Oxford University Press, 1956); B. Awe, 'The Ajele system: a study of Ibadan imperialism in the nineteenth century', *Journal of the Historical Society of Nigeria*, 3 (1964): 43–60.

6   See J. Iliffe, *The African Poor: a History* (Cambridge University Press, 1987), pp. 1–9, for a discussion of this characteristic of sub-Saharan Africa.

7   See N. Fadipe, *The sociology of the Yoruba* (Ibadan University

Press, 1978); B. Awe, 'The Yalode in the traditional Yoruba political system', in A. Schegel (ed.), *Sexual Stratification: a Cross-cultural View* (Columbia University Press, New York, 1977), pp. 144–60.

8   See Bade Onimode, *Imperialism and Underdevelopment in Nigeria* (Macmillan-Nigeria, London, 1983), Part II, pp. 29–128.

9   S. Afonja, 'Land control: a critical factor in Yoruba gender stratification', in Claire Robertson and Iris Berger (eds), *Women and Class in Africa* (Africana Publishers, New York, 1986).

10 For a general discussion of the way in which the imposition of colonialism affected women in sub-Saharan Africa, see Carolyne Dennis, 'Women in African labour history', *Journal of Asian and African Studies*, XXIII (1–2) (1988): 125–40.

11 B. Awe, 'Formal education and the status of women in Nigeria: an historical perspective', in F. A. Ogunsheye, K. Awosika, C. Dennis and C. M. Di Domenico (eds), *Nigerian Women and Development* (Ford Foundation, Ibadan), 1983, pp. 404–24.

12 A. B. Fafunwa, *History of Education in Nigeria* (Allen & Unwin, London, 1974).

13 *Third National Development Plan 1975–1980* (Government Printer, Lagos, 1975).

14 Adebayo Olukoshi 'World Bank/IMF structural adjustment programmes and the African working class: a Nigerian case study', Conference on the Impact of IMF and World Bank Policies on the People of Africa, Institute for African Alternatives, City University, London, 7–10 Sept. 1987, p. 8.

15 See S. O. Olayide (ed.) *Economic Survey of Nigeria 1960–78* (Aramolaran Publishing Co, Ibadan, 1976); C. E. F. Beer, *The politics of peasant groups in Western Nigeria* (Ibadan University Press, 1971), for a discussion of the political consequences of continued falls in cash-crop prices.

16 Paul Collins, 'The political economy of indigenisation', *African Review*, 4 (1975); E. O. Akerdolu-Ale, 'Private foreign investment and the underdevelopment of indigenous entrepreneurship in Nigeria', in G. Williams (ed.), *Nigeria: Economy and Society* (Rex Collings, London, 1976), pp. 106–22; S. A. Afonja and Carolyne Dennis, 'Social aspects of rural industrialisation: the Ado-Ekiti example', *Proceedings of the Conference on Social Research and National Development in Nigeria* (Ibadan, 1976), pp. 756–89.

17 'The Odama Report', *Africa Development*, IX (3) (1984): 75–115.

18 E. R. Fapohunda, 'Women at work in Nigeria: factors affecting modern sector employment', in U. G. Damachi and V. P. Diejamaoh (eds), *Human Resources in African Development* (Praeger, New York, 1978), pp. 225–38; C. M. Di Domenico, 'Male and female factory workers in Ibadan, Nigeria', in C. Oppong (ed.), *Female and Male in West Africa* (Allen & Unwin, London, 1983), pp. 256–66; Carolyne Dennis, 'Capitalist development and women's work: a Nigerian case study', *Review of African Political Economy*, 27/28: 109–19.

19 This process has been documented in the case of Kenya: see W. J. House, 'Redistribution, consumer demand and employment in Kenyan furniture making', *Journal of Development Studies*, 17 (4) 1986; and I.

Livingstone, *Rural Development, Employment and Income in Kenya* (Gower, Aldershot, 1986).

20   See Toyin Falola and Julius Ihonvbere, *The Rise and Fall of Nigeria's Second Republic 1979–84*, (Zed Books, London, 1985), pp. 83–121; World Bank, *Nigeria: Macro-Economic Policies for Structural Change*, Report 4506, UNI, Washington, 15 Aug. 1983.

21   Carolyne Dennis, 'Women and the State in Nigeria: the case of the Federal Military Government, 1984–1985', in Haleh Afshar (ed.), *Women, State and Ideology* (Macmillan, London, 1987), pp. 13–27.

22   This account draws heavily on Adebayo Olukoshi, 'World Bank/IMF structural adjustment and the African working class: a Nigerian case study', Conference on the Impact of IMF and World Bank Policies on the People of Africa, Institute for African Alternatives, City University, London, 7–10 Sept. 1987.

23   Adedotun O. Phillips and Eddy Ndekwu (eds), *Structural Adjustment Programme in a Developing Economy: the Case of Nigeria,* (Nigerian Institute for Social and Economic Research (NISER), Ibadan, 1987), p. 2.

24   Ibid, pp. 4–5.

25   Yusuf Bangura, 'Crisis and adjustment: the experience of Nigerian workers', Conference on the Impact of the IMF and World Bank Policies on the People of Africa, Institute for African Alternatives, City University, London, 7–10 Sept. 1987.

26   See Christine Oppong (ed.), *Female and male in West Africa* (Allen & Unwin, London, 1983), pp. 139–209.

27   Simi Afonja, 'Changing modes of production and the sexual division of labour among the Yoruba', *Signs*, 7 (2) (Winter 1981): 299–313.

28   Carolyne Dennis, 'The concept of a "career" in Nigeria: individual perceptions of the relationship between the formal and informal sectors', in Diane Elson (ed.), *Male Bias in Development Planning* (Manchester University Press, forthcoming).

29   E. Schildkrout, 'Women's work and children's work: variations among Muslims in Kano', in S. Wallman (ed.), *Social Anthropology of Work* (Academic Press, New York, 1979); Renée Pittin, 'Social status and economic opportunity in Urban Hausa society', in F. A. Ogunsheye, K. Awosika, C. Dennis and C. M. Di Domenico (eds), *Nigerian Women and Development* (Ford Foundation, Ibadan, 1982), pp. 633–8.

30   Adebayo Olukoshi, 'World Bank/IMF structural adjustment and the African working class: a Nigerian case study', Conference on the Impact of IMF and World Bank Policies on the People of Africa, Institute for African Alternatives, City University, London, 7–10 Sept. 1987, p. 30.

31   G. A. Cornia, R. Jolly and F. Stewart, *Adjustment With a Human Face* (Clarendon Press, Oxford, 1987), pp. 90–104.

32   D. F. Bryceson, 'Food and urban purchasing power in Tanzania', *African Affairs*, 84 (377) (1985): 499–522; Nici Nelson, 'Rural–urban child fostering in Kenya: migration, kinship, ideology and class', in J. Eades (ed.), *Migrants, Workers and the Social Order* (Tavistock, London, 1987), pp. 181–198.

33   A. Whitehead 'Gender and famine in West Africa', Development Studies Association (DSA) Annual Conference, Bradford, Sept. 1984.

34   Yusuf Bangura, 'Crisis and adjustment: the experience of Nigerian workers', Conference on the Impact of the IMF and World Bank Policies on the People of Africa, Institute for African Alternatives, City University, London, 7–10 Sept. 1987.

35   See G. A. Cornia, R. Jolly and F. Stewart, *Adjustment with a Human Face* (Clarendon Press, Oxford, 1987), pp. 218–31.

36   A. Whitehead, 'Gender and famine in West Africa', DSA Annual Conference, Bradford, Sept. 1984.

37   A. Bamisaiye and M. A. Oyediran, 'Female labour force participation and the care of pre-school children: a survey of mothers employed at LUTH/CMUL', National Workshop on Working Mothers and Early Childhood Education in Nigeria, NISER, Ibadan, 13–16 Sept. 1981.

38   A. Whitehead, '"I'm Hungry Mum": the politics of domestic budgeting', in K. Young, C. Woltiowitzc and R. McCullagh (eds), *Of Marriage and the Market* (CSE Books, London, 1981), pp. 88–111.

39   See 'Women in Nigeria and education briefing', *Review of African Political Economy*, 31 (Dec. 1984): 106–7.

40   See Carolyne Dennis, 'Women and the State in Nigeria: the case of the Federal Military Government 1984–1985', in Haleh Afshar (ed.), *Women, the State and Ideology* (Macmillan, London, 1987), pp. 13–27, p. 24.

41   R. Olukayode Jegede, 'Role strain and the health of Nigerian women', Seminar on Nigerian Women and National Development, Ibadan, 20–21 June 1985.

42   Yusufu Bala Usman, *For the Liberation of Nigeria* (New Beacon Books, London, 1979), pp. 79–92.

43   Tola Pearce, Seminar on Nigerian Women and National Development, Ibadan, 20–21 June 1985.

Chapter Six

CONCEPTIONS AND MISCONCEPTIONS: THE HISTORICAL AND CULTURAL CONTEXT OF DISCUSSION ON WOMEN AND DEVELOPMENT

Joanna de Groot

Any discussion or understanding of women's involvement in or experiences of 'development' will rightly emphasise the material aspects and contemporary relevance of the subject. However, contemporary situations are in fact the product of historical processes, just as developments at the material level are affected by political and ideological influences. This chapter places women's current relationship to development processes in a wider context, and argues that historical and cultural issues have had a significant effect on the terms in which development policies are conceived and applied. Established views of the needs, circumstances and problems of societies and people in the 'developing' or 'Third' world today have been shaped (for good and ill) by the historic experience of subordination to western political, economic and cultural power over the last two centuries, and by western perceptions and assumptions about non-westerners arising from this experience. More significantly, from the point of view of this study, these experiences and attitudes have had a profoundly *gendered* aspect; that is to say that particular definitions and interpretations of the distinctive character and roles of women, as opposed to those of men, were central to the encounters between western and non-western societies, and to the policies of control and 'development' devised for the latter.

The term 'development' which figures in the title of this volume is widely used in media, academic and everyday discourse, yet despite this fact (and indeed *because* of it) it is important to clarify our use of the term by pausing to consider its content, context and implications. The familiarity of the term leads us to assume that we 'know' its meanings, but in fact these meanings and their origins need to be unpacked and analysed. My contribution will take such an analysis as the starting point for an account of ways in which concepts and practices of development are *historically constructed* in such a way as both generally to *impose 'outsider' interpretations* and evaluations of societies and people experiencing 'development', and specifically to misinterpret and *marginalise women's roles and lives*. I stress the notion of historical construction as an explicit critique of non- or anti-historical approaches to development work (practical or theoretical) based on the dubious notion of 'value-free' social science, on the role of science and technology rather than human agency, and on assumptions about the 'timeless' character of development issues. I stress the problem of treating so-called 'under-developed' societies as passive objects of the views and policies of development 'experts' or academic theorists, since to ignore this problem is intellectually unsound and practically unhelpful, granted the obvious importance of the actual experiences and thinking within such societies for both analysis and policy implementation. I stress the marginalisation and misconception of women's lives partly because women's studies in the west need to confront the misunderstandings and prejudices which still influence approaches to Third World women, but more importantly because the female majority (in all its diversity) should be central, not peripheral, to development theory and practice.

In the late 1980s few practitioners or theorists of the processes associated with development would see the concept as either straight-forward or uncontentious. Diversities of past history, of social, economic or political structures, and of the direction or pace of change in particular societies make the distinctions between 'developing', 'developed' and 'under-developed' hard to use as more than general indicators. In this decade of crises in the Third World – from the debt crises in Latin America and subsistence crises in Africa to the crisis of Communist planning in China and the effects of war and revolution in Eritrea, Iran and Nicaragua – questions hang over many aspects of development, whether they are local or transnational, capitalist or socialist, state or private initiatives. Simple correlations between 'development' and betterment are hard to sustain in the face of the uneven and often unpredicted effects of planning, new technology or urban growth on Third World ecologies, economies and commu-nities, whether in the Amazonian forests, the export manufacturing zones of South-east Asia, or the shanty-towns of Cairo or Buenos Aires. Recent writing on development has addressed these questions and difficulties both through theoretical analysis and through specific and empirical studies of particular issues and societies.[1] It has also drawn on a range of new perspectives of which one of the most significant is growing awareness of the importance of women as a large, distinctive, and, until recently, neglected element in Third World societies, economies and 'development'.[2]

This volume is concerned with women's involvement in the devel-opment of Third World societies, and my contribution will examine some of the historical and cultural influences which have shaped ideas and discussions on the subject. However, the topic needs to be set in the context of a broader history of attitudes to societies in what is now called the Third World. These attitudes are the product of a historic relationship between such societies and external influences and interventions (material, political or cultural). The growing importance of that relationship in recent history shaped not only economic and political life in many societies, but also the very terms in which they perceived and understood one another. Although it is not appropriate to deal with the full range and detail of these developments here, certain aspects of the wider picture are worth considering if the history of debates and ideas about women and development is to be understood, and it is to these that we now turn.

It is an important, if familiar, starting point to say that those societies described today as 'underdeveloped' or 'developing' are by and large those which, until recently, have been for greater or lesser periods directly influenced and controlled by external powers, either European or North American. Between the seventeenth and the nineteenth centuries they became involved by diverse means and to varying extents in an extending and intensifying 'world system' of European-dominated financial and commercial networks, political relationships, communications, and territorial and colonial acquisition. This is not the place for a full account of the complex, diverse and contradictory processes involved in, say, the rise and fall of the Caribbean slave plantation economies, the European impact on textile manufacture in Asia, or the colonisation and decolonisation of Africa, to name only a few important elements in the history of this world system.[3] It is, however, worth drawing out a few points of particular significance to the history of development policy and development studies, and to the situation of women within that history. Rather than make such points at a bland and unhelpful level of generality, they will be addressed through particular examples.

Firstly, the notion of a 'world system' is meant to identify not merely a random set of specific relations between buyers and sellers, colonial rulers and subjects, investors and producers but a complex structure of many levels and interactions of material, political and cultural life. Thus the British domination of the Indian sub-continent is not so much a history of commercial or territorial expansion in isolation but of the impact of British investment on family production systems, or of government intervention on landlord–peasant relations. The 'incorporation' of Indians into a world system involved the emergence of an English-speaking and nationalist professional elite, new legal frameworks and education systems influencing class, caste and gender divisions, and new patterns of rural life and urbanisation.[4] Similarly, the French occupation of Algeria was part of a complex set of processes involving the creation of a settler community, the ambitions of the French state in the Mediterranean and as a major

European power, and a range of attempts to manage or modify in-digenous elites and communities combined with their responses to those attempts.[5] It is a question of appreciating the interrelations and many-sided character of processes in which the whole may be greater than the sum of its parts.

This can be demonstrated by examples at a more specific level. European interest in Iranian carpet manufacture began in the mid-nineteenth century as a response to the search for commodity trade in the context of Iranian economies only weakly linked to Euro-pean markets, and an Anglo-Russian interest in Iran which was more strategic than economic. It involved relationships with local mer-chants and subsequently direct relations with carpet producers, and re-directed a craft industry hitherto based on a local luxury market and local resources towards European and American consumer de-mand, the importation of dyes and yarn, and European influence on design and quality. Iranian entrepreneurs established putting-out sys-tems and workshops which reorganised and intensified family labour and the employment of women and children in specific sub-crafts in order to meet the new demands and profit from new opportunities. By the First World War a large-scale export industry based on these developments had not only affected regional economies in various parts of Iran, but had also altered urban life and politics as the carpet workers organised into craft associations which bargained with local government and European consuls, and intervened as a group in the radical nationalist movement.[6]

The second main issue which needs consideration if the growth of a world system is to be linked to the discussion of women and develop-ment is the cultural and ideological dimension involved. The diversity and extent of the material and political involvement of Iranians or Indians with European entrepreneurs, governments, missionaries or military men involved not only the structures of economic activity or daily life in community and family, but also people's consciousness and understanding of the world. Indian cultivators confronted new views of the relationships between land, kinship and power as well as demands for taxes or market pressures. Urban intellectuals and local politicians in Egypt and China faced new questions about edu-cation and technology, social and cultural values posed by printed newspapers and telegraphic communication or by challenging alter-natives to indigenous forms of schooling, administration and intel-lectual life.[7] Although the responses to these confrontations within the Third World (ranging from enthusiasm for European cultural imports to rejection of them) are of great historic significance, it is the shift in Europeans' consciousness arising from their encounters with non-European societies that has particular significance for our discussion.

The model of 'development' which emerged into modern times

was partly based on the nineteenth-century experience of these encounters, of radical change within European societies, and a corresponding interest in systematic study and explanation of change through the emerging 'scientific' disciplines of economics, history and sociology. European involvement in the expansion and intensification of the world system entailed not just trade, colonisation, investment or military aggression but also the construction of new, systematic interpretations of the different societies in the system. There is a rich literature dealing with the way in which these new interpretations evolved both in relation to actual experiences, and as bodies of ideas and images in their own right, and only a few major points will be made here.[8] While they may not do justice to the complex and sometimes contradictory aspects of the problem, they draw attention to some influential ideas, assumptions and arguments which passed into discussions of development.

Nineteenth-century European experience of substantial and rapid changes in their own societies, where new social, political and technological developments apparently increasingly differentiated them from non-western societies, provided the basis for new views of those societies. European successes in economic penetration, territorial acquisition, and political or military intervention, based on effective organisation of business, diplomatic or financial institutions and new technologies, appeared to give empirical proof of European superiority. British and French armies sustaining the Manchu rulers of China, British railway construction in Argentina or mining enterprises in southern Africa were the outward and visible signs of this superiority. The spread of Russian, German or British manufactured goods into Asian or South American markets, the political and territorial advantages gained in Africa or Peru or the Ottoman Empire, and the worldwide presence of European missionaries, technocrats and travellers were similar manifestations of European 'achievement'. European 'success' in transforming economic, political and social institutions and relations in their own societies, and in disseminating entrepreneurial or military or educational forms beyond Europe formed the context within which Europeans judged themselves and compared others.

The European sense of difference and superiority was expressed in a series of opposed definitions and contrasting images which reinforced negative concepts of Asian or African societies in terms of comparisons with western Europe, stressing what non-European societies were *not*. If forms of economic activity in Europe were seen as dynamic and acquisitive, the economic life of Palestinian cultivators or Masai pastoralists was judged hidebound and unproductive.[9] If political life in Europe was thought to be increasingly regulated by constitutional forms, public opinion and rational debate, that of Indian princely states or African chiefdoms was categorised as arbitrary, corrupt or violent.[10] If it was considered that social institutions in Europe were being continually improved by the application of progressive reforms and clear moral standards, those elsewhere were characterised as backward, disorganised and undesirable. Stagnation was posed against dynamism, chaotic inefficiency against rational organisation, and backwardness or decadence against progress and/or moral acceptability in either explicit or implicit judgements of non-European agricultural methods or family structures or political activity in terms of their failure to meet European norms.

Such negative judgements were constructed out of a mixture of cultural and ideological images ('oriental despotism', 'primitive customs', 'heathen beliefs') and detailed scholarship. One form of European power over non-Europeans lay in the establishment of dominant, even monopolistic, knowledge and expertise about languages, geography, customs, history or beliefs in non-European societies. Colonial administrators, learned institutions for the study and discussion of anthropology or oriental languages, detailed eye-witness accounts by western missionaries or explorers, soldiers or journalists about what other societies were 'really' like combined to construct a framework of 'actual knowledge' and expert testimony which defined and controlled the representation of those societies.[11] This framework interlocked with another, constructed from visual, verbal or religious images of the exotic, the primitive, the decadent or the savage.

Thus on the one hand Europeans asserted their capacity for unique and privileged rational understanding and knowledge of non-European societies, while on the other they suggested that the alien character of such societies put them beyond any fully rational account. Demonstrations of detailed learning about kinship among Africans or Islamic law and custom were interwoven with commentary about 'the mysterious orient' or 'the dark continent' – never to be fully explained or understood, except perhaps by the 'experts' who built careers in these fields. European religion could thus be set against 'primitive superstition' or 'irrational fanaticism' just as 'oriental despotism' could be opposed to 'proper' government, or 'backward' agriculture and banking systems contrasted with profitable and expanding production or investment, using a mixture of scholarship and mystification.[12]

This blend of information and imagination, of expertise and fantasy, established a dominant understanding of non-European societies which stretched across political and ideological spectra. The Utilitarian reformer James Mill, the conservative political analyst Fitzjames Stephen and the revolutionary socialist Karl Marx all discussed the Indian sub-continent in terms of the limitations or inadequacies of indigenous societies and their clear contrast with the superior alternatives offered by the British ruling regime, offering hopes of benefits or progress to their Indian subjects.[13] They might differ sharply in the characterisations, explanations or evaluations which they offered, but they operated within a hegemonic framework of discussion which coloured and dominated any alternative view. Similar patterns can be seen in the debates over the abolition of slavery, dominated by racialist perspectives on black Africans taken by both supporters and opponents of the institution, and in debates about colonial expansion in which assumptions about non-European backwardness influenced both sides. While the placing of non-European societies in an inferior position in a hierarchy, or on the negative side of a dichotomy, was neither a simple nor a universal process, it did represent the dominant trend of European theory and practice by the later nineteenth century.

Within this context discussions of women and of gender issues were not only part of the subject matter but also central to the intellectual and ideological construction of the non-European 'other'. A crucial element in the definition of Asian or African societies as primitive or decadent was the presentation of data and arguments about the disadvantaged position of women in the family, or production, or religious and social life. This was quite regularly depicted, however erroneously, as inferior to the situation of women in western Europe.

Legislators in British India made suppression of widow-burning, female infanticide and child-marriage part of a general mission to 'improve' society in the sub-continent, and their arguments linked these practices to general definitions of Indians as inferior. Missionaries, travellers and reformers presented sometimes highly coloured descriptions of foot-binding in China, polygamy in Africa, or the suppression of women in the Middle East which moralised and dramatised rather than analysed or understood the legal, familial or cultural frameworks of women's lives. These descriptions might be linked to campaigns for *zenana* education in India, or Cromer's discussions of health reforms in Egypt, but they stressed the image of women as the victims of an oppression intrinsic to the societies being described.[14]

The accumulation of information about the treatment of women in Islamic law or Yoruba custom, or about their roles as agricultural workers, victims of arranged marriages or lineage matriarchs was interwoven with a pervasive and influential set of cultural and ideological images and fantasies. These were rooted not in empirical observation but in a whole range of anthropological theory, fictional writing and imaginative description as well as in visual images generated in popular journalism, elite art and advertising.

The range and quantity of this material grew during the nineteenth century; there were popularising missionary accounts of women's experiences of slavery in East Africa from both British Protestant and French Roman Catholic perspectives; there were journalistic descriptions with cartoons and drawings of semi-nude black women and Middle Eastern dancing girls; there were travel books, ranging from the academic to the deliberately frivolous, depicting women in stereotyped roles; there were high-status paintings for affluent urban patrons, and novels like those of Rider Haggard for wider, middle-class audiences.[15] They reinforced various value judgements shaped by dominant European religious and secular ideologies ranging from devout Roman Catholicism to left-liberal progressivism. The exotic, alien but compelling images of women in Middle Eastern harems, or slave plantations in the USA, or Rider Haggard's Africa were products not of research or rational analysis but of a western imagination within which, as will be seen, such images had a powerful purpose. Languid odalisques lolling in the pages of European travel books like those of Nerval or Lane, and the paintings of the salons like those of Lewis or Gérôme, owed little to any substantive knowledge of the female part of aristocratic households in Cairo or Istanbul to which the term 'harem' might be applied.[16] The familiar descriptions of black mammies or sexually charged slave girls which were a staple of abolitionist pamphleteering or fiction bore little relation to the predominant experiences of Afro-American women as field labourers. Oriental dancing girls or African witch-women or sexually available Polynesian women might be the best-known 'types' which came to represent non-European womanhood, alongside the downtrodden wife or 'ignorant' village midwife; they revealed little about the complex realities of women's circumstances in the non-western world. However, it could be the stereotype rather than realities which influenced serious policy-making or scholarship as much as it shaped popular opinions.

Again it is important to grasp the powerful blend of information, imagination, pragmatic self-interest and prejudice which shaped received views on non-European women, the policies applied to them, and the whole definition of 'backwardness' (later, 'underdevelopment') within which non-European societies were understood. Where women's role as mothers or their role in production, or the rules governing their social conduct did not meet the norms accepted by middle-class Europeans, then their situation was by definition and necessarily 'inferior' to that of European women. 'Inferiority' in the treatment of women was part of the definition of non-European 'inferiority' in general, and debates or action concerning women were thus a central part of European entrepreneurial, imperial or missionary strategies in general. Images of the immovable power of 'native custom' and/or the energising power of market forces or colonial rule or western-style reform/Christianisation were central to the discussion and implementation of such strategies, alongside the dictates of political caution or ideologies of paternalism or improvement. These also incorporated ethnocentric assumptions about the 'proper' place of women in family, productive work or the community, reinforcing the close connection between discussions of women and of non-European societies generally. Cromer's comment of 1909 on Egyptian women's responsibility for infant mortality specifically reflects contemporary discussions in Britain.[17]

There were of course many contradictions and variations in the construction and representation of Third World women as exotic specimens, as oppressed victims, as sex objects or as the most ignorant and backward members of 'backward' societies. The painting of picturesque images could clash with the making of moral or 'scientific' judgements, or with the presentation of empirical knowledge. Nonetheless, the presentation of women played a central part in the conceptualisation of Third World societies, and, as will be seen, of European male views of their relationship to those societies. The images, arguments and explanations which were offered have been both pervasive and persuasive, operating in every dimension from academic scholarship to popular media culture, and from official policy-making to pornographic fantasy.[18] Since these constructions and representations of women entered the mainstream of European cultures through education, entertainment, arts and religion, they were able to exert their cultural influence on those brought up within those cultures who became policy-makers, missionaries or administrators shaping the lives of women in 'Third World' societies. While appreciating the significance of this situation, it is also important to examine some of the problems, contradictions and complexities within these western views of non-western women.

An obvious but important point to note about these views is that, despite their reliance on the 'knowledge' of European scholars, travellers and colonial officials, they actually offered inaccurate and partial accounts of the realities of non-European women's lives. Whether academic or exotic, these accounts emphasised *difference* between Europeans and non-Europeans at the expense of developed investigation or analysis.[19] Thus Europeans produced moralising or exoticising writing on institutions such as harems or polygamy in Africa or India rather than proper descriptions or explanations of the material circumstances or cultural context within which such institutions sustained kinship-based agricultural production, urban commercial interests or aristocratic households and lineages. The practice of 'arranged' marriage was much commented on by middle-class Europeans, when they encountered it in India or the Middle East, as an exotic and unfamiliar custom;[20] yet so-called 'free choice' marriage was a recent and by no means universal practice in nineteenth-century Europe, a fact overlooked by such comments; they similarly ignored the fact that family, property and community interests (rather than personal or emotional concerns) were as central to marriage in rural communities or elite families in England or France as in Anatolia or the Punjab. Campaigns against slavery employed depictions of tragic black mothers derived not from the lived experience of black women on plantations in the southern USA or in the slave trade of eastern Africa, but from the dominant values of white, middle-class motherhood and domesticity and white Christian morality (Roman Catholic or Evangelical).[21] The misleading divide created by western intellectuals, missionaries, experts and propagandists between themselves and 'others' obscured both the complex specific circumstances of women in particular societies in Europe and elsewhere, and the possibility of serious critical and comparative analysis of those circumstances.

If emphasis on the 'otherness' of non-westerners limited the possibility of any adequate account of women in non-western societies, neglecting both the range of influences upon their lives, and similarities or differences between societies and histories in Europe and elsewhere, European insistence that the 'oppressed state' of women in non-European societies proved their inferiority had its own misleading ironies. European discussions of Indian, African or Middle Eastern women in the nineteenth century focused on the legal, religious, social and educational restrictions which constrained them, and on their oppression at work and in the family. Yet at the very period when such accounts were being offered as sober assessments of women's position in non-European societies, it was equally possible to discuss, as many contemporaries did, the position of women *in European societies* in terms of comparable restrictions and oppressions. English and French legislation limited or denied married women access to property, divorce, or proper access to the courts; similar restrictions existed in most European countries denying women access to higher education, professional training, the right to vote or take office; trade unions and employers restricted their access to skills, jobs and adequate wages through exclusion, as in printing in Britain, and 'protective' legislation; exclusion from unions, political life, or economic independence was argued in terms of widely accepted beliefs about the domestic, reproductive role which shaped women's 'nature'.[22]

While circumstances of this kind in Europe differed in specific ways from those in Iran or Nigeria or Bengal, and were on occasion subverted or resisted by those who found them oppressive, they certainly show that comparisons between women's situation in Europe and that elsewhere which are expressed in terms of the superiority of the former over the latter make little sense. Indeed, in particular instances – as, for example, women's ability to defend their property and inheritance rights in the law courts of nineteenth-century Egypt, shown in Tucker's work, – comparison could well be to the advantage of the non-European situation.[23]

Above all, Europeans' partial and/or prejudiced analysis of women's situation in non-European societies needs to be understood as the expression of power relations rather than as ignorance or bigotry. The material and cultural dominance underlying European views of non-Europeans, and in particular non-European women, was a matter not only of the control wielded by powerful groups of European men in a world system, but of connected patterns of gender and class power sustaining male authority over women and the control of propertied and privileged groups over the labouring and popular classes. The organisation of production depended on this multi-faceted power structure in which the functioning of capitalist cotton industries relied on black plantation share-cropping or slavery, sexual divisions of labour in Egyptian agriculture and Lancashire textile mills, and wage and market forces within and between societies generating private profit and social production. It also depended on political systems using both exclusion and incorporation, whether it was the race-specific power structure of the post-Reconstruction southern USA, the widening of an exclusively male franchise in Britain, or the establishment of British control in Egypt in the 1880s. Culturally and ideologically these power structures were confirmed and represented in theories, beliefs and images of difference and inferiority. Such theories, beliefs and images often combined class, race and gender elements, as when journalists' descriptions of London slums were entitled voyages into 'darkest England', or when medical arguments about female biological weaknesses were published in anthropological journals usually concerned with racial questions.[24] Concepts of class, gender or race hierarchy and inequality were not merely parallel but mutually reinforcing in cultural as well as in material terms.

Both non-westerners and women (western and other) were understood and represented as less than adult through images and theories about their 'child-like', 'underdeveloped' character; their status as rational beings was denied through emphasis on their 'emotional', 'unreasonable', 'instinctive' qualities and behaviour as described by doctors, cultural commentators like Ruskin, and much abolitionist and anti-abolitionist literature. Adulthood and rationality were simultaneously equated with elite, white, male experience and outlook, thus ensuring that women and non-whites alike appeared as both different ('other') *and* inferior, to be understood in terms of their 'failure' to attain or 'incapacity' for such an experience and outlook. Such views explained and justified the exclusion of women and subordinate 'races' from access to material opportunity, political power or personal autonomy, and were closely linked to arguments that in view of their non-adult, non-rational characteristics they needed elite, white, male protection, control and subjection.[25]

On the other hand, the persistent power of such arguments and theories rested not just on their potential for legitimising male dominance or colonial rule, but on their expression of deep-seated contradictions, needs and anxieties among the elite, white males who put them forward. Purely functional explanations of the views under discussion as tools for the maintenance of particular power structures ignores their full implications and hence the full impact of these views within western cultures. If images and theories of non-European or female inferiority allowed elite, white males to define their rights to dominate those groups, they also allowed such males to deal with their own ambivalent relationships, to the 'alien' and 'emotional' whose desirability could be as significant as their 'inferior' status. This ambivalence appears in fiction from Walter Scott's juxtaposition of Rebecca and Rowena to Rider Haggard's *She* and *King Solomon's Mines* and in travel literature. The capacity and claim to control and dominate others (employees, wives, colonial subjects, social inferiors) was partly based on the ability to control the self by using the disciplines of work, schooling and authority to suppress feeling, 'weakness' or desire. The obsessive discussion and depiction of femininity or 'foreignness' as simultaneously attractive and subordinate expressed the conflicts produced by this process as well as the imperatives of class, race and gender power.[26] It was precisely the blending of practical and personal need, of internal and external aspects, of fantasy and empirical scholarship and of 'fact' and 'fiction', in a complex cultural and ideological whole which gave these concepts and images of non-European women a lasting and pervasive influence.

It is important to stress the power and persistence of this cultural and ideological legacy, with its material, intellectual and emotional underpinning, since it is often assumed that in the late twentieth century the outlook discussed above is no longer significant. Yet, in the era of post-colonial disillusionment, of gloomy development prospects, new levels of internationalisation of exploitation, and new forces of resistance, the views which have concerned us above still play an important role in debate and policy-making. The development of representations, definitions and explanations of non-European women and their lives in every form from the most scholarly to the most popular during the nineteenth century had lasting consequences for social scientific and policy approaches to women and 'development' in the twentieth century. Modern academic study and practical economic or administrative organisation in the 'development' field rested on Eurocentric, gender-blind foundations and powerfully sexualised and racialised understanding and scholarship, expressed in the 'neutral' languages of planners, researchers and experts.

The first aspect of twentieth-century discussion of 'development' worth noting is the way in which the female half of humanity became invisible to social scientists and policy-makers, whether they were concerned with western or non-western societies. Economists' discussions of 'employment', experts' and formulations of social policy, sociological discussion of 'the family' either accepted certain divisions of power, resources and roles as 'natural' and given, or dealt with 'women' and 'families' as though such divisions were unimportant. Sexual divisions of labour, male authority and privilege in family or political organisation, and discrimination against women by legal, education or welfare institutions, did not loom large in either the practical or the analytical work of governments and academics. The absence of women from positions of material and political power seemed to confirm their marginal or subordinate status within such work and its lack of concern with their experiences and interests as a priority.

Gender-blind theory and practice were reinforced by the establishment of modern methods and languages for social science research and writing (impersonal, 'objective', quantitative, technical) which marginalised women not through overt prejudices or stereotypes but through the 'scientific' use of neutral, abstract concepts and assumptions. This could be seen in British government statistics or in Marxist approaches to 'class', the use of the universal 'he/him' to describe groups which include men *and* women, or in the obscuring of women's reproductive and domestic work. Moreover, changes in women's situation, whether through legal and social reforms in the west or de-colonisation in Asia and Africa, encouraged the view that emancipation and quality, or at least 'progress' for women, had been or was being achieved, and was not a contentious issue.[27]

While the methods, assumptions and concepts used by economists, planners or social scientists in the middle of the twentieth century certainly differed from those prevalent in the nineteenth, the legacy of earlier observers, theorists or experts dealing with both western and non-western women had a shaping influence on their modern successors. The location of women in a familial domestic setting, and moralistic or voyeuristic concern with the forms and regulation of sexuality and gender difference were as noticeable in post-Second World War social science as in Victorian scholarship. Thus, for example, development studies in the 1960s paid little attention to women's activities in productive work, since the concept of 'worker', whether in England or Africa, was assumed to be male, reflecting the exclusion or marginalisation of women in western workplaces during both the nineteenth and twentieth centuries. Women as owners of property or as entrepreneurs likewise received little attention, as colonial administrators and development planners or anthropologists brought to their work their ethnocentric assumptions about the reality or desirability of women's presence in those spheres.[28] Furthermore, in so far as women were the subject of the concerns of social science or social policy-making, it was most often in respect of their sexuality and their marital and family situation. Nineteenth-century ethnography and anthropology discussed these questions in terms of exotic customs and fantasy scenarios of female subordination to

119

polygamy, slavery or harem existence in the non-European world, just as religion and modern social science confined western women to stereotypical roles as mothers, wives or sex objects.

This situation has been challenged by the growth of movements by and for women and of women-centred scholarship over the last twenty years. On the one hand, the lack of both empirical and analytical understanding of women's position in societies, economies and cultures round the world has been addressed by woman-directed and feminist research, theory and writing in history, social science and cultural studies. Practical demands by women in many societies for material, political and personal emancipation and empowerment have influenced and been influenced by the opening up of the study of women not only in academic institutions but also by local, national and international agencies with pragmatic concerns about development policy and planning. Knowledge, social change and political action have thus been interwoven in a whole series of initiatives that have given priority to women and refused the marginalisation and invisibility imposed upon them in their lives and in the investigation and analysis of their lives. It was indicative of the possibilities and limitations of these new developments that a feminist researcher and author with experience of development work should have written both on the mistreatment of women in development theory and practice, and also about their marginalisation in the politics and power structures of her own society, going on to edit a populist feminist magazine.[29]

On the other hand, feminist concern with the 'invisibility' of women in male-dominated societies and cultures also needed, and quite often failed, to confront the distinctive 'invisibility' of non-western societies and cultures within the western-dominated approach to policy-making, investigation or analysis in these societies. The legacy of bias within social science and colonial or post-colonial approaches to Third World societies combined with the effects of comparable bias against women and their interests to influence the treatment of Third World women as producers, as carers, as persons and as citizens. Their material needs, their legal rights and their social opportunities were either given low priority or treated within a framework of assumptions about the character of their 'backward', 'traditional', 'female' activities, identities and place in family, community, economy and society derived from those biased sources. In this situation, non-western women were doubly marginalised and misinterpreted; however, just as 'masculist' bias had been the focus for challenges from women-centred alternatives, so both mainstream and 'feminist' approaches to theory and practice have been addressed by those creating policy and scholarship within which Third World women are fully recognised. This has involved both a variety of critiques of inappropriate development policies and analyses of Third World societies and histories, and also the assertion of women's presence, needs and interests within the construction of theories and practices more appropriate to particular non-Western societies.[30]

Such critiques and alternatives, like the arguments put forward here, suggest bases or guidelines for more useful discussions on women and development. Instead of accepting and reproducing the gender-blind and ethnocentric assumptions which have influenced development studies and policy-making, such discussions would address and try to analyse the real complexities of women's lives. In order to redress the marginalisation and misinterpretation of Third World women, several major issues need to be addressed. It is particularly important to address women's dual and sometimes contradictory experience of structures and processes within their own societies on the one hand, and on the other hand the effect of external economic influences, of colonial and post-colonial interventions and of the presence of foreign experts, reformers and foreign examples and standards. Within their own societies women have had to deal with the structures and practices of male and class power embodied in the authority of male elders and relatives, the economic and political dominance of landlords, employers, kinship groups and government officials, and in cultural definitions (religious, secular, elite, popular) of 'proper' female roles and behaviour. In Indian caste systems, West African rural communities or Latin American urban slums such structures and practices have historically defined women's productive work, and patterns of marriage, childcare and education, or female status, and continue to influence governmental policies, family economic strategies and modern social and political activity.

However, these historic and contemporary processes *within* particular societies have confronted, coexisted with, or been transformed by other *externally* introduced elements. The impact of a growing, changing world system on production, trade and investment in many areas has affected women's productive activities, their movement within and between particular countries and their roles in consumption and services. The intervention of administrators and missionaries in the past, and of western experts and planners in the present has helped to re-shape communities and families as well as legal or educational systems. Moreover, models and standards of 'development' or 'progress' rooted in western experience and analyses of their own societies, and then unthinkingly generalised to all societies, have also transformed women's lives, for good or ill, by use of particular concepts of property rights or technology, or of western models of health care, literacy or urban planning. Whether we consider the situation of women in rural areas of Kenya dealing with the consequences of the rise of male wage labour or women's work in the export industries of South-east Asia, or the erosion of women's rights

121

to land by colonial and post-colonial legislation, we are looking at processes in which external economic influence or models play a shaping role. Investigation and analysis of these processes need to be part of the whole approach to women's experience of and involvement in development.[31]

If these experiences and involvements need to be understood in terms of interaction with both indigenous and external influences, whether material, cultural or political, women's own options and choices also need to be part of the discussion. The lives of Turkish or Ghanaian or Filipina women have been shaped by class and community solidarities and conflicts, by male interests and power, by kinship systems, and by state intervention in society. Thus they define themselves and are defined by others variously as gendered persons dealing with men, as cultivators, traders, wage labourers or professionals in relation to employers, clients, landlords or fellow workers, as members of kin groups with hierarchically defined positions as wives, mothers, sisters or daughters, and as objects of government political control and socio-economic policy. Indeed, it can be argued that concepts of class or kinship or ethnic identity or gender are best understood as definitions of identity and difference which *actually shape one another*, so that the notion of 'worker' or 'citizen' needs to be gendered and made culturally specific, just as notions of 'female' identity or inequality should be given a class and cultural content.

The existence of a complex range of overlapping, conflicting and interacting identities has clearly produced an equally complex range of needs and problems for women. Their commitments to their families may disadvantage them in relation to male relatives yet inhibit any defence of their interests against those relatives; trade-union organisation, anti-colonial activity or rural protest have created both opportunities for women to pursue their own interests and also dilemmas over the subordination of those interests to 'class' politics or 'national' causes which ignore or marginalise women; anti-colonial and nationalist movements have often failed to express class, gender or cultural interests adequately, just as family and kin interests have both stimulated and restricted those other interests and identities.[32]

It should be the task of any research, analysis and policy-making concerned with women and development to clarify both the central importance of gender divisions, inequalities and conflicts, and also the interweaving of gender with other inequalities in resources, power and influence. These need to be discussed in terms not only of structures and circumstances shaping women's lives, but also of women's own sense of their selves, their situation and their interests, and of the real and conflicting localities, choices or commitments which women have formed historically and in the present. Women's ambivalent relationships to the growth and aftermath of struggles against colonial rule in India since the 1930s or Algeria since the 1950s or Zimbabwe since the 1970s need to be seen as the product of the conflicts of gender, nationalism, caste, religion or family; women's disadvantaged position in production and reproduction should be understood as the outcome of complex interactions between economic needs, family interests, state intervention and male power, whether in post-1949 China or apartheid South Africa; the sexualisation and domestication of women in both ideology and practice in Iran or Latin America can only be grasped as an equally complex interaction of male self-interest, cultural and political anti-imperialism and chauvinism, and socio-economic conflicts over resources, status and autonomy.[33] Women themselves have to deal with these complex realities, and make difficult choices about their lives within the constraints and possibilities available and according to the priorities which seem relevant to them. Discussions of women and development need to take account of the dialectics of choice and circumstance, and to treat 'Third World' women not as passive, exotic victims either of external forces or local conditions, but rather as active participants in such dialectics.

While development theory and practice can draw on the inspiration, evidence and analysis within feminist studies in order to represent women properly as active subjects, it also needs to take on board the problems of ethnocentrism which have affected both intellectually and politically the discussions of women. Just as we would no longer accept the prejudices and assumptions about non-western women which social science inherited from Eurocentric, nineteenth-century predecessors, so too we need to explore non-western women's situation and interests in their own terms and not those of an agenda set elsewhere. There needs to be careful consideration of the relevance of themes and issues raised within western feminism to both historical and current circumstances facing women in the 'Third World', or to their problems, needs and desires. Concern with wage labour and trade unions may well not be appropriate for women whose productive work takes place in unwaged family settings. The politics of citizenship and participation in Central America or South Africa will not necessarily focus on the issues of suffrage or party politics which have been central for women in the west. Domestic violence or educational discrimination need to be addressed differently in India or North Africa than in Europe or China.

This is not to argue for some kind of unattainable (and, in fact, inconceivable) absolute cultural relativism, but for a thoughtful and fully comparative analysis of women's circumstances and consciousness which tries to account for both similarity and difference. Family and domestic commitments, divisions of labour and questions of sexuality may well be issues around which women in many societies are developing comparable theory and practice for themselves, but understanding of the specificities as well as of the common elements which shape these issues needs to be present in any adequate treatment of them.

It follows that it will be very important to grasp the specific and varied histories of kinship and property systems in, say, the post-emancipation Caribbean or colonial and post-colonial India or West Africa, and how these shaped women's involvement in reproduction, production, marriage and community life. Similarly, women's roles in agriculture need to be located in particular histories and structures of rice cultivation in South-east Asia, pastoralism in Iran, or various plough-and-hoe-based systems of grain production, just as their participation in manufacture needs analysis in terms of varied organisations and technologies of production, ranging from familial textile manufacture to large-scale trans-national enterprises. In cultural and political terms we need to approach different ideologies and practices of, say, segregation or exclusion of women through the particular histories of religion, popular culture and systems of political and power relations which have shaped the interaction of Islamic and secular forces in Turkey or of popular protest and rural communities in Latin America. While acknowledging the *common* problems which have been created for non-western women by the ways in which they have been represented, it is also important to challenge and de-construct the categories 'non-western' or 'Third World' in so far as they conceal or mystify the diverse interests and issues which concern women in non-western societies. Not to do so would be to reproduce the marginalisation and misconception which we wish to overcome, and to ignore significant divergences and contradictions in the experience of different groups of women.

Nevertheless, the significance of particular histories and social circumstances for women and development is matched by the significance of widespread and common experiences and issues which play their role in those histories and social situations. One of the most obvious of these has been the impact of colonial, semi-colonial and post-colonial influence, itself significantly varied. The common elements which need analysis are those associated with the power of colonial and international power to interfere directly at economic, political and cultural levels, and to place external pressure or controls on the lives and choices of individuals, groups and communities. These elements are part of the past and present experience of women in many societies and cultures. Another set of elements common to that experience arises from the persistence over time of kinship and community networks dominated by various forms of male authority over many aspects of the lives of other members of their households, families, caste groups, or communities. While such authority has remained a clearly male prerogative in many societies, it has also tended to be concentrated in the hands of senior/older males exercising material and ideological control or influence over women and younger people in what has been called a classic pattern of patriarchy. This patriarchal power could be manifest in the management of marriage, productive work and property rights, of authority in religious and political matters, and in the customs, values and ideas which shape socialisation, morality and popular culture.[34]

Discussions of women and development need to address these themes in a rigorous and comparative fashion. Colonial opposition to polygamy, to women-centred production, or to matrilocal–matrilineal social systems (labelled 'unnatural or grotesque' by one 1920s anthropologist)[35] should be analysed in terms of similarities and differences in both forms and effects. Changes in these practices might come through external economic pressure, the influence of social reformers and missionaries, or through colonial legislation. Such external changes were likely to generate new ideologies and aspirations and/or defensive resistance within colonial societies, often linked to anti-colonial and nationalist movements in which men played dominant roles. Themes and variations within this process can be seen in the history of India, Central America, the Middle East, and southern Africa, and should be linked to the multi-faceted character of the world system and of colonial power and their restriction of choice and control whether economic, political or cultural.[36]

The explanation of common and divergent elements in the structures and manifestations of male power will benefit from a similar approach. This will involve the analysis of property rights, of family relationships and systems of production as well as masculist influence over culture and ideology in forms ranging from the dominance of male priesthoods to popular stories and proverbs. It also involves the analysis of the *interactions* between cultural and material aspects of male power, as when cultural prescriptions about female modesty, obedience or seclusion affect women's ability to engage in public commercial or entrepreneurial activity with very differing outcomes in (for example) the Middle East and West Africa. None the less, the common element of concern for 'right and proper' female behaviour and of women's position in kin-groups or communities dominated by men is equally significant. The appearance of common themes, such as distrust of women in popular proverbs in cultures as separate as Zaïre, Bangladesh and Senegal, raises important questions about the cultural practices shaping the expectations and status of women either in specific roles (wife, daughter, mother) or in hierarchies of worth (inferiority, unreliability, uncleanliness).[37]

However, the exploration of common themes and variations is not just a matter of dealing with the exploitation, subjection or oppression of women, but needs to be equally concerned with women's positive ability to create and sustain both material and cultural autonomy and to subvert, adapt or resist within the structures of male power. One visible common phenomenon worth some discussion is

125

the importance of women's networks in various kinds of productive work, in community life, or the undertaking of household and family care. Such networks can show elements both of hierarchy and of co-operation, whether in the relationships of women market traders in West Africa, or women's formal and informal management of reputations and marriage arrangements in Middle Eastern communities, or joint female involvement in cultivation.[38] One historically significant and widespread form of female authority within families is that of older women, particularly of mothers-in-law, based both on a woman's status as a mother of sons and on her control over her son's wives. Paradoxically, the movement of women into their husband's households both opens a route to a position of respect and influence as a mother/mother-in-law while also contributing to the devaluation of daughters who will be no asset to the household of their birth. Other forms of female solidarity may involve the protection of women in their role as mothers from neglect or abuse, the enforcement of codes of female behaviour by senior women, or the transmission and application of health-care skills and services.[39] These varied forms of positive female activity and association, which are by no means unique to particular societies, play an influential role in shaping women's lives and consciousness and have both material and cultural aspects whose interaction merits analysis.

In arguing for a critical and comparative approach to the notion of 'Third World women', two points should be borne in mind. Firstly, this approach can reduce the dangers of misleading and dismissive simplification on the one hand and mystifying descriptive detail on the other. A critical view of the concept of 'Third World women' as a generality will enable us to avoid insulting women's varied experiences in diverse societies and cultures by implying that they are 'all the same'. A comparative approach to diversity and variety enables us to avoid using them to mystify and confuse ourselves or making them an excuse for not offering adequate explanations or analyses which take account of *both* difference *and* similarity. Secondly, a comparative and critical approach enables us to deal more adequately not only with features of women's subordination and inequality but also with the affirmative and positive aspects of women's lives, as well as linking gender analysis with other structures shaping women's experience and consciousness. It will allow flexible but coherent discussion of the complex and contradictory forms of class, gender and cultural difference, of external and internal pressure or change in particular societies, and of the combined and uneven forms of women's accommodation or resistance to the influences or controls upon them.

While discussions of women and development need to be critical and comparative in order to deal with both diversity and similarity, they also need a *historical* dimension, that is to take account of change over time. One of the classic stereotypes passed on to

twentieth-century social scientists by their nineteenth-century predecessors was the image of non-western societies as hidebound, stagnant
and indeed lacking the capacity to change without western assistance.
In the nineteenth century this was seen in terms of the benefits of
colonial rule, of the forces of the free market or of missionary efforts
for societies which were unable to generate 'progress' themselves.
By the twentieth century this image had been re-cast to represent
the problem as one of introducing 'modern' production, government
or technology into 'traditional' societies which by definition lacked
them.

Many historians or development specialists concerned with non-
western societies, whatever their views, have taken the penetration
of external economic forces or colonial intervention as starting points
for any processes of significant change in those societies. However, to
acknowledge the importance of such external influences, as indeed it
has been argued here that it is vital to do, in no way implies a denial of
the historical processes within non-western societies which pre-dated
and existed independently of those influences. The growth of a world
system influencing the development of those societies can be shown
to have intensified, redirected or altered the pace and character of
change; this is *not* to suggest that changing conditions and conflicts of
interest in the systems of production, of politics or of social relations
did not feature in the societies under discussion before the emergence
of that world system. The history of economic structures in the Ottoman Empire, or of state formation in West Africa, are cases in point.
This suggests the need for a clear distinction between using the growth
of the world system to periodise the history of non-western societies
and denying that they have histories which pre-date and persist across
the division created by that periodisation.

It follows that analyses of women's experiences in non-western
societies also need to acknowledge that women's histories do not just
begin with the colonial penetration of women's lives in the modern
period. The impact of population movements and the rise and fall of
state systems on the situation of women in African or pre-Columbian
America, like the effect of incoming nomadic pastoralism or new
religious influences on their lives in the Middle East, illustrate crucial themes in the histories of non-western women pre-dating their
encounter with the west.[40] The interaction between internal and external influences on women's lives which has been stressed earlier
as a crucial element in their involvement in development can only
be properly understood if it is given a historical dimension. The
impact of the British colonial presence in the Indian sub-continent as
compared with the same presence in East Africa is partly explained
by the different historic processes and social systems encountered by
the British in the two cases.[41] The absence or presence of large-
scale, elaborated government bureaucracies, commercial networks

127

or formalised property rights made crucial differences to women's experiences of colonialism and development in particular societies, and were the outcome of historical processes which need discussion in their own right. Only by dissolving the myth that women in non-western societies were sleeping beauties immobilised in static 'traditional' systems; waiting for western-style 'progress' to waken them, can any serious analysis proceed.

While critique and demystification of existing paradigms are essential if discussions of women and development are to improve, this 'negative' approach needs to be complemented by positive ideas about productive lines of enquiry which will take the discussion forward. Three areas suggest themselves as generally relevant fields within which many women's experience can be examined: the question of women's position within a system of production and division of labour is likely to be central in most societies, granted the centrality of the reproduction, development and use of human labour in any economic system, and women's involvement in both production and reproduction; the question of women's social identity, and how far that is organised around their differences from men as opposed to other forms of social difference (class, ethnicity) is an equally fertile way into the complex issues of legal, educational and customary construction of identity and difference; the question of sexuality as a crucial dimension of women's lives, and its development and regulation within cultures and communities as well as by the state also raises important general issues affecting women's participation in economic activity, in political life and social relations. By identifying topics such as these for further investigation, analysis and action around women's needs and interests discussion can advance beyond the constraints which have limited it until recently.

One specific example will illustrate the achievements which are being made. As its title implies, Judith Tucker's *Women in Nineteenth-century Egypt* is a treatment of women's lives in a particular period of Egyptian history.[42] It challenges prevalent western myths about Egyptian women's passivity, inactivity and oppression by investigating their economic activities, their family and social relationships and their legal position. This investigation reveals not only the high level of women's productive involvement in agriculture, domestic services, craft manufacture and petty commerce, but also their complex relationships to kin groups, landlords, communities and government officials. Women's action in defence of their rights in the law courts, and in social protest, is well analysed, and informed description of their lives in aristocratic households and the entertainment professions effectively challenges oppressive and inaccurate stereotypes of oriental harems and dancing girls. Women's lives are also situated within the framework of growing Egyptian involvement in the world economy, of foreign political intervention, and changing government structures and strategies. This allows the author to offer a complex account of women's subordination and their self-activity in relation to male power, to the dominant classes and to the colonial presence, as well as their place in families, occupational groups and neighbourhoods. Although one can take issue with specific aspects or emphases in this account, it succeeds in combining complexity with coherence, and, moreover, enables the reader to make links between the historical analysis set out in the book and the subsequent experiences and contemporary concerns of Egyptian women. Its blending of an empirical with an analytical approach, and of women-centred research with concern for other issues, provides an example of what can be successfully attempted and achieved by the approaches which have been advocated here.

For indeed these positive suggestions have not been plucked from the air, but on the contrary draw on recent initiatives in development studies which focus on women through more critical, comparative and historically aware theories and practices, of which Tucker's work is only one example. Both in the specific formation and implementation of development policies and also in the broader exploration of development issues there is now a body of serious work which offers alternatives to works based on the old-established assumptions which have been questioned here. Not only have the new approaches taken women's lives, ideas and activities seriously where they were formerly misunderstood and marginalised, but also women's situation has been addressed in relation to the historic and contemporary complexities of gender, class and community and internal/external influences. The new work ranges from analysis of Islamic ideologies in relation to women, to discussion of how co-operative production systems or investment in small enterprises can develop women's material opportunities. It draws on historical work on Caribbean slave systems, caste in India, or nationalist movements in the Middle East. It deploys concepts of gender, class and identity drawn from both social science and cultural studies. It is diverse, controversial and actively engaged in both theoretical debate and practical concerns. Only the existence of this body of work has made this discussion possible.

It has been the intention of this author to stand back from the substantive issues dealt with by other contributors and to assess not just women's past experience but also the representation of that experience in previous writing. There is both a history and a historiography of 'women and development' which we wish to confront, critique and transform in the process of researching, analysing and implementing development theories and practices which can address women's real situation, needs and interests. It is for this reason that there has been such emphasis on the historical formation of practical and theoretical expertise on women and on non-western societies and its continuing influence on modern scholarship and policy-making. Unless that history and legacy are clearly critiqued they will continue to influence and undermine future work on women and development, and thus cultural and historical analysis of discussions on women and development is indispensable for any adequate and useful initiatives in the field.

NOTES AND REFERENCES

1   Examples of debate about and re-assessment of the concept of development range from works such as I. Oxaal, *Beyond the Sociology of Development* (London, 1975), to L. Blusse and F. Gaastva (eds), *Comparative Studies in Overseas History,* (Leiden, 1981), and, in a different way, G. Kitching, *Development and Under-development in Historical Perspective,* (London, 1982). See also D. Seers (ed.), *Dependency Theory; a Critical Re-assessment* (London, 1981).

2   An early discussion of women's role in development was E. Boserup, *Woman's Role in Economic Development* (London, 1970); concern with the issue developed in such works as N. Yousef, *Women and Work in Developing Societies* (Berkeley, CA, 1974); B. Rogers, *The Domestication of Women* (London, 1980); K. Young, C. Wolkowitz and R. McCallagh (eds), *Of Marriage and the Market* (London, 1981). These works have drawn on and stimulated a large range of work related to more specific aspects of the question and to woman-directed literature on women, work, family and community.

3   Accounts of the earlier stages of this process can be found in I. Wallerstein, *The Modern World System,* 2 vols. (London, 1974, 1980), or F. Braudel, *Civilisation and Capitalism,* vol. 3 (London, 1984). Later stages can be traced in E. Hobsbawm, *The Age of Capital* (London, 1975); T. Smith, *The Pattern of Imperialism* (Cambridge, 1981); A. J. Latham, *The International Economy and the Under-developed World* (London 1978); D. Fieldhouse, *The Colonial Empires* (London, 1965); R. Owen and B. Sutcliffe (eds), *Studies in the Theory of Imperialism* (London, 1972).

4   See K. de Schweinitz, *The Rise and Fall of British India; Imperialism as Inequality* (London, 1983); E. Stokes, *The Peasant and the Raj* (London, 1978); A. Seal, *The Emergence of Indian Nationalism* (Cambridge, 1968); R. Frykenberg, (ed.), *Land Control and Social Structure in Indian History* (Wisconsin, 1969); H. Husain, *Tarikh-I-Jadid,* (1839).

5   See M. Bennoune, *The Making of Contemporary Algeria 1830–1967* (Cambridge, 1988); J. Ruedy, *Land Policy in Colonial Algeria* (1967) H. Brunschwig, *French Colonialism* (New York, 1964); A. Nouschi, *La Naissance du nationalisme algérien* (Paris, 1962).

6   See C. Issawi, *Economic History of Iran 1800–1914* (Chicago, 1971); J. Housego, 'The 19th century Persian carpet boom', *Oriental Art*

1974; A. C. Edwards, *The Persian Carpet* (London, 1953); H. Coxon, *Oriental Carpets; How They Are Made and Carried to Europe* (London, 1884); Great Britain, Foreign Office consular records for Tabriz, Kerman, Kermanshah.

7   See A. Haurani, *Arabic Thought in the Liberal Age* (Oxford, 1961); J. Levenson, *Confucian China and its Modern Fate* (London, 1958, 1964, 1965); T. Mitchell, *Colonising Egypt* (Cambridge, 1988); M. C. Wright, *The Last Stand of Chinese Conservatism* (Stanford, 1957).

8   V. Kiernan, *The Lords of Human Kind* (London, 1972); J. Haller, *Outcasts from Evolution* (Urbana, IL, 1971); N. Stepan, *The Idea of Race in Science* (London, 1982); D. Lorimer, *Colour, Class and the Victorians* (London, 1978); M. Biddiss (ed.), *Images of Race* (Leicester, 1979); E. Said, *Orientalism* (London, 1978); P. Curtin, *The Image of Africa* (Wisconsin, 1974); R. Hallett 'Changing European attitudes to Africa', *Cambridge History of Africa*, vol. V (Cambridge, 1976); J. Vatin and P. Lucas, *L'Algérie des anthropologues* (Paris, 1975).

9   G. Kitching, *Class and Economic Change in Kenya* (London, 1980), pp. 15, 143; R. Tignor, *The Colonial Transformation of Kenya* (Princeton, 1976), pp. 310–24; S. Graham-Brown, *Palestinians and Their Society* (London, 1980), pp. 14, 34–5, 42–3; M. Rogers, *Domestic Life in Palestine* (London, 1862), pp. 141–2; G. Franklin, *Palestine Depicted and Described* (London, 1911), p. 21; H. Luke and E. Keith-Roach (eds), *Handbook of Palestine*, (London, 1934), pp. 261, 279–80.

10   See P. D. Reeves (ed.), *Sleeman in Oudh* (Cambridge, 1971); Curtin, *Image of Africa*, pp. 407–8; C. Grant, *Observations on the State of Society among the Asiatic Subjects of Great Britain* (London, 1797–1832); Cairns, *Prelude to Imperialism* (London, 1965); R. Burton, *The Kingdom of Dahomey* (London, 18).

11   See Said *Orientalism*; R. Schwab, *The Oriental Renaissance*? Curtin, *Image of Africa*; Cairns, *Prelude to Imperialism*; T. Asad (ed.), *Anthropology and the Colonial Encounter* (London, 1973); references in note 8.

12   See, for example, the work of Maine and Lyall on India, discussed by R. Owen, 'Imperial policy and theories of social change', in Asad, *Anthropology and the Colonial Encounter*; or the role of Baker in equatorial Africa discussed in Cairns, *Prelude to Imperialism*, pp. 203–6.

13   J. Mill, *History of British India* (London, 1819), Book II, 'Of the Hindus'; Sir J. F. Stephen, letter in *The Times*, 4 Jan. 1878, and 'Foundations of the government of India', *Nineteenth Century* (Oct. 1883); K. Marx, in S. Avineri (ed.), *Karl Marx on Colonialism and Modernisation* (New York, 1969), pp. 39–40, 88–95, 449–53.

14   Examples from a large number of comparable works are E. Cooper, *The Harem and the Purdah* (London, 1915); *idem*, *My Lady of the Chinese Courtyard* (London); M. Hume-Griffiths, *Behind the Veil in Persia and Turkish Arabia* (London, 1909). J. R. Chilty, *Things Seen in China* (London, 1909), pp. 72–3; Cairns, *Prelude to Imperialism*, pp. 175–7; T. Winterbottom, *An Account of the Native Africans in the Neighbourhood of Sierra Leone* (London, 1803), vol. I, pp. 145–51, 176–7, 215–18; J. Tucker, *Women in Nineteenth Century Egypt* (Cambridge, 1985), p. 117.

15   The work of Livingstone and of French missionaries in East Africa
      are obvious examples; see D. Livingstone, *Missionary Travels and
      Researches in South Africa* (London, 1857), and E. Alpers, 'The
      story of Swema; female vulnerability in nineteenth century East
      Africa', in C. Robertson and N. Klein (eds), *Women and Slavery
      in Africa* (Wisconsin, 1983). The visual representation of women can
      be traced in magazines and periodicals both of a general and of a
      specifically travel-oriented kind (*Punch, Illustrated London News, Le
      Tour du Monde*).

16   For an analysis see J. de Groot, '"Sex" and "race", in the nineteenth
      century; the construction of language and image', in S. Mendus and J.
      Rendall (eds), *Sexuality and Subordination* (London, 1989); for some
      realities, see J. Tucker, *Women in Nineteenth century Egypt* (Cam-
      bridge, 1985), pp. 82, 92–3, 167–71, 190, 192; H. Shaarawi, *Harem
      Years* (London, 1986) (with M. Badran, 'Introduction'); M. Badran
      'The harem and Egyptian feminism', (Unpublished paper, 1975).

17   Tucker, *Women in Nineteenth century Egypt*, p. 117; the British de-
      bate is discussed in J. Lewis, *The Politics of Motherhood* (London,
      1980), and A. Davin, 'Imperialism and Motherhood', *History Work-
      shop Journal*, 1978.

18   The sexualised 'passivity' and 'concealment' of Middle Eastern women
      in western perceptions can be seen in sources as different as Egyptian
      government statistics (cited in Tucker, *Women in Nineteenth century
      Egypt*, p. 90), postcards sent by French people from North Africa – see
      M. Alloula, *The Colonial Harem*, (Manchester, 1987) and Flaubert's
      complex reactions, described in F. Steegmuller, *Flaubert in Egypt: a
      Sensibility on Tour* (London, 1984).

19   Examples include H. H. Johnston, 'Briton missions and missionaries
      and Africa', *Nineteenth Century* (Nov. 1887) (contrasting English and
      African women) and more generally (on clashes over polygamy)
      Cairns, *Prelude to Imperialism*, pp. 175–8; the framework of Cooper,
      Harem and Purdah, with all its variety and detail, is also one that
      emphasises difference; see also E. Wharton, *In Morocco* (London,
      1920), pp. 144–60..

20   See, for example, C. Doughty, *Arabia Deserta* (1888) (London, 1921),
      pp. 230–7; E. Lane, *Manners and Customs of the Modern Egyptians*
      (London, 1836); Cooper, *Harem and Purdah*, pp. 120–33.

21   See D. White, *Aren't I a Woman?* (New York, 1985), ch. 1, plus the
      references in note 15. A classic fictionalisation is Beecher Stowe's
      Uncle Tom's Cabin (1852); the religious aspect of white, middle-class
      concepts of domesticity is covered in J. Rendall, *Origins of Modern
      Feminism* (London, 1985), ch. 3.

22   See Rendall, *Origins of Modern Feminism*; L. Davidoff and C. Hall,
      Family Fortunes (London, 1987); S. Lewenhak, *Women and Trade Un-
      ions* (London, 1977); J. McMillan, *Housewife or Harlot* (New York,
      1981); B. Smith, *Ladies of the Leisure Class* (Princeton, 1981); B.
      Taylor, 'The men are as bad as their masters', *Feminist Review*, 1979;
      C. Cockburn, *Brothers* (London, 1983), ch. 1.

23   Tucker, *Women in Nineteenth Century Egypt*, pp. 43–60, 93–100.

24   W. Booth, *In Darkest England and the Way Out* (London, 1890); the

anthropology/gender point is made in de Groot, '"Sex" and "race" in the nineteenth century' quoting references to articles on women in *Anthropological Review* (1869), *Journal of the Royal Anthropological Society* (1875) and *Anthropologia* (1874).

25 De Groot, '"Sex" and "race" in the nineteenth century', pp. 95–9; one classic example is J. Ruskin, 'Of Queen's Gardens' in *Sesame and Lilies* (London, 1865), while child images of non-Europeans may be found in the writing of Livingstone and Speke, the poetry of Kipling ('half savage and half child') or comments by Dean Farrar (1867) and Captain Obsorn (1860) on the Chinese.

26 The image of women and/or foreigners as simultaneously attractive, dangerous and inferior can be traced from early nineteenth-century romanticism in art and literature to the symbolist creations of the late nineteenth century and the fiction of Kipling, Loti or Haggard.

27 Critiques of the neglect, concealment or marginalisation of women may be found in J. Acker, 'Women and social stratification; a case of intellectual sexism', *American Sociologist* (1973); R. Brown, 'Women as employees', in D. Barker and S. Allen (eds), *Dependence and Exploitation in Work and Marriage* (London, 1976); M. Millman and R. Kanker, (eds), *Another Voice*, (New York, 1975); S. Delamont, *The Sociology of Women* (London, 1980); L. Sargent (ed.), *The Unhappy Marriage of Marxism and Feminism*, and M. Barret, *Women's Oppression Today*, (1980) are both critiques of gender bias in Marxist work.

28 Classic examples from anthropology are C. Lévi-Strauss, *The Elementary Structures of Kinship* (London, 1969), p. 116 (on the 'absolute priority' of patrilineage and university of male control), and M. Godelier, *Perspectives in Marxist Anthropology* (Cambridge, 1977), pp. 105–6 (on the 'natural' control of women by men). The role of planners' assumptions is analysed in Rogers, *Domestication of Women*, chs 4, 6, 7.

29 I refer to the work of Barbara Rogers, author of *The Domestication of Women* and also of works on gender bias in British politics and on all-male institutions in Britain. She is currently an editor of *Everywoman* magazine.

30 See (for example) N. Hafkin and E. Bay (eds), *Women in Africa* (C. A. Stanford, 1975); M. Mackintosh, 'Reproduction and patriarchy; a critique of Claude Meillassoux', *Capital and Class* (1977); M. Molyneux, 'Androcentrism in Marxist anthropology', *Critique of Anthropology*, (1977); J. Nash, (ed.), *Women and Men in the International Division of Labour* (New York, 1983); C. Vidal (ed.), 'Des femmes sur l'Afrique des femmes', *Cahiers d'études africaines* (1977); D. Elson and R. Pearson, 'Nimble fingers make cheap workers; an analysis of women's employment in the third world', *Feminist Review* (1981); M. Swantz, *Women in Development; a Creative Role Denied* (London, 1985); R. Dixon, *Rural Women at Work; Strategies for Development in South India* (Baltimore, 1978); Maria Mies, *The Lace Makers of Narsapur* (London, 1982); S. Mitter, *Common Fate, Common Bond* (London, 1986); H. Afshar (ed.), *Women, Work and Ideology in the Third World* (London, 1985).

133

31   Kitching, *Class and Economic Change in Kenya*, pp. 8–14, 47–9, 82–6, 105–6, 121–6, 140–5, 167–79, 200–40; W. Chapkis and C. Enloe (eds), *Of Common Cloth* (Amsterdam, 1983); P. Roberts, 'The state and the regulation of marriage', in H. Afshar (ed.), *Women, State and Ideology* (London, 1987).

32   L. Bydon, 'The dimensions of subordination; a case study from Avatime, Ghana', in Afshar, *Women, Work and Ideology*; E. Sanasarian, *The Women's Rights Movement in Iran* (New York, 1981); D. Davin, *Womanwork: Women and the Party in Revolutionary China* (Oxford, 1976); J. Scott, *et al.* (eds), *Households and the World Economy* (London, 1984); G. Olmvedt, *We Will Smash This Prison*, (London, 1980).

33   On China, see Davin, *Womanwork*; N. Diamond, 'Collectivisation, kinship, and the status of women in rural China', *Bulletin of Concerned Asian Scholars* (1975); J. Stacey, *Patriarchy and Socialist Revolution in China*, (Berkeley, 1983). On South Africa see J. Cocks, *Maids and madams* (Johannesburg, 1980). On Iran see F. Azari, (ed.), *Women in Iran, the Conflict with Fundamentalist Islam* (London, 1983); A. Tabori (ed.), *In the Shadow of Islam* (London, 1982); G. Neshat (ed.), *Women and Revolution in Iran* (Boulder, (1983); H. Afshar, 'Women, State and Ideology in Iran', *Third World Quarterly* (1985); D. Gaitskell and E. Unkerhalker, 'Mothers of the nation', in F. Anthias and N. Yuval Davis (eds), *Woman, Nation, State* (London, 1989).

34   See D. Kandiyoti, 'Emancipated but "unliberated"', *Feminist Studies* (1987).

35   R. Rattray, *Ashanti Law and Constitution*, (London, 1929), p. 23.

36   For the Turkish context see D. Kandiyoti, in Anttias and Yuval-Davis (eds) *op. cit.* and also in *Feminist Studies*, 1987 and K. Brown *et al.* (eds) *The state, urban crisis and social movements in the Middle East* (Paris, 1989); for the South African context see C. van Onselen, *Studies in the economic and social history of the Witwatersrand*, (London, 1982) Vol. I, Chap. 2 and Vol. II, Chaps. 1 and 2 and J. Cock, '*Maids and Madams*', (London, 1980), as well as B. Bozzoli, 'Women in South Africa', *Journal of Southern African Studies*, Vol. 10, no. 1; for Indian material see B. Nanda (ed.) *Indian Women from Purdah to Modernity* (Delhi, 1976), M. Allen and S. Mukherjee (eds) *Women in India and Nepal* (Canberra, 1982), M. Mies, *Indian women and patriarchy* (Delhi, 1980).

37   See M. Schippe *Unspoken Words* (London, 1987).

38   See L. Abu-Lughod, *Veiled Sentiments; Honour and Poetry in Bedouin Society* (Berkeley, CA, 1986); E. Friedl, *Women of Deh-Koh* (London, 1989); C. Okali, *Cocoa and Kinship in Ghana* (London, 1983); J. Bukh, *The Village Woman in Ghana* (Uppsala, 1979).

39   See for example P. Jeffery, *Frogs in a Well*, (London, 1979), Chaps. 4, 5; Friedl, *op. cit,;* M. Llewelyn-Davies, 'Two contexts of solidarity among pastoral Masai women' in P. Caplan, and J. Bujra (eds) *Women united, women divided*, (London, 1978); L. Abu-Lughod, *op. cit.*

40   Thus the establishment of Aztec imperial structures in the valley of Mexico, or of nomadisation, Seljuq political power and Muslim

practices in Anatolia, or of Muslim city states and trade networks in pre-colonial West Africa had implications for women's position in production, kin systems or communities which are nonetheless real for not being studied.

41 Thus, compare attempts at socio-cultural intervention in existing treatment of girl children or widows in nineteenth-century India with the involvement of the British colonial power in female-dominated sectors of agriculture in Kenya in the 1930s.

42 J. Tucker, *Women in Nineteenth Century Egypt* (Cambridge, 1985).

Part Two

THE RURAL EXPERIENCE

Chapter Seven

GENDER, FOOD PRODUCTION AND PROPERTY RIGHTS: CONSTRAINTS ON WOMEN FARMERS IN SOUTHERN AFRICA

Anne V. Akeroyd

It is too often assumed that women farmers are interested in consumption expenditure, not in capital investment, that their domestic work is non-productive and reduces the time which they can allocate to farming tasks, and that, where production is increasingly left to women, productivity will necessarily decline or at best stagnate. Women are blamed *qua* women: the ideological, economic and legal constraints on their autonomy and the real economic nature of their labour time and activities are often not fully appreciated. This chapter discusses the reasons for the under-evaluation of women's productive labour, and examines constraints on women farmers arising out of their subordinate position in the domestic and public domains in southern Africa.

Throughout southern Africa women are faced with discrimination and disadvantage; and the difficulties are exacerbated for single women and female heads of households. Assumptions about women's roles and the nature of gender relations, in many cases constructs of the colonial period, may be exacerbated by post-colonial policies. Women are primarily responsible for food production but may receive little in the way of training or extension services. They may benefit but little from their labours though, paradoxically, they may be better off – at least in nutritional terms – in the subsistence sector than in the commercial or semi-commercial farming sector. The unfavourable lot of women and children in male-headed households on agricultural development and rural settlement schemes shows that those may offer no panacea. Poverty is increasing throughout the region, as a consequence of climatic disasters, civil strife and South Africa's destabilisation measures, economic recession, the debt crisis and international monetary policies; and the feminisation of poverty is advancing apace, reflecting in part the growing proportion of households which are female-headed.

The chapter is written from the perspective of an outsider, and is based on publications by national and expatriate researchers in the region, not on new fieldwork. Its intention is to illustrate selected aspects of rural women's lives, to highlight particularities as well as features shared with women in other parts of Africa and the Third World[1].

THE LOT OF RURAL WOMEN: FOUR CASE STUDIES

What is expected of, and by, rural women in southern Africa? What does 'development' offer them? What are the opportunities and constraints affecting the daily and long-term survival of themselves and their dependants? Is their situation inevitably that of a second-class and subordinated category of citizens? Before discussing some of these issues I start with some contrasting accounts of women's lot in farming communities.

CASE STUDY 1: SUBSISTENCE FARMERS IN MUKUNASHI, NORTH WEST ZAMBIA, 1979–81[2]

During her fieldwork in a Kaonde community Kate Crehan found a list of family duties in a girl's schoolbook: the father's duty was to work hard and pay for everything the family needed including house, land, and food; the mother's duties were purely domestic and caring tasks, such as buying and cooking food.

The reality of life was markedly different. The Kaonde lived in hamlets consisting of from one to twenty-two households in the sparsely populated North Western Province, practising *chitimene*-based grain cultivation. Women were subordinate to men, and men dominated village politics, though matrilineal descent governed social relations. Nearly one-third of the households in the study were female-headed, and eight men were polygamists. Women and men were interdependent: a clearly defined gender division of labour established reciprocal obligations between spouses; and failure to fulfil these was grounds for divorce. Women with their children formed the basic unit of production and producers of household food, working on fields: only maize fields worked by men were called 'farms'. Husbands were expected to make fields for wives (and sometimes for female kin), to provide tools, a house and clothing, and might choose to help with planting and weeding. Women harvested grain and had exclusive rights over fields and granaries: a wife had to provide food for her husband and entertain his friends. Children were expected to help their mothers, though boys aged nine or ten became increasingly reluctant to perform 'women's work'. Men therefore knew how to perform 'women's tasks' but were not economically self-sufficient, since only an eccentric man would live and farm alone. A woman was only recognised as a household head if there were no adult male present; and although female-headed households did provide for themselves, normally such women lived in the village of their male matrikin on whom they relied for the fulfilment of 'male tasks'. There was one very small, poor settlement of four female-headed households which, simply by existing independently, contravened the norms of village life and the pattern of basic authority relations between the sexes which gave men access to women's production and women access to male labour and skills.

Women provided food for the men: men did not provide women with money to buy food. Production for the market was small-scale and money was a 'problem'. Proceeds from the small crop sales were subject to the normal claims of wives and kin for help but, being relatively new, grain sales were less trammelled by customary obligations and the proceeds could be retained more easily for the producer's own use or deposited in the post office. Official measures encouraging production for the market were aimed at men: as elsewhere, 'progressive farmers' were assumed to be men and extension workers were men. Women were not 'farmers'; their fields were not 'farms'; and they did not practise cash-cropping. Their only source of cash earnings was derived from brewing, though divorced and widowed women sometimes worked as casual labourers for more prosperous villagers.

So, *pace* the ideological representation which reflected western concepts about nuclear families and male breadwinners, the daily reality for Kaonde women was that they were dual providers of domestic services and economic provisioning for themselves, their children and their husbands. That women sustained a very heavy workload *qua* women was explicitly recognised by them, as their common reproach to their daughters showed: ' "What are you doing just sitting there, do you think you are a man?" '3

But was the Kaonde situation just the result of isolation and relative insulation from the money economy? How different is the situation of women in families which are fully engaged in commercial agriculture?

CASE STUDY 2: MEDIUM-SCALE COMMERCIAL
FARMERS IN MSENGEZI 'PURCHASE AREA',
ZIMBABWE, 1973–4[4]

The medium-scale commercial farmers studied by Angela Cheater
owned freehold farms and practised fairly intensive mixed farming.
Most of the Msengezi families were monogamous, and less than 18
per cent were polygamous, whereas polygyny rates went up to 43 per
cent in other freehold areas.

Women had a very heavy workload, though family labour was supplemented by casual hired labour and forms of labour co-operation.
A woman worked on different types of fields: fields owned by the
husband/father; 'farm fields', the produce from which was distributed
among those who worked on them; fields allocated directly to a wife
for cash crops (on some polygamists' farms); and household gardens
(on 8 per cent of farms). Though women from landowning families
would not normally hire themselves out as individuals, women's collective work groups based on membership of a church or women's
club might hire themselves out to farmers unrelated to their members
to earn extra cash or 'pocket money'. The labour of adult and young
children was expropriated as well, and the hours children worked on
agricultural tasks approximated to those of adult women. Polygynists
recognised the value of daughters' labour and they demanded high,
even extortionate, bridewealth as compensation for the loss of labour.
Profits were mostly appropriated by husbands and fathers. Cheater
comments that the rights wives and dependent children had in crops
represented a derisory return for their labour input and in no cases
were they given control over the means of production.

Some women were directly involved in farm management: 11.5 per
cent of the farms were run by women who owned, leased or managed them; and some farmers (both monogamists and polygamists)
treated their wives as co-decision-makers and field supervisors. Male
farmers and women farmers/managers alike utilised the various types
of labour; and the men drew on the organisational skills of wives,
especially in polygamous households – senior wives were involved in
the exploitation of junior wives, often being in charge of organising
their domestic and agricultural labour. There was, however, a marked
difference in power and authority between those women who were
wives of absentee landowners who returned only at weekends, and
those who were widows, the mothers of men who had inherited farms.
The former could not take the lead in decision-making; whereas the
latter usually took full responsibility for all decisions, marketed the
crops in their own names (usually through the co-operative), and the
heir was not usually involved in the farm work. Even farm managers
who were sisters of the owners had more power than wives.

This study shows that in certain forms of commercial agriculture polygyny may be a very important strategy of labour recruitment; that through the co-optation of certain women into the 'male' category of controllers of the means of production, women may be exploited by their peers on behalf of men; and that in some circumstances the relations of production characteristic of a peasant system may be the mainstay of a basically capitalist mode of agricultural production, entailing the appropriation of surplus through control of the labour of the young and of women and the masking and mystification of this by 'custom'. Cheater did not think that the exploited would either recognise the full significance of the system and practices in which they were enmeshed or be able to alter their situation. However, some women did tell her that husbands were lazy and irresponsible and it was only the women who kept those men's farming enterprises from collapse. So in Msengezi, too, women were aware of their indispensability, of their workloads, of their vital contribution to the family exchequer, but were caught in the coils of 'custom' and ill-equipped to alter the status quo.

If Msengezi women were not in a position to alter the basic structures of gender and generational relations, even less so may be the female dependants of male farm tenants on estates owned by commercial companies.

CASE STUDY 3: SETTLERS OR TENANTS? RESIDENTS ON THE TABEX TOBACCO COMPANY SCHEME, MOUNT DARWIN, ZIMBABWE[5]

In 1981 the Tabex Company planned to settle a 6,000-acre farm with peasants from the surrounding communal areas who would grow burley tobacco. In principle, the unit of selection was the nuclear family, since the tillage unit was planned for the joint labour of husband and wife. By mid-1983, 275 families (out of a planned 400) had joined: twenty to fifty families lived in a 'village', each in a rented hut with a (free) drying barn alongside, and each was allocated two 0.6 ha fields for tobacco and maize. A 'growth centre' contained a supermarket, butchery, mill, meeting place and a primary school staffed by government teachers, which had 600 pupils; but there was no clinic and medical facilities were 6 miles away from the farm.

Peasants were subordinated to the production process of the company and took all the risks. The management could dictate to the growers and evict inefficient and unproductive ones; it provided inputs (which had to be paid for from crop sales) and some technical assistance (though most work was done with basic tools such as hoes), and controlled the growing and marketing of the crop. Only nuclear family labour was available; the patterns of selection and settlement precluded the use of hired labour or extended family labour. Some peasants and their families, especially elder children, worked in the processing factory as well as on their fields.

Residence, however, was not intended to be permanent; peasants were supposed to leave after five years to run their own farms independently elsewhere and let other families move in. This might imply that growers had opportunities for accumulation of capital, but the need to purchase inputs such as fertiliser and inbuilt constraints on expansion presented obstacles. Mohammed Sato concluded that the growers could not be described as settlers: in all respects they were dependent on a private company and in effect its tenants – even though the scheme was called a 'co-operative' and treated as such by government ministries.

The Tabex farmers, like the Msengezi ones, come from societies with a patrilineal mode of descent and inheritance which privileges agnatic bonds. Does matriliny necessarily entail female power and autonomy, even dominance? The Kaonde case suggests that it does not, since there the land was controlled by men, and women were subordinate. But might the situation differ if women were the effective holders of the means of production and lived with their matrikin?

CASE STUDY 4: WOMEN FARMERS IN ZOMBA DISTRICT, MALAWI, 1981[6]

Megan Vaughan and David Hirschmann examined the situation of women farmers in Zomba District which offered greater access to urban wages and markets than did other parts of Malawi. It was also characterised by a considerably higher growth rate for females than males, and a percentage of divorced or separated women nearly twice the national average. The 1977 Census found that 34 per cent of District households were female-headed, and in 12.6 per cent of households with women working full-time on the land the husbands were in full-time employment; the 1980–1 National Sample Survey for Agriculture found 39.6 per cent of households were female-headed. The study focused on seventy women from fifty-four villages, of whom 31.4 per cent lived in female-headed households and 12 per cent had absentee husbands.

Most married and almost all widowed and divorced women lived either in their natal villages or in a village containing maternal relatives. Most had obtained land from the village headman (usually land previously worked by a mother, grandmother or maternal relative) or from a mother or grandmother; and 80 per cent said their tenure would be secure even on divorce or separation. Twelve women had no land or only a token plot, five had more than sufficient, and 57 per cent said they had insufficient to grow enough food, even had they been able to afford labour and fertiliser.

Food sufficiency depended greatly on the presence of husbands (or on remittances): the great majority of women could not cover their food needs for the year, but whilst half of those with husbands present could produce enough, only a quarter of those without husbands or whose husbands were absentees could do so. Both sexes worked on maize fields, but even those women whose husbands were present were often solely responsible for harvesting, storage and selection of seed. In those households, too, hired labour was more common; when husbands were absent, child labour and the help of female relatives was important. The most labour-deficient households were those without husbands and containing young children.

Most women grew maize, 98 per cent favouring the local variety rather than those promoted by extension services which were more demanding and required cash inputs. Cassava was a cash crop for many and was also used for beer. Few women had had any contact with the extension services, which favoured the richer farmers, and most regarded the advice offered as inappropriate and irrelevant. But they did not reject all facilities; 60 per cent used fertilisers because land shortage and declining fertility had affected maize production, and some had experimented with new crops or different methods.

Whilst women had control over disposal of crops, when men were present in households growing a cash crop they had a considerable degree of control over sales and, though decisions tended to be made jointly in such households, men mostly made decisions about spending large sums of money and in 75 per cent of such cases employed and paid for labour. In all households, though, women seemed to have retained control over 'women's gardens', well-watered sites on which vegetables could be grown throughout the year for consumption or sale. Among them, 91 per cent had earned some cash themselves, mostly from selling small quantities of fruits, legumes and vegetables, and some sold beer. Those women without much land and without husbands were least able to adopt this strategy; and in poorer households one or both partners sometimes worked as casual agricultural labourers, though unattached women thereby forfeited time on their own plots. Female relatives, mainly sisters and mothers, operated a support system, providing mutual aid, food-sharing, and co-operating with food-processing; but generally the only farming task which was shared was harvesting. Cash was mainly provided by male relatives and children of both sexes; 47 per cent, mainly those with absentee husbands, had received gifts of money, mostly from brothers, sons and married daughters.

Economic differentiation was produced mainly by two factors: access to land and opportunities for trade or wage labour. But arguably the availability of male assistance was becoming equally important and seemed likely to increase in significance, since the authors pointed out that with growing pressure on land women were likely to become even more dependent on the marital bond and off-farm sources of 'male' income for their livelihood.

So, even in this case, though women directly controlled land and provided their husbands with fields – the key factor keeping men at home appeared to be availability of land for them to farm – they still were faced with decreasing power and loss of autonomy in the domestic domain, as factors beyond their control intensified women's dependence on male earning power.

The case studies have illustrated different facets of women's domestic and economic responsibilities in contrasting social and economic settings, and show their immediate or ultimate subordination to the interests of men and of the wider society. I turn now to consider some of the issues they raise.

THE POSITION OF WOMEN

The problems faced by women farmers, their exploitability and vulnerability, arise out of ideologies, structures and customs in the spheres of kinship and marriage, politics and law, and education and religion. Many practices and ideas in southern Africa, far from being 'traditional' and of long standing, were constructed during the colonial period through the formalisation of 'customary' law;[7] and even in those countries where women have legally attained full adulthood they still lack many rights available to men, and there may be differences between the rights enjoyed by single and married women. Women's confinement to the status of jural minors under the tutelage of husbands, fathers or other kinsmen in the colonial period limited, and may still constrain, their freedom of action and their economic and decision-making powers. Particularly difficult is women's position with regard to property rights: they usually have minimal or non-existent control over marital property, and sometimes even over their own (whether brought into the marriage or purchased from the proceeds of their own labours).[8] Other problems originated in the changes wrought by the colonial economy which altered the gender division of labour and thereby affected marital and household relations.[9] Far from being in the powerful economic position of the market traders of Nigeria and Ghana, the women of southern Africa are trammelled in a straitjacket not of their making, out of which is hard to break, and which is too often justified on the grounds of 'custom'. As a Malawian official stated bluntly:

> Our custom is that women should be subordinate to men. This is how it always has been and it won't change easily. We have always been a male dominated society. Men were hunters, but made most of the important decisions. Then they became migrant workers and brought home money. Ask any woman about decisions. They will talk but in the end they will say: you must ask the man. So this is a cultural thing.
>
> In this country men are always above women. The women who are struggling to get on top of men are fighting against their own consciousness. They know and are brought up to know that men are above them.
>
> Men's superiority here is customary – also it's Christian – it's in the Bible. We expect our wives to respect us and despite the talk of equality, we must lead – we can compromise a bit, but we must lead.[10]

FEMALE-HEADED HOUSEHOLDS

The assumption that women have men to run affairs for them is not always the case in the domestic domain. Southern African women are increasingly fending for themselves in female-headed households in both town and countryside. Africa's population is basically rural, and the region (excluding South Africa) is no exception. There are high incidences of women and of female-headed households in the rural areas, though these vary considerably between and within countries. Rural dwellers comprise some 80–90 per cent of the populations, only Zambia (at *c.* 40 per cent) and Zimbabwe (*c.* 25 per cent) have sizeable urban populations; and over half the rural population is usually female. For example, in Zimbabwe 52 per cent of the rural population in 1982 was female and 78 per cent of all women lived in the rural areas; in Botswana in 1981 54 per cent of the rural population and 63 per cent of rural dwellers in the 25–29-year age cohort were female; in Malawi in 1977 93 per cent of women lived in rural areas.[11]

Estimates for female-headed households in the rural areas generally range between 20 and 50 per cent; for example, in Botswana 20–42 per cent; and in Malawi 28–35 per cent; and in Zambia the 1980 Census showed 33 per cent of rural households were female-headed, but percentages varied widely; for example, ranging from 4 to 52 per cent in Northern Province districts.[12] Contributory factors include the heavy dependence on migrant labour and commuter labour systems in the regional and national economies, high rates of marital instability and divorce in some parts (such as Zambia), and women's increasing preference for remaining unmarried (as in Botswana). The incidence of female-headed households may be correlated with the economic potential of an area;[13] the latter may be linked to the incidence of male labour migration and thus to marital instability, as well as to the location of development projects and their bias towards male-headed conjugal households. The statistics, of course, reflect static entities, whereas a household's status may vary over time: a female head may be a characteristic of a stage in a household's developmental cycle or in a woman's own life cycle.

Though not all female-headed households are inevitably poor, this type falls disproportionately at the lower end of scales and indices of well-being; and single female heads (unmarried, deserted, separated, divorced or widowed women), especially elderly women, are often in the worst financial straits and have least access to resources of all kinds. Numerous studies in the region and elsewhere attest to the economic, institutional and social problems which such women face and their limited or non-existent involvement in development efforts.

Women's households are not only poor in terms of income and material and human assets: frequently they also face deficiencies in jural rights. Single women, even those living 'independently', may find their freedom of action limited by law and custom, and particularly by the restrictions placed on legal minors. The position of women in households which are *de jure* male-headed but *de facto* female-headed varies greatly. Women with absentee husbands may have daily responsibility for household affairs but frequently lack *de jure* power and authority; sometimes they do not even have the right to make the decisions which perforce they take. Women whose husbands are present may also face similar constraints. For example, a married woman may need her husband's approval before she can make decisions about buying items such as equipment, goods or land for investment or consumption, dispose of her own money or property, undertake paid work or make gifts or loans to her own kin. She may be powerless to prevent the husband in the case of divorce, or his heirs after his death, from seizing all the household's property, though the goods might have been bought with agricultural income to which she had contributed her labour; and even gifts to her or items bought with her own money may not be secure. Such practices, often justified by 'custom', hardly conduce women to invest in capital goods which would increase their productivity; they present severe constraints for women farmers with absentee husbands; and they may leave a woman destitute after the dissolution of a marriage by death or divorce.

The position of individual women may differ markedly, for both married and single women, at one extreme resembling the general unfavourable situation propounded for single female-household heads and, at the other, being analogous to that of men in the case of those women who have considerable power and influence, share in decision-making and so forth. The latter are often wives who are not 'relict' but are part of a conjugal household with both spouses present, as Peters[14] points out; but far too little is known about female labour in male-headed households, and

> Until we have more systematic studies of 'women's contribution' in the '*male*-headed households' and in the advantaged households, we shall have partial understanding of both these *and* of 'female-headed' and disadvantaged households.[15]

The disadvantaged and female-headed households are linked through labour recruitment with members of other households, sometimes female-headed ones; but little, too, is known about such linkages. These lacunae should not surprise us, but they are easily overlooked when the focus (whether of research or policy) is on female-headed households.

Neither women's households nor their problems are homogeneous, though their very singling out tends to encourage us to overlook differences. Their household units may not even be strictly comparable: any analysis must include the life-cycle stage of the household head and the developmental stage of the household[16]. There is considerable evidence that factors such as age, dependent children, access to means of production and/or money and/or labour, customary age of marriage, external linkages such as exchange and support networks, personal misfortunes, and other factors which vary over personal and family life trajectories create differential outcomes for the economic well-being of women farmers and of female-headed households in the short term and the long term, with different effects according to their class and rank position.

WOMEN AND PRODUCTIVITY: ASSUMPTIONS AND REALITIES

The preponderance of women in rural areas and in agriculture means that they do much of the drudgery of farm work, yet their work is often inadequately rewarded, their contribution too often disparaged and/or not formally recognised and the constraints they face not always understood. Four assertions recur about the consequences of leaving farming to the women:

1   if male labour is replaced by female labour in the agricultural sector (the 'traditional' sector), there is a reduction in the output per unit of labour;[17]

2   women are less efficient and less cost-effective than male farmers/workers;[18]

3   women are not (or are less) interested in investing in capital goods, and instead spend their money on items for consumption;

149

4   women's domestic duties mean that they do not do as much
     farm work as men, primarily because of a shortage of time.[19]

The tone of such statements often suggests that women are at fault
because they are *women*: women are the problem. Chipande,[20] on
the contrary, whilst similarly noting the lower output and apparent
lack of interest in high-priced crops of Malawian women farmers,
took the trouble to find out *why* the women behaved as they did.
He showed how economically rational their choices were given the
economic and institutional constraints they faced: gender relations
and roles and power structures were the problem for women.

On average, African women do 60 per cent of the agricultural work
and *c.* 44 per cent of services for the family;[21] some sources say that
60–80 per cent of the agricultural labour force is female or, alternatively, that women do 60–80 per cent of food production, processing
and marketing (though many general statements are based on 1975
data). Women's work and their full contribution to the economy,
though, are often not officially recognised and recorded because of
conceptual deficiencies in the statistics and data collection methods.
Bardouille has pointed to the gross under-estimation of Zambian
women's contribution to the household and national economies in
statistics which classify just over one-third of women as economically
active, even though women do most of the subsistence agricultural
production, work in cash-crop production and on commercial farms
and are responsible for domestic provisioning and services.[22] A 1984
official estimate is even worse: that gave an average activity rate for
Zambian women aged 15+ years of 17.4 per cent, with a range from
24.0 to 42.3 per cent (whereas the 1983 Labour Force Survey for
Malawi gave an average activity rate for women aged 10+ years of
51.7 per cent with a range of 52.0–91.6 per cent).[23]

At issue are the measurement and valuation of women's domestic and non-domestic work, highly problematical and increasingly
contentious matters.[24] What factors might help explain such discrepancies, and the disparaging assertions about women farmers? There
is space only to mention a few contributory factors, but it should
be noted that: first, there are problems with the measures used and
comparisons being made; second, erroneous or partial data often lead
to inaccurate or biased conclusions about women's work; and third,
there are various constraints which might genuinely reduce women's
productivity and/or make it difficult for them to make up the labour
shortfall caused by men's exit from the agricultural sector.

1   *Bias in comparisons of productivity, its formulation and meas-*
     urement: Cloud[25] argues for the use of more than one measure
     of productivity when comparing men with women; and suggests
     that *time* should be taken as the denominator since access to
     other inputs varies and women may use time to compensate

for deficiencies in those. Though time is a complex concept, a number of studies have shown that women frequently do the same or as nearly as much farm work as men, despite their domestic load. Over a decade ago Malawian women spent 25–65 per cent more time than men on productive activities per year and the same or more per day, in addition to domestic work[26]; a more recent study found they worked 2–3 times as many hours as men overall and frequently even twice as long in the sphere of production[27].

2 *Bias in calculating women's labour input:* Farming systems research usually weights a woman's productivity at 0.75 or 0.8 of a man's, even though empirical data may refute this.[28] So, like the tortoise, women can never catch up!

3 *Problematical assumptions about 'domestic labour':* The category of 'domestic activities' usually includes tasks such as the provision of water and fuel, food-processing and storage that are too rarely given an economic value or an accounting value whether in national accounts or individual studies. Equally problematical is the fact that men's domestic responsibilities are frequently ignored, which could create bias and entail spurious or inaccurate conclusions from comparisons of male and female workloads. For example, a report on differences between joint and female-headed households in Zambia gives the hours per day spent by women and children on household tasks but not comparable data for men.[29]

4 *Measures of output:* What is being measured productively is usually output marketed in the monetary sector, in the urban and export sectors, rather than in the local economy.

5 *Differential investment in capital goods and/or labour power, access to extension services and other institutional provision which may increase output and/or reduce labour time:* Men's productivity levels may only be the result of their privileged or greater access to these inputs. Women's access may be constrained by their limited control over money or their need to make up shortfalls in other provision, technical design of tools, lack of education and/or suitable extension provision, or cultural constructs about gender-appropriate practices and behaviour. Much domestic drudgery could be relieved by appropriate technology[30] and provision of water supplies, thus freeing women's time and energy for agricultural production or for leisure.

6 *Differentially valued crops:* Women may not grow the crops which are considered important by officials, planners and economists alike. Men may reserve growing of cash crops for themselves. Women may dislike crops promoted by development programmes because they create labour bottlenecks which cannot be overcome because of domestic responsibilities or limited

resources, or cash-crop varieties (especially hybrid maize) may not be favoured for home consumption.[31]

7   *The 'customary' gender division of labour:* This may define tasks which women cannot or are not allowed to do or have not had the opportunity to learn. In the absence of a resident adult male or the wherewithal to purchase assistance (even from kin), vital agricultural tasks may not get done.[32]

8   *Access to child labour:* Women's productivity may depend on the availability of children for agricultural or domestic tasks, but vicissitudes of demography, health, the extension of schooling or men's labour demands on children may reduce or remove this.

9   *Poverty and paid labour:* Poverty or the refusal of husbands (especially absentees) to meet their economic obligations to wives and children may force some married women, as well as the single or elderly, on to the local labour market, often in work for more prosperous farmers. Their own production is thus neglected.

The problem of comparison in this area is acute; and it is compounded by lack of data. Kydd and Christiansen, for example, noted that their argument about the consequences of the feminisation of the labour force depended on an 'educated guess' about the role of male labour before its withdrawal from agriculture.[33] It may well be the case, too, that the individuals and household units whose productivity is being compared are not always comparable; we may be dealing with not simply an apparent gender differential in productive ability but one situationally determined by family or individual developmental stages. The great variety of residential and economic arrangements found in southern African domestic units exacerbates the difficulties for analysts as well as for planners.

Women's apparent reluctance to invest in agricultural equipment and inputs may have several causes other than lack of interest. They may have to spend what cash is available on consumption goods to meet their responsibilities for domestic provision and the needs of their children, such as school fees, especially when husbands have failed to make adequate provision. They may be interested in investment but be unable to use the available equipment; be unable to afford it or to get (or be reluctant to apply for) credit; and/or they may be unable to get their husbands' permission to invest in such items. They may also be reluctant to spend money on capital goods which may be seized by the husband or his heirs in the case of divorce or his death.

Assumptions about women's lower productivity are not necessarily accurate; and neither women's workload nor in all cases their productivity are necessarily reduced by the absence of men. What may be curtailed (by men's absence or women's involvement on cash-cropping schemes) is women's leisure time. When men desert farming, the agricultural labour force is reduced, and the absolute production of cash crops may be expected to fall even if the productivity of the remaining (women) workers does not alter. If custom, technology and/or extension programmes cannot make up for missing *man*power, then something has to give: it is not always women *qua* women who are at fault.

TECHNICAL ASSISTANCE AND SKILLS

The improvement of productivity is linked to improvements in farming methods, which are usually the result of access to education, training, credit and extension facilities.

Agricultural training and extension services

If women farmers are to increase their production, both on their own behalf and to make up for that lost through male defections, they must have access to training and extension services. That such services be provided by women officers may also be essential, since in many areas cultural constraints on male–female interaction may prevent women from benefiting from existing provision.

There are few women extension officers in the region (and throughout Africa), and they are mostly restricted to offering advice about home economics. This is partly a consequence of training opportunities, partly of assumptions about appropriate skills for women. In Malawi, women field officers in the Ministry of Agriculture almost invariably teach home economics (which homecraft workers and community development assistants also provide). In Zambia, some of the few women holders of agricultural certificates become Home Economics Officers: in the Northern Province in 1982–3 only one of the ten District Agricultural Officers and ninety-eight (7.1 per cent) of the agricultural extension staff were women (only half of them married). The situation is likely to have worsened since the local Agricultural Colleges were due to withdraw the certificate course in 1987 because there was no prospect of increasing the establishment of agricultural assistants' posts. There are other examples – for example, from Kenya – of the restricted range of courses and the compulsory component of home economics offered to female trainees in agricultural colleges or by extension services to women farmers. Zimbabwe would seem to be an exception: women were not allowed to attend agricultural colleges until after independence, but by 1985 they formed 25 per cent or more of the intake and apparently take the same courses as men though as yet they form only 5 per cent of extension staff.[34]

Other restrictions on women's full participation in the agricultural sector may lead to male extension workers having little or nothing to impart to women because they deal with matters such as credit, for which women may not be eligible, or cash crops, which it is assumed women will not grow or for which they have not the necessary land, equipment or skills. A quarter of participants on the GTZ Lima programme in north-western Zambia were women, but extension workers tended to favour men and those already established in market production. Receiving credit in Malawi was linked to using extension techniques, which was linked to having sufficient land and resources to practise them; thus in effect most women were excluded.[35]

There are similarly large discrepancies between numbers of male and female producers who have participated in training programmes and in the training offered them. The ratio of women to men receiving agricultural training in Malawi in the early 1980s was probably 1:30, and agricultural departments offered men courses on 'General Agriculture', but 'Home Economics' to women ('farmers' wives'). In contrast, the SIDA Lima development programme in central and southern Zambia provided agricultural training, extension services and loans for farming inputs directly to women, even though such schemes might come up against into culturally based objections. The evaluators suggested that excluding other members of the household from services might be counter-productive in the long run; and they pointed to the problems (and western ethnocentrism) entailed in a programme aimed at making women self-reliant and 'independent' of men, suggesting that this aim should be 'sold' tactfully by emphasising instead the opportunities for improving women's farming abilities.[36]

The provision of credit

One of the major stumbling blocks to the expansion of women's farming activities has been their limited access to credit facilities, compounded by failure to recognise this discrepancy. One Malawian official informed Hirschmann that women were sharing fairly fully in credit, especially in the Lilongwe Land Development Programme, which provided about 50 per cent of all credit in the country. Further investigation revealed that only *c.* 7 per cent of the 52,810 recipients of credit in the LLDP were women – yet they made up over 50 per cent of operating farmers and *c.* 25 per cent of household heads in the area. Similarly, Due found only two women among 123 small-scale farmers with loans from the Zambian Agricultural Finance Company. The manager allowed credit only to divorced or widowed women on the grounds that a married woman would be more likely to sell her crops in another's (the husband's) name to avoid repayment. He admitted, though, that men also engaged in that practice yet were not refused loans.[37]

Like male smallholders, though, women may be particularly reluctant to apply for credit and risk falling into the 'debt-trap', the paradox that faces so many peasant and subsistence farmers who try to expand production or to grow cash crops which have to meet specific standards. This happened to some women on the SIDA Lima scheme in Zambia: intensifying their dependence on the household to meet repayments reduced the attractiveness of the programme, and repayment difficulties encouraged a fairly high drop-out rate[38].

Women may also be directly precluded from obtaining credit because they do not control other resources and therefore may be unable to provide the necessary collateral. The matter is made more complex since the type of marriage contracted affects their rights in property (marital and personal), and in some circumstances married women may be prevented (whether legally or not) from receiving credit. For example, in Zambia a married woman is treated as an independent applicant for loans from the Agricultural Finance Company, but in practice must provide a letter from her husband consenting to the use of his land, so that most applicants tend to be single women. Few women received loans: between 1970 and 1985 only 8.6 per cent of all AFC loans in the Northern Province went to women; the district rates varied from 0.2 to 69 per cent, the highest rate being in a district where 50 per cent of household heads were women. The Village Agricultural Programme, in order to overcome the problems presented by married women, provided credit only to single women who were unlikely to marry or remarry during the period of the loan, which created other problems and accusations of unfairness from married women[39].

Farmers' organisations

Another hindrance to women's full participation in agricultural development may arise from the official view that farmers' organisations are an appropriate vehicle for the provision of services. These may be used for granting credit on a group basis with every member standing as guarantor for the others (thus helping to overcome the problem of defaultors), and for providing farmers' education and extension advice for those who are not already 'progressive farmers'[40].

Farmers' organisations often tend to exclude women and smallholders because they do not grow the necessary cash crops or because other barriers are used to bar them from membership. Bratton found that in the communal areas of Zimbabwe such organisations mainly involved middle peasant households and drew attention to the problems they may pose for women, citing features which recur elsewhere in the region, pointing out that unless women occupy executive positions, such organisations may reinforce existing patterns of gender inequality[41]. (Co-operatives may be a way of overcoming some of these problems, but they are not always a vehicle for women's advancement and autonomy; but this form of association cannot be discussed further here.)

Income-generating projects

The Zambian Lima programme, aimed at increasing women's self-sufficiency, is one way in which some of these handicaps facing women can be overcome. Another, more common one, is through developing specific income-generating projects, often in vegetable or small livestock and poultry production.

By late 1984 there were in Zimbabwe 8,237 such projects, with 163,000 members (70 per cent women), of which 39 per cent were engaged in gardening, stock or poultry-keeping and tree-planting or timber. Batezat *et al.* point out, though, that this meant that women were still seen primarily as producers for the household, not for the market; and this further maintains a gender-based division between domestic food crops ('women's crops') and cash crops ('men's crops'). Paradoxically, the Zimbabwean government's concern with household nutrition is aimed at encouraging women to cultivate the more nutritious foods (which are often 'women's crops', such as groundnuts), yet most agricultural research is directed towards improving 'men's crops' (which may also be food crops but less nutritious ones), as are delivery and marketing procedures.[42]

Such projects, however, may not prove an adequate way of enriching and empowering women. Batezat *et al.* draw attention to specific problems, to the failure of projects elsewhere and to the likelihood that they will become increasingly marginalised from the main areas of production.[43] Such projects, even if conceived with an economic rationale, often become welfare-oriented, a paradox analysed by Buvinic[44]. If they are economically successful, then men may usurp control of women's gardens, a difficulty which Cleveland and Soleri raise.[45]

THE LAND QUESTION

LAND TENURE AND ALLOCATION ISSUES

Arguably, the most crucial issue facing women farmers in southern Africa is the question of access to land; and whether they have this in their own right or only by virtue of a prior relationship with a man. Without direct access to (or, better, control of) land, women's access to opportunities for investment, credit and marketing, may be limited or non-existent.

Throughout much of the region the 'family' and men are regarded as the natural units to which land should be allocated. Where the family unit predominates the direct recipient is the male head; in turn he allocates land to his wife and perhaps adult children (and may also be responsible for widowed and divorced female kin). If a woman is directly allocated land, this is normally *qua* 'substitute man' responsible for children. But the position is complex, both within and between countries. African farmers hold land governed by different forms of tenure – customary, leasehold and freehold – and, whatever the customary form in a community, normally the introduction of statutory forms privileges men and may remove rights enjoyed by women. The position of wives and widows varies according to whether they were married under customary or statutory law, which type of marital property regime applies, and which mode of inheritance (customary or testamentary) is followed. Women's subordinate position in relation to landholding is also partly related to their civil legal status as minors or majors. Two examples will suffice here.

In Zimbabwe women's legal status was altered by the Legal Age of Majority Act 1982, and they have also become eligible for land allocations: yet most women still only have access to land through a man. On individual family (Model A) resettlement schemes plots are normally given to a man as 'head of the household', and married couples do not have joint tenure; but widows, and now also divorced women, can obtain land in their own right.[46] Though women have been urged to apply for land, very few have been successful and some allocatees have withdrawn, perhaps because of societal pressures.[47] The power to allocate land in the communal areas has been vested in local councils, but 'custom' still prevails: men are still allocated land on behalf of their families and thereby control women and farms. Batezat *et al.* (1988) point out that Zimbabwean women want some control over land, their labour and its products, but such demands were not reflected in draft proposals for the Communal Lands Development Plan, and policy-makers did not fully recognise the conflicts and contradictions in their assumptions that farmers are men and that the family is the basic unit of production[48].

Women suffer considerable discrimination in Swaziland and are still legal minors; there too the situation is complicated by the co-existence of different legal systems, marriage rites and marital property regimes and by varying official interpretations.[49] Generally, only men receive cultivable land on Swazi Nation Land (communal land) which they are then deemed to 'own'. Married women are allocated fields by their husbands; and the eldest son of each 'house' inherits

157

these – daughters rarely inherit land. It is, however, increasingly accepted that unmarried, divorced or widowed women with dependent children must be given land. On long-term leasehold schemes developed around irrigation schemes only men with families receive leases; but there a lease is automatically inherited by a widow. One interesting anomaly is the case of land in irrigation schemes on Swazi Nation Land, which is distributed by chiefs but not governed by customary tenure; there, women can be plotholders since the holder is an individual rather than the family.[50]

Direct allocation of land rights to women as individuals is still rare in southern Africa. Women normally acquire their use rights in land by virtue of a prior and dependent relationship with a man – as daughter, wife, mother, sister, sister's or brother's daughter and so on. Their position is precarious: the temporary nature of women's use rights may become only too obvious when a relationship through which they are derived is severed by disagreement, desertion, divorce, or death.

SETTLEMENT SCHEMES AND CASH-CROPPING MAY NOT BE 'GOOD' FOR WOMEN

It is not only with respect to land held under customary law that women fare worse than men. They are usually disadvantaged by allocation procedures in new settlements, in tenant farming schemes, and in the areas set aside for the use of 'improved' or 'advanced' farmers[51]. Whether women fare any better in these schemes is frequently doubtful; and there is mounting evidence that their situation may actually be worsened.

One of the myths of the development process is that settlement and cash-cropping schemes benefit the 'family': in practice they often have deleterious consequences for wives and children. Development and settlement schemes serve various economic and political functions but, whatever the rationale, their main agricultural aims are the upgrading of male farming skills: normally men are the settlers, lessees or tenants, and procedures for land allocation, tenure and usufructory rights reflect this. Even where 'family' provision is made, women are rarely designated beneficiaries: they and children are expected to be dependents and helpers, and it is assumed that the benefits which should accrue to the male settlers or tenants will also benefit their families. Even more rarely is any provision made for women to acquire land rights in the event of separation, divorce or death of the male landholder.

Here I am less concerned about tenure than with some other consequences for women of agrarian reform which are increasingly being found in southern Africa and which throw yet more doubt on the view that development schemes are 'good' for women: demographic skewing, stress, malnutrition and the abrogation of reciprocity.

Demographic structures and labour demands

Women are directly affected by the often marked skewing of the age structure in many settlement and farming schemes. Such schemes are usually based on family units; and they may also have an inherent pro-natalist tendency.[52] Settlement schemes and development programmes usually require farmers to take on heavy debt repayments and additional farming tasks on cash crops. Those willing to get involved, or who meet the selection criteria, are usually younger men with families in the first expansion phase of the developmental cycle since older farmers are rarely thought to be suitable risks or are unwilling to take on such a burden. Consequently the population in such settlements or tenant farming areas will initially consist of two generations, fall within a relatively restricted age range, and may be far from sources of labour supply other than that of the conjugal family. Since families are still growing there is likely to be a high demand for schooling, maternity and child welfare services.

The land allocation may be planned for the joint tillage of husband and wife; or planners may assume that wives will provide the family's food without necessarily providing adequate resources for them. Farmers may find themselves short of child labour for agricultural or domestic work; and extra labour power may also be needed if farming operations are to be expanded. These demands may be met by directing labour of wives and children into cash crops at the expense of subsistence production, domestic labour, education (of younger children) and economic independence (of older children) and, in the long term, by having more children. The practice of polygamy as a method of labour recruitment has been reported on settlement schemes in Zambia as well as in Zimbabwe and seems to be on the increase. It accords with the notion of 'family' units, and may be more profitable for the male farmer since government legislation rarely regulates family labour relations and remuneration. This is yet another way in which women may be exploited and used to provide cash benefits for their husbands but with meagre returns to themselves.

Labour may also be acquired by exploiting the need for money of single women and other poor female household heads even though working for others inevitably has deleterious consequences for the women's own production. In some areas refugees from civil strife provide a reserve labour force; again, women are likely to be involved. Women farm owners or managers, often older women or senior wives in polygamous households, may be equally implicated in such practices. In north-west Zambia, richer women farmers hired labour to help on their subsistence fields (freeing themselves to work on their Lima project fields), mostly from the poorer single women in the village or refugees from Angola. Similar practices have been reported from Malawi and Botswana.[53]

Stress

Rural women in southern Africa are no strangers to stress, as studies of communities affected by male labour migration have demonstrated. Women on settlements, too, face a stressful environment. Upheaval and adjustment to life in a new environment surrounded by strangers may produce a situation analogous to that found in refugee and relocatee populations.[54] Settlement schemes may induce stress because they are rarely planned with women's activities in mind and the settlers are usually men, so that wives accompanying husbands become involuntary settlers; provision is rarely made for women's activities, and their economic opportunities may be severely curtailed[55].

The skewed demographic structure on settlements adds to women's difficulties. Supportive networks are likely to be lacking at the outset and will take time to develop, especially when the settlers have no prior connections with one another. Women may well find themselves isolated and, in the early stages at least, even more subject to their husbands' control, and their customary autonomy in various domains may be curtailed or abrogated. Where, as is not uncommon, welfare and other services are lacking, especially if demand for these is increased by additional child-bearing or overwork on the farm, then again difficulties for women are increased and claims on their time increased.

Malnutrition

Stress and isolation are not the only maleficent effects of development projects. In Zambia and Malawi the nutritional status of women and children has been found to be worse in the families of emergent and commercial farmers than in those of subsistence farmers.

Various causes for this decline in health have been suggested.[56] Cash-crop production increases the labour burden of women and often children but may add no food to their diet, and may even reduce their calorific consumption. Malnutrition is also worse where the cash crops are not food crops (tobacco, coffee, sugar); and less so when food crops (such as groundnuts) are grown since part of the crop may be used for home consumption. The demands of cash-cropping may override those of production for home use and transfers within the local community; women's (and children's) labour may be diverted from household or women's independent fields to men's cash crops at periods of peak demand or even permanently. Mambwe women in north-east Zambia had to spend time brewing beer for sale in order to pay for fertiliser used on their husbands' fields;[57] and on another Zambian scheme husbands further appropriated their wives' labour by insisting they sell part of their 'woman's crops' if the men's implements had been used on the women's fields.[58] Even when food is available, women may have to reduce time spent on food preparation and on weaning foods for children, and this problem may be compounded by the absence or unavailability of older daughters to help with food preparation. Failure by the husband to make adequate provision is a not infrequent problem: women rarely receive more than a little cash to buy food and other necessities, and face further problems when the responsibility of providing for children (for example, school fees) is borne by them (as is not uncommon in the dual household exchequer schemes found in Africa).

This problem is still little studied;[59] but it is clear that when cash-cropping is important to men (let alone to the state), wives (and children) are expected to work much harder and when time is scarce to neglect their own household production and domestic activities.

The abrogation of reciprocity

Lastly, not only women's daily well-being but also their long-term interests may be jeopardised because of their difficulties in engaging in the exchanges expected between kin.[60] Though married women's involvement with their kin varies according to custom and factors such as wealth and propinquity, they may be expected, or find it necessary, to maintain links by making gifts and meeting obligations, thereby ensuring their well being in the present, help in emergencies and insurance against future difficulties.

In order to appreciate fully the effects on women of agrarian reform, settlement and tenancy schemes and the like, we need to know what 'customary' obligations between spouses, between parents and children, between men and their kin and between women and their kin are likely to be recognised and what might have to be abrogated. Women are particularly vulnerable, given their often-dependent position in households in development schemes, and because of their limited control over resources in cash or kind of which they can dispose. Women who have perforce breached the norms of exchange and reciprocity might be in an extremely weak position should they need help from their own kin if their marriages break down, if they are widowed, or if emergencies leave them or their dependants short of necessities.

Although I have highlighted some of the less favourable aspects of land issues and development schemes, their common appearance throughout southern Africa hardly suggests that only a few women are affected by disadvantage, exploitation and discrimination. On the other hand, as Cheater[61] has pointed out, the varying modes of involvement of women and the labour practices in family-based commercial farming may create a far more exploitative situation than that faced by peasant women. The work involved in commercial or semi-commercial agriculture, too, may be much harder and, on schemes under the aegis of transnational companies, much more organised and less under the control of the farmers, and puts wives more firmly under the control of husbands. Yet such schemes are currently being seen as the economic saviours of the region: huge tracts of central Africa, in Zambia and elsewhere, have been handed over to companies and independent peasant farmers dispossessed and turned into tenants. Zambia may benefit, though there are grounds for doubting this. Will Zambian women gain or lose thereby from their involuntary involvement?

CONCLUSION

Too often women *qua* women have been presented as *the* problem by analysts concerned with the problem *of* women or problems posed *by* women for development programmes, agricultural productivity and the like. Those writers concerned with the problems *for* women have focused on institutional constraints and the underlying causes of women's difficulties, and the problems caused for women by *men*. Muntemba, for example, focused on land, labour and the sexual division of labour; the Zambian women she studied more bluntly construed the sources of their problems and exploitation as the state (and its policies) and men (husbands, headmen and male kin)[62].

Whatever their rationale and proffered solutions, most writers are agreed that the role of women producers in African agriculture, with respect to both subsistence food crops and cash crops, is vital to the well-being of their families, communities and nations. Yet, despite studies substantiating the importance of women's farming, and the apparent recognition of this by politicians, planners and researchers, similar problems for women continue to be 'discovered', similar assumptions are made *about* women farmers, similar demands are articulated by women, similar recommendations are made. The reiteration of women's importance has become almost ritualistic: a new book[63] on food security in the region barely mentions women, and not at all in the chapter on small-farmer agricultural strategy, yet ends with fifteen lines on the 'Central Role of Women', concluding that the success of food security programmes in southern Africa will depend on their reaching women!

Women are farmers: farmers are women. The recognition of this, practically and conceptually, is the essential first step[64]. Despite abundant evidence to the contrary, too often farmers are officially assumed to be men and the provision made for women is non-existent, trivial or subsumed under the concept of the 'family'. The issue of productivity is linked to the acquisition of knowledge, and the provision of agricultural training, extension services, and credit and other facilities. Throughout the region there is a gender-based hierarchy in these matters, these are gender-biased perceptions about women's progress, not least because gender-specific records are rarely kept, and a gender-imbalance in agricultural training, personnel and extension services.

Development projects and policies are often premised on the assumption that the nuclear household maintains a single exchequer and that its members have a unitary interest: it may be this which above all puts women in such a weak position *vis-à-vis* their husbands and, potentially, *vis-à-vis* their own kin. The 'neat' household units, normally male-headed, envisaged by development planners soon become transformed by 'untidy' reality, and socio-economic and demographic differentiation develops between and within the social units. Any study or evaluation of such schemes and/or land tenure reforms, and their particular impact on women, therefore, needs to disaggregate the social and economic units within the family and household, so as to specify who benefits and who does not and in what ways.[65]

What women often face in relation to land allocation and tenurial systems, settlement schemes and development policies is the abrogation of their customary rights, the loss of autonomy, the appropriation of their labour and the profits therefrom, and the appropriation of their children's labour. That is hardly 'betterment' let alone empowerment; rather, in many cases, it is depowerment.

NOTES

1   For an overview by Third World women, see G. Sen (with C. Grown), *Development, Crisis and Alternative Visions: Third World Women's Perspectives* (London: Earthscan Publ., 1988).

2   Based on K. Crehan, 'Women and development in North Western Zambia: from producer to housewife', *Review of African Political Economy*, 27/28 (1983): 51–66.

3　Ibid., p. 58.

4　Based on A. Cheater, 'Women and their participation in commercial agricultural production: the case of medium-scale freehold in Zimbabwe', *Development and Change,* 12 (1981): 349–77.

5　Based on M. Sato, 'Capital's initiative and the development of cooperatives in post-independence Zimbabwe', unpublished paper presented at the annual conference on Research in Progress, Centre for Southern African Studies, University of York, (1988). I am grateful to Mr Sato for letting me use his material, which forms part of his Ph.D. research, University of Leeds.

6　Based on D. Hirschmann and M. Vaughan, 'Food production and income generation in a matrilineal society: rural women in Zomba, Malawi', *Journal of Southern African Studies,* 10(1) (1983): 86–99.

7　See M. Chanock, *Law, Custom and Social Order: the Colonial Experience in Malawi and Zambia,* African Studies series 45 (Cambridge, Cambridge University Press, 1985); and A. Cheater, 'The role and position of women in pre-colonial Zimbabwe', *Zambezia,* XIII (1986), 65–79.

8　See, e.g., A. Armstrong (ed.), assisted by W. Ncube, *Women and the Law in Southern Africa* (Harare, Zimbabwe Publishing House, 1987); J. Kazembe, 'The women issue', pp. 377–404 in I. Mandaza (ed.), *Zimbabwe: the Political Economy of Transition 1980–1986* (Dakar, CODESRIA, 1986); A. Armstrong and R. T. Nhlapo, *Law and the Other Sex: the Legal Position of Women in Swaziland* (Kwaluseni, University of Swaziland, 1985); J. May, *Changing People, Changing Laws,* Mambo Occasional Paper, Socio-Economic Series no. 22 (Gweru, Mambo Press, 1987).

9　For a general account, see C. Robertson, 'Developing economic awareness: changing perspectives in studies of African women, 1976–1985', *Feminist Studies,* 13(1) (1987): 97–135; and for some Zambian examples, S. Muntemba, 'Women as food producers and suppliers in the twentieth century', *Development Dialogue,* 1–2 (1982): 29–50.

10　D. Hirschmann, 'Bureaucracy and rural women: illustrations from Malawi', *Rural Africana,* 21 (Winter) (1985): 54.

11　Figures calculated from United Nations, Department of International and Economic Affairs, *Demographic Yearbook 1985,* 37th issue (New York, United Nations, 1987), Table 7.

12　On Zambia, see G. G. Geisler, B. M. Keller and P. M. Chuzu, *The Needs of Rural Women in Northern Province: Analysis and Recommendations. A Report Prepared for NCDP and NORAD* (Lusaka, Government Printer, 1985), p. 7; and R. Bardouille, 'Women's opportunities in economic work in Zambia', *Zimbabwe Journal of Economics,* 2(1) (1988): 26–46. For Botswanan sources, see P. Peters, 'Gender, developmental cycles and historical process: a critique of recent research on women in Botswana', *Journal of Southern African Studies,* 10(1) (1983): 100–22. On Malawi, see G. H. R. Chipande, 'Innovation adoption among female-headed households: the case of Malawi', *Development and Change,* 18 (1987): 315–17.

13　In Malawi the incidence varies inversely with the economic potential (Chipande, 'Innovation', p. 316).

14   Peters, 'Gender', p. 118.

15   P. Peters, 'Women in Botswana', *Journal of Southern African Studies,* 11(1) (1984), 152 (her emphasis).

16   H. Moore and M. Vaughan, 'Cutting down trees: women, nutrition and agricultural change in the Northern Province of Zambia, 1920–1986', *African Affairs,* 86(345) (1987): 539. See also W. Izzard, 'Migrants and mothers: case-studies from Botswana', *Journal of Southern African Studies,* 11(2) (1985): 258–80; Peters, 'Gender', and 'Women'; and Geisler *et al., Needs of Rural Women.* Whether the 'household' is an appropriate unit for analytical purposes has been hotly debated with respect to the great variety of residential and economic arrangements found in this region; see J. I. Guyer and P. E. Peters' Introduction to special issue on 'Conceptualizing the household', *Development and Change,* 18(1) (1987): 197–214.

17   See J. Kydd and R. Christiansen, 'Structural change in Malawi since Independence: consequences of a development strategy based on large-scale agriculture', *World Development,* 10(5) (1982): 366, regarding Malawi, though note they say that this is an hypothesis for empirical investigation.

18   Carol Kerven (cited in Peters, 'Gender', p. 109) drew this conclusion about female-headed households in Botswana.

19   Kydd and Christiansen, 'Structural change', p. 366.

20   Chipande, 'Innovation'.

21   M–A. Savane, 'Women and rural development in Africa', in International Labour Office, *Women in Rural Development: Critical Issues* (Geneva, ILO, 1981), p. 27.

22   Bardouille, 'Women's opportunities' pp. 29–30.

23   International Labour Office, *Yearbook of Labour Statistics 1987,* 47th edn (Geneva: ILO, 1987), Table 1, p. 18.

24   See, e.g., L. Beneria, 'Conceptualizing the labor force: the underestimation of women's economic activities', in N. Nelson (ed.), *African Women in the Development Process* (London, Frank Cass, 1981) pp. 10–28; and R. B. Dixon, 'Women in agriculture: counting the labor force in developing countries', *Population and Development Review,* 8(3) (1982), 539–66. The UN System of National Accounts includes some types of activity concerned with primary production for *own* consumption, but excludes much other domestic processing and service work done by women; see the details in M. T. Dupré, R. Hussmans and F. Mehran, 'The concept and boundary of economic activity for the measurement of the economically active population', *Bulletin of Labour Statistics 1987–3,* pp. ix–xviii. Women and other family members are usually categorised as 'unpaid family labour'; see E. Hoffman, 'Issues concerning a possible revision of the International Classification of Status in Employment (ICSE)', *Bulletin of Labour Statistics 1987–4,* pp. xii–xiii, on finding a more appropriate classification.

25   K. Cloud, 'Women's productivity in agricultural households: How can we think about it? What do we know?' pp. 11–35 in J. Monson and M. Kalb (eds), *Women as food producers in developing countries* (Berkeley, CA, UCLA African Studies Centre/African Studies Association/OEF International, 1985), p. 12.

26   B. A. Clark, 'The work done by rural women in Malawi', *Eastern African Journal of Rural Development,* 8(1/2) (1975): 80–91.

27   L. E. Engleberg, J. H. Sabry and S. A. Beckerson, 'Production activities, food supply and nutritional status in Malawi', *Journal of Modern African Studies,* 25(1) (1987): 139–47.

28   Cloud, 'Women's productivity', p. 15. Children's labour is similarly weighted, though studies in the region and elsewhere refute this undervaluation; and the threshold age for becoming economically active varies considerably between countries in official statistics and between studies.

29   J. M. Due and M. White, 'Contrasts between joint and female-headed farm households in Zambia', *Eastern African Economic Review,* 2(1) (1986): 97, Table 3.

30   See J. D. C. Osuala, 'Extending appropriate technology to rural African women', *Women's Studies International Forum,* 10(5) (1987): 481–7; and Geisler *et al. Needs of Rural Women,* for some Zambian examples.

31   See Chipande, 'Innovation', on such objections and constraints.

32   See Y. Sugiyama, 'Maintaining a life of subsistence in the Bemba village', *Africa Study Monographs,* Supplementary issue 6, (1987): 24–5, for an account of Bemba women in north-east Zambia paying their sons and other kin and neighbours to do essential tasks.

33   Kydd and Christiansen, 'Structural change', p. 374, n. 23.

34   On Malawi, see D. Hirschmann and M. Vaughan, *Women Farmers of Malawi: Food Production in the Zomba District of Malawi* (Berkeley, CA, University of California, Institute of International Studies, 1984), pp. 131–2. On Zambia, see Geisler *et al. Needs of Rural Women* pp. 23—7. On Zimbabwe, see E. Batezat, M. Mwalo and K. Truscott, 'Women and independence: the heritage and the struggle', in C. Stoneman, (ed.), *Zimbabwe's Prospects* (London, Macmillan, 1988); and C. Stoneman, personal communication, 1987 (re. content of courses). On Kenya, see R. Feldman, 'Women's groups and women's subordination: an analysis of policies towards rural women in Kenya', *Review of African Political Economy, 27/28,* (1983): 67–85 (published 1984).

35   On Zambia, see K. Crehan and A. von Oppen, 'Understandings of "development": an arena of struggle;' *Sociologia Ruralis,* XXVIII (2/3) (1988): 113–45. On Malawi, see Hirschmann and Vaughan, 'Women farmers', pp. 131–4, and Chipande, 'Innovation'.

36   On Malawi, see Hirschmann, 'Bureaucracy and rural women', p. 58; on Zambia, A. Chilivumbo and J. Kanyangwa, *Women's Participation in Rural Development Programmes: the Case of the SIDA Lima Programme* (Lusaka, University of Zambia, Rural Development Studies Unit, (Occasional Paper no. 22, 1985).

37   On Malawi, see Hirschmann, 'Bureaucracy and rural women', pp. 58–9; on Zambia, see J. M. Due and R. Summary, 'Constraints to women and development in Africa', *Journal of Modern African Studies,* 20(1) (1982): 161.

38   Chilivumbo and Kanyangwa, *Women's Participation in Rural Development;* see also M. Bratton, 'Farmer organizations and food production in Zimbabwe', *World Development,* 14(3) (1986): 367–84 on this problem in Zimbabwe.

39 Geisler *et al.*, *Needs of Rural Women*, p. 46. For other examples of marriage types and their effects on women's rights and ability to obtain credit, see Armstrong (assisted by W. Ncube), *Women and the Law;* and A. Armstrong and M. Russell, *A Situation Analysis of Women in Swaziland* (Kwaluseni, University of Swaziland, Social Science Research Unit, 1985).

40 For examples of credit schemes in Zimbabwe, see Bratton, 'Farmer organizations', p. 370; and in Malawi, Chipande, 'Innovation'.

41 Bratton, 'Farmer organizations', p. 374. See also Geisler *et al.*, *Needs of Rural Women*.

42 Batezat *et al.*, 'Women and independence'. That subsistence foods are not only 'crops' but also 'cash' crops, if only in the local economy, needs official recognition, as does the economic importance of 'kitchen gardens', respectively argue P. D. Little and M. M. Horowitz, 'Subsistence crops *are* cash crops: some comments with illustrations from Eastern Africa', *Human Organization,* 46(3) (1987): 254–8, and D. A. Cleveland and D. Soleri, 'Household gardens as a development strategy', *Human Organization,* 46(3) (1987): 259–70.

43 Batezat *et al.*, 'Women and independence'. For an extremely ill-conceived Zimbabwean women's project, see B. M. C. Sibanda, 'Impacts of agricultural microprojects on rural development: lessons from two projects in the Zambezi Valley', *Land Use Policy,* 3(4) (1986): 311–29.

44 M. Buvinic, 'Projects for women in the Third World: explaining their misbehaviour', *World Development,* 14(5) (1986): 653–64.

45 Cleveland and Soleri, 'Household gardens', p. 259.

46 S. Jacobs, 'Women and land resettlement in Zimbabwe', *Review of African Political Economy,* 27/28 (1983): 41 (published 1984); and Batezat *et al.*, 'Women and independence'.

47 L. Cliffe, personal communication, 1987.

48 Batezat *et al.*, 'Women and independence'.

49 See T. Nhlapo, 'Law versus culture: ownership of freehold land in Swaziland', in A. Armstrong (ed.) (assisted by W. Ncube), *Women and the Law in Southern Africa* (Harare, Zimbabwe Publishing House, 1987), pp. 35–55.

50 Armstrong and Russell, *A Situation Analysis*, pp. 35–6.

51 Various terms have been used for these farmers, such as master farmer (Rhodesia), small-scale commercial farmer (Zimbabwe) and emergent farmer (Zambia).

52 On pro-natalist tendencies, see I. Palmer, *The Impact of Agrarian Reform on Women* (West Hartford, CT, Kumarian Press, 1985), pp. 44–5.

53 On Zambia, see Crehan and von Oppen, 'Understandings of "Development" ' and Crehan, personal communication, 1988. On Malawi, see Chipande, 'Innovation', and Hirschmann and Vaughan, 'Food production'. On Botswana, see Peters, 'Gender'.

54 T. Scudder and E. Colson, 'From welfare to development: a conceptual framework in the analysis of dislocated people', in A. Hansen and A. Oliver-Smith (eds), *Involuntary Migration and Resettlement: the Problem and Responses of Dislocated People*, (Boulder CO, Westview Press, 1982), pp. 267–87.

55 Ibid. pp. 284–5.

56 See, e.g., Engleberg, Sabry and Beckerson, 'Production activities', Moore and Vaughan 'Cutting down trees'; and Zambia Association for Research and Development, *An Annotated Bibliography of Research on Zambian Women* (Lusaka, ZARD, 1985) on which this compilation is mainly based.

57 J. Pottier, personal communication.

58 Muntemba, 'Women as food producers'.

59 For a general survey, see B. M. Purvis, 'Family nutrition and women's activities in rural Africa', *Food and Nutrition,* 11(2) (1985): 28–36.

60 Exchange networks and the transfers involved, as Peters 'Gender', p. 109, points out, are difficult to investigate, let alone fully to elucidate. More studies are needed of transfers at the intra- and inter-'household' level. Economists have begun considering such flows but the transfers considered are limited. The categories used for donors and recipients tend, too, to be translated as western terms like 'uncle', which are often too generalised and ethnocentric adequately and meaningfully to reflect African concepts.

61 Cheater, 'Women', p. 364.

62 Muntemba, 'Women as food producers'.

63 C. Bryant (ed.), *Poverty, Policy, and Food Security in Southern Africa* (Boulder, CO, Lynne Riener Publishers; London, Mansell Publishing Ltd, 1988).

64 On this point see also J. K. Henn, 'Feeding the cities and feeding the peasants: what role for Africa's women farmers?' *World Development,* 11(12) (1983): 1043–55.

65 For discussions about household concepts, see Guyer and Peters 'Conceptualizing the household'; and for how conflicting interests over time altered a situation in ways unenvisaged by planners, see Crehan and von Oppen, 'Understandings of "development" '.

BIBLIOGRAPHY

Armstrong, A. (ed.) (assisted by W. Ncube) (1987) *Women and Law in Southern Africa.* Harare: Zimbabwe Publishing House.

Armstrong, A. and Nhlapo, R. T. (1985) *Law and the Other Sex: the Legal Position of Women in Swaziland,* Kwaluseni: University of Swaziland.

Armstrong, A. and Russell, M. (1985) *A Situation Analysis of Women in Swaziland,* Kwaluseni: University of Swaziland, Social Science Research Unit.

Bardouille, R. (1988) 'Women's opportunities in economic work in Zambia', *Zimbabwe Journal of Economics,* 2(1): 26–46.

Batezat, E., Mwalo, M. and Truscott, K. (1988) 'Women and independence: the heritage and the struggle', in C. Stoneman (ed.), *Zimbabwe's Prospects.* London: Macmillan.

Beneria, L. (1981) 'Conceptualizing the labor force: the underestimation of women's economic activities', in N. Nelson (ed.) *African women in the development process.* London: Frank Cass, p. 10–28.

Bratton, M. (1986) 'Farmer organizations and food production in Zimbabwe', *World Development,* 14(3): 367–84.

Bryant, C. (ed.) (1988) *Poverty, Policy, and Food Security in Southern Africa,* Boulder, CO: Lynne Reiner Publishers; London: Mansell Publishing Ltd.

Buvinic, M. (1986) 'Projects for women in the Third World: explaining their misbehaviour', *World Development,* 14(5): 653–64.

Chanock, M. (1985) *Law, Custom and Social Order: the Colonial Experience in Malawi and Zambia* (African Studies series 45). Cambridge: Cambridge University Press.

Cheater, A. (1981) 'Women and their participation in commercial agricultural production: the case of medium-scale freehold in Zimbabwe', *Development and Change,* 12: 349–77.

Cheater, A. (1986) 'The role and position of women in pre-colonial and colonial Zimbabwe', *Zambezia,* XIII: 65–79.

Chilivumbo, A. and Kanyangwa, J. (1985) *Women's Participation in Rural Development Programmes: the Case of the SIDA Lima Programme.* Lusaka: University of Zambia, Rural Development Studies Unit (Occasional Paper no. 22).

Chipande, G. H. R. (1987) 'Innovation adoption among female-headed households: the case of Malawi', *Development and Change,* 18: 315–27.

Clark, B. A. (1975) 'The work done by rural women in Malawi', *Eastern African Journal of Rural Development,* 8(1/2): 80–91.

Cleveland, D. A. and Soleri, D. (1987) 'Household gardens as a development strategy', *Human Organization,* 46(3): 259–70.

Cloud, K. (1985) 'Women's productivity in agricultural households: How can we think about it? What do we know?' in J. Monson and M. Kalb (eds) *Women as food producers in developing countries.* Berkeley, CA: UCLA African Studies Centre/African Studies Association/OEF International, pp. 11–35.

Crehan, K. (1983) 'Women and development in North Western Zambia: from producer to housewife', *Review of African Political Economy,* 27/28: 51–66.

Crehan, K. and Oppen, A. von (1988) 'Understandings of "development": an arena of struggle', *Sociologia Ruralis,* XXVIII (2/3): 113–45.

Dixon, R. B. (1982) 'Women in agriculture: counting the labor force in developing countries', *Population and Development Review,* 8(3): 539–66.

Due, J. M. and Summary, R. (1982) 'Constraints to women and development in Africa', *Journal of Modern African Studies,* 20(1): 155–66.

Due, J. M. and White, M. (1986) 'Contrasts between joint and female-headed farm households in Zambia', *Eastern African Economic Review,* 2(1): 94–8.

Dupré, M. T., Hussmanns, R. and Mehran, F. (1987) 'The concept and boundary of economic activity for the measurement of the economically active population', *Bulletin of Labour Statistics 1987–3:* ix–xviii.

Engleberg, L. E., Sabry, J. H. and Beckerson, S. A. (1987) 'Production activities, food supply and nutritional status in Malawi', *Journal of Modern African Studies,* 25(1): 139–47.

Feldman, R. (1983) 'Women's groups and women's subordination: an analysis of policies towards rural women in Kenya', *Review of African Political Economy,* 27/28 67–85 (published 1984).

169

Geisler, G. G., Keller, B. M. and Chuzu, P. M. (1985) *The Needs of Rural Women in Northern Province: Analysis and Recommendations. A Report Prepared for NCDP and NORAD*. Lusaka: Government Printer.

Guyer, J. I. and Peters, P. E. (1987) ('Introduction' to special issue on 'Conceptualizing the Household'), *Development and Change*, 18(1): 197–214.

Henn, J. K. (1983) 'Feeding the cities and feeding the peasants: what role for Africa's women farmers?' *World Development*, 11(12): 1043–55.

Hirschmann, D. (1985) 'Bureaucracy and rural women: illustrations from Malawi', *Rural Africana*, 21 (Winter): 51–63.

Hirschmann, D. and Vaughan, M. (1983) 'Food production and income generation in a matrilineal society: rural women in Zomba, Malawi', *Journal of Southern African Studies*, 10(1): 86–99.

Hirschmann, D. and Vaughan, M. (1984) *Women Farmers of Malawi: Food Production in the Zomba District of Malawi*. Berkeley, CA: University of California, Institute of International Studies.

Hoffman, E. (1987) 'Issues concerning a possible revision of the International Classification of Status in Employment (ICSE)', *Bulletin of Labour Statistics 1987–4:* ix–xv.

International Labour Office (1987) *Yearbook of Labour Statistics 1987*, 47th edn. Geneva: ILO.

Izzard, W. (1985) 'Migrants and mothers: case-studies from Botswana', *Journal of Southern African Studies*, 11(2): 258–80.

Jacobs, S. (1983) 'Women and land resettlement in Zimbabwe', *Review of African Political Economy*, 27/28: 33–50 (published 1984).

Kazembe, J. (1986) 'The women issue', in I. Mandaza (ed.), *Zimbabwe: the Political Economy of Transition 1980–1986* Dakar: CODESRIA, p. 377–404.

Kydd, J. and Christiansen, R. (1982) 'Structural change in Malawi since Independence: consequences of a development strategy based on large-scale agriculture', *World Development*, 10(5): 355–75.

Little, P. D. and Horowitz, M. M. (1987) 'Subsistence crops *are* cash crops: some comments with illustrations from Eastern Africa', *Human Organization*, 46(3): 254–8.

May, J. (1987) *Changing People, Changing Laws* (Mambo Occasional Paper, Socio-Economic Series no. 22). Gweru: Mambo Press.

Moore, H. and Vaughan, M. (1987) 'Cutting down trees: women, nutrition and agricultural change in the Northern Province of Zambia, 1920–1986', *African Affairs*, 86 (345): 523–40.

Muntemba, S. (1982) 'Women as food producers and suppliers in the twentieth century', *Development Dialogue* 1982: 1–2: 29–50.

Nhlapo, T. (1987) 'Law versus culture: ownership of freehold land in Swaziland', in A. Armstrong assisted by W. Ncube, *Women and the Law in Southern Africa*. Harare: Zimbabwe Publishing House, p. 35–55.

Osuala, J. D. C. (1987) 'Extending appropriate technology to rural African women', *Women's Studies International Forum*, 10(5): 481–7.

Palmer, I. (1985) *The Impact of Agrarian Reform on Women*. West Hartford, CT: Kumarian Press.

Peters, P. (1983) 'Gender, developmental cycles and historical process: a critique of recent research on women in Botswana', *Journal of Southern African Studies*, 10(1): 100–22.

— (1984) 'Women in Botswana', *Journal of Southern African Studies,* 11(1): 150–3.

Purvis, B. M. (1985) 'Family nutrition and women's activities in rural Africa', *Food and Nutrition,* 11(2): 28–36.

Robertson, C. (1987) 'Developing economic awareness: changing perspectives in studies of African women, 1976-1985', *Feminist Studies,* 13(1): 97–135.

Sato, M. (1988) 'Capital's initiative and the development of cooperatives in post-independence Zimbabwe', unpublished paper presented at the Annual Conference on Research in Progress, Centre for Southern African Studies, University of York, York.

Savane, M–A. (1981) 'Women and rural development in Africa', in International Labour Office, *Women in Rural Development: Critical Issues.* Geneva: ILO.

Scudder, T. and Colson, E. (1982) 'From welfare to development: a conceptual framework in the analysis of dislocated people', pp. 267–287 in A. Hansen and A. Oliver-Smith (eds) *Involuntary migration and resettlement: the problem and responses of dislocated people.* Boulder, CO: Westview Press.

Sen, G. (with C. Grown) (1988) *Development, Crisis, and Alternative Visions: Third World Women's Perspectives.* London: Earthscan Publ.

Sibanda, B. M. C. (1986) 'Impacts of agricultural microprojects on rural development: lessons from two projects in the Zambezi Valley', *Land Use Policy,* 3(4): 311–29.

Sugiyama, Y. (1987) 'Maintaining a life of subsistence in the Bemba village', *Africa Study Monographs,* Supplementary issue 6: 15–32.

United Nations, Department of International and Economic Affairs (1987) *Demographic Yearbook 1985.* 37th issue. New York: United Nations.

Zambia Association for Research and Development (1985) *An Annotated Bibliography of Research on Zambian Women.* Lusaka: ZARD.

Chapter Eight

AGRICULTURAL MECHANISATION AND LABOUR USE: A DISAGGREGATED APPROACH[1]

Bina Agarwal

The debate on the employment implications of agricultural mechanisation in South Asia is now an old one. Yet, in spite of a proliferation of studies,[2] there are still gaps in our knowledge about the exact effects. One major shortcoming of many previous studies is their aggregative approach.[3] Most have limited themselves to considering the effect (principally of tractors) on total farm employment, failing to take account of the fact that mechanisation is essentially a mixed package. Different operations and crops allow different mechanisation alternatives, which are likely to have varying implications.

A disaggregation by operations becomes particularly important in the case of a multi-purpose technique such as a tractor which, even in the cultivation of a single crop, lends itself to a wide range of agricultural operations, such as soil preparation, sowing/manuring and the powering of irrigation pumps, harvesters and threshers. A farmer may, however, choose not to utilise it for all the functions it is capable of performing, and its actual use could vary from farm to farm. The flexibility increases further when we consider that a farmer could hire a tractor for specific operations. Its employment effects would differ depending on both the nature and the number of operations it performed. Similarly, disaggregation by crops becomes important because different crops lend themselves to different levels of tractor use. Failure to disaggregate the effects of a technique by operations and crops implies that farms are uniform in the use to which they put it, an assumption that cannot be justified *a priori*.

Also, by looking at the aggregate effects alone, it is not possible to identify the operations where mechanisation is likely to have the maximum impact. And in so far as certain operations tend to be performed by certain types of labour, questions relating to which type of labour is likely to be affected can only be answered adequately through disaggregation.[4]

Preoccupation with the aggregate effects, however, is not the only limitation of previous studies. Often inaccuracies in measurement are introduced in one or more of the following ways:

–   taking ownership of a technique as a surrogate for use (where hiring of machines is common, this is likely to bias the results);
–   attributing to a mechanised technique the effects of other techniques or inputs;
–   studying the employment effects without diffentiating between different types of labour, that is, family, permanent and casual labour.

My own study was an attempt to fill some of these gaps in earlier research. In order to highlight the disaggregated employment effects of alternative techniques, I shall be presenting in this chapter a crop-specific analysis[5] for high-yielding variety (HYV) wheat in the Punjab.[6] In this context three broad but related questions will be addressed:

1   What alternative techniques or combinations of techniques are being used for each operation on the farm plots in the sample studied?
2   Do different techniques vary significantly from one another in their use of labour time for a particular operation?
3   What is the composition (in terms of family, permanent and casual labour units) of the labour used for different operations, with alternative techniques and on farms of different sizes?

The reasons for choosing HYV wheat for the crop-specific analysis are spelt out in the next section.

DATA USED

The empirical exercise undertaken here relates to plots belonging to a sample of 240 owner-cultivator farms taken from the principal wheat-growing areas of the Punjab and covering all its districts, for the crop year 1971/72. The data were collected under the 'Comprehensive Scheme for Studying the Cost of Cultivation of Principal Crops' by the Punjab Agricultural University (PAU) for the Directorate of Economics and Statistics (DES), New Delhi. The cost-accounting method was used, that is, information was obtained on the basis of day-to-day observation of selected cultivators by a full-time research worker residing in the villages. This method provides much more precise and accurate information than does the often used 'recall method' which relies on the memory of the respondent, since it is virtually impossible to recall precisely, at any given point in time, the number of hours or even days spent by different types of labour on various agricultural tasks over the year.

In comparison with the Farm Management Studies (FMS) data (also collected by the PAU for the DES, using the cost-accounting method), on which most previous research on mechanisation in the Punjab is based, the Cost of Cultivation data used here have a number of advantages. They have a wider coverage (the FMS data for the Punjab are confined to the Ferozepur district), a larger sample size (the FMS sample contains only 150 farms), and provide more detailed information (the FMS data do not, for instance, include details about the operations for which the machinery is used, and whether it is owned or hired).

The choice of HYV wheat for the crop-specific analysis was determined by two considerations. First, the highest level of mechanisation in the Punjab (and indeed in India) is found in wheat cultivation and the range of observable techniques is therefore greater than with other crops in this region (or even elsewhere);[7] second, this is the main crop grown on the farms in the study area.

RESULTS AND INTERPRETATION

ALTERNATIVE TECHNIQUES USED, BY TYPE OF OPERATION

Tractors, tubewells and threshers were found to be the main mechanical aids being used in the Punjab. The level of mechanisation was observed to vary considerably between farm operations[8] (see Table 8.1 page 176). At one end of the spectrum came harvesting, which was still being carried out by hand on almost all the plots, and interculture (essentially weeding); at the other end was threshing, which was completely mechanised for 72.5 per cent of the plots and at least partially mechanised (with bullocks supplementing the thresher or tractor) for another 22.4 per cent. Like threshing, irrigation was done largely by modern means – tubewells were used on 86.5 per cent of the plots, either on their own or along with canals or wells; 42 per cent of the tubewells were being run by diesel engines and 58 per cent by electric motors. Ploughing and sowing used both traditional and modern techniques, the bias being towards the former. On the majority of plots the two operations were still being done primarily with the help of bullocks. Even when tractors were used, bullocks were often retained as an insurance against the risk of mechanical breakdown or to make up for the inadequacy of hired tractor services.

Hiring of tractors was in fact fairly common: 42.2 per cent of the plots ploughing with a tractor used a hired one, while 27.9 per cent of the tractor-sowing plots did so. If ownership of tractors had been taken as the criterion for differentiating between tractor-using and bullock-using plots, as in some recent studies,[9] then these tractor-ploughing and tractor-sowing plots would have been misclassified as bullock-using. Machine hiring was also common for threshing. Among the plots whose output was threshed mechanically (with either a tractor or a thresher), 63.7 per cent used an owned machine and the rest a hired one.

It is noteworthy that even on farms owning tractors, their use was largely confined to ploughing, with some limited use in sowing. They were rarely employed to power irrigation pumps and their use in threshing, whether on their own or to provide power to threshers, was not common to all tractor farms either.[10]

LABOUR TIME REQUIRED WITH ALTERNATIVE TECHNIQUES, BY TYPE OF OPERATION

The labour time required for a given operation was found to differ considerably between different techniques. Table 8.1 gives the mean use of human, bullock and mechanical energy for each operation and technique in hours per hectare and hours per unit of output, as appropriate.[11] To test the statistical significance of the differences in the mean human labour hours used for each operation with alternative techniques, 't' values were also computed (the results are summarised in a footnote to Table 8.1).

We note from the table that, for both ploughing[12] and sowing, the non-mechanised, exclusively bullock-using plots use substantially more human labour hours per hectare (L/H) on average than the partially mechanised bullock+tractor plots, and these in turn use more L/H than the exclusively tractor-using ones. In ploughing the decrease in L/H from exclusively bullock to exclusively tractor plots is as much as 82.4 L/H (or 81.4 per cent), and in sowing it is 23.6 L/H (or 59 per cent). Pair-wise comparisons of the mean L/H used with the three techniques indicates that the differences are significant at the 1 per cent level in all three comparisons relating to ploughing. The displacement of human labour time in this operation closely complements that of bullock-pair time and largely reflects the reduced demand for a driver's services (one man being used to drive one bullock-pair).

In interculture, L/H used with the manual method is significantly higher (at the 1 per cent level) than when bullocks are used. In irrigation, among the five methods of irrigation being used – namely, well, canal, tubewell+well, tubewell+canal and tubewell alone – the

175

TABLE 8.1 Human, bullock and mechanical energy used in HYV wheat cultivation, by operations and techniques

Operation and technique	No. of plots (N = 790)	% of plots	Hours per hectare[1] (mean values)		
			Human labour[2]	Bullock-pairs	Machines
Ploughing:					
Bullock	463	58.76	101.27	97.10	—
Bullock + tractor	229	29.06	61.28	45.16	7.60
Tractor	96	12.18	18.86	—	12.41
Unknown[3]	2	—	—	—	—
Sowing:					
Bullock	617	79.72	40.06	20.74	—
Bullock + tractor	44	5.68	18.48	4.55	2.33
Tractor	103	13.31	16.41	—	2.54
Other[4]	10	1.29	—	—	—
Unknown[3]	16	—	—	—	—
Interculture:					
Absent	154	19.49	—	—	—
Manual	576	72.91	109.42	—	—
Bullocks	60	7.59	67.82	13.56	—
Irrigation:					
Well	10	1.28	241.79	—	—
Canal	96	12.24	51.93	—	—
Tubewell[5] + well	12	1.53	177.17	—	68.42
Tubewell[5] + canal	105	13.39	93.30	—	49.26
Tubewell[5]	561	71.56	140.53	—	106.94
Unknown[3]	6	—	—	—	—

176

TABLE 8.1 (Cont.) Human, bullock and mechanical energy used in HYV wheat cultivation, by operations and techniques

Operation and technique	No. of plots (N = 790)	% of plots	Hours per hectare[1] (mean values)		
			Human labour[2]	Bullock-pairs	Machines
Harvesting:[1]					
Manual	781	99.24	129.21	—	—
Other[6]	6	0.76	—	—	—
Unknown[3]	3	—	—	—	—
Threshing:[1]					
Bullock	39	5.08	7.61	1.97	—
Bullock + thresher/tractor	172	22.43	4.84	0.46	0.54
Thresher/tractor	550	71.71	3.51	—	0.63
Other[6]	6	0.78	—	—	—
Unknown[3]	23	—	—	—	—

[1]Hours per quintal (100 kg) of wheat in the case of threshing.

[2]Pair-wise comparisons were also made of the mean human labour used with alternative techniques for each operation and the significance of the differences so obtained was tested, using a one-tailed 't' test. It was found that for ploughing, interculture and threshing the differences were significant at the 1 per-cent level. For sowing, too, they were significant at the 1 per-cent level for all comparisons except that relating to 'bullock + tractor' and 'tractor', which was insignificant at the 5 per-cent level. For irrigation, again, the differences were significant at the 1 per-cent level in all cases except those relating to 'well' compared with 'tubewell + well' (significant at the 5 per-cent level) and 'tubewell + well' compared with 'tubewell' (insignificant at the 5 per-cent level).

[3]'Unknown' denotes cases where the technique used was not known. These cases have not been included when computing the percentages.

[4]Under sowing 'other' includes cases where both sowing and manuring are done together with a seed-cum-fertiliser drill.

[5]The tubewell category includes pumpsets.

[6]Under harvesting and threshing, 'other' includes cases where a combine has been used to perform both operations jointly.

177

most *L/H* is used in well irrigation, followed by tubewell+well. Canal irrigation makes the least use of *L/H* and tubewell+canal irrigation the second lowest. Exclusively tubewell-irrigated plots fall between the tubewell+well and tubewell+canal categories. All these sources differ significantly (at the 1 per cent level) in their mean use of *L/H*. The results are in keeping with an expected pattern. With canal irrigation no labour is needed for operating the source and a minimum of labour is needed for preparing the field, which is usually left to be flooded. Well and tubewell irrigation, on the other hand, require more labour for preparation of channels, for operating the source and for closer over-all management. Operating a well requires more labour time than operating a tubewell.

For threshing, the mean human labour hours used per unit of output (*L/O*) – that is, per quintal of wheat threshed – were computed. Broadly, three methods of threshing can be distinguished: the traditional one of bullock threshing, the modern one of using a power-operated thresher or tractor, and the intermediate one where part of the output is threshed by bullocks and part by a thresher or a tractor. We note that when threshing is done exclusively by bullocks, *L/O* is significantly greater (at the 1 per cent level) than when a thresher/tractor as well as bullocks are used, and *L/O* with the latter method is, in turn, significantly higher than when a thresher/tractor alone performs the operation.[13]

It is worth noting here that while the technique of cultivation used for an operation is the most important factor affecting the input of labour per hectare, it is not always the sole factor. In the case of seed-bed preparation, in particular, the crop rotation pattern and soil type also tend to be of significance.[14] More intensive ploughing is required after certain crops and on heavier soils. In my sample different zones served as broad surrogates for differences between plots in cropping patterns and soil conditions. The three zones had the following crop rotations: in the *rabi* season (October–April) HYV was the predominant crop on all the plots and in *kharif* (May–September) the principal crops were paddy and maize in Zone I, some combination of groundnuts/paddy/maize/cotton in Zone II, and mainly cotton in Zone III. Cotton usually leaves the most stubble while in groundnut cultivation some soil digging takes place during harvesting itself. Hence, as one might expect, the labour input per hectare in seed-bed preparation for wheat was the greatest in Zone III and the least in Zone II, with Zone I coming in between. Also, not unexpectedly, the differences were found to be larger on bullock-ploughed plots than on tractor plots, since with tractors difficult field conditions do not necessarily require an increase in human effort, either by itself or associated with a larger number of ploughings.

Another variable which was seen to affect the input of human labour per hectare, albeit only in some operations such as interculture, was farm size, which was found to be inversely related to labour use in this operation. For seed-bed preparation, however, the labour input varied little with farm size.

TYPE OF LABOUR AFFECTED BY MECHANISATION

Given that mechanisation leads to a decrease in the aggregate use of labour time, an important complementary question is: what kind of labour is affected? Here a distinction between *labour time* effects and the effect on *labourers* is useful. A reduction in requirements of family labour time, for instance, may lead to no particular hardship for the workers (and may in fact constitute a benefit in terms of increased leisure), since they would usually be able to continue subsisting on the farm if no alternative full-time employment were available. Similarly, permanent labourers, even if under-utilised during some parts of the year, may be retained to reduce the risk of a labour shortage during the peak periods. On the other hand, a reduction in demand for casual labour time would usually mean a displacement of labourers, apart from having an immediate effect on the subsistence earnings of those workers who are hired on an hourly or daily basis. We thus need to break down the total labour time effect by the categories of workers affected.

My results indicate that the type of labour likely to be affected by mechanisation will depend essentially on which agricultural operation is mechanised and on the size of the farm concerned.[15] From Table 8.2 it may be noted that, for every operation, the percentage use of family labour time decreases steadily, almost without exception, as farm size increases. This decrease is accompanied by an increase in the use of either permanent or casual labour time, or both. Ploughing, sowing and irrigation are done largely by either family or permanent labour, with a predominant use of the former on the smaller farms and of the latter on the larger ones. There is relatively little use of casual labour for these operations even on the larger farms. In interculture, harvesting and threshing, on the other hand, there is relatively greater use of casual labour, and the decrease in family labour use with an increase in farm size is accompanied by an increase in the use of both permanent and casual labour. In harvesting, in particular, casual labour is the predominant type in all size groups except the smallest, where family labour continues to be more important.

The observed pattern suggests a task specificity in the use of different types of labour. It also suggests that in operations such as ploughing and in the sowing and irrigation of wheat, given the observed close inverse relationship between family and permanent labour, the latter tends to be a much closer substitute for the former

179

TABLE 8.2 Composition of labour time used in HYV wheat cultivation, by operations and farm size (%)

Operation and type of labour	Farm size (in hectares)					
	All sizes	0–4	4.1–8	8.1–12	12.1–16	16.1–20	>20

	All sizes	0–4	4.1–8	8.1–12	12.1–16	16.1–20	>20
Ploughing							
Family	64.6	87.8	67.8	54.5	36.7	64.0	42.3
Permanent	32.1	11.6	31.1	36.0	62.4	35.9	52.1
Casual	3.3	0.6	1.1	9.5	0.9	0.1	5.6
Sowing							
Family	63.3	88.2	71.5	55.4	32.6	30.2	22.3
Permanent	31.0	8.1	25.5	33.2	63.8	66.5	64.9
Casual	5.7	3.7	3.0	11.4	3.6	3.3	12.8
Interculture							
Family	53.0	77.9	57.6	41.5	34.9	35.7	24.1
Permanent	24.2	6.3	24.2	27.4	42.3	34.6	38.2
Casual	22.8	15.8	18.2	31.1	22.8	29.7	37.7
Irrigation							
Family	58.8	87.1	65.6	47.0	30.9	29.6	26.2
Permanent	39.0	12.3	32.4	50.2	68.8	69.2	63.8
Casual	2.2	0.6	2.0	2.8	0.3	1.2	10.0
Harvesting							
Family	39.8	70.9	40.6	27.6	20.6	30.1	12.8
Permanent	14.3	6.5	12.0	17.8	25.0	19.5	28.3
Casual	45.9	22.6	47.4	54.6	54.4	50.4	58.9
Threshing							
Family	55.3	77.5	61.3	44.7	33.6	43.3	19.2
Permanent	24.0	6.0	18.7	33.2	40.5	44.9	48.8
Casual	20.7	16.5	20.0	22.1	25.9	11.8	32.0

than does casual labour. This is probably because these operations are considered to be more vital than the others and to require greater skill (and/or responsibility), which permanent labour is expected to have acquired.

We now return to the question of the differential effect of mechanisation on various categories of labour. Table 8.3 shows the change in the number of hours worked (for a given area or unit of output) by different types of labour, broken down by farm operations and farm size. In each case the effect has been measured by comparing

TABLE 8.3 Effect of mechanisation on different types of labour used in HYV wheat cultivation, by operations and farm size[1] (hours per hectare[2])

Operation and type of labour	Farm size (in hectares)					
	All sizes	0–4	4.1–8	8.1–12	12.1–16	16.1–20	>20
1 *Tractor ploughing*	−82.4	−91.5	−88.9	−80.3	−76.6	−70.5	−78.6
Family	−59.6	−81.2	−59.2	−50.7	−31.4	−26.9	+1.0
Permanent	−21.3	−10.4	−29.2	−24.0	−45.2	−43.3	−57.7
Casual	−1.5	—	−0.5	−5.6	—	−0.3	−21.9
2 *Tractor sowing*	−23.7	−18.8	−25.0	−27.3	−13.7	−8.1	−16.9
Family	−23.2	−24.1	−19.2	−24.8	−9.5	−1.2	−2.3
Permanent	−2.5	−0.7	−6.8	−5.6	−2.7	−5.8	−16.6
Casual	+2.0	+6.0	+1.0	+2.5	−1.5	−1.1	+2.0
3 *Tubewell irrigation*	+88.6	+100.8	+97.0	+66.8	+45.5	+84.6	+87.3
Family	+46.8	+82.9	+56.7	+22.4	+13.8	+2.1	+6.2
Permanent	+38.7	+16.8	+38.7	+39.9	+31.2	+80.1	+59.2
Casual	+3.1	+1.1	+1.6	+4.5	+0.5	+2.4	+21.9
4 *Power threshing*[2]	−4.1	−4.9	−4.7	−4.0	−3.5	−3.9	−2.9
Family	−2.3	−3.9	−2.9	−1.7	−1.2	−3.2	−1.6
Permanent	−1.0	−0.3	−0.9	−1.4	−1.4	−0.8	−2.6
Casual	−0.8	−0.7	−0.9	−0.9	−0.9	+0.1	+1.3
Combined effects							
1 + 2	−106.1	−110.4	−113.9	−108.2	−90.3	−78.6	−95.5
Family	−82.8	−105.3	−78.4	−75.5	−40.9	−28.1	−1.3
Permanent	−23.8	−11.1	−35.9	−29.6	−47.9	−49.1	−74.3
Casual	+0.5	+6.0	+0.4	−3.1	−1.5	−1.4	−19.9
1 + 2 + 3	−17.5	−9.6	−16.9	−41.4	−44.8	+6.0	−8.2
Family	−36.0	−22.4	−21.7	−53.1	−27.1	−26.0	+4.8
Permanent	+14.9	+5.7	+2.8	+10.2	−16.7	+31.0	−15.0
Casual	+3.6	+7.1	+2.0	+1.5	−1.0	+1.0	+2.0

[1] The mechanisation effect has been measured by subtracting the mean labour used with the modern technique from the mean labour used with the traditional technique for the operation and size group concerned. The techniques considered are as follows: for ploughing and sowing, tractors instead of bullocks; for irrigation, tubewells instead of canals; for threshing thresher/tractor instead of bullocks.

[2] Hours per quintal in the case of threshing.

labour time on plots using exclusively one technique with those using exclusively the other technique. Plots using some combination of both techniques do not enter into the computations.

We note from the table that in keeping with our observations so far, the type of labour most affected varies with farm size and operations. In ploughing, on the smallest farms (4 hectares or less) the use of tractors tends to affect mainly the input of family labour time, the decrease in which accounts for over 88 per cent of the reduced requirement of total labour time for ploughing on these farms. As farm size increases the proportion of family labour time displaced decreases, while that of permanent and casual labour time displaced increases.[16] Similarly with sowing, tractors tend primarily to reduce requirements of family labour time on the smaller farms and of permanent labour time on the larger ones, with some slight increase in the use of casual labour time. In irrigation, mechanisation (the use of tubewells instead of canals) leads not to a decrease but to an increase in the use of labour time on farms of all sizes. On the smaller ones the increase is largely in terms of family labour time, and on the larger ones of permanent and, to a lesser extent, of casual labour time. Finally, in threshing, where mechanisation is labour-displacing, the displaced labour consists mainly of family and, to a limited extent, of casual labour on the smaller farms, and of family and permanent labour on the larger ones.

So far we have been looking at mechanisation in different farm operations separately. When their combined effects are taken into account it is noted that:

1 On the smaller farms of 12 hectares or less the reduction in labour hours per hectare through the use of a tractor for ploughing and sowing primarily concerns family and also, to a limited extent, permanent labour. The use of a tubewell on these farms increases the use of all labour, but particularly of family labour. Tubewells, in other words, help to offset the labour displacement effect of tractors. The combined effect of a tractor and a tubewell on these farms is to decrease the use of family labour time, though to a lesser extent than if tubewells had not been introduced; and to increase the use of permanent and casual labour time, the increase in the former being less than if tubewells alone had been introduced.

2 On the larger farms of over 12 hectares tractor ploughing and sowing lead primarily to a reduction in the use of permanent labour time and, to a lesser extent, of family and casual labour time. Again, the introduction of a tubewell increases the use of all labour, but this time particularly of permanent labour. The net result of introducing both a tractor and a tubewell on these farms is, however, less clear-cut. Broadly, there tends to be a decrease in the use of family labour time and the negative effect of tractors on permanent labour time is not completely offset in all the larger farm size groups by the positive effect of tubewells.

3 With the addition of a thresher on farms already having a tractor and a tubewell there is a further reduction in the use of family labour time, and any increase in the use of permanent labour time is curtailed. This holds true for farms of all size groups.

TABLE 8.4 Use of female labour in HYV wheat cultivation, by operations[1]

Operation	Labour time (in hours)				Female labour time as % of	
	Total	Female Total	Family	Casual	total labour time in operation concerned	female labour time in all operations
Ploughing	20,547	—	—	—	—	—
Sowing	2,154	403	367	36	18.7	5.1
Interculture	3,383	78	78	—	2.3	1.0
Irrigation	3,779	57	37	20	1.5	0.7
Harvesting	43,552	6,940	396	6,544	15.9	87.8
Threshing	6,769	426	424	2	6.3	5.4
All the above operations	80,184	7,904	1,302	6,602	9.8	100.0[2]

[1] The table relates only to the 66 farms using female labour.
[2] Of this, female *family* labour accounts for 16.5 per cent and female *casual* labour for 83.5 per cent.

EFFECT ON FEMALE LABOUR

I have till now concentrated on categories of labour in terms of employment status (family, permanent and casual). When a further disaggregation by gender is undertaken, it is found that the involvement of women in field activities connected with wheat cultivation is limited. Of the 240 farms in the sample only 66 (27.5 per cent) use any female labour for the crop and even fewer use any women family workers.[17]

Table 8.4 gives the operation-specific use of female labour time on the 66 farms using at least some female labour (family and/or hired). Women are seen to contribute 9.8 per cent of the total labour used for the specified operations on these farms. Most of this labour – 83.5 per cent – is casually hired and the rest is contributed by women family workers, there being no permanent female labourers involved in crop production activities. The two operations in which the contribution of female labour is seen to be of some importance are sowing and harvesting, where it constitutes 18.7 and 15.9 per cent respectively of total labour time. Almost all the female labour in sowing is provided by family workers and almost all of that in harvesting by casually hired women.

Harvesting is seen to account for 87.8 per cent of the total female labour time in HYV wheat cultivation. In so far as wheat harvesting is still largely performed manually, mechanisation associated with this crop is not yet a threat to women's wage employment. Any introduction of combine harvesters, however, is likely to have a major displacing effect for both female and male casual labour.

IN CONCLUSION

At the beginning of this chapter the need to disaggregate the employment effects of mechanisation by specific operations and crops was emphasised. From the results, it was noted that such a disaggregation assisted in highlighting a number of aspects which would have been obscured in an aggregate analysis. For instance, it helped to bring out the differences between operations such as ploughing and sowing in the labour displacement effect of tractor use. It also helped to separate the divergent effects of different types of mechanisation, such as the negative labour use effect of tractor ploughing and sowing from the positive effect on labour use of mechanising irrigation through tubewells. Most important of all, it helped to trace the differential effect on different types of labour, and hence to identify the contexts in which mechanisation is likely to have the most impact on them. In so far as a differential social weighting needs to be given to the incomes received by different types of labour – for example, a higher weighting for casual workers (most of whom will usually be landless) than for family workers – this will have implications for the estimation of the social cost of certain mechanised techniques and for decisions about the social desirability of promoting such techniques.

NOTES

1   I am grateful to Ingrid Palmer and the *Review's* referee for comments on an earlier draft. The chapter is based largely on my doctoral dissertation, *Mechanisation in Farm Operations – Choices and their Implications: a Study Based on Punjab* (University of Delhi, Department of Economics, Dec. 1977).

2   For an analytical review of a number of these studies, see Agarwal, *Mechanisation;* and Hans P. Binswanger. *The Economics of Tractors in South Asia – an Analytical Review* (New York, Agricultural Development Council; and Hyderabad, International Crops Research Institute for the Semi-Arid Tropics, 1978).

3   One of the rare (and best-known) exceptions to this is the study by Martin Billings and Arjan Singh, 'Mechanisation and rural employment,

with some implications for rural income distribution', in *Economic and Political Weekly* (Bombay), 27 June 1970. They consider the possible effects of mechanisation separately for each operation. However, their estimates consist of a set of norms evaluated from a variety of data sources and do not relate consistently to any one sample of farms. Hence their study at best provides only a broad idea of possible effects.

4 This is not to say that the aggregate effects are unimportant. In fact such an analysis is necessary as a *complementary* exercise, since certain effects of mechanisation, as on the farm's cropping intensity (which in turn has a crucial bearing on the total employment-generating capacity of a given piece of land over the year), are not brought out in a crop-specific study. We might say that a disaggregation by operations gives an insight into the crop-specific effects, and the latter along with the cropping intensity effects help us to understand the aggregate implications better.

5 The fuller study included, in addition, an analysis of the cropping intensity and the aggregate employment effects (see Agarwal, *Mechanisation*).

6 The analysis is limited to the *direct* impact on employment. Any *indirect* employment generated through mechanisation, such as in the manufacturing and servicing of machinery or in the marketing of any additional output produced, has not been considered. For a discussion on this see R. G. Ridker, 'Agricultural mechanization in South Asia', in *Development Digest* (Washington), Jan. 1971, and Raj Krishna, who spells out a methodology for quantifying the indirect effects in 'Measurement of direct and indirect employment effects of agricultural growth with technical change', in Edgar O. Edwards (ed.), *Employment and Developing Nations: Report on a Ford Foundation Study* (New York, Columbia University Press, 1974).

7 It is also noteworthy that the level of mechanisation in India, particularly in terms of tractors, is higher in the Punjab than in any other state. In 1972 the Punjab had 42,400 tractors, or 28.6 per cent of the total in the country. See *Statistical Abstract, India, 1975* (New Delhi, Central Statistical Organisation, 1977), p. 58.

8 Data on labour used in fertiliser application were incomplete; hence this operation has not been included in the analysis.

9 See, for instance, C. H. Hanumantha Rao, *Technological Change and Distribution of Grains in Indian Agriculture* (Delhi, Macmillan Company of India Ltd, 1975); and Prem Vashishtha, *Issues in Technological Adaptations and Agricultural Development – an Analysis of Production Junctions on Punjab Farms*, Ph.D. dissertation (University of Delhi, Department of Economics, April 1975).

10 Factors contributing to the limited use of tractors for crop production activities include inadequate investment in supplementary tractor equipment, a lack of experience in the early years of tractor use, and poor tractor repair facilities. See, for instance, Bruce Johnston and Peter Kilby, *Agricultural Strategies, Rural–Urban Interactions, and the Expansion of Income Opportunities* (Paris, OECD Development Centre, 1973).

11 To compute the total labour time used for an operation, one hour of female labour was assumed to be equivalent to one hour of male labour, and one hour of child labour to be equivalent to half an hour of adult labour. Most studies take one hour of female labour to be equivalent to only half an hour of male labour, but the available evidence on relative male/female productivity does not justify this assumption *a priori*. See, for example, Bina Agarwal, *Work Participation of Rural Women in the Third World – Some Data and Conceptual Biases* (Institute of Development Studies, University of Sussex, 1979; mimeographed).

12 The labour time indicated for ploughing in fact includes that spent on all activities connected with seed-bed preparation. However, since ploughing is the main activity involved, the operation will be referred to simply as 'ploughing'.

13 Combine harvesters were in use on only six plots belonging to two farms in the sample. The number of observations was too small to make a definitive statement on their labour displacement effect.

14 Inderjit Singh, Richard Day and S. S. Johl in their Punjab-based study also note that the crop rotation and soil conditions are important determinants of the number of ploughings needed for seed-bed preparation for a given crop. See *Field Crop Technology in the Punjab, India* (Madison, University of Wisconsin, Social Systems Research Institute, 1968).

15 Among the few studies that have disaggregated the effect of mechanisation by the type of labour affected are: Billings and Singh, 'Mechanisation and rural employment'; Ashok Rudra, 'Employment patterns in large farms of Punjab', in *Economic and Political Weekly*, 26 June 1971; and R. K. Sharma; *Economics of Tractor versus Bullock Cultivation (a Pilot Study in Haryana)* (University of Delhi, Agricultural Economics Research Centre, 1972; mimeographed). Of these and other studies that have looked at the composition of labour used, only Billings and Singh consider the effect by each farm operation. However, even they provide only a limited insight since their inferences are drawn largely from their field observation of the types of labour commonly seen to perform different operations, and not from an actual quantification. Also, their conclusions do not adequately highlight the importance of farm size in determining the type of labour affected.

16 Billings and Singh, 'Mechanisation and rural employment', conclude that mechanisation of preparatory tillage primarily displaces family labour and that the effects on casual and permanent labour are slight. My results indicate the importance of taking size effects into account. It can be seen that the Billings and Singh finding holds true only for small farms and that as farm size increases it is not family but permanent and casual labour time which is likely to be reduced.

17 The low involvement of female family workers may be attributable to prestige reasons, which cause women to withdraw from or opt out of participating in the fields on farms where the family can afford hired help. The women may of course be doing off-field work indirectly related to cultivation, such as preparing meals for farm labourers,

particularly during the peak harvest periods when extra hands are often hired and the provision of meals is customary. However, in the absence of information on such off-field work, it is not possible to substantiate or quantify this.

Another point which has a bearing on agricultural female labour in general is that its use tends to be not merely operation-specific but also crop-specific, women being more frequently involved in the cultivation of some crops, such as rice (particularly for transplanting), than of others, such as wheat.

Chapter Nine

MALAY WOMEN AND RICE PRODUCTION IN WEST MALAYSIA

Cecilia Ng[1]

The purpose of rural development in West Malaysia is to increase agricultural productivity, and consequently farm income, through the introduction of modern farming methods and institutions in the rural sector. It is hoped that a commercially oriented farming population would emerge to replace what is usually viewed as a more traditional and backward agricultural sector.[2] Hence, through the years there has been an increasing penetration of capital in the rural areas, subsequently transforming the social organisation of production. This chapter will discuss the changes, particularly in the realm of gender relations and labour utilisation patterns in rice cultivation in a West Malaysian village.

Modern technological innovations have been introduced in the rice sector since the early 1960s, albeit in different stages of technological adoption. At the most basic level of this 'Green Revolution' package is the introduction of double-cropping through the utilisation of high-yielding varieties (HYV) and other biochemical inputs (fertilisers, weed-killers and so on), complemented by improved infrastructure facilities. The more advanced stage sees the introduction of mechanised rice production where the tractor and the combine replace the hoe and the sickle. The establishment of rice mills also take over traditional post-harvesting processes such as winnowing and manual-pounding of padi. What is also significant here is the increasingly important role of the state, via formal rural institutions, in determining the direction of agricultural change.

What has been the impact of such transformation on rural women? In terms of female labour utilisation, studies undertaken in some Asian countries point out that, while technology in rice production increases female labour input in the early stages, the more advanced stage of farm mechanisation reduces female participation. However, this phenomenon is not universal as it varies from country to country. For example, female labour use in a rice-farming village in the Philippines declined both absolutely and relatively, between

188

1970 and 1980, as a consequence of modern technology.[3]

On the other hand – in Japan, for instance – while overall labour input has decreased substantially due to modern technology, female participation in rice production has remained quite high – at 41 per cent.[4] This is because Japan's industrialisation policies have led to an emigration of male labour to the urban areas, leaving the middle-aged and older women to tend the fields and even to operate farm machines.[5] It would seem that the issue is not technology *per se*, but the nature of the existing social and gender relations under which technology is being introduced which determines the extent of female participation in mechanised agriculture. As Agarwal has succinctly pointed out,

> More often than not, the problem cannot be located in the technological innovation *per se*, since what is often appropriated about the innovation is not its technical characteristics but the socio-political context within which it is introduced. This gives the innovation its specific class and gender bias and mediates the distribution of costs and benefits from its adoption.[6]

My earlier studies in the Krian District on the impact of the early diffusion of modernisation practices on female labour utilisation and the status of rural women examined an area much neglected by studies on the impact of the Green Revolution in Malaysia.[7] This present chapter is a continuation of that study, albeit in another rice-bowl area called Tanjong Karang where mechanisation processes have been widely adopted.

The primary question asked in this chapter is 'What happens to the division of labour and gender relations when advanced mechanisation is practised in the rice sector in rural Malaysia?' In other words, what are the implications for rural women's status in terms of their access and control of agricultural resources? Given that the rural community is not homogeneous, how are women from different socio-economic strata affected? What sort of policies should be pursued to ensure that modernisation programmes benefit the rural women, especially the poorer ones?

After describing the village setting and study methodology, this chapter will examine the changing role of women in rice production under advanced mechanisation. This will be related to their increased role in reproduction and the implications in terms of their access to household and agricultural resources. Several case studies will be highlighted to provide a more personal insight to the study. The final section will summarise the changing nature of gender relations under the onslaught of rural modernisation and propose some policy recommendations for the advancement of rural women's status.

THE VILLAGE SETTING

The village of Sawah Sempadan, consisting of 23 blocks (about 6,000 acres), is located within the Tanjong Karang rice belt along the coast of the state of Selangor.[8] Originally conceived in the late nineteenth century by the colonial authorities to convert jungle swamp into productive rice cultivation, the Tanjong Karang Scheme attracted pioneers who came from various parts of the country and as far as Java and Sumatra from neighbouring Indonesia. However, irrigation work for single cropping began only in the mid-1930s whereby settlers were awarded 3 acres of rice land each and 1 acre for domestic cultivation.[9] It was only in the early sixties, in line with the Green Revolution strategy, that double-cropping was introduced, followed by the use of the two-wheeled tractor. By 1978 the four-wheeled tractor was in operation, and in 1982/83 broadcasting by hand and machine-harvesting were introduced.

The scheme is at present administered under the Northwest Selangor Integrated Agricultural Development Project (henceforth IADP or the Project). Launched in 1978, the Project covers an area of approximately 247,405 acres, consisting of the rice areas in the districts of Sabak Bernam and Kuala Selangor. The initial projected cost, estimated at M$148.73 million, 43 per cent of which was funded by the International Bank for Reconstruction and Development, will be increased to M$265.72 million by the end of 1990.

The Project objectives as spelt out in its briefing report are:

1   to increase the yield and quality of various crops;
2   to maximise farm income;
3   to alleviate rural poverty; and
4   to develop a self-reliant, progressive and commercial-orientated farming society.

Strategies towards achieving these objectives include the strengthening of existing infrastructure and support services as well as the provision of training to farmers in modern farming techniques.[10]

The actual research area comprises four blocks within Sawah Sempadan.[11] All rice-farming households with married couples (101 households) were interviewed between June and December 1987 – that is, during the rice-planting season.[12] Out of this, forty households were selected for detailed study of their labour utlisation patterns in the various rice-production tasks. Another visit was made in October 1988 to verify certain data and to interview selected families.

Although the original settlers started on an equal footing, by the time of the study it was found that there were variations in the socio-economic standing of the 101 households sampled. For example, twenty-six households did not own any land at all. The size distribution of rice-holdings owned and operated ranged from less than one acre to as high as 21 acres. Out of this, three-quarters of the farmers owned less than 3 acres of padi land, while half of them rented in extra land in order to increase production.

In terms of income, 62 per cent of the households earned a monthly income of less than M$300 a month, 24 per cent between M$301 and M$500, while a minority of 14 per cent earned more than M$500 a month. The average income per household was approximately M$330 per month.[13] It is understandable then that household members seek other income-earning activities, although the opportunities for off-farm employment are more limited for the women. Half of the husbands are involved in off-farm employment, mainly as rural labourers within the rice scheme or in the nearby palm-oil estates or factories. However, less than 20 per cent of the wives, mainly from the poorer households, are engaged in short-term rural wage work.

The households have been stratified into poor (*susah* – 44 per cent), middle (*sederhana* – 45 per cent) and rich (*senang* – 11 per cent) categories based on broad categories of land ownership, per capita income and employment status. Here again is further evidence of the unequal benefits derived by farmers through the Green Revolution strategy implemented under conditions of a market economy geared towards personal as against social gain.[14] Consequently, the ability to reproduce the household will involve different survival strategies for households from different strata. Women belonging to such households will also be differently affected. If labour utilisation and income-earning patterns are differentiated by one's socio-economic and gender status, then this should be an important point to be considered by policy-makers. With this background, it is now possible for us to delve into the impact of advanced technology on rural women's productive and reproductive activities.

THE CHANGING DIVISION OF LABOUR UNDER ADVANCED TECHNOLOGY

As noted earlier, the majority of farm households have more or less adopted *in toto* the various technological innovations recommended by the IADP office. For example, all land preparation is undertaken by machine, 97 per cent of the households use direct seeding (broadcasting) as a planting method, either by hand or by machine;

TABLE 9.1 Average labour utilisation (hours/acre) of 40 households by operation in Sawah Sempadan, 1987

Type of Operation	Family labour Male	Family labour Female	Wage labour Male	Wage labour Female	Total labour Total	Total labour % M	Total labour % F
1 Land preparation	7.4	1.9	2.7	—	12.0	84	16
2 Seed preparation	0.7	1.8	—	—	2.5	28	72
3 Broadcasting	1.1	0.4	0.7	—	2.2	82	18
4 Crop care, application of:							
(a) Weedkiller	2.2	0.1	0.2	—	2.5	96	4
(b) Fertiliser	5.7	1.7	0.7	—	8.1	78	21
(c) Insecticide	3.3	0.3	1.1	—	4.7	94	6
5 Machine harvest	—	—	0.9	—	0.9	100	—
6 Transportation	—	—	0.3	—	0.3	100	—
Total	20.4 (61%)	6.2 (19%)	6.6 (20%)	—	33.2 (100%)	81	19

Total acreage   = 158.5 acres
Average acreage =   3.96 acres

and about 96 per cent utilise fertiliser, weed-killers and insecticide as methods in crop care. Moreover, 99 per cent use the combine harvester for harvesting their crops after which the padi, upon being weighed by the middlemen, are sent directly via lorries or motorbikes to the rice mills for processing.

The end result of such widespread use of technology is a significant reduction in labour utilisation among men and women. Table 9.1 depicts the intensity of labour use per acre of padi land among the forty households as compared with similar padi operations in the mid-seventies as shown in Table 9.2. A more detailed breakdown of labour utilisation in rice production by strata is provided in Tables 9.3, 9.4 and 9.5.

It can be seen from Tables 9.1 and 9.2 that mechanisation has brought about a five-and-a-half-fold decrease in average labour input; that is, from a total of 185.18 hours per acre in 1975/76 to a mere 33.2 hours per acre in 1987. Nursery preparation has been completely eliminated while a drastic reduction in labour has taken place in the three labour-intensive tasks of planting (from 50 to 2.2 hours), harvesting and threshing (from 76 to 1.2 hours). The contribution of family labour remains at 80 per cent, with the remaining 20 per cent being accounted for by hired labour primarily during field preparation, broadcasting, harvesting and transportation of padi sacks. Reciprocal labour relations (*berderau*), prevalent in other less commercialised rice communities, are entirely absent in this area.

TABLE 9.2 Number of hours and man-days utilised by field operation per acre of padi cultivated, average over two seasons 1975/76

Operation	Family labour (Hours)						Hired labour	
	F^b	M^b	P^b	C^b	Total	Man-days	Hours	Man-days
Nursery preparation	9.56	3.27	5.95	0.26	18.99	2.38	—	—
Field preparation	10.67	2.05	4.38	0.16	17.25	2.16	—	—
Transplanting	17.03	6.99	15.45	0.46	39.93	4.99	9.90	1.24
Crop care^a	15.56	1.57	4.94	0.18	22.24	2.78	0.27	0.04
Harvesting, threshing and transportation	21.05	9.35	20.58	0.40	51.38	6.43	25.22	3.15
Total	73.87	23.23	51.30	1.46	149.79	18.74	35.39	4.43

a Including weeding, application of fertilizer, insecticide, herbicide, etc.
b F = Farmer; M = Male adults; P = Female adults; C = Children (under 16 years old)

Source: L. J. Fredericks (1977), 'Patterns of labour utilization and income distribution in rice double cropping system: policy implications'; Occasional Papers on Malaysian Socio-economic Affairs, No. 8, University of Malaya, Kuala Lumpur

TABLE 9.3 Average labour utilisation (hours/acre) of poor households by operation in Sawah Sempadan, 1987 (N= 24)

Type of operation	Family labour		Wage labour		Total labour		
	Male	Female	Male	Female	Total	% M	% F
1 Land preparation	7.1	4.1	2.8	—	14.0	71	29
2 Seed preparation	0.8	2.8	—	—	3.6	22	78
3a Broadcasting by hand	0.8	0.7	0.7	—	2.2	69	31
3b Broadcasting by machine	0.1	—	0.07	—	0.17	100	—
4 Crop care, application of:							
(a) Weedkiller	1.9	0.25	0.1	—	2.25	89	11
(b) Fertiliser	4.6	3.0	0.7	—	8.3	64	36
(c) Insecticide	3.2	0.6	0.8	—	4.6	87	13
5 Machine harvest	—	—	0.9	—	0.9	100	—
6 Transportation	—	—	0.2	—	0.2	100	—
Total	18.5 (51%)	11.45 (32%)	6.27 (17%)		36.22	68	32

Total acreage = 63.5 acres
Average acreage = 2.64 acres

TABLE 9.4 Average labour utilisation (hours/acre) of middle households by operation in Sawah Sempadan, 1987 (N= 11)

Type of operation	Family labour		Wage labour		Total labour		
	Male	Female	Male	Female	Total	% M	% F
1 Land preparation	5.4	0.8	4.1	—	10.3	92	8
2 Seed preparation	0.6	1.4	—	—	2.0	30	70
3a Broadcasting by hand	0.8	0.3	0.4	—	1.5	80	20
3b Broadcasting by machine	0.07	0.07	0.3	—	0.44	84	16
4 Crop care, application of:							
(a) Weedkiller	1.9	0.03	0.5	—	2.43	99	1
(b) Fertiliser	3.8	1.3	0.8	—	5.9	78	22
(c) Insecticide	2.9	—	1.7	—	4.6	100	—
5 Machine Harvest	—	—	1.0	—	1.0	100	—
6 Transportation	—	—	0.4	—	0.4	100	—
Total	15.47 (54%)	3.9 (14%)	9.2 (32%)		28.57	86	14

Total acreage   = 57.5 acres
Average acreage = 5.22 acres

This disintegration is also manifested in a significant change in the division of labour by gender. Whereas traditionally, certain padi production functions are gender-specific, the situation in Sawah Sempadan seems to point to a reduction of female labour even in what is ideologically conceived as 'women's work', such as transplanting and harvesting. These two tasks have been taken over by male family and male hired labour. Broadcasting of padi seeds by hand or by machine is invariably a less laborious task than the earlier method of actually bending one's back to transplant the padi seedlings.

Similarly, harvesting by machine does not require the usual hard labour experienced in manual harvesting and threshing, the latter being acknowledged as threshing your bone (*membanting tulang*) in Malay proverbial language to denote hard work. Indeed, the role of harvesting has been taken over by the combines operated by richer farmers, state rural institutions or other middlemen who rent their combines for M$5.50 per *guni* sack of threshed padi.

Advanced mechanisation has deprived poor women and men of substantial income-earning opportunity as rural labourers, although women seem to be more adversely affected. Indeed my sample households found that all hired labour in the various padi operations were men.

TABLE 9.5 Average labour utilisation (hours/acre) of rich households by operation in Sawah Sempadan, 1987 (N= 5)

Type of operation	Family labour		Wage labour		Total labour		
	Male	Female	Male	Female	Total	% M	% F
1 Land preparation	10.9	0.1	0.5	—	11.5	99	1
2 Seed preparation	0.5	0.8	—	—	1.3	38	62
3a Broadcasting by hand	0.2	—	—	—	0.2	100	—
3b Broadcasting by machine	1.5	—	0.3	—	1.8	100	—
4 Crop care, application of:							
(a) Weedkiller	3.1	—	—	—	3.1	100	—
(b) Fertiliser	10.7	—	0.6	—	11.3	100	—
(c) Insecticide	4.4	—	0.6	—	5.0	100	—
5 Machine harvest	—	—	0.9	—	0.9	100	—
6 Transportation	—	—	0.2	—	0.2	100	—
Total	31.3 (88%)	0.9 (3%)	3.1 (9%)		35.3	97	3

Total acreage   = 37.5 acres
Average acreage = 7.5 acres

In this sense the introduction of machine broadcast and machine harvest has been appropriated by the male, both in terms of the nature and type of work as well as in the time utilised for such tasks. Female family labour contributes only 19 per cent of total labour input and mainly comprises the lighter tasks of burning off the dried stalks during field preparation and in seed preparation. This is a far cry from their previous participation rate of 34 per cent in 1975/76. Furthermore, my study in another rice-bowl area in the north revealed that women provided 60 per cent of the total labour input in rice production.[15]

It seems that the opposite phenomenon is happening – that is, a masculinisation of agriculture instead of a feminisation of land – a conclusion often reached in studies on rural women.[16] With the drudgery of work being eliminated, it is now relatively easy to operate by machines and this is undertaken by men while the women are left to their reproductive tasks. The question arises – is technology gender-specific?

I argue that pre-existing gender relations constrain women to take up such 'heavy' and more lucrative tasks. Malay and Islamic gender ideology, as expressed by the villagers, pre-supposes women's primary role in the domestic sphere. The majority of husbands and wives interviewed felt that religion defined women's role at home although at the same time, interestingly enough, about half of the women and one-third of the men did not believe that the fundamental duties of the wife are confined to home and children. However, it was strongly felt by both parties that learning new technology was the responsibility of the men. Concretised so clearly here is the contradiction and struggle between abstract notions of women's role and their actual work reality although other external social forces are also at play.

For example, equally important is the impact of the labour market, because, unlike in Japan, the lack of other wage-earning opportunities, especially during the recession, means that male labour is not pulled away to the capitalist sector. On the contrary, young girls opt for the city as electronics workers and domestic servants, settling within the lower rungs of the segmented labour market. These circumstances provide the conditions towards the emergence of a patriarchal household, particularly within the rich and middle stratum, in which males provide the management and labour in the farm and women undertake the reproductive function, sharpening the ideological distinction between the idea of man as the producer and women the reproducer.[17] On the other hand, the existence of a substantial number of female-headed households belies the fact that poor men do migrate, leaving women to manage the farm and household.[18]

It is not surprising, then, that the division of labour is a little different when one breaks down the rural community by strata. As shown in Tables 9.3 – 9.5, women from the poor households contribute 32 per cent of total labour input, compared to 14 per cent of the middle households and only 3 per cent of the rich households. It is interesting to note that women from the poor households provide a substantial contribution in land and seed preparation, broadcasting and fertiliser application. Women from the middle and rich households are mainly involved in seed preparation, a relatively light task which is undertaken in the house compound. The middle households have the means to command the labour of others while the rich households have the means to buy their own machinery as a form of investment to hire out to others.

It is also significant to note that wage labour comprises 17, 32 and 9 per cent of total labour in the poor, middle and rich households respectively. Wage labour is used among poor households only when necessary; if not, most of the work is shared between the men and women. It can be seen that half the hired labour utilised here is in the area of land preparation and harvesting which necessitates the use of machines. A similar situation exists with the middle households although they are probably in an economically more secure position to hire labour. None the less, the rising costs of production are a continuous source of lament among the majority of the people in the village. For example, the cost of labour has risen from M$1.20 in the sixties to the present M$6 per day; while the rent per acre has risen from M$50 to between M$125 and M$200 within the same period. Ploughing the land takes up another M$130, and this does not include the costs of weed-killer and pesticide, all of which were not necessary before.

The rich households use a minimum of hired labour, which is actually not surprising when one realises that the few rich families in Sawah Sempadan have bought their own four-wheeled tractors, mechanical broadcasters and sprayers which they can operate themselves rather easily. They then hire out their tractors, which they or their sons handle, to the surrounding villagers. This is a lucrative venture. According to one rich farmer, he bought a four-wheeled tractor for M$36,000 and after four years he had earned M$60,000, a sum sufficient to cover his mortgage and to make a tidy profit. To be sure, women from this stratum are visibly absent from the various padi operations. One of them said that she hardly goes down to the padi fields and is relatively ignorant of what is happening in the fields. She just 'sits in the house' (*duduk rumah sahaja*) and has been elevated to the status of a housewife.

To sum up, the impact of advanced rice technology has serious, long-term implications for the role and status of rural women and men. It has definitely transformed the division of labour by gender, whereby rural women's contribution in general has been reduced significantly both in terms of the type performed and the intensity of the work process. Although the women are invariably happy with the elimination of such hard work, they have also lost many skills coupled by a concomitant decrease in knowledge about rice production and technology. For example, about 40 per cent of the wives interviewed did not even know the name of the type of seeds utilised in their fields – a rather shocking discovery, at least to me.[19] The new skills created in the operation of the new technology are possessed by the men who have basically taken over the management of the rice farms. This is mainly true of the middle and rich households, as in the poorer households women still have a substantial say in padi production given their significant contribution.

Another important dimension is the increasingly coercive role of the state in directing agricultural modernisation. With double-cropping, work has to be completed at a much faster pace, so that one is forced to mechanise whether one can afford it or not. For the future, the Project is planning to convert the entire padi scheme into mini-estates in which all agricultural operations will be synchronised and unified by the state machinery. As one farmer said, 'If you do not plough your land in time, the Farmers' Organisation will do it for you and you have to pay, whether you like it or not.' Again the benefits will accrue to the richer farmers, who will rent out their machines to the state, which will mediate any conflicts arising with the poorer farmers.

WOMEN'S INCREASED ROLE IN REPRODUCTION

With their displacement in rice production, it seems that rural women play an increasingly pivotal role in household reproduction. As mentioned earlier, women, especially those from the middle and rich households, are now becoming full-time housewives, confirming earlier myths of 'women only helping in the farms'. Table 9.6 informs us about the nature of involvement of husbands and wives in home tasks and responsibilities. It can be seen that certain domestic activities like food preparation, serving, cleaning, washing are clearly the responsibility of the wives. However, tasks which involve the use of money, like shopping for food, the purchase of household appliances, furniture, land and other productive assets, are the purview of the husbands.

This dichotomous pattern in household responsibilities reflects the decreasing access and control of women to non-agricultural household resources, probably as a consequence of their decreased role in agricultural production. Indeed, some women remarked that since they do not work and earn income now they have less say in the 'business of running the house'. And even if the women wanted to work outside the home, there are very limited opportunities available. Moreover, they are often discouraged to do so by their husbands who feel that they should stay at home since there is 'enough to eat in the house' (*dah cukup makan*).

The distinction between production and reproduction is made sharper with the male taking a dominant role in agricultural tasks, and women being more responsible for domestic work. It seems that the ideology of woman as the helper has caught up with the reality of her actually becoming a housewife. This is particularly real to the women from the middle and upper strata, while for those from the lower strata, their workload is intensified in both reproduction and petty commodity production. However, women in both groups still play the role of maintaining and reproducing labour at no cost to capital; for example, maintaining migrant workers, the sick and unemployed. The implications for women's status are discussed in the following section in the context of their access and control of the available resources in the household and village.

TABLE 9.6   Wives' and husbands' performance of home tasks

Task	W	W+	W=H	H+	H	O	NA
				Task performer* (percentage, N = 101)			
1 Food shopping	14.9	14.9	30.7	15.8	20.8	3.0	—
2 Food preparation	76.2	13.9	1.0	—	—	8.9	—
3 Setting plates, glasses, etc. on dining table/floor	73.3	11.9	1.0	—	—	12.9	—
4 Food serving	73.3	11.9	1.0	—	—	13.9	—
5 Dish washing	73.3	13.9	—	—	—	12.9	—
6 In-house cleaning	75.2	10.9	1.0	—	—	12.9	—
7 Yard cleaning	70.3	12.9	2.0	—	—	14.9	—
8 Washing clothes/ bedsheets/curtains	70.3	11.9	2.0	—	1.0	14.0	—
9 Ironing clothes	49.5	11.9	—	—	—	32.9	5.9
10 Sewing and mending clothes	67.3	11.9	2.0	—	—	13.9	5.0
11 Bed-making	81.2	12.9	2.0	—	—	4.0	—
12 Buying household appliances/furniture	9.9	3.0	34.7	9.9	30.7	5.9	5.9
13 Buying piece of land and other productive assets	—	1.0	11.9	5.0	40.6	4.0	37.6
14 House repair and improvement	—	—	15.8	5.9	48.9	18.8	10.9
15 Fetching water	19.8	7.9	5.0	3.0	14.9	8.9	40.6
16 Gathering firewood	9.9	4.0	4.0	6.9	29.7	5.0	40.6
17 Caring sick family members	26.7	21.8	39.6	4.0	2.0	5.9	—

*Code

W	=	wife only
W=H	=	wife and husband about equally
H	=	husband only
NA	=	not applicable
W+	=	wife more
H+	=	husband more
O	=	neither husband nor wife

RURAL WOMEN AND RESOURCES

Land, as one of the most important means of production, is highly valued by the villagers in Sawah Sempadan. Rural women are supposed to have equal access to property under the customary (*adat*)

law of inheritance which recognises and thus rewards their important contribution in agricultural production. Alternatively, under the
Islamic law of inheritance, daughters are legally entitled to one-half
of the male share of inherited property.

However, with the increasing commoditisation of padi production,
the price of land has soared from a low M$400 per acre in the 1960s
to as high as M$12,000 per acre at the time of writing. Hence, only
the better-off farmers have access to bank and other credit facilities
to purchase land now. And if the men are the ones working on the
land, then the opportunities would automatically accrue to them since
they would be the ones in contact with the representatives of financial
institutions. What are the implications on women's traditional rights
to land?

My data show that women own only 11 per cent of total land in
Sawah Sempadan; 87 per cent of the land is owned by men, while
only 2 per cent of husbands and wives jointly own land. One of the
reasons could be that land registered by the colonial state reflected
a patriarchal bias, in that title deeds were put under the husband's
name, as head of household. It is possible also that with women's
decreasing role in rice cultivation, there could be a similar decrease
in their access to land ownership.

Indeed, this could be a critical juncture in that there could be
other legal implications pertaining to land ownership. For example,
it could be more difficult now for a divorced woman to demand land
jointly acquired as a result of shared input (*harta sepencarian*) even
though the land is not legally under the name of both spouses. Since
housework and/or subsistence production is not legally recognised as
work, the divorced woman could lose out economically in terms of
obtaining any kind of land compensation with the justification that
she did not contribute to the land and hence did not 'work'.

As for other resources, the data revealed that farm assets are also
under the control of men. Table 9.7 shows that the majority of farm
implements (tractors, sprayers, motorcycles), except bicycles, are
owned by the men, irrespective of socio-economic position. There
is more flexibility in the ownership of household assets, some of
which are jointly owned. However, it is interesting to note that
many wives do not want to acknowledge themselves as owners or
co-owners of household implements since it is not 'their money' which
buys the goods. Bigger household items like stoves, televisions and
fans, belong to the men, while the kitchen utensils, such as blenders
and rice cookers, are the property of the women.

Farmers under the Project rely heavily on state aid and extension
support systems for continued access to other agricultural resources
such as credit and training facilities regarding technological innovations. In fact, as discussed earlier, education and training in new
technology is one of the main aims of the Project. It would be

TABLE 9.7   Ownership of farm and household assets

	Poor			Middle			Rich			Total		
	J	H	W	J	H	W	J	H	W	J	H	W
Farm assets												
1 Hand/pedestrian tractor	1	3	–	–	4	–	–	2	–	1	9	–
2 Four-wheeled tractor	–	–	–	–	1	–	–	2	–	–	3	–
3 Seed broadcaster	–	4	–	–	2	1	–	1	–	–	7	1
4 Sprayer	3	30	2	5	31	2	1	9	–	9	70	4
5 Car	–	3	–	–	3	–	–	1	–	–	7	–
6 Motorcycle	5	22	3	8	26	–	1	6	–	14	54	–
7 Bicycle	13	5	6	9	7	8	1	1	6	23	13	20
Household assets												
1 Gas range	3	5	2	6	3	1	1	2	4	10	10	7
2 Electric/gas stove	1	1	2	–	4	6	1	1	2	2	6	10
3 Refrigerator	3	2	–	5	4	2	2	1	2	10	7	4
4 Washing machine	–	–	–	2	2	–	–	–	–	2	2	–
5 Blender	2	4	4	5	4	12	2	1	3	9	9	19
6 Flat iron	9	9	8	7	9	17	3	2	5	19	20	30
7 Television	7	23	1	9	26	7	3	3	4	19	52	12
8 Electric fan	3	14	2	5	22	4	3	6	1	11	42	7
9 Wall clock	3	15	10	9	21	3	3	4	2	15	40	15
10 Radio	4	14	8	8	11	6	3	3	2	15	28	16
11 Sewing machine	3	4	9	6	2	19	1	2	5	10	8	33
12 Rice cooker	2	4	6	4	4	7	–	2	3	6	10	16

Note: J = joint ownership
        H = husband
        W = wife

really beneficial if the farmers were encouraged to participate in the planning, implementation and evaluation of their crops together with the extension agents on the ground. This type of process would then encourage a two-way communication between farmers and policy-makers in the direction and strategy of rural development. However, it seems that not everyone has equal access to the benefits of this increasing dependence on formal state institutions.

A series of questions were directed to the husbands and wives regarding their perceived access and actual utilisation of agricultural resources and training within the past twelve months. It is useful to note that the men and women across the three strata perceived things differently, although the difference was more significant between the genders than across strata.

Table 9.8 shows the actual utilisation of the various facilities in terms of visits by extension agents, attendance at training/seminars, use of printed materials produced by the Project office, discussion

TABLE 9.8   Utilisation of agricultural resources and training

	Poor		Middle		Rich		Total	
	M	F	M	F	M	F	M	F
1 *Personal visits by Extension Officers*								
Not at all	24	32	29	37	6	8	59	77
A little	13	8	12	9	1	1	26	18
A great deal	7	4	5	–	4	2	16	6
2 *Consultation at office with Extension Officers*								
Not at all	27	42	27	43	6	10	60	95
A little	13	2	17	1	2	–	32	3
A great deal	4	–	2	2	3	1	9	3
3 *Attendance at training/seminars*								
Not at all	35	42	38	46	8	17	81	99
A little	6	2	8	–	3	–	17	2
A great deal	3	–	–	–	–	–	3	–
4 *Printed utilisation of agricultural materials*								
Not at all	32	35	30	32	7	8	69	75
A little	10	8	15	14	3	3	28	25
A great deal	2	1	1	–	1	–	4	1
5 *Discussion with farmer leader*								
Not at all	11	32	14	33	3	7	28	72
A little	20	9	20	11	2	4	42	24
A great deal	13	–	12	2	6	–	31	5
6 *Discussion with fellow farmers*								
Not at all	11	23	14	22	5	7	30	52
A little	23	17	24	22	3	3	50	42
A great deal	10	4	8	2	3	1	21	7
7 *Attendance at field demonstrations*								
Not at all	33	42	35	44	6	10	74	96
A little	7	2	7	2	3	1	17	5
A great deal	4	–	3	–	2	–	9	–

Note: M = Male   F = Female

with block leaders under the Training and Visiting System, and attendance at field demonstrations. The latter is especially important especially when there are attacks of padi diseases, a common occurrence in the area.

The majority of farmers (between 60 and 90 per cent) felt that they did not have much access nor did they actually utilise the resources available. More women than men registered a negative use of such resources. For example, more than three-quarters of the women interviewed felt that they never met the extension officers while more than 90 per cent had never attended any meetings, training nor attended field demonstrations. The statistical findings for the men are not impressive either, although a higher percentage of men utilised the existing resources and training.

The diffusion of technology according to the training and visiting system is through the block leader, who will then disseminate the new information to his block members. However, it appears that this trickle-down effect is not very effective because many of the farmers do not receive such communication from the leaders. Communication among the farmers themselves, in defiance of the diffusion of innovation concept, seems to be a more popular process of obtaining and sharing information. In fact, many of the women stated that the block leaders and extension officers spoke only to the menfolk. As a consequence, rural women are deprived of knowledge of new techniques and access to credit facilities, which in the long run will mean a lowering of their status as rural producers. Rural women are in fact encouraged to attend family life education programmes conducted by community teachers (*guru* KEMAS). Perhaps it is not by coincidence that these programmes prepare women to be housewives, foreseeing their displacement from agricultural production. Moreover, would it not also conveniently conform to the existing gender ideology of the model homemaker?

Hence it is seen that while there has been a shift in the locus of control to the state and its auxilliary agencies in terms of access and control over agricultural resources, not all farmers partake of such benefits. Poor farmers are left out and so are women. I shall try to illustrate this by providing two cases.

NAPSIAH AND MAT

Napsiah's father came from Indonesia when he was in his late forties. He later settled down and married her mother, who was only 9 years old. They had fifteen children, four of whom died. Napsiah herself married Mat when she was 14 years of age. At that time they were 'squatting' on Mat's grandfather's land. He later bought half an acre of land, all that they could afford. 'Nowadays land is very expensive. . .only the rich can buy. It is also difficult to rent in land as the landowners want us to pay the rent in cash and in advance. . .not like before, when you could pay after the harvest', she adds.

Both of them work on the land, but the produce is insufficient for household expenses. To obtain more income Mat works in a padi processing mill, earning M$300 a month. That is not enough to feed their six children, five of whom are still in school. As a result, the eldest daughter has gone to the city to work in an electronics factory.

Before mechanisation, Napsiah used to be a wage labourer in transplanting and harvesting. However, now there is no work, so she helps a neighbouring relative to make cakes, earning M$2 – 3 a day. She says she feels exploited by the relative but she cannot say anything – she feels bad (*malu*) to ask for more money. In fact she claims she had a miscarriage due to the hard work involved. She wants to migrate somewhere else but Mat says there is nowhere for them to go. To avoid being exploited, Napsiah is now looking after the two children of the community teacher, obtaining a wage of M$80 per month.

Money is a continual problem but they survive by cutting down on various expenses. For example, in rice cultivation they do not use weed-killer; so she does the weeding by herself. They don't sell all their produce, keeping several sacks for a rainy day. Both husband and wife try to obtain any kind of wage work while their daughter is in the city, Napsiah is not happy that the daughter is away but there is no choice. Napsiah also tends some mango trees and sells the fruits when they ripen. They usually discuss family and farm matters together before any decision is taken.

Napsiah does not have much free time, but when she does she attends the classes conducted by the community teacher – programmes mainly related to cooking, embroidery, religion and so on. She says she likes to go to these classes to learn new things. However, Mat does not go to the meetings organised by the Farmers' Association due to the lack of time.

MUKARAH AND ZAIN

Unlike Napsiah, the husband, Zain did most of the talking, although efforts were made to direct questions to Mukarah. So this story comes from the male perspective.

Zain's father came from Java and bought 3 acres of paddy land. When Zain was 16 years old he dropped out of school and decided that he wanted to be a farmer – and a good one – since he was interested in agriculture. So he rented in 1.5 acres of land for M$50 per year for two years. It was a good crop. Consequently, with the money obtained from the sale of the produce he rented in another 1.5 acres. By the time he was 18 years he was a tenant with 4.5 acres of land. It was time to marry. He married Mukarah, and with her additional help he rented in another 3 acres of land for M$50 per acre. Besides padi, he also planted sweet potato and he made a huge profit from the sale.

Mukarah and Zain worked very hard on the land. In fact, he added that people in the village said that he was treating his wife like a coolie, but he did not care. He was only interested to increase his yield and to make money. Finally, he was able to buy a piece of land – 1.5 acres – from his accumulated savings.

When double-cropping was introduced in 1963, Zain worked very closely with the Farmers' Association. During the land blight in the sixties he continued to work on the land, although this time he could rent in land for free. Whatever he could save he did. That paid off because he began buying land and machinery. In 1965 he bought 3 acres for M$1,200 and in 1968 he bought a two-wheeled tractor for M$3,000 through a loan from the Farmers' organisation.

By the 1970s he was a big owner-operator and tenant, cultivating 29 acres of land, hiring fifteen men from the neighbouring state, Perak, to work on his land while Mukarah cooked for the workers. In fact, she was slowly disengaging herself from actual work in the field. He also made money by renting out his tractor to the neighbouring villagers. At that time he was active in the Farmers' organisation, being the unit head. He was also active in the local party politics (of the ruling party), being the head of the Information Section. His credibility was growing, so to speak.

In the 1980s Zain continued accumulating more rice land. Altogether he bought 8 acres of land for a tidy sum of M$64,000, which he borrowed from the Agricultural Bank. He also bought a four-wheeled tractor for M$36,000, although within four years he had made M$60,000 from the hire of this tractor.

Now Zain says that his wife can stay at home and do anything she wants. She does not have to work any more and can sleep the whole day long. However, Mukarah said that she felt bored at home and wanted to work. But because he does not allow her to do so she has to stay at home. In fact, they have a big double-storey concrete house which sticks out like a sore thumb in the village surroundings. He continued to point out that in Islam the man has the power and control (*kuasa*) over the women and if he has sufficient income, the wife need not work. She needs his permission to do so.

It can be seen that the Green Revolution has benefited Zain and Mukarah. He has been able to make use of the opportunities offered in terms of loan and credit facilities due to his close contact with the state agencies. In the process he has become confident of his abilities as an entrepreneur and in his ability to make money if 'one works hard enough'. The wife remains in the shadow and only listens to him while he talks about his life.

CONCLUSION

Capital penetration has brought about various changes in the organisation of padi production in Sawah Sempadan. This can be seen in the patterns of labour utilisation, although at the initial stages of commodity production, the division of labour by gender was not significantly altered. Indeed, the labour process was not, and is still not significantly commoditised, unlike production inputs and outputs.

It is only with advanced mechanisation that there is a reduction in labour utilisation as well as a shift from communal and gender-specific work parties to the use of mainly male family workers and male hired labour. This is made possible by the prevailing gender ideology which, while according an equal status to women in the economic realm, also places priority on her singular role as reproducer. Hence, although technology is not gender-specific, rural women seem to have lost out in the wake of technological progress, not least due to village and state patriarchal biases. Community home economics education programmes for rural women bear this out.

At the same time with increased commercialisation, peasant differentiation has also emerged with different implications for the various peasant strata. Women from the rich and middle households, displaced from agricultural production, retire to the kitchen, so to speak – donning their new role and status as rural housewife. However, women from the poor households need to work as there is not sufficient cash to command labour nor to buy the whole range of inputs for increased productivity. To make ends meet, younger women from this stratum leave for the city as domestics or as workers in the manufacturing sector, particularly in the electronics industry. The men also find work in the capitalist sector, usually returning during the harvest time if they are away from the village.

There seem to be two broad trends, one leading to the emergence of a patriarchal household within the middle and rich stratum, and the other, female-headed households among the poorer strata. Because of their participation in agriculture, gender relations in poor households seem to be less unequal than those in the other two strata, although the women in general are slowly being displaced by the advance of mechanisation.

With the sharper distinction between production and reproduction, rural women begin to lose their power base in agriculture and subsequently have decreased access and control of household and agricultural resources. State intervention consciously or unconsciously contributes to the emergence of a patriarchal household, and women could begin to lose their legal status as rural producers in property inheritance dealings. Moreover, existing gender ideology of the glorification of the housewife status also influences this possible trend towards the shift in rural women's role from production to reproduction. Unless some steps are taken to overcome this situation, rural women could well become short-changed despite the benefits and progress introduced by technological advancement.

As an immediate stop-gap measure, formal state institutions should actively encourage the participation of rural women in all their development and credit programmes. Knowledge and training in new technology should also be provided for the women in order for them to be involved in farm management and crop care. As a long-term policy, alternative employment opportunities should be provided for those displaced by mechanisation, with special focus on the poorer farmers.

At another level, the attitude towards work, especially women's work, should be changed. Reproduction should be recognised as a necessary process in the overall production process and should be legally and culturally acknowledged. Rural women's organisations, free from political control, should be set up to struggle genuinely for their rights and should provide educational programmes to cultivate values of co-operation, social and gender equality and dignity. Of course, all this also entails a reorienting of existing gender relations and ideology but it is imperative that a start is made before it is too late.

NOTES

1   This is a revised version of a paper presented at the Twelfth Annual Canadian Research Institute for the Advancement of Women Conference, Quebec City, 11–13 Nov. 1988. I would like to thank the Commonwealth Foundation for sponsoring my participation in this Conference.

2   See the National Agricultural Policy as discussed in the Fifth Malaysia Plan (Government of Malaysia, 1986).

3   Lyda Reys, 'Changing labor patterns of women in rice farm households: a rainfed rice village, Iloilo Province, Philippines', in *Women in Rice Farming* (International Rice Research Institute, Philippines, 1985).

4   Ryohei Kada and Yukiki Kada, 'The changing role of women in Japanese agriculture: the impact of new rice technology on women's employment', in *Women in Rice Farming*, (International Rice Research Institute, Philippines, 1985).

5   The study by Reiko Ohki notes that the increased role of women in padi cultivation has led to their increased access to farm machinery. As early as 1977, 53 per cent of 4,628 farm women sampled could operate a variety of agricultural machinery ranging from tractors to combines. Refer to Reiko Ohki (1985), 'Women's labor and the technological development of rice cultivation in Japan', in *Women in Rice Farming*.

6   Bina Agarwal, 'Women and technological change in agriculture: the Asian and African experience', in Iftikar Ahmed (ed.), *Technology and Rural Women: Conceptual and Empirical Issues* (George Allen & Unwin, London, 1985), p. 112.

7   See articles entitled 'Gender and the division of labour: a case study', in Hing Ai Yun and R. Talib (eds), *Women and Employment in Malaysia* (University of Malaya, Kuala Lumpur, 1985); and 'Agricultural modernization and gender differentiation in a rural Malay community 1983–1987', in Cecilia Ng (ed.), *Technology and Gender* (Universiti Pertanian Malaysia, Serdang, 1987).

8   L.J. Fredericks, 'Patterns of labour utllization and income distribution in rice double cropping system: policy implications', Occasional Papers on Malaysian Socio-economic Affairs, no. 8 (Faculty of Economics and Administration, University of Malaya, 1977).

9   Abdul Halim Taib, 'Tanjong Karang Survey – Phase II: Socioeconomic survey of Sawah Sempadan, a study of Blocks E, Q, S, W', Graduation Exercise, University of Malaya, 1963. What was interesting was that Malay and Chinese farmers worked together in the early stages. It was only later that Sawah Sempadan was allocated to the Malays and another area, Sekinchan, to the Chinese farmers.

10   'Brief information on the Northwest Selangor integrated agricultural development project', Pejabat Pengarah Projek Barat Laut Selangor (July 1986).

11   Each block is identified by a letter in the alphabet. The four blocks selected – E, Q, S and W – are adjacent to each other and stretch for several kilometres from one end of the village to the other.

12   I am extremely grateful to Fe Dagoy for assistance in the data collection and analysis, especially when I was incapacitated for several months in 1987 and 1988.

13   This figure is lower than the monthly income of M$420 per month provided by the Project office. However, it is acknowledged that the poverty rate has been reduced from 65 per cent to 41.7 per cent in 1985, with a projected decrease to below 35 per cent by 1990. See 'Brief information on the Northwest Selangor integrated agricultural development project'.

14   Henry Cleaver, 'The Contradictions of the Green Revolution', *Monthly Review*, 24 (2) (1972).

15   Cecilia Ng, 'Gender and the division of labour', (1985).

16   Studies of rural women in Africa point to their important contribution in agricultural production and processing. Nearer to home, rice cultivation in the state of Kelantan is also predominantly a female responsibility. What these two studies have in common is the vacuum created by the emigration of male labour to mines (in Africa) and factories (in Malaysia) to seek to alleviate their poverty-stricken conditions. For further details see Maria Rosa Cutrufelli, *Women of Africa* (Zed Press, London, 1983), and Janet Rodenburg, *Women and Padi Farming: Sociological Study of a Village in the Kemubu Scheme* (University of Amsterdam, 1983).

17   This important issue is brought up by Ben White (1985) who sees this as a possible trend with adverse implications for rural women. See his article entitled 'Women and the modernization of rice agriculture: some general issues and a Javanese case study', in *Women and Rice Farming*.

18   This point is also brought up by Hart in the Muda region about the nature of labour circulation. However, she also cautions us that women's 'major role in farm management does not necessarily ensure their control over farm income', since by returning to the village during harvest time they do take charge of the marketing and proceeds of the crop: Gillian Hart, 'The mechanisation of Malaysian rice production: will petty producers survive?', Working Paper, World Employment Programme Research, International Labour Office, Geneva, 1987.

19   In the Krian area I was suitably impressed with the wide knowledge the women there had of the different padi varieties used within the past ten years. They could name about fifteen different varieties and could differentiate their growing patterns, plant structure, and so on.

REFERENCES

Abdul Halim Taib (1963) 'Tanjong Karang Survey – Phase II: Socio-economic survey of Sawah Sempadan, a study of Blocks E, Q, S, W'. Graduation Exercise, University of Malaya, Kuala Lumpur.

Agarwal, Bina (1985) 'Women and technological change in agriculture: the Asian and African experience', in Iftikar Ahmed (ed.), *Technology and Rural Women: Conceptual and Empirical Issues*, George Allen & Unwin, London.

Cleaver, Henry (1972) 'The Contradictions of the Green Revolution', *Monthly Review*, 24 (2).

Cutrufelli, Maria (1983) *Women of Africa*, Zed Press, London.

Dagoy, Fe (1988) *Wives' Work Roles in Two Padi-Farming Villages in Malaysia*, Masters' thesis draft, Centre for Extension and Continuing Education, Universiti Pertanian Malaysia, Selangor.

Fredericks, Leo (1977), 'Patterns of labour utilization and income distribution in rice double cropping system: policy implications', Occasional Papers on Malaysian Socio-economic Affairs, no. 8, Faculty of Economics and Administration, University of Malaya.

Government of Malaysia (1986) *Fifth Malaysia Plan 1986–1990*, Government Printers, Kuala Lumpur.

Hart, Gillian (1987) 'The mechanisation of Malaysian rice production: will petty producers survive?', Working Paper, World Employment Programme Research, International Labour Office, Geneva.

Kada, Ryohei and Kada, Yukiki (1985) 'The changing role of women in Japanese agriculture: the impact of new rice technology on women's employment', in *Women in Rice Farming*, International Rice Research Institute, Philippines.

Ng, Cecilia (1985) 'Gender and the division of labour: a case study, in Hing Ai Yun and R. Talib (eds), *Women and Employment in Malaysia*, Kuala Lumpur.

(1987) 'Agricultural modernization and gender differentiation in a rural Malay community, 1983–1987', in Cecilia Ng (ed.), *Technology and Gender*, Universiti Pertanian Malaysia, Serdang.

Ohki, Reiko (1985) 'Women's labour and the technological development of rice cultivation in Japan', in *Women in Rice Farming*, International Rice Research Institute, Philippines.

Pejabat Pengarah Projek Barat Laut Selangor (1986) 'Brief information on the Northwest Selangor Integrated Agricultural Development Project', July.

Reys, Lyda (1985) 'Changing labor patterns of women in rice farm households: a rainfed rice village, Iloilo Province, Philippines', in *Women in Rice Farming*, International Rice Research Institute, Philippines.

Rodenburg, Janet (1983) *Women and Padi Farming: a Sociological Study of a Village in the Kemubu Scheme*, University of Amsterdam.

White, Ben (1985) 'Women and the modernization of rice agriculture: some general issues and a Javanese case study', in *Women and Rice Farming*, International Rice Research Institute, Philippines.

Chapter Ten

WOMEN AND THEIR FAMILIES IN THE MOVEMENT FOR AGRICULTURAL COLLECTIVISATION IN VIETNAM

Le Thi Nham Tuyet

BACKGROUND

The movement for agricultural collectivisation in Vietnam began in the North (lying between latitudes 17° and 23°22′) in 1958, and it has undergone different stages of development: setting up low-level co-operatives (1958–60); building high-level co-operatives (1960–5); now, after the completion of collectivisation, the movement embarked on consolidating and perfecting co-operatives with the form of 'contractual quota system' (taken since 1981)[1]. In the South (which lies between latitudes 17° and 8°30′), though the movement was officially started in 1977, it has initially taken shape in liberated areas before 1975 and now it has been in the flush of satisfactory and healthy development.

In some aspects, this movement belongs to the 'Revolution in the relations of production', while in others, it is considered part of the 'scientific and mechanical revolution' and the 'ideological and cultural revolution'. For Vietnamese women and their families, the three revolutions are of greater significance as they seem to serve as a broader 'social environment' embracing a narrower one, the movement for agricultural collectivisation (MAC). There were, however, at least two other movements coinciding with the MAC: the movement for 'socialist industrialisation' (which, to some extent, means urbanisation) and the 'anti-US imperialist movement for national salvation', which was specified for women as the 'Five Good' emulation movement (1961–5),[2] and then the 'Three Responsibilities' movement (1965–5).[3] These movements were of historical significance. Together with the MAC these movements exerted a great impact on Vietnamese women and their families that should not be underestimated, which however, is beyond the scope of this chapter.

211

The MAC has actually become an important revolutionary movement in Vietnam's countryside. It has involved women and their households in drastic changes in economic, political, cultural and social fields. As a result, the women and their families have made enormous contributions to building, consolidating and developing the movement.

This chapter will deal with the MAC in North Vietnam, since we are not able to present here all the facts and figures concerning the movement in the South. However, we do hope that it still can give an outline of the general situation and deal with major problems related to women and their families in the course of agricultural collectivisation in Vietnam.

AGRICULTURAL COLLECTIVISATION

Before the MAC started, 89.34 per cent of Vietnamese women were peasants in the private sector. In the course of agricultural collectivisation, 45.8 per cent of Vietnamese women have been employees in public offices and state-run factories (as compared with 5 per cent in 1954). Women workers, including those working at state farms, account for 67.5 per cent of the total workforce in agriculture, 65 per cent in light industry and 61 per cent in the food and foodstuff industry. Their participation in other services and mass organisations is also considerable, such as 60 per cent in education and 56.7 per cent in art and cultural service (in which many women are writers, poets, stage directors and art critics). A great number of women have joined the army (among them many have become officers and voluntarily served the army for good). The MAC has, thus, drawn a good number of women from agricultural production for non-agricultural services, lowering the ratio of women peasants in the whole social structure. It is, however, necessary to say that the retrospective influence of women workers, who originally were farmers, on those women who still live on farming is also considerable.

In the course of agricultural collectivisation, the Vietnamese women – once almost 100 per cent illiterate – have caught up with men with regard to their standard of primary and secondary education. Women graduated from universities and colleges account for 39 per cent of the total with many having obtained postgraduate degrees. They are working in various public offices and factories or joining the army. However, about half of Vietnamese women still stay in their home villages and take part in agricultural production. The MAC has, therefore, also created favourable conditions for considerably improving the intellectual quality of Vietnamese women in general and those in rural areas in particular.

However, the most fundamental point is the change in peasant women's social position. From being private peasants, they have now become collective masters of social and production (economic) units, which employ tens of thousands of work-hands to till thousands of hectares of cultivated land, and which have, besides agricultural production, practised many other collectively-run side-line occupations such as handicrafts, fishery, forestry and trade. Peasant women have thereby become real masters of these units. They are taking part in a variety of work, including organisation, management, business practice and allocation of labour.

Right from the beginning of the MAC, which coincided with the revolution in the relations of production in agriculture, three principles – namely, 'voluntariness', 'mutual benefits' and 'democratic management' – were introduced, in which the first principle is the kingpin of scientific character. The MAC has helped liquidate the system of private ownership of land, eradicate the exploiting class, and build the system of public and collective ownership in agriculture. Women played a very active role in this revolution, the most profound in its socio-economic form. More than 90 per cent of peasant women voluntarily applied to join co-operatives, and they have become a powerful workforce of collective labour. (In many places, they make up 60 per cent of the co-operative's workforce, and the figure rises to 80 or 90 per cent in some places.) Experienced in farming, they have played a decisive role in the development of agricultural production[4] and in the building of co-operatives. Tens of thousands of women have been elected to managerial boards of co-operatives, many of them are entrusted with the post of the co-operative's managers or deputy managers, while hundreds of thousands of others have been appointed as heads of production teams or other leading positions of marketing and credit co-operatives.

The MAC has not only liberated women from class oppression and exploitation but also freed them from the backward customs and practices bequeathed by the old feudal and colonialist regimes. That is why Vietnamese women have spared no efforts to build and consolidate their co-operatives. However, during the lengthy course of collectivisation, things have not always run smoothly. The women had to become involved in criticism and self-criticism in order to help promote their sense of collective mastery. These activities are not only aimed at enforcing the co-operative's rules and regulations (adopted by all co-operative members at their congresses– but also at improving and perfecting them.[5] At times, the women have to persuade their husbands to give up their conservative methods.

The collectivisation of agriculture is always linked with the peasants' comprehension and the application of science and techniques in order to boost production.[6] In this connection, such questions as irrigation and drainage, fertiliser quality, improved farm tools, livestock breeding techniques and sowing, transplanting and harvesting techniques have captured the attention of peasants who stand in the vanguard of the struggle against conservative and backward farming practices. In the early days of collectivisation, for instance, when new farm tools were introduced, many people were suspicious of their usefulness and were afraid of costly investment, it was the women who secretly tried them on rice-fields on moon-lit nights and when they testified to the superiority of the new tools over the old ones, all the doubts and fears of co-operative members were cleared. Another example can be found in the movement of intensive cultivation and application of new techniques in the selection of rice seeds and in transplanting. Young women make up 80 per cent of technical teams in co-operatives.[7]

The introduction of scientific and technical progress in agricultural production is of much greater significance for women of ethnic minorities living in mountainous regions where farming is still very hard work, with low and unstable productivity, and where backward habits and superstitions still hinder the application of new techniques (not only in farming but in many other social fields).[8] In the process of agricultural collectivisation, women of ethnic minorities have not only engaged in all the activities of co-operatives, such as production, cultural, scientific and educational services, but have also participated in the building of new industrial centres in mountainous regions in the service of agriculture and worked in state farms, local offices and factories. They have, therefore, changed their lives. From a life which was fenced in by wild forests and mountains, they have now learned to operate machines and have eventually become skilled workers and engineers. Together with other changes, this change has brought new life to peasant women in Vietnam's mountainous regions. The socialisation and division of labour in accordance with state plans have gradually taken shape and enhanced the collective dignity of peasant women. That is the spirit – all for one and one for all. Together with a new style of work (well-organised, disciplined and technically guided), that spirit has created favourable conditions for each peasant woman to make better contributions to the cause of building a new countryside.[9]

On the other hand, while discharging the assignments of society, women are, in return, given due attention in various domains by that society. Social services have been instituted widely in rural areas in the form of marketing and credit co-operatives and so on. Material provisions for daily life and production of peasant women and their families are supplied by different services of each co-operative. In addition, there are many other social welfare facilities such as hospitals (dispensaries and maternity homes), crèches, kindergartens, schools, clubs, libraries, cultural houses, traditional houses (local museums), amateur art groups, mobile projection teams and so forth. Women's demands for artistic and cultural entertainments have also been better met, though these have not yet been completely met and are still unsatisfactory due to many difficulties and shortages in the country. However, the progress and fundamental changes which have improved women's social position in the course of the MAC are of great significance.

FAMILY LIFE

Agricultural collectivisation has brought about changes in women's families. In the course of agricultural collectivisation, the family no longer retains all the functions it had in the past, functions closely associated with the private ownership of means of production which was characterised by autarchy and spontaneity. The so-called 'household economic sector' in present day Vietnam is a component of the socialist economy. It is aimed at partially improving the economic life of the household. However, it is no more limited within the side-line occupations which earn more income in order to meet the daily needs. Today, together with state and collective economic sectors, the household economic sector takes part in social production. The household economic sector is now really accelerating the production of material wealth for the society and has become an important part in the reorganisation of production, the development of productive forces and the consolidation of socialist relations of production. The socio-economic functions of a new family, which at present still depend on side-line jobs practised by its female members, have brought about not only changes in various elements of women's social life but also an improvement in their position in family life as well. And, together with other factors, these changes have helped to abolish many old, backward customs and the former life-style of rural families.

With the change in the functions of the household economic sector and the gradual perfection of the new productive forces, there is no longer a need for large families, comprising many persons of different generations, and there are now an increasing number of small families. Demographic figures concerning families have been split into smaller units, each including a father, mother and their children, or a father, mother and their oldest son's own family.[10] In country families in Vietnam at present there are five or six persons. The aspiration for an independent existence for small families, separated from their larger components (which is that of 84.5 per cent of fathers and mothers in rural areas now) is, however, relieved of many difficulties and complications formerly vested in the women.

215

Parallel to the tendency of reducing family size is the change in the social attitudes of young people of marriageable age. The preparation for an independent family life automatically requires a higher age for marriage. Thus, immature marriage has now become a thing of the past.[11] The following table shows the average age of marriage in Vietnam:

TABLE 10.1   Average age of marriage in rural Vietnam

Sex	Before 1960	1960–4	1965–9	1970–5	1975-80
Male	23.6	24.5	24.7	23.0	23.0
Female	20.1	24.0	22.8	26.7	21.0

The rise in the age of marriage among rural young people is due to the impact of various socio-economic factors, the most important of which is the development of the collective economic sector and the socialisation of labour in the countryside. Besides the aforesaid fundamental changes, the agricultural collectivisation that we are discussing has also created important changes in education,[12] in Vietnam's rural areas, the family has assumed among others a function of great social significance, that is, to rear and educate the children. In fact, that work has been paid much attention not only by members of every family but also by the whole society.

Many parents in rural areas have become aware that this function is of both a social significance and a scientific character. With the new idea that the young generation must be educated to become fully developed persons in all fields (moral, intellectual, physical, aesthetic and occupational), parents at the same time reject bringing up their children with underlying obsolete concepts. Such parents think that they cannot bring up their children well with such old maxims as 'spare the rod and spoil the children', 'bad behaviour should only be corrected at home' and 'parents care for their children by themselves alone'. They now deem it necessary to promote joint efforts, and for that reason, they have set up an organisation called 'The Parents' Society', serving to connect school and family in order to improve social education. Such organisations are backed by the co-operative through its mass medium in order to disseminate scientific knowledge and experience concerning education. In that sense, family education is no longer a separate undertaking but it has actually become a component part of the whole process of building new kinds of people in the countryside. The changes in the role played by mothers in rural areas in the eduction of their own children are obviously considerable, and differ from the former concept of women as representing the 'beauty and virtue' of the family but who had no actual weight in its affairs and were fully dependent on their husbands.[13] In today's collectivised countryside the women, with their greater role in social production, have all round a higher footing because of their higher intellectual standard.[14] Modern social conditions have opened up new ways for women in rearing and educating their children. They have learnt not only effective methods of educating children[15] but also scientific measures for taking better care of children and sick people. Manifestations of superstition and the outbreak of contagious diseases have been much fewer than in the past.

I have mentioned above some fundamental changes in the structure and functions of rural families in the course of agricultural collectivisation in Vietnam. Yet, a more important change is that Vietnamese women have now found for themselves factors of a new life in each family – the fundamental cell of society – where they play a constructive and creative role. Among those factors are real equality, mutual help, genuine love and judicious respect among family members of opposite sexes. The communal life, with wholesome collective and high social character, has thus rendered obsolete the paternalism of the large families of the past, which entitled the father or the oldest son to the right to inherit all the property and even decide the destiny of every female member of the family. Gone are the days when husbands could legally beat, insult and even betray their wives. Gone also are the scenes of jealousy between the first wife and concubines or the exchanges of sharp and vulgar words between mothers and their daughters-in-law. and there is no longer the scene once described by a folk saying, how sad it is for those women who suffer like a half-felled bamboo.[16] With agricultural collectivisation, rural women's contributions to their families are, for the first time, duly considered. They turn out, more often than not, to earn more than the male members of their families. And, where favourable conditions are already created, rural women are becoming family chiefs, playing a leading role in bringing to reality the new functions of their families. That is why their voice in household affairs is now completely different from what once was described in a saying as the explosion of a burnt bamboo tube in the depth of the jungle. It has become a voice full of trust and commanding respect.

CONCLUSION

I have sketched some glimpses of the fundamental changes, chiefly positive, in the role of Vietnamese rural women and their families in the MAC. In fact, the question is much more diversified and the improvement in women's roles faces many difficulties and there are many shortcomings in the process of execution, especially in the struggle to eradicate the legacies of the feudal ideology and the influence of non-proletarian trends formed in some social strata, including those women who have an inferiority complex because they set more store by men than women. However, it is impossible that those ideologies and influences can be rooted out overnight. It would also be unfair to become sceptical of the whole trend of development of our time just because of some shortcomings in certain of its aspects.

The fact is that in Vietnam the emancipation of women, especially rural women, measured by the achievement of equality between women and men in all socio-economic respects, has made substantial progress and, in fact, an unprecedented advance. The enhancement of women's roles in all fields of social and family life has long been a state policy, enforced by various social, economic and juridical measures, among which agricultural collectivisation is of paramount importance. These facts allow us to come to another conclusion: it will be possible to effect the emancipation of women even before the industrialisation of the economy, and this emancipation will become a source of active backing to such industrialisation.

NOTES

1   The contractual quota system is a mode of economic management in the production and distribution of goods. It is based on economic and technical quotas allocated to each co-operative member according to the principle of remunerations and bonuses according to the amount of work done.

2   The 'Five Good' movement called for good solidarity, production and thrift; good observation of government policies; good knowledge of politics, culture and techniques; good handling of one's own family and children; and good participation in economic management.

3   The 'Three Responsibilities' movement encouraged women to be capable of production and work; of family affairs, and of fighting and serving the struggle.

4   The great success in reaching the target rice output of 5 tons per hectare (especially during the anti-US war) was, in the main, due to women: in 1965, 1,200 co-operatives reached that target; in 1972, 3,768; and in 1974, nine northern provinces did so.

5   Regulations banning careless work, encouraging conscious work and observation of technical requirements.

6   The process of peasants' comprehension and the application of technical progress in their production in North Vietnam could be generalised, having developed through four stages:

   1   1958–60: the peasants began to join co-operatives and started to learn new techniques;

   2   1961–5: the peasants participated the first Five Year Plan and began to apply new farming techniques widely;

3   1965–73: the peasants took part in the struggle against the US air war of destruction, and, at the same time, increased their knowledge of science and techniques and combined them in the improvement of their economic management; and

4   since 1973: the peasants have carried out the reorganisation of production and, at the same time, promoted their knowledge of science and techniques to new heights.

7   In production emulation movements in co-operatives, hundreds of women have been recognised as 'Emulation Fighter', eleven have been awarded the 'Heroine of Labour' title, and thousands of production units awarded the title of 'Unit of Socialist Labour'.

8   Old and backward customs have prevented women of ethnic minorities from ploughing and harrowing (H'mong, Dzao); growing cotton and making fabrics (Phula, Cosung Puoc).

9   From the early years of the MAC, women of competence were assigned to various tasks of managing co-operatives. Many of them have won the trust of co-operative members and have been re-elected time and again to the co-operative's managerial board. Many others were elected to higher administrative posts in their village, district or province, and even entrusted with assignments of much more importance.

10 A sociological survey on families shows that in Tam Son village, Ha Bac province, families of two generations account for 72 per cent, while those of three generations 25.6 per cent, and those of one generation 1.6 per cent (according to Mrs Nguyên Thi Quang's documents).

In Dong Duong village, Thai Binh province, families of two generations make up 90.3 per cent, families of three generations, 6.7 per cent; and families of one generation 3.1 per cent (ibid.).

11 According to Nguyen Khanh Bich Trâm's documents.

12 In the early years after the revolution and during the anti-US war the state was in no position to afford all the financial needs of the educational field, and most of the basic general education and complementary schools had to be financed by co-operative welfare funds.

13 In patriarchal families of the past, a woman had to follow the traditional custom of 'three obediences': before marriage, obedience to her father; on being married, to obey her husband; and after the husband's death, to obey her eldest son.

14 According to Mrs Nĝuyên Thi Huong, a recent sociological survey of the countryside shows that the difference in basic education knowledge between young men and women has been bridged, while that in secondary education is insignificant.

15 Most members of 'Parents' Societies' in the countryside are women. The majority of rural women, irrespective of their ages, have attended various courses on motherhood regularly held by the Vietnam Women's Union.

16 A comparison of a woman in a desperate situation when she can neither die of grief nor recover from all her sufferings and just flickers on like a helpless 'half-felled bamboo tree'.

Part Three

RESOURCES, SKILL AND WAGED EMPLOYMENT: THE INDIAN EXPERIENCE

Chapter Eleven

THE INTEGRATED RURAL DEVELOPMENT PROGRAMME FOR WOMEN IN DEVELOPING COUNTRIES: WHAT MORE CAN BE DONE? A CASE STUDY FROM INDIA

Leena Mehendale

SUMMARY

Women are always the worst sufferers from any social evil or economic constraints. In the Third World countries which are passing through difficult phases, especially with widening income inequalities, the number of exploited and exploitable women is increasing. The Integrated Rural Development Program (IRDP)[1] is one of the very few programmes available for any poverty-ridden group of women. But it puts great emphasis on self-employment without recognising and providing for all the aspects of self-employment. The present success story points out the role of beneficial motivation, leadership, managerial efficiency and personal involvement in the greater use of the IRDP for women beneficiaries. It also suggests that such programmes have a better chance of success if women officers occupy more significant posts, in larger numbers, in administration rather than being confined merely to a social welfare of education department.

INTRODUCTION

The Integrated Rural Development Programme, popularly known as IRDP, is being tried as an important strategy by many developing countries in their attempts to alleviate poverty and reduce inequalities of income. This chapter concerns a case study in which the benefits of

223

the IRDP were extended to some groups of socially and economically exploited women called *devdasis*. The case study is important because it poses many questions regarding the underlying assumptions of the IRDP, especially in the context of women beneficiaries. It suggests ways in which the IRDP can be modified better in order to achieve its objectives. It illustrates the developmental role of the public sector and possible problems faced due to its bureaucratic structure. It shows how leadership, organisational efficiency and motivation of beneficiaries act as key prerequisites for the success of any potential development programme. Lastly, it also provides some guidelines for voluntary agencies.

This chapter will give a short background of *devdasis*, the women who are the focus of this case. It will then give an account of the structure of the bureaucratic machine in India and its role in implementing the IRDP. This will be followed by an account of how the IRDP was used for the rehabilitation of *devdasis*, the barriers encountered and the story of the final success. While so doing, it will highlight some important issues regarding programme implementation and gender considerations.

THE CUSTOM OF DEVDASIS

Indian society is characterised by exploitation which has been perpetuated because of poverty, illiteracy and deep-set traditions whose sanctity has not been effectively questioned. One such tradition is the custom of *devdasis*. These are women who were offered or sacrificed to God in early childhood by the parents in order to ensure family well-being against the perceived anger of God, or, more importantly, in order to ask for a son. Although there is no basis for this system in the Hindu religious scriptures and though the custom has been banned by law, every year nearly 10,000 girls are thus offered to God. The offering takes place ceremonially on all full moon days at the Renuka temple at Soundatti in Karnataka state, but only on Pausha Pournima (the day of the full moon in February) at a few other Renuka temples. In some cases the girls are offered as family tradition. The daughters of *devdasis* are also normally offered. Tradition and superstition ban them from marrying and settling down to a normal life, and finally they often succumb to prostitution and begging.

To my mind the *devdasis* qualify to be called the most deprived class of the society. They lack money and education, they have the disadvantage of their sex and scheduled caste, and coming from villages they also miss the exposure to modern conveniences which are known, if not available, to the urban poor. They cannot acquire the social status of a married woman and secure family life. To top all this is their own mental barrier of superstition which stops them from aspiring to better life.

In the past twenty years some social and voluntary organisations have started undertaking programmes for the uplifting of *devdasis*. Their main emphasis has been on social and health aspects. Their efforts include regular medical guidance to *devdasis*, organising them, settling them in married life and removing superstition. Economic rehabilitation was tried in the present programme because it was felt that the poor succumb to this tradition because it partly solves the problem of their livelihood.

Devdasis live in groups in villages, with older ones acting as chaperones, although nowadays it is not uncommon for them to stay with their parents. They have no rights in the family, least of all the right to property, but the parents have a right to their income because they provide them with lodging, boarding and shelter. They have no right to marry but they can and do live as the kept women of wealthy clients. Most of the offered girls, aged between four years and their early twenties, eventually land up in the flesh market of big cities, but many stay back in the villages. Some return at old age. They have to go begging for alms in the name of the goddess at least on Tuesdays and Fridays, and on several occasions they have to visit the temple of Renuka, spending day and night singing and dancing before the deity. For survival they mostly resort to prostitution and unskilled jobs. They also have to provide for their children.

It is estimated that every year 8,000–10,000 girls or women are offered. The system is prevalent in the states of Karnataka, Tamilnadu, Andhra Pradesh, Goa and parts of Maharashtra. The girls are offered by their parents, and rites are performed by temple priests in spite of many laws declaring both the acts as crimes. Most parents are extremely poor, uneducated, superstitious and are from scheduled classes, though some offerings are also made from other communities. There are many variations in the reasons leading to the offerings, the rites to be performed, the subsequent living arrangements of the women, their means of survival and so on. But the common factor is the cause of perpetuation, which is undoubtedly poverty combined with superstition and lack of education.

THE IRDP

The Integrated Rural Development Programme is intended to assist the rural population. A specially conducted survey of families living in poverty, conducted in 1980, showed that nearly 350 million (48 per cent) people live below the poverty line, out of whom 300 million are in rural areas. These families consist largely of landless labourers, small and marginal farmers and rural artisans who have, to a large extent, lost their traditional skills and earning power because of the lack of upgrading of skills and unfavourable competition from industrial production. Since most of the women were traditionally engaged as partners with the male artisans, and suffer worse from this poverty-accentuating phenomenon, the IRDP could play a special role for them. The programme has three areas of emphasis. One is to give bank finance to individual beneficiaries whose families are listed as living below the poverty line, for the creation or purchase of assets such as irrigation wells, cows or machinery. Of the cost 25 per cent comes from the government as a subsidy, which banks treat as equity to give an additional 75 per cent as a loan. The second part is to run short-term vocational courses under a scheme called TRYSEM (Training of Rural Youth in Self-employment). The third is to create infrastructure for the use of a group of beneficiaries. Normally a budget of 15 million rupees ($1 million) is available per district per year for subsidy disbursement, TRYSEM expenses and infrastructure creation. The programme is implemented for the district as a unit. A senior officer of the Indian Administrative Service (IAS) is in charge of a district unit.[2]

THE JAT EXPERIENCE

Attempts to rehabilitate *devdasis)* in the present case were first started in 1984 when, as Collector of Sangli district, I attempted to prevent the ritual of offering *devdasi* girls at a *taluka*[3] called Jat. These attempts met with opposition from village leaders, priests and older *devdasis*, all of whom came to the village to perform several tasks during the ritual, and who have a vested interest in the perpetuation of the system (older *devdasis* are supported financially by the younger *devdasis*). The resistance died down quickly, once they realised that I was prepared to use the Devdasi Abolition Act to arrest them. They had never faced such a threat before. Secondly, there were many local level politicians in the group who did not want to be seen before a woman collector as the perpetuators of an evil system that undermined the dignity of women. Jat is a small place; similar action later created a violent situation at Soundatti, and a show of force or threats of arrest have not worked there.

I also had a meeting with about fifty *devdasis* whom I had arranged to call from other villages. We discussed issues of human dignity and self-respect, social rights and their deprivation, the questions of religion and faith and superstition – all abstract principles – till one of them asked 'What alternatives will society offer to us?' They were roused at least to argue and think of alternatives. I grabbed the opportunity, and registered them as trainees under TRYSEM, by making an exception to the rule that they should have passed at least seventh standard. They were all illiterate. When training was offered, they came forward to meet our challenge. They were registered for a three-month poultry training course. This case study deals with the second and subsequent groups of trainees who were in the making of knitwear and in other occupations.

In order to understand why subsequent training batches were successful, something may be said about the first training batch. They could not utilise their training and start their own poultry units. In that sense the attempt was a failure. Although the IRDP is intended precisely for people like the *devdasis*, in many ways it was an unusual attempt and was thwarted with many queries, lack of precedents, procedural bottlenecks and so on, which a team of well-meaning officials cannot cope with without risks. A few also feared that I was inviting the wrath of God, to which they must not be a party. Some officials questioned why so much effort should be wasted on *devdasis*. However, the immediate success was that on the last day of training, nearly 100 *devdasis* gathered to request to be enrolled for training. The stamp of failure was not yet put on the first batch. So, I and the CEO decided to organise another group of twenty-six *devdasis* for training in woollen knitwear.

THE CHALLENGE

During their training I had insisted on one condition: that they would not go begging for alms, because this would be the biggest affront to their self-respect. Did they continue with prostitution during the night? I would not ask. Should I have tried to stop it? I have asked myself this question only once and have, since then, fully believed in my answer: in a society which denies then fulfilment of their financial, physical and social needs, I, as a privileged member of that society, have no right to put that condition. My boundaries could be stretched only up to offering them alternatives from which they must choose themselves. With my government job I could offer them an alternative way of earning and I could not even claim that it was better in monetary terms. But the training might break down their social barriers and superstitions, and bring an awareness of their potential to learn and do something worthwhile. That would be the reward, even if they continued in prostitution.

Our second training programme (March 1988) was started in machine knitwear. We faced typical problems – how to get vocational trainers who were prepared to live in a village for six months? Whether or not these were good teachers? This question arose because under the TRYSEM programme it is neither possible, nor I think advisable, to have a cadre of trainers. To give high and regular remuneration to the trainers, which in the past has not always occurred, is essential. Their own motivation is also extremely necessary.

Moreover, could they train a totally illiterate group? Could the trainees be asked to spend additional time on literacy lessons? Is money available under TRYSEM to cover the salary of a special literacy teacher? (No, it is not.) The training in operating a knitting machine had obvious, recognisable economic prospects, but what was the use of literacy classes? This question was asked both by the trainees and the TRYSEM authorities. These questions are faced in all TRYSEM programmes, and the success of such programmes in developing countries will depend on whether their bureaucratic structures can provide a systematic answer to them.

A further question was one regarding the attitude of the banks. Even in India, where banks are nationalised and have directives regarding making some definite lending under the IRDP, banks will prefer to process loan cases in order to benefit small or marginal farmers who have been engaged in agriculture in the past. Loans can be given for cattle-keeping or a shop or a photographic unit. All these loans are given to those who are already in that occupation, and the loan strengthens them economically. But, where a new skill is to be acquired, banks are reluctant to give loans to trainees who have no previous experience. How can banks give finance for capital investment without asking what was the guarantee that the *devdasis* would complete training and that they would be adequately trained and thereafter could market their goods? What guarantee can be given by the *devdasis*, or by any voluntary organisation prepared to run their training programme, or by a collector (who can be transferred the next day)? Such problems have arisen and have been solved in certain cases in which the crucial factor seems to be the personal initiative of the organiser. They are not solved routinely and certainly not without much persuasion. The answers are not available within the given pattern of the IRDP. So long as that remains the case the benefits of the IRDP cannot be widespread.

Other vocational courses are also run under TRYSEM. They may be tailoring, carpet-weaving, pottery or shoe-making; I am talking of all those vocations where the final product must be approved and purchased by the consumer. These courses are run not only under TRYSEM but also by other institutions for vocational training.[4] What happens to the trainees later? Most developing countries do not have a system whereby they can follow up cases, and in India we do not have statistics about the future pursuits of the trainees.

This brings us to a much more important question. These training courses assume that the trainees inherently possess four skills: first, of marketing their goods; second, of inventory control; third, of correctly pricing the product; and fourth, of managing working capital – and all they need to be taught is some vocational skill. The courses are therefore typically devoid of any entrepreneurial or managerial development component. In our training programme it was sharply becoming clear that within the funding pattern of TRYSEM it was not possible to appoint extra staff who would keep the accounts or suggest designing and market strategies or who would liaise with banks. The important point to make here is that rural development departments are normally not orientated towards commercial management, and hence the IRDP in its present form in India will not achieve much towards self-employment unless the aspects of business management and project management are emphasised, both among the implementors and the beneficiaries.[5]

Lastly, there are always problems related to implementation. When large quantities of training material are needed, as in this vocational course, the funding is not adequate. The cost of repair and maintenance of machines is not provided. If the training needs to be extended, extra money is not provided. In spite of all this, the IRDP is the only existing programme which contains some hope for a group like the *devdasis*.

In short, the trainee group at Jat faced the problem of banks not giving loans initially, then the trainer moving away leaving behind a semi-trained mechanic, the raw material being quickly exhausted and not replenished, and so on.

THE INTEGRATED APPROACH

During the training project I was transferred[6] to the post of managing director of the Western Maharashtra Development Corporation (WMDC), which is a public-sector undertaking of the government of Maharashtra based in Pune under the Department of Industries. Its responsibility is to promote balanced industrial growth, especially of small-scale industries. I recognised that I could use the industrial and promotional activities of the WMDC to combine with the *devdasi* training programme at Jat. It was a lucky coincidence that I was posted to the WMDC, whose geographical jurisdiction included Sangli district. What I was planning and advocating was new; namely, to combine the organisational skills and capacity of financial investment of the WMDC with the rural, woman-orientated training programme. Many people doubted the wisdom of doing so, but luckily I won the support of the chairman of the board (who is a politician) and the officers of the WMDC, who were willing to share this extra burden.

Many outside the WMDC felt that this activity was best left to someone in the Rural Development or Social Welfare Department, since in their view it could not be considered as industrial development. My argument was that those departments do not have managerial and entrepreneurial skills, which is the main factor missing in the training and management of rural development programmes. I pointed out that as soon as the training was over these women would need working capital, marketing arrangements and accounting skills. They would thus need to become entrepreneurs and on their own they could be successful.

Such debates are inevitable in administration. But I was surprised by the attitude of many senior colleagues, who would ridicule my efforts by claiming that no person working in the Department of Industries needed to concern themselves with these downtrodden women, as the department was meant for high-flying industrialists, and that the *devdasis* would be better left to the Social Welfare Department. I was told that I was attaching too much personal emotion to the whole issue, which meant that I was not able to come out of my complex of being a woman and so on. On the other hand, many officers supported my efforts precisely because I was promoting the cause of needy women and they shared my concern for them. Perhaps I did get emotionally attached to the project, which I think is necessary for implementing any project successfully. This case has taught me that a detached efficiency is not always the best tool for achieving development, as is normally believed in the running of bureaucracy.

We started by giving the trainees of Jat an order for knitwear with some money in advance (about £2,000). The results were very good. The trainer mechanic, who was also by this time frustrated and prepared to quit, decided to stay on. Attendance improved. The trainees started to discuss marketable colour combinations. The government allowed an extension of the training period for a further six months with costs. The WMDC used the knitwear for a market survey. Costing, accounting and even procurement of input and transportation were all arranged by the WMDC. It was, in a true sense, the nurturing of an infant industry. When the first batch of knitwear received a good response, the WMDC thought of larger participation.

During this period the WMDC also used the help of a voluntary agency named Bhagini Nivedita Pratishthan Sangli, whose participation could not continue for long because they had a staff shortage. Also, their main field was nutrition and the health care of pre-school children. Since then I have been acutely aware of two factors that undermine the working and potential of voluntary agencies. First is their lack of voluntary workers, resulting perhaps from their paucity of funds, and second is the lack of managerial ability, efficiency and technical knowledge of their well-meaning and hard-working volunteers. These qualities are as necessary as sincerity. The combination of sincerity with knowledge and efficiency is extremely rare. But is it less rare or less needed in government jobs?

Next, the WMDC prepared a scheme to run a training-cum-production centre for the *devdasi* trainees. The idea was that this scheme would run for three years, during which the WMDC would invest money and provide all support, like accounting, inventory management, marketing and so on. These services were identified as crucial. The scheme would need an investment of nearly $50,000.

We were faced with two sets of questions, some bureaucratic (a few of them arising from my own bureaucratic rigidities) and some having much wider implications. The bureaucratic questions were the most trivial and the most time-consuming. For example, why are the *devdasis* not being trained instead in vegetable-selling? Or did the programme come within the purview of the Department of Industries, or of Social Welfare or of Rural Development, and if it was not of the former, then why should the others accept the methodology of someone in another department? Thus, the WMDC had to enter into lengthy correspondence with several departments before funds for this scheme were given by the Woman and Child Welfare Department of the Government of India.

What I want to point out is that this is not a unique situation. In all developing countries such conflicts (and, no doubt, many others) will arise because of the limitations of bureaucracy. Traditionally, bureaucracy is characterised by accountability, which means that one must be seen to be acting strictly within the given job description and within the set rules of financial control. This ignores two aspects vitally important in any development programme. First, every development programme will require the co-ordination of functions of many departments, out of which only one will have to be accepted as the 'lead department' for one project. This should not lead the other departments to withdraw their support. In the present age of specialisation, all government sectors must draw from the expertise of one another rather than try to build up their own cadres in every field. The second aspect concerns financial propriety. Financial rules are necessary in order to prevent misuse of the vast funds which a government officer handles. However, because the present rules do not recognise the element of risk in any development project, they insist that any project selected for implementation must be in effect 100 per-cent risk-free. This is never possible, but because of this approach there is no attempt or methodology to quantify a reasonable risk, or assess possible areas of failure. Thus there can be no risk monitoring during the implementation of the programme.

While tackling these issues in December 1986 the WMDC had started another training group in knitting at Gadhinglaj in Kolhapur District for forty trainees. Gadhinglaj *taluka* has an estimated *devdasi* population of 5,000, whereas their population in Jat is about 500. This training was also funded by DRDA of Kolhapur District and supplemented by the Social Welfare Department. Later (from December 1986 to December 1988) two training groups for silk-reeling and one more for making knitwear were also started. The total number of beneficiaries had thus risen to 120 by December 1988. Thus, despite all initial bottlenecks, the WMDC has systematised a way of using the IRDP more effectively. The trend to involve more women will continue in future years. The number added per year has been deliberately kept low for reasons to be discussed later.

The policy issues have to be settled more carefully and the role of leadership becomes important. The issues must be based on clear philosophical principles if they are to provide continuous guidance. The first principle in selecting trainees was that *devdasis* must feel themselves to be a part of the mainstream of society. So we included 20 per-cent non-*devdasis* in every batch and we also tried to select the *devdasis* from different educational levels. A few *devdasis* have attended schools up to different standards. This was considered necessary so as to have a bigger demonstrational effect on those lagging behind, and has worked out better. Literacy and numeracy had to be a part of their training, and this was found very difficult to impart. We also insisted that each trainee group formed itself into a co-operative society in which the WMDC would be a shareholder but not a sharer of profits accruing to the society. The members would earn wages from the co-operative society according to their output. When the co-operative society published its yearly accounts and declared profits, they would share the profits too. Some part of the profit was to be kept aside by each co-operative society in an educational fund, to be used for future training groups if needed. The WMDC would provide the clerical and managerial support to every batch initially for three to five years.

The members were to train themselves to run the affairs of the society. They had to spend some time in acquiring managerial skills, thus forgoing some wage-earning. This is, of course, too much to demand from an uneducated, unprivileged, downtrodden group of women.

Even well-educated people are not necessarily good managers. Yet, their real emancipation will come only when they are no longer pliable and manageable by others, easily surrendering before all forms of exploitation and victimisation. The *devdasis* also understand this. Each of them has to travel this tough path with endurance and a strong will till she has learned enough to fight further exploitation. The women's learning speed may be slow and different for every individual, but there is no escape from this learning process.

And this brings me to the best part of the project. The desire to learn comes not from the lure of increased earnings: in fact, the *devdasis* earned more when their time was not spent on learning these different skills. The argument that learning will prevent their exploitation is understood by them. Still, this argument was not sufficient in motivating them in learning managerial skills because, in their opinion, if their management continued to be the WMDC, this would, in fact, protect them from exploitation. They would far prefer it if management were to remain with the WMDC forever and if they did not have to train themselves in management. I do not share this view. First, no dependence can be free from exploitation, and second, the burden of this faith would be too heavy on the WMDC. But there is a third and more important reason, which I will discuss shortly.

Their willingness to learn came through self-confidence which we systematically tried to build through personality development programmes. For this purpose we arranged visits by university teachers and students and promoted their mixing with the trainees. We had personality development camps for them lasting from three to seven days, conducted by visiting voluntary organisations. In groups of four or so they were called to Pune for a week's training, during which they were trained by WMDC staff in basic office management skills such as filing, stapling, punching, telling the time, making phone calls, using xerox machines and calculators and such innumerable trivial things which at our level we never notice and at their level they had never seen. Gradually, their interest grew as we took them to secondary and higher levels of learning such as purchasing wool, managing their stalls during exhibitions, making out receipts, marketing their items by procuring small orders, operating their bank accounts, measuring the work output, making wage payments, writing up cash books, visiting other offices, explaining their problems to those officers, and so on. With different speed this has proceeded. Some learned to ride bicycles, and want to learn to drive jeeps. Some are trying photography, some have learned computer data-feeding, and at the end of the day they feed the data of the total work done by each individual. In turns they undertake inspection and quality control. Some have taken an examination in co-operative accounting. Some are appointed as instructors for subsequent trainee groups. A

233

few still have to show any worthwhile progress, but this was to be expected.

As for work quality, the silk reeled by them is sold at the silk exchange in Bangalore (the main silk market in India) for the best prices, while the sale of knitted garments has exceeded $40,000 per year (600,000 rupees). Their average earning is 400 rupees per month. (The Minimum Wage Act prescribes 300 rupees per month as the lower limit.) On the whole the project was very successful.

One reason for the justification of such a great involvement by the WMDC was that here was a group whose members could not be expected to get any benefit from various government schemes, simply because government departments do not know about the *devdasis* (who are unfortunately not the only such group). They cannot knock at the doors of offices to take advantage of various schemes. In that sense the WMDC has acted in the role of a voluntary agency, providing supporting services and also filling short-term financial gaps. The WMDC approached many offices for them, trying to get whatever benefits were available under different schemes. We thus secured a grant of $200,000 for building a working women's hostel for them from the Women and Child Welfare Department. The National Chemicals and Fertiliser Corporation agreed to provide funds for a work shed and nursery, and for expert staff for our proposed training group in forest nursery work. The CEO Sangli built twenty houses for them at Jat under the programme of houses for the homeless. The IRDP agencies in both Sangli and Kolhapur districts gave money for training and subsidies for equipment. Now the Central Silk Board is in a position to support some more programmes in sericultural activities because the World Bank has asked them to undertake women's programmes. In the space of three years the WMDC has been able to integrate the beneficiary programmes of many departments and get not only the money but also their expert staff to use for the benefit of a larger number of devdasis. However, such help is slow to come, so that any other agency which tries to provide a similar co-ordinating service must have its own financial standing and expertise in accounting and marketing dealing, and knowledge of various departments which run different beneficiary programmes. This is especially a guideline for the voluntary agencies.

However, the other side of such support must also be considered. The *devdasis* have often asked why the WMDC must withdraw its support at a later date. The answer, which is obvious to me, is that the role of the WMDC must be limited to that of an initiator in the beginning and as a stand-by in later years. Such work needs staff members who are both dedicated and efficient. No organisation has a large number of them. Hence there has to be a scheme by which the work of these staff members is handed over to a different group, so as to use them for subsequent trainee batches. And those who are taking over must come from the beneficiaries themselves. The WMDC achieved what it did because of the high level of efficiency and dedication of the staff and their sense of immense satisfaction that they were contributing to a vital social cause. Very often I have received useful suggestions from such staff members who were not directly doing this work. Their participation and skills in entrepreneurial management were equally important.

Those who were involved in training, and especially those who were involved in personality development and literacy training, were puzzled as to why I insisted that every beneficiary should be asked to learn everything. Would it not give much quicker results if only a core group was identified as potential managers and was given much more concentrated attention? That can be one way to proceed. However, I would accept a much slower speed if it meant better understanding of the running of the organisation by a larger number, than a system in which a few managed and others remained as ignorant as before and therefore as prone to exploitation as before. That is why we have arranged the training in such a way as to include each beneficiary in the learning process. In my opinion the most important point of this success story is that there is no substitute to learning and no short cuts to the process of learning.

Digressing slightly, I have often seen voluntary agencies running training programmes in a similar way. They either restrict their role to training only, or if they have to get involved with management as well, then they cannot extend their help to more groups because all their manpower is used up just in the management of one group. I do not want to undermine the work of those voluntary agencies which have remained confined to the management of only one group. But it reduces the scope of help by that voluntary organisation. I hope that the example narrated here will suggest a different strategy to voluntary organisations.

Another small digression is about the role of women officers. It would perhaps be wrong to make a generalisation that only women officers can become aware of or sensitive to problems of women trapped in a situation like that of the *devdasis*. In my opinion any officer sensitive to such social problems would have acted similarly. However, I question the normal belief that women officers are only suitable for working in the departments of Social Welfare or Health or Child Care and that they can be more useful in those departments to solve the problems of women. This case shows that the solution to women's problems does not lie necessarily in the schemes of the Social Welfare or Rural Development Department. It is therefore important that women officers be posted in all departments without bias.

There was also the question of giving such market and organisational support to many other groups of educated unemployed, who had been trained for some skills under TRYSEM, but thereafter remained stranded because no attempt was made to develop their entrepreneurial skills. As I said, that component is not built into the training schedule of TRYSEM. Many such groups approached us. Giving these groups support would bring us faster results because they have an educational background. We would have more success stories to our credit. However, to provide comprehensive support to TRYSEM beneficiaries is not the assigned role of the WMDC, it is not the assigned role of anyone. To my mind, this lack of recognition of the need for comprehensive support for trainee groups reduces the potential of programmes like TRYSEM or the IRDP. Many of the public-sector corporations can fill this gap.

Indeed, some have tried it in the past. However, they have been trapped in the roles of permanent managers because they did not have the express policy of withdrawing after an initial period of support. As for the WMDC, as this support which we extended to the *devdasis* was not our assigned role it can be taken up only selectively. The WMDC does not have a large enough staff to undertake similar activity for a large number of groups (at least, not unless it is an assigned role of the WMDC). Till then, it was felt by all in the organisation that we should not worry so much about collecting success stories and should restrict our small capacity to help this most neglected section of the society. Other groups are much higher up in the social hierarchy and have a better chance of survival without the WMDC. However, in the system of the IRDP and TRYSEM, something must be included for them. That is another main point in this case study.

In conclusion, I must add that to my mind even the IRDP is not the best programme for imparting the necessary managerial and entrepreneurial skills. This training must be built into the Indian educational curriculum and should be taught much earlier rather than having the students spend eight to fifteen years before they are taught these skills. Our educational system must recognise the fact that at least 60 per cent of children drop out before they have spent four years in school. At that stage they and their parents realise that their wage-earning capacity has not been improved by the four years of schooling. The returns of expenditure on universal education for society as a whole can be infinitely high when fully realised, but to an individual in the present system, they come too slowly and the situation is frustrating. Often the returns are beyond the individual's means in terms of a time investment that ranges from a minimum of eleven years to a maximum of twenty years. This is especially true of developing countries. On the other hand, we have supposedly quick-gain programmes like TRYSEM in which vocational expertise is supposed to be achieved in three to six months with a further assumption that any one who has the vocational expertise can automatically market it. Both assumptions are wrong. All our educational experts must do some heart-searching on the validity of these assumptions, on the one hand, and on redundancy and time wastage in our educational system, on the other. Only then shall we be able to tap the full potential of poverty alleviation programmes like the IRDP.

NOTES

1   For more information on the IRDP, the reader is referred to the Sixth Five Year Plan of India.

2.   The administrative hierarchy in India is as follows. The central government functions from Delhi. The federation of India is divided into several state governments. The smallest unit is a village; about 500 villages make a *taluka* and about fifteen *talukas* make a district, which is the most important administrative unit. Each state has several districts.

The Indian Civil Service is responsible for carrying out all development programmes within the perspective outlined by the political leadership, although the bureaucracy itself is required to remain apolitical. Most of the key functions of bureaucracy are performed by the officers of the Indian Administrative Service (IAS), which is the prime civil service of India, and has continued on the lines of the Indian Civil Service of the British period. The recruitment for the IAS is on an all-India basis and is highly competitive. In general, the IAS officers are known for high efficiency, sincerity and their apolitical functioning.

Unlike in the colonial days, now the bureaucratic machinery of most developing countries is given the task of carrying out speedy development. In India, the IAS officers at district level work either as district development officers (or CEO) who are in charge of all developmental activities in the district, including the IRDP, or as collectors, who look after revenue collection, maintenance of law and order through police, district planning, and overall co-ordination of government functioning in the district. More senior IAS officers work as heads of public-sector corporations and secretaries of various departments.

The author is herself an IAS officer and was actively involved in implementation of the case study presented here.

3   See note 2.

4   In India, formal vocational education starts after schooling and is conducted mainly by the Industrial Training Institutes (ITIs) and to a small extent by the Kadi and Valley Industries Committee (KVIC) or the Districts Industries Centre (DIC).

5   Some readers may even question the whole ideology of giving low-level skills to the TRYSEM beneficiaries and requiring that they turn

into small-scale entrepreneurs. Knowing the tough competition which the small-scale business faces from large concerns, this may be a valid question. However, the purpose of this case study is not to go into those long-term questions but to suggest how best the IRDP can be utilised when it is the only available programme for the groups like the *devdasis*.

6   I have learnt from subsequent collectors of Sangli that the practice of offering women at the temple in Jat has stopped. At Soundatti also, the government has partly succeeded, as no offering now takes place openly.

238

INSTITUTIONAL CREDIT AS A STRATEGY TOWARDS SELF-RELIANCE FOR PETTY COMMODITY PRODUCERS IN INDIA: A CRITICAL EVALUATION[1]

Jana Everett and Mira Savara

Studies have been made which have revealed that lack of access to institutional credit has limited the economic potential of female home-based producers in the Third World (Schumacher, Sebstad and Buvinic, 1980). They lack the capital necessary to buy raw materials in bulk at the source or from wholesalers. Instead, they have to make more frequent trips to buy small amounts from retailers at much higher prices. They become indebted to money lenders charging exorbitant rates of interest or become involved in exploitative relationships with contractors supplying the raw materials. Thus one of the strategies most often recommended in the Women and Development literature is to provide these female workers with access to institutional credit.

Since bank nationalisation in 1969, the government of India has instituted a number of polices designed to provide credit for the production needs of the weaker sections (a term designating the poor). The programme most relevant for home-based producers from the lower classes is the Differential Rate of Interest Scheme (DRI) operated through banks. DRI provides loans of up to 5,000 rupees for fixed assets and up to 1,500 rupees for working capital to those self-employed meeting certain eligibility standards[2]. DRI began in certain backward districts in 1972 and expanded throughout the nation in 1977. Since 1978 the DRI target has been 1 per cent of each bank's advances of the previous year. As of 1980 there were 2,253,000 DRI accounts and Rs. 1581.14 crores (1 crore = 10 million) outstanding.[3]

Although the reach of DRI is woefully inadequate in the light of India's poor population, the government plans to allocate a growing share of bank credit to the weaker sections in coming years.

It is difficult to judge the extent of the participation of women home-based producers, vendors, and petty service workers in weaker section lending in India. Anecdotal evidence suggests that women constitute a very small proportion of DRI borrowers on a national basis. However, in some cities women's organisations have facilitated access to weaker section lending for large numbers of women. Studies have revealed that, even apart from the efforts of women's organisations, women constitute a significant proportion of DRI borrowers in some cities and towns. A State Bank of India (1978) study of DRI in eight localities found that 25 per cent of the borrowers were women, and in a survey of DRI borrowers in Baroda, Agarwal[4] reported that 29 per cent of the borrowers were women. In our case study of DRI in Bombay,[5] we found that 80 per cent of DRI loans in Bank A and 72 per cent of the DRI loans in Bank B were to women. In several of the branches, most of the women borrowers had been recruited by women's organisations. However, this was not always the case. For example, in Bank A, branch 1, women received 75 per cent of the approximately 2,200 DRI loans advanced in 1979, and none of the women had been recruited by women's organisations.

Does access to institutional credit provide a strategy towards self-reliance for women home-based producers in India? We do not think so, for female home-based producers occupy a position of overall vulnerability and dependence in the political economy of petty commodity production. Under these conditions, the operation of weaker section lending often serves to reinforce women's vulnerability and dependence by providing opportunities for local power holders to connect banks and borrowers through patron–client relationships. Women's organisations can improve the conditions of women's access to weaker section lending. But credit alone (even if obtained through a women's organisation's auspices) cannot transform the political economy of petty commodity production. Nevertheless, women's organisations potentially provide a means for attacking the other constraints preventing the self-reliance of women home-based producers.

In this chapter we attempt to substantiate the above argument. First we look at the political economy of petty commodity production. Next we investigate the operation of weaker section lending in Bombay, paying particular attention to the experience of women borrowers. Then we examine two different models developed by women's organisations to improve the conditions of women's access to weaker section lending. We inspect various survey findings on the impact of weaker section lending on women borrowers. Finally, we briefly review the efforts of women's organisations to address the other problems faced by female home-based producers.

Our analysis is intended to be suggestive, not conclusive, as the data are sketchy and problematic. Further research is needed to test the usefulness of the petty commodity production framework for various groups of female home-based producers in India. The data on DRI are incomplete. Banks do not keep sex disaggregated data on borrowers.[6] At the time of our research, there were no nationwide representative surveys of DRI borrowers. Most of our information pertains to the experience of urban women. Finally, in our review of existing empirical studies and our own case study in Bombay we group together information on lower-class female vendors and service workers with information on female home-based producers because in our opinion they all face similar constraints.

POLITICAL ECONOMY OF PETTY COMMODITY PRODUCTION

In the early 1970s researchers began to use the concept of 'the informal sector' to describe the economic activities of small producers, vendors and service workers in the Third World. According to the International Labour Officer[7] the informal sector was 'characterised by (a) ease of entry; (b) reliance on indigenous resources; (c) family ownership of enterprises; (d) small scale of operation; (e) labour-intensive and adapted technology; (f) skills acquired outside the formal school system and (g) unregulated and competitive markets'. Interest in the informal sector enterprises arose out of a concern over the persistence of poverty in the Third World. Early work in this area emphasised the disadvantageous position of the informal sector, relative to the formal sector (modern, industrial), *vis-à-vis* the state (in terms of regulations and benefits), and recommended that the state begin to discriminate in favour of the informal sector through loan programmes and so forth.[8] Radical scholars criticised the concept of the informal sector because they saw fragmentation and not dualism in the labour force (Breman, 1976) and subordination of the informal sector to the capitalist mode of production instead of the benign relationship between formal and informal sectors implied by the mainstream scholars.[9]

In recent years most researchers have come around to accept that the informal sector is internally differentiated[10] and that the poverty of poor producers is fundamentally the result of the uneven distribution of private resources and not of discriminatory state policies (themselves shaped by the distribution of resources).[11] Researchers have also begun to realise that women are clustered in enterprises at the bottom of the informal sector hierarchy, involving the lowest remuneration and least capital investment.[12] This holds true in India where official statistics (which grossly undercount the number of women workers) show 60.4 per cent of the rural female workforce and 44.2 per cent of the urban female workforce to be self-employed, the vast majority of whom are in the informal sector.[13]

The concept of petty commodity production, based on the writings of Karl Marx, serves as an alternative way to analyse the economic activities of micro-producers in the Third World.[14] According to this perspective, the petty commodity sector has a dependent relationship to the capitalist sector. The forces of production are characterised by rudimentary technology, the labour power of an individual and perhaps other family members, and meagre resources. The social relations of production involve labour being directly or indirectly subsumed by capital. Others control the means of production by supplying one or more of the following: raw material, tools, credit and marketing outlets. Sometimes the petty commodity producer is dependent on a subcontractor or merchant; in other cases the dependence relationship is with a money lender.

A distinction is often drawn between self-employed and dependent workers involved in petty commodity production.[15] Self-employed workers own their means of livelihood (tools and raw materials) and handle all parts of the processes of production and distribution. These workers are in a sense 'free' to select raw materials as they choose, but their options are sharply constrained because of their position of weakness in the political economy. Supplies may be unavailable or cost more than they can afford. They may not be able to sell their products. Dependent workers participate in a putting-out system. The tools and raw materials used belong to outsiders who pay the workers on a piece-rate basis for their labour and collect the final product. The insecure existence of self-employed workers and their lack of resources usually force them into dependent relationships with middlemen to obtain finances and/or raw materials or compel them to become full-fledged dependent workers. Moving from self-employment to dependence means exchanging one situation of powerlessness for another and continuing to get a very low return for one's labour.

Pushpa Sundar has categorised the activities of female petty commodity producers in India into two main groups. First there are self-employment activities which involve extensions of traditional household activities (such as making *papads*) and craft skills (for example, lace-making) for the market. Sundar emphasises the constraints experienced by these women workers:

the high rate of illiteracy, lack of mobility, lack of working space, lack of capital, lack of skills and lack of access to training along with socio-cultural taboos and constraints. Coupled with these are restrictions, regulations and harassment by local authorities and lack of reliable sources for raw materials and supplies. The shortage of funds and lack of staying power limit the self-employed women's scale of operation, particularly in relation to introduction of technology, and therefore limit the profits made. Moreover, the small self-employed woman has to manage all the levels of operation herself.[16]

Women in these activities usually become dependent upon money lenders and may become dependent workers if middlemen calculate there is a sufficient market for their products. The second group of petty commodity production activities in which women are concentrated, according to Sundar, are ancillary processes associated with large industries such as *bidi*-making and electronics. In order to increase profits, entrepreneurs decentralise the production process and pay women low wages on a piece-rate basis. Obtaining raw materials and securing markets are taken care of by the entrepreneur or his agents, but the unequal power relationship between the woman worker and middleman means among other things that the woman may not get enough work and that unfair deductions may be taken out of her earnings.

Women in both types of petty commodity production activities lack the protection of state labour laws. Even when laws in India have been framed to protect workers in home-based industries, they are not enforced. A combination of sexist assumptions about female workers and the power of the entrepreneurs deters officials from implementing existing policies, as the following exchange between Ela Bhatt of the Self-Employed Women's Association (SEWA) and the Labour Commissioner over the eligibility of women *bidi* workers for the Bidi Workers Welfare Fund illustrates:

'These are all home workers, they are not proper employees,' the Labour Commissioner says doubtfully.

'But the Bidi and Cigar Act specifically defines homeworkers as employees,' Elaben replies.

'They are all housewives doing some leisure work. If we press the owners, they will stop giving them work and these poor families will have less income,' says the Labour Commissioner and refuses to take any action.[17]

In addition to exploitative social relations of production, the dependent relationship between petty commodity production and the capitalist sector leads to certain macro-trends that constrain petty commodity producers. The transformation of the rural economy and the slow growth of the modern industrial sector in India contribute to a labour surplus that results in extreme crowding in many petty commodity activities.

International recessions threaten the export markets for which some craft items are aimed, and industrial strikes threaten the working-class markets at which many utilitarian items are aimed. Finally, petty commodity production is caught up in the cycle of growth and destruction which characterises capitalism.[18] Petty commodity production exists where capital-intensive industry has not penetrated. According to Gerry, the prospects are either involutionary growth or absorption by the capitalist sector if it expands in that direction.

For female petty commodity producers an additional dimension shapes their lives. Patriarchal relationships operate at the level of the household, the economy and the culture. In the household male–female power relationships, female responsibilities in the reproductive sphere (fertility, housework, child care), and male violence decrease a woman's control over her income, time and body.[19] Desertion leaves her with the sole responsibility for her family's survival. In the economy and culture, the identification of women as 'only housewives', women's market work as an extension of women's 'traditional' tasks, and the selection of women as out-workers in order to reduce the labour costs and the threat of disruption for large entrepeneurs – these are phenomena that reflect patriarchal values and result in a low monetary return for women's labour. In addition, cultural restrictions tying women to the home affect many groups of Indian women and further constrain their options.

The structural position of female petty commodity producers results in a number of constrains that must be overcome in order for them to achieve self-reliance.

1   They are trapped in exploitative relations of production.
2   They lack the organisational and technical capacity to generate adequate income through marketing arrangement, holding capacity, credit, access to raw materials and improved technology.
3   They experience increasing competition and fluctuating markets.
4   They are excluded from state protective policies and harassed by regulatory policies.
5   They are vulnerable to male domination in the household and in the wider society.

The preceding theoretical analysis casts doubt on the proposition that institutional credit alone can overcome the myriad constraints facing home-based producers. How do such credit programmes operate? What are their effects on female home-based producers? What difference do women's organisations make when they organise the participation of women borrowers in weaker section lending? It

244

is to these questions that we turn in the subsequent sections of the chapter.

THE OPERATION OF WEAKER SECTION LENDING IN BOMBAY

An interest in studying women borrowers' experiences with weaker section lending led us to do a case study of DRI in Bombay. Our findings have been reported elsewhere.[20] Here we want to examine the way in which the banks interface with the political economy of petty commodity production discussed above. We organise our observations around the theory of street-level bureaucracy developed by Michael Lipsky (1980). In our study the street-level bureaucrats are those bank employees who interact with weaker section borrowers and exercise discretion in the loan-granting and collection processes. According to Lipsky[21] street-level bureaucrats have to solve the following problem: 'How is the job to be accomplished with inadequate resources, few controls, indeterminate objectives and distressing circumstances?' The conditions of work lead street-level bureaucrats to adopt coping responses to get the job done. These constitute patterns of practice that are the public policy experienced by clients. We cannot be sure that the conditions of work and patterns of practice that we observed in Bombay characterise DRI operations in any other areas of India, but available studies of DRI contain descriptions consistent with our findings.[22]

We selected two of the largest public-sector banks in Bombay for our case study of weaker section lending.[23] In Bank A, weaker section lending services were centralised in branches we have labelled 'Weaker Section Advancement Departments' (WSADs). There were specialised procedures and personnel for the weaker section borrower: simplified forms, passbooks, and cash collectors whose jobs entailed visiting the slums to investigate loan applicants and to collect loan payments. In 1979–80 there were two WSADs in Bombay. The original WSAD was located near the enormous Dharavi slum. This WSAD to which we refer as A1, disbursed approximately 2,200 DRI loans in 1979 and about 1,000 other weaker section loans. There was also a newly opened WSAD located in a working-class neighbourhood inhabited by many textile workers. This WSAD, A2, disbursed approximately 350 DRI loans in 1979 and about 150 other weaker section loans. In 1979 there were ten cash collectors in A1 and one at A2. We have identified the cash collectors as the street-level bureaucrats at Bank A.

In Bank B weaker section lending was decentralised within each of Bank B's eighty-five Bombay branches, and concentrated in branches in working-class neighbourhoods. There were simplified forms for DRI borrowers, but the same staff handled 'regular' and weaker section accounts. No employees were assigned exclusively to outreach work as were the cash collectors of Bank A. We studied the four branches of Bank B with the largest number of DRI loans. In 1980 these four branches together made 212 DRI loans. Each of these branches was small, and DRI work (investigations and collections) was the responsibility of the sole loan officer. The four loan officers comprised our street-level bureaucrats in Bank B.

After receiving a DRI loan application, the bank was supposed to conduct an investigation of the applicant and record findings on the application. A subsequent interview usually conducted by the branch manager in Bank A and the loan officer in Bank B was mostly pro forma. Almost all those interviewed were granted loans, as the staff tried to weed out problem cases earlier in the application process. The banks were supposed to send their staff out to make collections from delinquent borrowers. Although in both banks the branch manager had the formal decision-making authority in approving loans and in deciding whether and how to collect overdue payments, the individuals conducting the investigations and doing the collection work had enormous discretionary power. The loan officers of Bank B had more authority than the cash collectors of Bank A because the former were officers and the latter, clerks; but the cash collectors had much more day-to-day experience with weaker section borrowers.

The majority of DRI borrowers in the branches studied were women working in the petty commodity sector. They obtained bank loans ranging in size from 500 rupees to 1,500 rupees for working capital needs. Two of the enterprises – broom-making and glass making – involved production and trading activities. The broom-makers fashioned brooms and baskets out of raw material from the jungle. The women sold the brooms to lower-class households with dirt floors and the baskets to wholesale markets. The glass-makers bought used bottles, made glasses out of them, and sold the glasses on the street. The *bidi*-makers were merely involved in production activities. Merchants sold them tobacco and then bought the finished product, so these women were really out-workers. Two of the businesses involved trading activities. The vegetable vendors bought produce at the wholesale market and sold the vegetables on the street. The utensil barterers bought stainless steel cookware and hawked it in the middle-class neighbourhoods. They exchanged the cookware with housewives for old clothes, which they then sold to merchants. The *khanawallis* (food providers) were involved in a service activity: cooking meals for the male workers who came to Bombay without their families. The daily earnings of these women ranged from 5 rupees (broom-makers) to 15–20 rupees (*khanawallis*). There was great variation among them in the level and stability of overall family income. Some were the sole supporter of their families. Others had husbands and/or sons in permanent or temporary jobs (for example, in the mills) or in self-employed activities like themselves. Many of the borrowers probably exceeded the DRI income standard (which was itself below the Indian 'poverty line',) but all that we spoke to were poor, although there were many levels of poverty. The male DRI borrowers in the branches studied were mainly vendors, *bidi*-makers and cobblers.

For the street-level bureaucrats in DRI lending the job involves expanding the reach of banking to the poor. It is a job most of them did not expect to be doing. We will look at the conditions of work that shape the practice of street-level bureaucrats in Indian banking: distressing circumstances, inadequacy of resources, untrained clients, ambiguity of goals and alienation.

For middle-class employees visits to Bombay slums are bound to be distressing: crowds of children following them down narrow, winding paths littered with garbage being eaten by chickens, and criss-crossed by open sewers amidst ramshackle huts constructed of scrap material. Investigating loan applicants is difficult. Slum residents are reluctant to give directions to outsiders. As one bank employee told us, 'In the slums it often takes us four or five hours just to find the address if we have no one to help us.' Collecting loan payments can be even more problematic. A cash collector told us: 'There was this story of a person being beaten up when he went around for repayment.'

Apart from these occupational hazards the bank's street-level bureaucrats experience an extreme inadequacy of informational resources in their investigations of DRI applicants. Residence can be verified by hutment occupancy card, rent receipt or ration card, but it is difficult for an outsider to verify income level, business volume, or level of indebtedness. For example, one bank employee told us: 'If you tell the people you are coming on such a day, then even if they do not have a legitimate business, they will get somebody else's vegetable basket and keep it in their house. It is really very difficult for us to check if the people are genuine.' The street-level bureaucrats also lack sufficient information in loan recovery work. Some of the borrowers do not speak any language understood by the bank employees. The borrowers are usually illiterate and do not know how much they owe. Previously Bank A issued passbooks in which stamps were posted to let borrowers know how much had been repaid. The size of the stamps suddenly increased so that they filled an entire passbook before the loan was paid off, and the posting of stamps had to be discontinued. The passbook, containing a photo of the borrower, continues to be issued, but it is sometimes lost. One woman told a cash collector that her passbook had been eaten by the rats. Without a borrower's passbook, the cash collector has difficulty crediting a payment to the correct account, as many individuals in the slums have the same name. In addition, women sometimes give their husband's names and other times give their father's names,

Lipsky implies that street-level bureaucrats fear that their clients will act in an uncontrolled or inappropriate manner. Many of the bank employees we encountered were put off by the appearance and behaviour of the DRI borrowers. Although in our presence the employees were usually courteous to the borrowers, activists who have worked with weaker section women borrowers tell a different story. In a study of the Self-Employed Women's Association (SEWA), Devaki Jain[24] quotes a SEWA publication describing the experience of association members with the nationalised banks:

> Being all women, accompanied by children, filthy in appearance, unaccustomed to manners and business talks, they were annoying to and not much welcome by the bank staff at their premises. Being illiterate they would go to the wrong bank, go at wrong hours, could not fill the slips . . . the bank staff has neither time nor understanding to deal with this class of borrowers and would start doubting their bonafides.

Some of the bank employees we interviewed wanted to change the attitudes and behaviour of the borrowers in areas extending beyond finances. As one employee stated, 'Part of the job is to give advice. They produce many children. They are illiterate. They even sleep with pigs.' In the South Asian context with its traditions of sex segregation, a factor contributing to the discomfort of the street-level bureaucrats we studied was that all of them were men and most of their clients (DRI borrowers) were women. One cash collector said that a women 'defaulter' claimed he had held her hand in order to get him in trouble because he was trying to collect on the loan.

As Lipsky found in the US agencies he studied, street-level bureaucrats in weaker section lending are apt to experience ambiguity in goals. It is not at all clear what they are supposed to be doing. Three divergent goals emerged from our discussions with bank employees: (1) careful investigation and aggressive collection in order to promote high recovery rates (conventional banking); (2) assisting the slum borrowers with their problems and/or changing their attitudes and behaviour (social work); and (3) lending money to the poor for purposes of populist rhetoric and writing off the loans (symbolic politics).

Some of the cash collectors were proud of the strategies they had devised to increase collection rates (for example, collecting on days when many of the borrowers' family members in wage employment were paid), but they were frustrated that managers did not seem to evaluate their performance on the basis of their recovery rates. Most of the employees were confused about whether they were to emphasise conventional banking or social work and had divergent attitudes toward the latter as a goal. One said, 'If I am going to do social work, I will do it full time, not work in a bank.' But another stated, 'The bank should be teaching the weaker sections they have the right to use the bank.' Unpredictability in the availability of funds for DRI loans contributed to cynicism on the part of some of the street-level bureaucrats. Yearly targets existed, and sometimes there would be no loans disbursed for months on end followed by a large volume of disbursals at the end of the year. Pressure to achieve targets sometimes led to questionable tactics. In one of the branches of Bank B we found that a large number of DRI loans had been disbursed on 30 December for 2,000 rupees. When we enquired about the larger-than-usual amount, the loan officer said it was a mistake, and all of these individuals had repaid 1,000 rupees the next week. Most probably an arrangement had been made by the officer to ensure that DRI targets were met. The loan repayment on these accounts after the initial 1,000-rupee repayment was negligible.

Finally, Lipsky states that street-level bureaucrats tend to become alienated from their work. In our study this was especially evident among the cash collectors, the bank employees who spent the most time with weaker section borrowers in the slums. Many of them aspired to be bank officers. Their main grievance was that their work did not prepare them for the bank officer examination and thus they had less chance of promotion to officer than other bank clerks. One cash collector had failed the examination three times. All of the cash collectors had applied for jobs as conventional bank clerks and had not envisaged the kind of outreach work they were doing. In addition, most of the cash collectors felt there was very poor communication with management. On the one hand they wanted more discretion (for example, being able to approve small loans) and on the other hand they wanted management to pay more attention to them. One cash collector complained that the programmes had deteriorated in the last few years with turnover in management. He stated, 'Higher management should watch what happens instead of just sitting there in their air-conditioned cabins.' In the early 1970s Bank A1 had been a pioneer in weaker section banking. But by 1982 the original implementors had been promoted out of this sector of banking, with the most far-sighted officer now manager of the London branch of the bank. The frequent transfers of bank officers exacerbated communication problems with the cash collectors. The only branch-level officer we found who understood the dynamics of the borrowers at Branch A1 was a former manager who now headed a commercial branch in another part of Bombay.

The cash collectors also complained about lack of support by management. One told of an incident in which he had recommended against an individual getting a loan. This individual filed a legal case against him. The branch manager, rather than involving the bank in a court suit over a small amount of money (a 500-rupee loan), granted the individual a loan on the condition that he drop charges. As a result the cash collector became very disillusioned.

Based on our observations in Bombay, we saw that the primary way in which the street-level bureaucrats in DRI organised their work in response to the conditions described above was to rely on intermediaries to manage the relationship between bank and weaker section borrowers. One most common type of intermediary was an individual – a slum leader, raw materials supplier, a politician, or someone else from the community. The bank employees referred to these individuals as 'social workers'. Other types of intermediaries were a government agency, the Backward Classes Corporation (BCC), and women's organisations (which will be discussed later). The intermediaries brought prospective borrowers to the bank, took some or all of the responsibility for investigation, and played a greater or lesser role in the other aspects of the loan transaction and in recovery.

Street-level bureaucrats in both Banks A and B utilised intermediaries, although the intermediaries associated with the centralised system of Bank A dealt with larger numbers of borrowers. In both banks there were some borrowers who did not work through intermediaries, but almost all of the women borrowers did. Even though the cash collectors of Bank A went into the slums, they depended upon a relationship established with an intermediary to contact a particular borrower. Some employees in the branches of Bank B went out to verify the investigations made by the intermediaries, but most did not. As one loan officer put it, 'If the BCC recommends an individual we don't do an investigation. For a 400-rupee loan it is not worth it; for 5,000 rupees we go.' He also admitted that he rarely went out to collect on DRI accounts, as he had too much work to do, and that his experience with loans recommended by the BCC had been so bad that he would no longer work with that agency.

The solution of using intermediaries in turn created new problems for the banks' street-level bureaucrats. Sometimes the 'social workers' would collect money from borrowers and fail to turn it into the bank. There were other allegations of 'social worker' fraud. One 'social worker' was accused of taking the loan money from his women borrowers and then having them impersonate other women to get more loans. In some cases 'social workers' would accuse cash collectors of misconduct. For example, Y, a political broker in Dharavi slum who has received loans for over 2,000 *bidi*-makers and utensil-barterers, accused a cash collector of accepting a bribe and then not recommending that a particular loan be granted. The cash collector cleared his name only after hauling Y (a Muslim) off to a mosque and demanding that he swear the charges were true on holy ground. Y withdrew the charges, but continued to make life difficult for the bank employees by threatening a hunger strike in front of the bank unless more loans were granted.

We observed that in some cases the street-level bureaucrats tried to put off all responsibility for the borrowers on to the intermediaries. For example, while accompanying a cash collector to Dharavi slum, we encountered a group of women who began to ask about loans. One asked if it was possible to go directly to the bank. We said yes, but the cash collector yelled instead, 'Tell Y your name, he'll put you on the list.' After some insistence on our part, the cash collector gave the women his name and the day he was at the bank office. When several more women asked for this information, the cash collector shouted, 'I have given it to her, now take it from her. I can't write my name down for everyone.'

The patterns of practice of the street-level bureaucrats in DRI establish an additional obstacle to self-reliance for female petty commodity producers and other DRI borrowers. When borrowers are recruited by social workers, their chances for increased vulnerability are high and their chances for increased power are low. The patron–client relationship establishes vertical ties that the social worker can use to his advantage but no horizontal ties through which the borrowers can fight for collective goals. Under these conditions the lending programme merely provides new channels through which ties of dependence and exploitation are established, maintained or strengthened. This situation is reflected in the repayment rates of DRI borrowers. The repayment record for DRI on a national basis was a dismal 30 per cent in 1980.[25] In our case study the repayment rates for DRI borrowers recruited by intermediaries ranged from 44 to 71 per cent for loans disbursed in 1979 and 1980.[26]

WOMEN'S ORGANISATIONS AND WEAKER SECTION LENDING

As we have seen in the preceding section, a major shortcoming in the operation of weaker section lending programmes is the inability of banks to establish a relationship with borrowers, and especially with women. This inability serves as an opportunity for local brokers to connect the banks and borrowers through patron–client relationships. There are two existing alternative models to patron–client relationships between female petty commodity producers and the banks. Women's organisations have devised these alternatives in an effort to make weaker section lending work for women. They are (1) women's organisations as intermediaries and (2) women's banks.

The three best-known women's organisations involved in weaker section lending – the Self-Employed Women's Association (SEWA) of Ahmedabad, Annapurna Mahila Mandal of Bombay, and Working Women's Forum (WWF) of Madras – originated as intermediaries between the banks and lower-class women home-based producers,vendors and casual labourers.[27] In all three cases women leaders with long histories of political activism began to investigate the needs of women in the slums and found indebtedness to money lenders to be a serious problem. The women leaders – Ela Bhatt of SEWA, Prema Purao of Annapurna, and Jaya Arunachalam of WWF – developed organisational strategies to enable banks to advance production loans to SEWA, Annapurna and WWF members. The organisational strategies were similar. The core of the organisation was the loan group – a group of women borrowers in a neighbourhood who would act as guarantors of the loan and as a support group for the women. Group leaders investigated prospective members, attended regular organisation meetings, and helped in the collection of loan payments.

When women's organisations operated as intermediaries, their borrowers achieved high repayment rates, much higher than the DRI averages. For example, in Bombay repayment rates of Annapurna borrowers to Bank A from 1976 to 1978 ranged from 94 per cent to 98 per cent on more than 3,500 loans.[28] A Bank of India (1981) study showed almost all WWF loans disbursed in 1979 were repaid in full. Nevertheless, two of the three organisations – SEWA and WWF – became dissatisfied with the intermediary model and they started their own women's banks. The reasons for their dissatisfaction were the lack of courtesy shown their members by bank officials and the many difficulties in communication between banks and borrowers which resulted in extra trips to the banks and forgone work. Furthermore, both organisations wanted to encourage their members to save. SEWA and WWF raised share capital and obtained outside funding to open their banks, which offered both saving and lending opportunities to members.

SEWA opened the Mahila Seva Sahakari Bank in 1974, and for two years it handled (for a fee) application and repayment work for the nationalised banks with SEWA borrowers. This arrangement did not succeed, for over-expansion in loans granted resulted in a drastic decrease in repayment rates. According to Sebstad (1982), of the approximately 9,000 loans that were advanced to SEWA members (by the nationalised bank and the SEWA bank) during 1973–76, less than one-half were recovered in full (this was still above average for DRI loans). The relationship between the nationalised banks and SEWA became strained. The SEWA Co-operative Bank ceased disbursement of nationalised bank funds and relied solely on its own resources. Both the volume of lending and number of defaults decreased dramatically. Between mid-1976 and mid-1981, 1,668 loans were advanced and defaults were negligible.[29]

WWF began a Co-operative Credit and Service Society in May 1981 and disbursed its first loan in October 1981. Through July 1982 WWF members had obtained 7,000 loans from the nationalised banks and 1,800 loans directly from their own bank.[30] While the WWF bank relied on its own resources, the WWF also began negotiations with the government to enable the nationalised banks to lend directly to co-operative societies of self-employed women.

The Annapurna Mahila Mandal remained generally satisfied with its role as intermediary between bank and borrower. Between 1976 and 1982 Annapurna members obtained over 6,000 loans from the nationalised banks.[31] An important factor explaining Annapurna's greater satisfaction with the nationalised banks was that Prema Purao's late husband had been a leader in one of the major unions of bank employees.

There are advantages and disadvantages in each model of women's organisation involvement. When the women's organisation is an intermediary, it is at the mercy of some of the shortcomings of the staff and policies of the nationalised banks. In the women's bank much of this can be changed. Sympathetic, motivated and knowledgeable staff can build strong relations of trust with female home-based producers. Loans can be disbursed in a timely fashion and in amounts appropriate for both production and consumption needs. If the woman's bank is solvent, the problem of lack of availability of funds for months on end should not arise.

However, issues of finance and scope make the women's bank model impractical except under special circumstances. It is questionable whether lending to the poor can be a break-even proposition financially. For the nationalised banks more profitable operations (such as foreign branches) subsidise weaker section lending. Both SEWA and WWF have outside funding which subsidises their activities. WWF receives an annual grant of 25,000 rupees from the Indo-German Service Society to pay staff salaries. From the perspective of SEWA organisers, their bank is self-supporting, but the organisation as a whole has received funds from the government and international organisations which, for example, paid for the building in which the bank is housed. Other women's organisations without access to these resources would find it hard to make a go of it. SEWA's experience suggests that as the size of a women's bank increases, repayment rates decrease. Women's banks appear to operate most effectively when their scope is small. The labour-intensive character of weaker section lending work suggests that women's organisations operating as intermediaries have the potential to reach more women borrowers than do women's banks.

EFFECTS OF THE LOAN PROGRAMMES ON WOMEN BORROWERS

We have seen that women's organisations improve the conditions of access to weaker section lending for women borrowers and facilitate higher repayment levels. But what are the effects of weaker section lending on borrowers? Do the effects vary by gender? Do women's organisations make a big difference in the economic and political effects of loans on women borrowers? These questions are difficult to answer definitively, as the existing studies on economic effects are methodologically flawed and there is little attention to political effects in the literatures.[32]

The picture that does emerge suggests that DRI borrowers tend to experience increases in income but these increases are small and the borrowers remain below the poverty line. Many of the surveys of DRI borrowers do not disaggregate their results by gender, but when they do, women appear to receive smaller loans and experience smaller increases in income than men.[33] Data on women's organisation borrowers fit the general pattern of small increases in income although their experience may be slightly better than other women borrowers. Surveys indicate that most women borrowers were in the financed activity before obtaining loans. When new businesses are financed, women's organisation borrowers are more likely to earn income from the new business than are other women borrowers.

A fairly consistent pattern of loan utilisation emerges in both the general surveys and the surveys of women's organisation members. Some of the money is invested in the business, but some was also used for paying off old debts and/or meeting current consumption expenses (day-to-day needs, special events such as marriages, and crises such as serious illness). Business-related uses of the loan proceeds included switching from retail to wholesale suppliers, increasing inventories and making improvements in their workplace homes. Most of the borrowers remain in debt to money lenders. This is true for a majority of WWF and Annapurna members and for 28 per cent of SEWA members.[34]

None of the general surveys examines the issues of social and political effects of weaker section lending. Surveys of women's organisation members do contain information on borrower attitudes, and report increased awareness, confidence and assertiveness on the part of members. WWF members oppose dowry, a position in keeping with WWF ideology. To what extent these changes result from the conditions of access provided by the women's organisations and to what extend they result from the loans themselves cannot be determined without a comparative analysis of women member borrowers and non-member borrowers. However, it seems likely that greater attitudinal changes would be found among women's organisation members. One piece of supporting evidence is that women's organisation group leaders show greater attitudinal changes than other members.

These findings appear consistent with the implications of the theoretical framework examined earlier in the chapter. The provision of institutional credit does not by itself overcome the other constraints facing female petty commodity producers. This is true even with the improved conditions of access to weaker section lending developed by the women's organisations. Of course the women's organisations do not only focus on bank loans. To a greater or lesser extent they are mounting an assault on the other constraints as well. Pushpa Sundar (1981) analyses several models developed by women's organisations to replace the existing exploitative relations of production and provide improved productive capacity. She advocates in particular efforts to create production co-operatives with collective workplaces (which SEWA has implemented on a small-scale basis in several trades). The women's organisations also use pressure group tactics to combat harassment of their members by government authorities and merchants. The leaders of the women's organisations lobby for policy changes in the interests of their constituencies. The organisations provide health and social insurance programmes for their members. Most importantly, they build a sense of collectivity among female petty commodity producers and provide a forum for discussing and solving problems. These activities constitute the potential base for the political mobilisation of these women around issues of economic, political and gender equality. All of these efforts have grown out of the organisation-building mechanism of weaker section lending. Thus the real issue is not women's organisations making the loan programme work but, instead, the loan programme facilitating organisational development among women petty commodity producers.

NOTES

1   This chapter is based on a paper presented at the Asian Regional Conference on Women and the Household at the Indian Statistical

Institute, New Delhi, January 1989. An earlier version of this chapter was also published in *Invisible Hands, Women in the Home-based Production*, edited by Andree Meneree Singh and Anita Kelles-Viitanen (Sage Publications, Delhi, 1987).

Jana Everett's fieldwork was made possible through a grant from the American Institute of Indian Studies. She wishes to acknowledge the help received from the Research Unit on Women's Studies, SNDT Women's University, Bombay, with which she was affiliated while in India.

2   An annual family income not exceeding 3,000 rupees in urban areas, or 2,000 rupees in semi-urban and rural areas (as well as little or no assets in land). 1 crore = 10 million. At the time of our research, 1 rupee = US$10. The DRI interest rate is 4 per cent.

3   Reserve Bank of India, 1981:127.

4   R.B.L. Agrawal, 'Concessional Finance: Do weaker sections benefit?' *Economic Times*, Bombay, 10 Nov. 1981 and 16 Aug. 1982.

5   Everett and Savara, 1983, 1984a, 1984b.

6   Sundar, 1981.

7   ILO, 1972:6.

8   Weeks, 1975.

9   Bromley, 1978.

10   House, 1984.

11   Papola, 1980.

12   Nelson, 1979.

13   Planning Commission, 1980:219.

14   Moser, 1978.

15   Eg., Harris, 1982.

16   Sundar, 1983, 'Credit and Finance Needs of Women Workers', New Delhi *Political Weekly*, **18** 26 November, 1983 M171.6.

17   Jhabwala, 1984:20.

18   Gerry, 1979.

19   Beneria and Sen.

20   Everett and Savara 1983, 1984a, 1984b.

21   Lipsky 1980:82.

22   These are surveys of DRI borrowers undertaken by the banks and others, and most contain descriptions of individuals playing intermediary roles between the banks and borrowers: State Bank of India, 1978, 1981, 1982; Central Bank of India, n.d.; R.B.L. Agrawal, 1981, 1982; Oommen, 1980.

23   For a discussion of our methodology, see Everett and Savara, 1984b.

24   Jain, 1975:10.

25   Reserve Bank of India, 1980:125.

26   Everett and Savara, 1983, 1984a, 1984b.

27   This section relies heavily on the following sources: for SEWA – Jain, 1980; Sebstad, 1982; Bhatt, 1982; for WWF – Jeffers, 1981; Arunachalam, 1982, Bank of India, 1981; for Annapurna – Mistey *et al.*, 1979; Krishna Raj, 1980; Savara, 1981; Purao, 1982.

28   Everett and Savara, 1983:104.

29   Bhatt, 1982.

30   Arunachalam, 1982.

31 Purao, 1982.
32 The major limitation of the studies, based on surveys of DRI bor-
    rowers in one or more localities, is that economic impact is assessed
    by asking borrowers about their income and so forth in the pre- and
    post-loan periods so that conclusions rest on fallible memories and
    we cannot be certain that any changes experienced were due to the
    loans. For references to these studies see note 22, and to studies of
    women's organisation members, see note 27.
33 Eg., Agrawal cit.
34 Jeffers, 1981, Mistey *et al.*, 1979, Sebstad, 1982.

REFERENCES

Agrawal, R.B.L. 'Concessional finance: Do weaker sections benefit?' *Eco-
    nomic Times*, Bombay, 10 Nov. 1981 and 16 Aug. 1982.
Arunachalam, Jaya (1982) Interview, New Delhi. 4 Sept.
Bank of India (1981) *Promotion of Self-employment through Bank Fi-
    nance: a Case Study of DRI Scheme for Slum Dwellers in Madras.*
    Bombay,
Beneria, Lourdes and Gita Sen (1981) 'Accumulation, reproduction, and
    women's role in economic development: Boserup revisited,' *Signs Jour-
    nal of Women in Culture and Society*:279–98.
Bhatt, Ela (1982) Interview, Ahmedabad. 25–26 Oct.
Breman, Jan (1976) 'A dualistic labour system? A critique of the informal
    sector concept', *Economic and Political Weekly*, 27 Nov., 4 and 11, Dec.
    1870–76, 1905–1908.
Bromley, Ray (1978) 'Introduction – the urban informal sector: why is it
    worth discussing?' *World Development*, 6, (9/10):1033–9.
Central Bank of India (n.d.) *Report on Differential Rate of Interest Scheme
    – Sample Survey*, Bombay.
Everett, Jana and Mira Savara (1983) 'Bank credit to women in the
    informal sector: a case study of DRI in Bombay City', Bombay:
    Research Unit on Women's Studies, SNDT Women's University.
    (1984a) 'Bank loans to lower class women in Bombay: problems and
    prospects', *Economic and Political Weekly*, 19 25, Aug.:M113–M
    119.
    (1984b) 'Bank loans to the poor: do women benefit?' *Signs Journal of
    Women in Culture and Society*, 10 (2), forthcoming.
Gerry, Chris (1979) 'Small scale manufacturing and repairs in Dakar: a
    survey of market relations within the urban economy', in Ray Bromley
    and Chris Gerry (eds), *Casual Work and Poverty in Third World Cities*
    (New York, John Wiley), pp. 229–250.
Harris, John (1982) 'Character of an urban economy: small scale pro-
    duction and labour markets in Coimbatore', *Economic and Political
    Weekly*, 5 and 12 June: 945–54, 993–1002.

House, William J. (1984) 'Nairobi's informal sector: dynamic entrepreneurs or surplus labour?' *Economic Development and Cultural Change*, 32: 277–302.

International Labour Office (1972) *Employment Incomes and Equality* (Geneva, ILO).

Jain, Devaki (1975) *From Dissociation to Rehabilitation: Women in a Developing Economy* (New Delhi: ICSSR).

(1980) *Women's Quest for Power* (Bombay: Vikas).

Jeffers, Hilde (1981) 'Organizing women petty traders and producers: a case study of Working Women's Forum, Madras', MA Thesis, Department of City and Regional Planning, University of California, Berkeley.

Jhabwala, Renana (1984) 'Neither a complete success nor a total failure. Report of a SEWA campaign to organise bidi workers', *Manushi*, 22:18–22.

Krishna Raj, Maithreyi (1980) *Approaches to Self-Reliance for Women: Some Urban Models*. Bombay: Research Unit on Women's Studies, SNDT Women's University.

Lipsky, Michael (1980) *Street-Level Bureaucracy: Dilemmas of the Individual in Public Services*, Russel Sage Foundation: New York.

Mistey, Mani, *et. al.* (1979) 'A study of repercussions of bank loans to Annapurnas financed by the Multi-Service Agency of the Bank of Baroda', Parts I–IV, MSW thesis, College of Social Work, Bombay University.

Moser, Caroline O.N. (1978) 'Informal sector or petty commodity production: dualism or dependence in urban development', *World Development*, 6:1041–64.

Nelson, Nici (1979) 'How women and men get by: the sexual division of labour in the informal sector of a Nairobi squatter settlement', in Ray Bromley and Chris Gerry (eds), *Casual Work and Poverty in Third World Cities* (New York, John Wiley), p. 283–302.

Oommen, M.A. (1980) *Banks in the service of weaker sections* (New Delhi, Oxford and IBH Publishing Co.).

Papola, T.S. (1980) 'Informal sector: concept and policy', *Economic and Political Weekly*, 15 3 May:817–24.

Patel, Mutokhshi (1979) 'A descriptive study of cash collectors employed under the MSA scheme of the Bank of Baroda and the organiser of Annapurna borrowers who benefit from this scheme', MSW thesis, College of Social Work, Bombay University.

Planning Commission (1980) *Sixth Five-Year Plan: 1980–85*, New Delhi. Government of India.

Purao, Prema (1982) Interviews. Bombay, (Aug.-Nov.).

Reserve Bank of India (1980, 1981) *Report on Currency and Finance*, vol. I *Economic review*, 1979–80, 1980–81. Bombay: Government of India.

Savara, Mira (1981) 'Organising the Annapurna', *Bulletin of the Institute for Development Studies*, 12 (3) (July):48–53.

Schumacher, Ilsa, Sebstad, Jennefer and Buvinic, Mayra (1980) *Limits to Productivity: Improving Women's Access to Technology and Credit* International Center for Research on Women, Washington, DC.

Sebstad, Jennefer (1982) *Struggle and Development among Self-Employed Women: a Report on the Self-Employed Women's Association, Ahmedabad, India*. United States Agency for International Development, Office of Urban Development, Washington, DC.

State Bank of India (1978) *Impact of Credit on Weaker Sections: a Report Based on Eight Case Studies*. Bombay.

State Bank of India (1981) *A Report of the Impact of Bank Credit on Weaker Sections: a Report of a Field Study in Bolangir District in Orissa*. Bombay.

State Bank of India (1982) *A Study of the Impact of Bank Credit on Weaker Sections: Report of a Field Study in Kashmir Valley*. Bombay.

Sundar, Pushpa (1981) 'Credit and finance needs of Women workers'. New Delhi, mimeo.

    (1983) 'Women's employment and organization modes' *Economic and Political Weekly*, 18 (26 Nov.): M171–M176.

Weeks, John (1975 'Policies for expanding employment in the informal urban sector of developing economies', *International Labour Review*, 91 (1) (Jan.):1–13.

Chapter Thirteen

WOMEN WORKERS IN MANUFACTURING INDUSTRY IN INDIA: PROBLEMS AND POSSIBILITIES[1]

Rohini P. H.

As a result of the gender division of labour in manufacturing industry, women have always been a disadvantaged minority within the workforce in India. This division takes place along several lines. The first is not actually *within* industry but has to be taken into consideration because without it none of the other divisions are completely explicable. This is the division into unwaged labour in the home, traditionally the preserve of women, and wage labour in the factory, where men predominate. Within wage labour there is the segregation of women and men into different types of jobs – for example, the preponderance of women in jobs like packing and assembly while engineering jobs are monopolised by men. This division partially overlaps with another – that into low-paid and well-paid jobs – because in general the jobs where women predominate are more poorly paid than those from which they are excluded. Not always, however; most of the heavy unskilled jobs involving carrying and loading are handled by men who are often on even lower wage-scales than most of the women. On the other side are the cases where women do the same jobs as men but get paid less for them. Here again there are two possibilities: (1) within the same enterprise, men and women may get paid different rates for the same work; or (2) they may be paid different rates because wages are on the whole higher in the kind of enterprises where men work than in those where there are more women in the workforce. The picture is further complicated by the fact that these lines of division are not independent of one another but interact to reinforce the tendency for women to be pushed into the occupations which receive least social recognition and remuneration.

However, despite these problems, the participation of women in the industrial workforce opens up possibilities for collective action which can substantially improve the position of all women in society. Once again, these possibilities often remain unrealised, due to the limitations of the organisations through which women workers have hitherto struggled – namely, the trade unions. None the less, there are enough instances of successful action to indicate the tremendous potential strength of organised women workers.

WAGED AND UNWAGED LABOUR

The attitude of trade unions and the government in India to the division between waged and unwaged labour can best be summed up in the words of Dr S. Radhakrishnan in his inaugural address to the National Committee on Women's Education set up in May 1958 by the government: 'While the greatest profession of a woman is, and probably will continue to be, that of home-maker, yet her world should not be limited to that relationship.'[2] The recognition that large numbers of women will have to work for wages if they and their families are to survive has meant that there was never any systematic attempt by trade unions to exclude women from the wage-labour force as there was in countries like Britain. And although unions have acquiesced in the exclusion of women from certain trades, this has not resulted in their exclusion from union membership as such, since craft unions are virtually non-existent.

If trade unions and the government have recognised the right of women to enter employment outside the home, however, the implicit condition for this entry has been that they continue to shoulder the entire responsibility for running the home and taking care of children. The concern they express for the welfare of the woman worker has been genuine enough, but the remedies proposed have been aimed at helping her to take up the double burden more effectively rather than relieving her of part of it. And since they recognise that she is not super-human, this means accepting the consequence that she cannot possibly be as effective a wage-worker as a man. Hence the understanding is that men will be the primary bread-winners; women will take sole responsibility for unwaged work in the home and will also earn if necessary, but only in a supplementary capacity. Either total economic dependence on men, or a degree of independence but at the cost of an increased workload: that is the choice for women underlying union demands for protective legislation as well as a living wage.

JOB SEGREGATION

Given these assumptions, there has been no reason for unions to try to break down the traditional segregation of jobs by gender in the form it has taken in factory production. An extensive discussion of the principles behind this segregation is not possible here, but it appears to be based on some notion of 'prestige': that is, women are allotted jobs which are considered less prestigious. Traditionally women have not been excluded from heavy work, probably because in Hindu culture no prestige is attached to heavy manual labour; thus large numbers of women are employed in such strenuous occupations as road-building, construction work and hand-cart pulling. But within traditional family-based handicrafts, women have consistently been allotted a subordinate role. They were not allowed to belong to the ancient craft guilds, although they assisted their husbands in their home workshops.[3] Even today among handloom weavers in South India the eldest male decides on the division of labour and allots the preparatory work to women and children; women do the actual weaving only if there are no male family members to perform this function.[4] In other traditional handicraft communities too, such as the makers of Sanganeeri prints and the sari weavers of Varanasi, women are assigned the more peripheral tasks.[5]

In the context of manufacturing industry, it might be expected that jobs involving a higher degree of education and skill would be more prestigious, and this is certainly true of many jobs. In these cases, women are scarcely represented in such jobs because they have less access to skills and education due to (1) the attitude of parents, who are usually willing to spend more on educating a boy, sometimes even sending a daughter out to work so that they can afford to pay for a son's education; (2) the attitude of schools and colleges, which tend to channel girls into arts and especially commerce courses in the expectation that if they get a job at all it will be a clerical one; (3) the attitude of technical institutes, which usually take girls for courses like embroidery and dress-making but very rarely for training in engineering and technical skills; and (4) the policy of employers, who hardly ever recruit women for technical jobs or provide them with on-the-job training. For all these reasons women tend to be excluded from most skilled jobs,[6] apart from a very few qualified women who work as chemists, draughtsmen and so on. However, there are other cases where the claim that there is more 'skill' involved in the more prestigious jobs is not so easy to justify. For example, it is not at all clear that operating a packing machine requires more skill than doing the same operation manually. Yet there is certainly more prestige attached to working with the machine, probably because it embodies a much greater amount of capital, and it very often happens that when an operation is mechanised, it passes to men, even if no shiftwork is involved. This seems to be the specifically capitalist form of the more universal

tendency to give women less than equal access to means of production. That is to say, in women's occupations there is less capital input per unit of labour either in the form of improved tools or in the form of arrangements for using non-manual sources of power.[7]

TABLE 13.1 Statement showing trade-wise break-up of total capacity and students on roll as on 31 March 1978, under Craftsmen Training Scheme[8]

Serial No.	Trade	Capacity	Men	Women
1	Building construction	384	269	—
2	Draughtsman (civil)	3413	3545	82
3	Draughtsman (mech.)	3998	4041	43
4	Electrician	16339	17169	7
5	Electroplater	432	329	—
6	Fitter	25567	25744	9
7	Instrument mech.	2425	2218	41
8	Machinist	11955	11894	17
9	Machinist (grinder)	2052	1990	—
10	Mechanic (N & V)	8749	8513	—
11	Refrigeration and air conditioning	2188	2017	14
12	Mechanic (Radio and television)	4150	3773	123
13	Pattern maker	1168	852	—
14	Surveyor	1795	1625	19
15	Turner	16003	15973	20
16	Watch and clock maker	304	244	11
17	Wireman	10275	9887	5
18	Electronics	1228	1157	54
19	Tool and die making	924	935	3
20	Millwright mech.	232	269	—
21	Farm mechanic	224	175	—
22	Blacksmith	2371	1625	4
23	Carpenter	3808	2721	22
24	Mechanic (diesel)	2944	3143	—
25	Mechanic (tractor)	2478	2358	—
26	Moulder	3790	3531	20
27	Painter	819	717	55
28	Plumber	1305	1219	3
29	Sheet metal worker	2846	2247	70
30	Upholstery	48	32	—
31	Welder (gas and electric)	9778	9381	3
32	Wireless operator	146	123	—
		144138	140212	625

Source: Papers of Planning Commission Working Group on Women's Employment, 1978

This is accompanied by an under-valuation not only of skills like precision and dexterity which supposedly come naturally to women, but even of the greater physical effort involved in the manual operations they perform. In India, where many companies do not even claim to evaluate jobs scientifically, the under-valuation of women's jobs passes virtually unnoticed.[9]

The consequence of this job segregation is that women are concentrated in the more labour-intensive and therefore lower-paid industries. Within the organised industrial sector in 1977-8, 'the amount of invested capital per worker in industries where women formed a significant portion of the labour force was significantly below the all industries average'.[10] Within each industry, women are employed in the most labour-intensive jobs. Right from the inception of the Bombay textile industry, 'women seem to have been employed predominantly in the cotton cleaning, winding and reeling departments – sections in which power equipment was not generally used until well after the end of World War I. (Note: Women largely dominated the winding and reeling department.)'[11] In the pharmaceutical industry women are found mainly in packing and visual inspection jobs, which are among the most labour-intensive. And in electronics they are predominantly found in manual assembly departments.

TABLE 13.2 Invested capital per worker in industries with a significant participation of *women* (all India, 1977–8)[12]

Industry	Invested capital per worker (Rs)
All industries average	53680
Grain milling	20647
Cocoa, chocolate and sweetmeat industry	22475
Tobacco processing and bidi	2224
Cotton ginning and baling	5731
Cotton textiles	20908
Coir and coir products	19136
Matches	6359

Source: CSO, *Annual Survey of Industries*, vol.1, Government of India, New Delhi 1979

EQUAL PAY

Although trade unions have not felt it necessary to break down the segregation of women into particular jobs, they *have* fought for equal pay for equal work (though not for work of equal value), against the resistance of employers and initially against the resistance of the government too. The Report of the Royal Commission on Labour in India (1931) found that in the cotton textile industry,

> in all departments where men and women worked at the same jobs, the average daily earnings of women were distinctly lower than those of men. . . . In cotton ginning factories in the Madras State in 1928, women's wage rates were 63 per cent of men's wage rates and in pressing factories, 61 per cent. In ginning and pressing factories as a whole, women's wage rates were about 60 to 70 per cent of men's wage rates in the Punjab, in UP and in Bombay State.[13]

One of the demands of the Bombay Strike Committee in the textile strike of 1928-9 was that the minimum wages of all workers should be raised to 30 rupees per month. The Bombay Strike Enquiry Committee set up by the government of Bombay replied that

> the payment of an equal minimum wage has not been adopted anywhere and that a higher wage is fixed for men because 'a large proportion of adult male workers are responsible for the maintenance of a wife and children, whereas the proportion of women who have dependents is comparatively small.'[14]

In 1940, the Government of India Textile Labour Enquiry asked, 'Should the rates of men and women differ?' and replied,

> We believe the answer inevitable. They will have to be different. A considerable gap in fact exists today between the lowest wages earned by men and women in industry. Any violent disturbance of the existing differentiation is bound to affect the proportion of employment offered to the two classes of workers.[15]

The Labour Investigation Committee reported around fifteen years after the Royal Commission. Wherever it gave information separately for men and women, it showed that in the cotton textile industry women still had lower wage rates than men in the same occupation. Committees and tribunals continued to find good reasons for paying women less. The Report of the Committee on Fair Wages, 1949, observed that

> where . . . women are employed on work exclusively done by them or where they are admittedly less efficient than men, there is every justification for calculating minimum and fair wages on the basis of the requirements of a smaller standard family in the case of a woman than a man.

Apart from being based on rather muddled reasoning, this could, as Subramanian observed,

> encourage the perpetuation of the questionable practice of demarcating jobs as 'men's jobs' and 'women's jobs' and of relegating the latter to the bottom of the wage rate schedules. . . . When jobs are labelled as

'women's jobs', it is so easy to declare that they are less arduous than men's or that women are less efficient than men.[16]

As recently as 1958 a West Bengal Cotton Textile Industrial Award argued that, 'In view of the fact that the employer has to bear additional burden on account of maternity benefits and other welfare measures for the female workers, some differentiation in the matter of wage of the female workers should be made.' It therefore decreed that while men and women doing the same work should receive the same basic wage, a woman should receive only three-fourths of a man's DA or dearness allowance.[17] Now DA, the inflation-linked cost-of-living allowance, actually amounted to more than the basic wage, so the impact of the award on women's wages was drastic. It not only defeated the purpose of providing maternity benefits and crèches, but penalised all women – not just women with small children but *all* women – by making them pay for these benefits with a substantial part of their wages.

TRADE-UNION POLICY: WAGES

Trade-union policy on wages has been based on the principle that where women *do* enter the labour force, they should be paid the same as men for doing the same work. An Ordinance was issued on 26 September 1975, ensuring 'equal pay to men and women workers for the same work or work of similar nature',[18] and unions have been able to use this to obtain equal wages for men and women in the same occupations, although the issue of 'work of a similar nature' (or 'work of equal value') has by and large been neglected by them. The consequence can be seen in the contrasting wage differentials in large-scale organised industry where unions are active, and in the unorganised sector, where unions are virtually non-existent. In a survey we carried out in large-scale pharmaceutical and food factories in Bombay, we found only one case where women doing the same work as men were given a different job designation and put on slightly lower pay-scales. On the other hand, in another survey we found women in non-unionised, small-scale factories being paid as little as 50 per cent of what their male counterparts were being paid.[19] These results are confirmed by investigations carried out in 1955-6 which contain

> some interesting information on how the earnings of women were generally below those of men in the same occupational group. . . . The ratio of women's to men's earnings was somewhat higher, around 80–90 per cent, in the better-regulated and higher-paying occupations than in activities which we would classify as unorganised where it was 50–65 per cent.[20]

These observations are not surprising; given the way in which even tribunals often upheld the arguments by which employers sought to justify the payment of lower wage rates to women, it was only a relatively well-organised workforce which could demand and obtain a uniform rate for the job.

However, trade-union arguments for a 'living wage' also reveal an underlying assumption that many women will *not*, in fact, enter the wage-labour force but will be dependent on male earners who will therefore have to be paid enough to support them. Two union officials in Bengal who were interviewed by the Royal Commission on Factory Labour (1931) argued for a wage which would be sufficient to support female dependents as well as children;

> although not formulated explicitly as a demand for a 'family wage' based on a male breadwinner/dependent wife conceptualisation of the family, the complaints of the Bengali trade unionists over wage levels certainly involved the assumption that the typical worker was a married male with a range of non-employed dependants whom he had increasing difficulty in maintaining.[21]

The Delhi Agreement of 1935 between the Ahmedabad millowners and the Textile Labour Association made this assumption explicit by specifying that married women workers whose husbands were employed in the mills would be retrenched.[22]

In one respect these arguments represented an advance on those of the employers who insisted that account should be taken of the wages of women and children, as well as of the fact that many male workers left their families behind in their villages to subsist as best they could on uneconomical plots of land. The millowners would have preferred to leave no time or space for the reproduction of the working capacity of their labour force, either from day to day or from generation to generation. By contrast, the union leaders recognised the need for children to be cared for and educated, and acknowledged implicitly that running a household and caring for children was a full-time job for which someone had to be maintained. But it was assumed that women alone would do this work while it would be paid through the man's wage, and it was this assumption which was in the long term detrimental to the interests not only of women but of male workers too.

TRADE-UNION POLICY:
PROTECTIVE LEGISLATION

The assumption that women will take sole responsibility for running the home becomes even clearer when we look at the introduction of protective legislation. Much of the earliest protective legislation was inspired by the concern of the government and labour leaders for the welfare of women and children working in the textile mills – though also, incidentally, by pressure from Lancashire textile interests who feared unfair competition from Indian manufacturers working with unregulated labour.[23] In 1890, women were getting up at 4.30 a.m. and working till late at night in order to complete their household duties as well as their mill work. They had only two holidays a month, and while overall rates of sickness were high, they were even higher for women than for men. Infant mortality rates showed an interesting pattern. Most women workers stayed away from work at least one or two months before and two to six months after delivery, and up to the age of six months, mortality rates were higher among children of non-working mothers than among children whose mothers were mill workers; but this pattern was dramatically reversed between six months and one year, when most mothers would have returned to work. A woman with a baby would either have to bring it to the factory and keep it beside her while she worked, or leave it at home, in which case it would either be brought to her for feeds or fed on buffalo milk. The administration of opium to these infants was a routine matter, so the high mortality rates between six months and one year (102 deaths per 1,000 live births) is hardly surprising.[24]

The Indian Factories Act of 1881 only restricted the working hours of children, but the Factories Act of 1891 limited the working hours of women to eleven a day and required that all employees be given a Sunday holiday unless some other holiday occurred during the week.[25] Despite the demands of workers, working hours of men were not limited at this time. The agitation for shorter hours continued, especially after electric lighting began to be introduced in the mills at the end of the nineteenth century and many millowners took advantage of this to extend the working day to fifteen hours. This caused serious unrest among the workers, culminating in riots in 1905. A Factory Commission was established in 1908 to investigate the long hours, and its recommendations were the basis for the Factories Act of 1911, which restricted the hours of men to twelve per day; women's hours continued to be eleven per day, and their employment between 7.00 p.m. and 5.30 a.m. was prohibited.[26] The unrest died down after this, but in the general strike of January 1920, a Marathi leaflet signed by two or three men calling themselves 'Joint Secretaries' of the Mill Hands' Association once again demanded a shorter workday.[27] Only in the Factories Act of 1922 was the number of hours for men made equal to those for women. Subsequently the statutory maximum working week was gradually reduced to forty-eight hours, which is where it stands today.

Meanwhile, the International Labour Conference of 1919 which adopted the Childbirth Convention passed a resolution requesting the Government of India 'to make a study of the question of employment of women before and after confinement, and of maternity benefits, . . . and to report on these matters to the next Conference'. The report was submitted in 1921, and argued that legislation on this matter would be premature, but that the government would encourage and assist the principal organised industries to start voluntary benefit schemes.[28] Subsequent enquiries showed that the provisions being made were totally inadequate, and in 1924 N. M. Joshi attempted to make maternity benefits statutory throughout India. The attempt failed, but in 1929 the Bombay government passed an Act providing for eight weeks of paid maternity leave, and this was followed by similar Acts in other states.[29] The Employees' State Insurance Act of 1948, which applied to the whole of India, extended the period of paid leave to twelve weeks, but restricted the benefit to employees earning 400 rupees or less per month. Unlike the Maternity Benefit Acts, which require the employer to pay the entire amount, the Employees' State Insurance Scheme (ESIS) benefits are financed by contributions from the worker, employer and government, which are the same for men and women. The income limit was later raised to 1,000 rupees, but the rate of inflation had been so great that it still covered only low-paid workers.

The Factories Acts of 1934 and 1948 prohibited the employment of women in dangerous or excessively strenuous operations. The Factories Act also stated that separate toilets and washrooms must be provided for women workers, and that a suitably equipped crèche must be provided for the children (under the age of six) of women workers, wherever fifty or more of them are employed in one workplace. (This number has subsequently been reduced to thirty.)

EMPLOYER RESPONSES IN THE TEXTILE INDUSTRY

The final outcome of struggles to implement protective legislation was a decline in the number of women workers. Part of the decline can be accounted for by mechanisation of the operations in which the vast majority of women were employed; given the drastic reduction in the number of these jobs and the failure of women to gain admission to other occupations, a reduction in the number of jobs available to women was inevitable. But even in the jobs which remained, there was considerable replacement of women by men, and this is what accounts for the rest of the decline. What we have here is a one-sided breakdown in the gender division of labour, with men taking over what were traditionally 'women's jobs' without any corresponding breakthrough of women into traditional male preserves. The process began earlier and was especially acute in Bombay, but was repeated elsewhere and mirrored in other textile industries, especially jute.[30]

In Bombay, the major reason for the reduction of the number of women workers in the cotton textile industry was the restriction on night work. From the 1920s onwards a process of rationalisation took place, and by 1930 most mills were running a night shift. Knowing that they had no possible alternative sources of employment in the organised sector, women opposed the attempts of millowners to retrench them, arguing instead that they should share whatever work was available. Hence there was no catastrophic decline in their numbers, but recruitment virtually stopped so that there was a gradual reduction in the number of women, from 32,396 in 1925 to 22,962 in 1947, while the proportion of women in the workforce dropped from a peak of 25.87 per cent in 1893 to 11.17 per cent in 1947.[31] Nor did the decline stop there, but has continued since then, till today the proportion of women in the cotton textile industry is negligible.

For other employers, dismissing women or depriving them of permanency was a way of evading legislation on maternity benefits or crèches. Report after report documents these evasions: for example, 'An enquiry into conditions of labour in the cashewnut processing industry of India',[32] 'A Report on labour conditions in tanneries and leather goods factories', 1946,[33] 'Report on labour conditions in the glass industry', 1945.[34] One common method was to employ women as temporary or casual workers so that their names did not appear on the attendance registers; another was to dismiss women at the first sign of pregnancy.

> The annual note on the working of the UP Maternity Act during 1938 admits that many women workers were discharged immediately after the Act was passed . . . . The Labour Investigation Committee found that the Maternity Benefit Acts were not properly observed or enforced especially in the smaller concerns . . . . Similar is the conclusion of a . . . study made by the International Labour Office: 'Women fail to file claims . . . because they fear such an application may be followed by dismissal. In some cases, women workers are unable to prove completion of the requisite period of service because their employers have not kept the proper records.'[35]

WOMEN IN NEW INDUSTRIES

However, the reduction of women in the organised sector of the textile industry has not been matched by a reduction of their proportion within organised industry as a whole. The number of women

TABLE 13.3   Women's employment in factories, 1952–62[36]

Year	Total no. of employees ('000)	No. of women employees ('000)	Percentage of women
1952	2561.5	278.4	10.84
1953	2528.0	269.9	10.67
1954	2589.8	285.2	11.01
1955	2690.4	295.1	10.96
1956	2882.3	301.4	10.45
1957	3074.1	346.1	11.26
1958	3102.2	343.9	11.08
1959	3202.9	344.6	10.76
1960	3367.8	367.3	10.91
1961	3497.0	372.3	10.65
1962 (P)	3648.6	394.1	10.80

(P) = Provisional

Source: Statistical Abstract, 1961, p. 563; Indian Labour Statistics 1964, pp. 28–9

in registered factories (that is, those employing ten or more workers if using power, and twenty or more workers without power, and registered under the Factories Act) rose fairly steadily between 1952 and 1962, while their proportion in the workforce remained constant:

By 1980-1 the proportion of women workers was slightly lower, at 9 per cent.[37] But their decline in textiles was largely offset by their increase in other industrial sectors, especially in 'food except beverages' and 'tobacco'. In 'chemicals and chemical products', where women are employed mainly in pharmaceuticals, there is an interesting pattern, with their numbers and proportion increasing up to 1955 and then declining.

TRADE UNION STRUGGLES

From the 1940s onwards, there was an expansion of the chemical and pharmaceutical industry in Bombay. By contrast with textiles, where the companies are almost exclusively Indian, the chemical and pharmaceutical industry is heavily dominated by multinational companies, even though many of them have diluted their equity below 50 per cent and a few companies are purely Indian. The type of unionism is also totally different, with centralised bargaining and industrial unionism in textiles while plant-based bargaining predominates in chemicals and pharmaceuticals, with some of the unions being entirely controlled and run by workers whereas others rely to a varying extent on an outside leader. The women who worked in the textile mills were largely uneducated, and drawn from sections of the population where girls were married off very young, so that almost all of them were either married or widowed. By contrast, the women recruited into the modern industrial sectors were generally educated at least up to the tenth standard, and came from communities where marriage at a latter age was customary: they tended to enter employment immediately after leaving school and before getting married. This gave employers an opportunity to use a different strategy to avoid the consequences of legislation on maternity benefits and crèches: some of them explicitly stated in their employment contracts that female employees would be dismissed when they got married, while others operated the same system in a less formal way. This not only saved them from the necessity of paying out benefits but also gave them a very flexible workforce. The pharmaceutical employees' unions took up this issue in the late fifties and began a more systematic fight after forming themselves into a federation in February 1960. When May & Baker in 1961 terminated a woman employee on her getting married, the Pharmaceutical Employees' Federation took the matter to court and also agitated against the dismissal in various other ways. The case dragged on for years, and went by stages up to the Supreme Court. On 20 February 1965, women from all the pharmaceutical companies staged a one-day fast, organised a huge procession, burnt an effigy along with the anti-marriage clause and threw the ashes in the Arabian Sea. As a result of their protest, an unofficial bill to amend Standing Orders prohibiting employers from dismissing women workers on their getting married was discussed in the Maharashtra Assembly, and the government put pressure on employers not to implement the marriage clause. Finally, that same year, the Supreme Court ruled that the clause was illegal.

Along with job security, the pharmaceutical unions won for women as well as men a working week which is substantially shorter than the statutory maximum – in some factories only forty hours – and relatively high pay scales, with automatic annual increments and a cost-of-living linked component, DA, which quickly increased to become by far the most important part of their salaries; also a range of benefits and allowances which contribute substantially to total earnings and provide some security on sickness or retirement. In almost every case, pay scales are the same for men and women doing the same work, and in Glaxo, where initially women were being retired at 55 and men at 60, the union in 1977 demanded and got the retirement age for women raised to 60. A highly significant indication

TABLE 13.4 Employment in factory industries, 1952–62 (in thousands)[38]

Name of industry	1952	1953	1954	1955	1956	1957	1958	1959	1960	1961	1962(P)
Food except beverages											
Total employees	311.7	305.8	317.5	336.7	353.0	409.4	412.0	429.1	454.3	473.7	496.6
Women employees	55.2	54.3	56.9	58.7	53.2	85.3	85.6	82.7	96.1	106.3	119.2
Percentage women	17.7	17.8	17.9	17.4	15.1	20.8	20.8	19.3	21.2	22.4	24.0
Tobacco											
Total employees	110.7	116.3	130.6	134.1	147.6	145.5	149.0	140.4	149.2	136.2	140.0
Women employees	43.3	44.3	53.7	57.3	72.4	71.4	76.8	76.8	84.6	84.2	87.6
Percentage women	39.2	38.1	41.0	32.7	49.0	49.1	51.5	54.8	56.8	61.0	62.6
Chemicals & chem. prods											
Total employees	73.6	76.6	77.4	85.9	87.0	94.3	109.5	118.1	124.6	133.3	140.9
Women employees	11.4	12.2	13.9	16.3	16.1	15.8	15.3	15.4	15.3	14.5	14.0
Percentage women	15.5	15.9	18.0	19.0	18.5	16.8	14.0	13.0	12.2	10.9	9.9

(P) = Provisional

Source: Figures up to 1956 have been taken from *Women in Employment (1901–1956)*, p.16. Figures for 1957 onwards are based on returns received by the Labour Bureau, Simla, under the Factories Act, 1948, and relate to factories submitting returns only.

of the strength and self-confidence of these women workers is the virtual absence of sexual harassment in this sector.

In 1961 the diverse statewide Maternity Benefit Acts were replaced by a single all-India Maternity Benefit Act providing for twelve weeks' maternity leave on full pay, six weeks before and six weeks after delivery. Employers were slow to comply with this legislation, and in 1974 a delegation of women workers presented the Labour Minister with a memorandum containing thousands of signatures in support of their maternity benefit demands. There were also agitations in individual factories, and by 1983 almost all the large pharmaceutical companies were paying maternity benefit according to the Act, apart from a few like Roche, Boehringer-Knoll and German Remedies, which gave only two months' fully paid leave, and Boots which gave only half-pay for the three months of maternity leave.[39]

Obtaining crèche facilities too was often a struggle. Glaxo, which got a crèche in 1956, was one of the first pharmaceutical factories to do so. In Pfizer, in spite of repeated demands from the union, it was 1964 before a crèche was established; and in 1983 there were still companies like E. Merck and Indo-Pharma which had not complied with the law.[40] However, other amenities like separate toilets, washing facilities and rest-rooms for women were provided without much resistance.

CONTINUING DISCRIMINATION

It may appear that these women have all the advantages of the men working in their factories and a few more besides. But they too are affected by discrimination. On average, women earn less than men, and the main reason for this is that the vast majority of women are confined to the lower-paid, 'semi-skilled' jobs, whereas men have jobs at all levels. This is largely because, with a very few exceptions, women are recruited only into these jobs; apart from a few chemists who work in the laboratory, the women are invariably found in jobs like packing, checking, labelling and bottle-washing. The workers in the manufacturing departments where the drugs are actually made are all men. The reason usually given for this, and accepted by women, is that the work is heavy, it involves lifting heavy sacks of chemicals, it is sometimes hazardous, and so on. However, many of the jobs which were once heavy or hazardous are no longer so because of automation. Also, the heaviness or otherwise of jobs is partly a function of the way machinery is designed and work is organised. In Parke-Davis, for example, women suffered from strain and fatigue because the discs used for capsule-filling were unnecessarily heavy;

the older machines were easier to operate because the discs were lighter. And even where something heavy has to be lifted, it may be possible to do it without strain if two people do it together rather than one person alone. This solution, adopted by some women in Pfizer, is obviously preferable to the more usual one of requesting management to transfer the job to a man – which may in fact be no solution at all since most jobs which are too heavy or too hazardous for a woman are also likely to be too heavy or hazardous for a man. So it appears that the real reason for the exclusion of women from the manufacturing departments is the traditional segregation of 'men's' and 'women's' jobs. Yet unions have never taken this up as an instance of discrimination, and this is partly a reflection of the fact that the women themselves have not pressed unions to make it an issue.

On the other hand, a reason given for the absence of women in skilled engineering jobs is lack of qualification. At first sight this appears to be a valid objection, since as we saw earlier, it is true that very few girls are trained for these jobs. However, the director of a technical institute explained that a major reason for the low intake of girls into these courses is the difficulty of their finding jobs afterwards, given the tendency of employers not to recruit women for engineering jobs. It is interesting that women themselves do not see these jobs as being inherently unsuitable for them, and often point out that in the course of operating a machine they do in fact learn how to set it up and do minor repairs; yet here again, neither the women nor the unions have taken any action to correct this bias either by insisting that employers recruit women for these jobs, or by tackling discrimination in training. Thus here, as in other industries, women are concentrated in the most labour-intensive operations which are rapidly being eliminated with the advance of automation.

The other reason why women remain restricted to lower-paid jobs is that they seldom get promoted – either because the jobs are such that there is little scope for promotion, or because even where there *are* avenues for promotion, women get passed over in favour of men. A very frequent complaint of women workers is that after working for twenty years or more, they still remain in the same grade. However, unlike their restriction to lower-paid jobs, their restriction to lower-paid grades is something about which women feel strongly enough to take action, and even male-dominated unions are forced to take notice of their grievances on this score, although this could also partly be because grade stagnation and arbitrary promotions affect male employees too and generate enormous dissatisfaction. The device most commonly used to deal with grievances due to stagnation in a job like packing where there is little scope for promotion is to create a new grade – for example, Senior Packers – or split the grade into, say, Packers A, B and C, so that after ten or more years in one grade, workers can be upgraded into a higher one. In Hindustan Lever in

1983, after a new job evaluation, the union succeeded in getting the majority of packing jobs in Grade C (the next but lowest grade) upgraded to a new Grade E. However these are not promotions in the strict sense of the term because although grades and wage scales are raised, the work remains essentially the same.

The policy which many unions have tried to press managements to follow in order to minimise disputes over promotions is to promote workers strictly in accordance with their seniority (length of service) within a department, unless they can be shown not to be competent to do the jobs. Many managers refuse to adopt this policy, not only because they prefer to keep promotions within their control, but also because flexibility is impaired when workers refuse to be transferred from one department to another on the grounds that they lose their promotion rights thereby. However, where the principle has been established, its contravention can have dire consequences. The most dramatic instance was in Philips Pune in 1983, when management, with the consent of the union, promoted a woman from one department into a vacant post in another. This not only provoked a massive strike but also resulted in bitter hostility between the union leadership and the women in the department concerned.

In some cases managers justify promotion of a man over the heads of more senior women by saying that the person in the higher grade has to be able to work shifts, which women cannot do. And often they give this same reason for not recruiting women at all, especially where with increasing automation and rationalisation there is pressure for more shiftworking. In Roche, for example, women were 56.7 per cent of the workforce in 1962, but by 1983 were reduced to a mere 9 per cent, and in Hindustan Lever, where recruitment of women stopped in 1952, their share of the workforce declined from 30 per cent to less than 5 per cent by 1987; consequently the company was able to close down the once-flourishing crèche since none of the women had young children any longer, some of them in fact being grandmothers by then. The dramatic increase in women's employment in this sector was reversed after 1955; we have, in fact, a process which looks very much like a repetition of what happened to women's employment in the textile industry.

And yet we cannot conclude from all this that women's employment in manufacturing industry as a whole is declining. Many of the big companies which stopped recruiting women years ago are now subcontracting out parts of their production processes to small units, and this is a sector where women are still well represented. What is happening is that not only women's but also men's jobs are being lost in the large-scale sector, but are reappearing in the unorganised sector. In the process it is likely that there is actually a net generation of women's jobs – *but* under employment conditions very different from those of the jobs which were lost.

THE UNORGANISED SECTOR: EXPANDING FEMALE EMPLOYMENT?

The unorganised or small-scale sector is distinguished from the organised sector by the fact that the legal rights of the workforce are much weaker – the Factories Act and other legislation is not applicable – and the virtual absence of trade unions means that even the few rights which do exist are not implemented. A few examples demonstrate very clearly the transfer of jobs from the organised to the unorganised sector. In Coimbatore in 1951, 79 per cent of total cloth production was in the mill sector; by 1981, only 38 per cent of total cloth production was in this sector. Between 1971 and 1981, women declined from around 19 per cent to 15 per cent of the mill workforce, where the cost of labour rose by 20 per cent in the same period.[41] On the other hand, production of cotton cloth in the low-wage, decentralised powerloom sector grew by 8.7 per cent in the fifties, 10.6 per cent in the sixties and 8.0 per cent in the seventies; employment increased correspondingly, with women constituting 33 per cent of the workforce. Almost 80 per cent of these women worked more that eight hours per day, six days a week, working night shifts on alternate weeks.[42] Most interesting was the relationship between the mills and the powerlooms:

> Four out of six composite mills in the Coimbatore sample have adopted powerloom units in and around Coimbatore . . . . SIMA, the millowners' association, is helping set up powerloom centres by way of SITRA (the research organisation financed by SIMA), so that powerloom producers have access to technical advice on machinery and cloth production (SIMA Year Reports 1974, 1975) . . . . All these factors taken together show a clear indication of great interest by the mill sector (especially the composite mills) in subcontracting out their production to the decentralised sector, where income levels for producers are lower than those for mill workers, and labor legislation does not apply.[43]

In the Coimbatore textile industry, although the proportion of women employed is much higher in the powerloom sector than in the mill sector, there does not seem to be a positive preference for women over men in the former. In the *bidi* (indigenous cigarette) industry of Calcutta, on the contrary, the shift of production from one sector to the other was accompanied by a transfer of employment from relatively well-paid men to poorly paid women:

> In our 1976-77 study of unorganised sector workers in Calcutta . . . we found that in the bidi rolling industry men and women did identical tasks; but men got Rs 8/- for 1000 bidis plus a daily dearness allowance while women got only Rs 3/- per 1000 bidis. There was no perceptible difference in the work since payment was strictly by results after a check for quality. However, while essentially the work was the same, the main difference from the point of view of employers was that men worked in bidi factories

277

while women did the same work at home. In fact this industry of Calcutta was at the time of that survey in a process of transition and employers were increasingly putting out the work to cheap female labour because men workers in factories had got organised and had obtained an officially fixed, fairly reasonable piece rate for the work. Over the next few years, the industry has increasingly shifted production to home-based women workers and can now be regarded as a women's occupation which apparently justified the payment of the significantly lower piece rates.[44]

A similar process of subcontracting has led to the generation of women's jobs in the unorganised sector in the fish processing, cashew and coir industries in Kerala.[45]

MANAGEMENT CHOICES: MALE/FEMALE, ORGANISED/UNORGANISED

What emerges is that employers prefer to recruit men rather than women into the organised sector, whereas the opposite is true of the unorganised sector. It is not difficult to see why employers prefer to employ men once the workforce is unionised and claims its rights. Legal recognition of women's domestic responsibilities involves granting them maternity leave, paying maternity benefits, and providing a crèche for their children under the age of 6 – which also means employing trained personnel to look after the children. Flexibility is impaired because women cannot be employed on shift systems involving night work; it is impaired even more because women are less willing than men to work overtime. In India, where payment of often pitiful shift allowances to men is sufficient to obtain continuous or semi-continuous production, and with workers sometimes being forced to work two shifts one after the other if workers from the next shift fail to turn up to replace them, there are obvious advantages in hiring men who are presumed to have no responsibility for domestic work. Moreover, women seem to pose greater resistance to increasing workloads. Automation ought to result in lighter workloads, but in practice managements often use the introduction of new machines as a way of intensifying work. This took an extreme form in Parke-Davis, and it was the women there who found themselves too exhausted to do the housework by the time they got home and therefore chose a new union leadership to take up the struggle to increase line strength and reduce work speeds. In Hindustan Lever, up to 1965 four women worked on each soap-packing machine, but then management wanted to reduce the number to three. The women refused to accept the reduction, so they were shifted out and replaced by men.

Clearly, women in this sector have not lived up to their early promise; a manager whom we interviewed ruefully observed that 'When we first employed women, we thought they would be docile and easy to manage, but after the union was formed, they have become as bad as the men!' In fact, not merely as bad as the men but much worse, not only demanding to be provided with extra benefits and facilities but also refusing to give in return extra production and flexibility. This is why, as one male unionist put it, 'When it comes to physical work in the factories, management prefers men' wherever the workforce is unionised. Whether it is because of their masculine ideology of pride in physical strength, or because they don't have to perform several hours of domestic drudgery after work, or because they feel their presence at home is not crucially important, men have more easily accepted long or inconvenient hours and heavy workloads, and it is not surprising that managers prefer them.

However, the same reasoning does not apply in the unorganised sector. Here, at one level, the domestic role of women gets no consideration: they may be required to work long hours and night shifts, crèches are not provided, maternity benefits are evaded by employers; and yet, paradoxically, the presumed primary domestic and secondary wage-earning role of women is used as an excuse for paying them less than men for the same work and laying them off or dismissing them at will. In fact, many of these women may be primary or even sole breadwinners in addition to being responsible for the care of their families, and this very dependence on their wages makes them more vulnerable to pressure, forcing them to accept wretched wages and conditions; in extreme cases they might even submit to sexual harassment, although usually they leave their jobs under such circumstances.[46] Thus here, by contrast with the organised sector, they are actually cheaper and more flexible than men.

So we have a fairly clear hierarchy, with unionised women in large-scale industry being the most expensive and least flexible type of labour force, men in this sector being more convenient from the employers' point of view, men in the unorganised sector being even more convenient, and non-unionised women being most convenient of all. And, as we would expect, we find jobs slipping down the hierarchy – that is, jobs which are lost at the higher levels often reappear lower down. How can this be prevented from happening?

MALE ATTITUDES

Until fairly recently, the loss of jobs at the top affected mainly women, and most unions did not consider it a serious problem; but now men's jobs too are being affected significantly by management strategies to decentralise production through ancillarisation and subcontracting, and union concern is increasing. Clearly, so long as the wide disparity in the legal rights of workers in the two sectors remains, employers have a strong incentive to practise such a policy; a necessary step, therefore, would be to obtain for workers in small-scale industry the same legal rights and benefits as those which are enjoyed by workers in registered factories. However, these employers are well practised in evading such legislation, and conditions would not improve unless the larger and stronger unions helped workers in small-scale industry to organise and fight for their rights.

Even if the major disparities between the two sectors were to be removed, this would still leave the problem of what is to be done about the decline in the percentage of women. Solving this problem would involve not simply ensuring that women are not completely replaced by men in the traditional 'women's jobs', but also helping women to enter other occupations as the number of jobs previously available to them is cut by automation. Even the Federation of Pharmaceutical Employees which in an earlier period was such a fervent champion of women's rights has not taken any steps to combat this decline in their numbers. Other unions are ambiguous in their attitudes to the problem. One unionist has already been quoted as expressing an opinion which implies that women may be physically unsuited to factory work. Here is another, trying to explain why women are displaced when automation takes place:

> [Management] demand more flexibility in work, so that when every new machine comes you can adjust to it and so on and so forth . . . but actually I don't think that women will not be able to adjust to the machines which are there in our factory – the job is not so highly complicated that women will not be able to do it.

The implication, presumably, is that anything more complicated would be beyond the mental capacities of women to handle. These men are sincere and militant unionists, yet it is easy to see why their own attitudes would make it difficult or impossible for them to combat management strategies aimed at replacing women with men. In fact, in Hindustan Lever it would be easy to take up the issue legally, because the company has agreed to a policy of giving preference in recruitment to children of employees, yet not a single daughter of an employee has ever been put on the waiting list. The union committee has taken this up with management, but complain that without support from the workforce they can go no further. The predominant feeling among workers is that it is better for a son to get a job, since a daughter will be lost to them when she gets married and goes to live with her in-laws; and when the company refuses to put a daughter on the waiting list, the majority who want their sons to get a job are secretly pleased because it means that there is one person less on the list. In the face of such attitudes the union leadership say they feel helpless to fight on the issue, and it would indeed be difficult; but on the other hand, there is no indication that they have ever tried to confront sexist attitudes within the workforce.

WOMEN AND UNIONS

But why have the women allowed this to happen? What has changed since they were so militantly demanding their rights thirty years ago? One obvious change is the decline in their numbers: the sense of being a disappearing minority is demoralising and there is a real erosion of their power within the unions as their numbers go down. Secondly, this is not an issue which affects them personally; with their own jobs secure and retirement a few years away, they are in no mood to fight on an issue which only affects future generations of women. Thirdly, as a discouraged woman trade unionist who had once been president of the Pfizer Employees' Union explained, most of the women became inactive long ago when they got married – not only because they found it impossible to cope with union activity on top of their jobs, housework and childcare, but also because in many cases husbands were not happy about their going out after working hours. Even a glance at the routine of union activists makes it clear why it would be virtually impossible for a married woman, especially if she has small children, to play such a role. Day after day they are out till late in the evening, and holidays are often eaten up by union work. When we consider that a large proportion of male unionists are married men with children, it becomes clear that unionism today in fact presupposes and survives on the gender division of labour in the home, since these men would not be able to spend so much time on union work unless there were someone else to look after their children and home.

However, the same division of labour which releases men for the gruelling routine of union work prevents women from participating in the same capacity and ensuring that the union fights for their interests too. The vicious circle is complete, and the ex-president of the Pfizer union could see no way out except for autonomous women's organisations *outside* the unions to take up the issue of women's employment. Yet she herself pointed out that such organisations have shown little interest in this issue. Not that they have never campaigned around issues of interest to women workers; in Bombay, for example, the Forum Against the Oppression of Women has taken up cases of sexual harassment of women in non-unionised workplaces. But this remains within the general area of violence against women and sexual exploitation, which is what most of these organisations have concentrated on, so that in a sense their struggles have remained purely defensive. The further process of empowering the mass of women by increasing their social weight and confidence has never really been undertaken; which means that, paradoxically, the trade unions, male-dominated as they are, are still the only mass organisations through which women workers can get a sense of their collective strength.

ALTERNATIVE STRATEGIES

A possible solution is an organisation which includes women unionists as well as women outside existing unions who wish to organise around issues of women at work. What could such an organisation fight for? There are many possibilities. One which is immediately obvious is to attempt to break down job segregation. This would involve both trade-union action, pressing employers to train women for and recruit and promote women into jobs from which they have hitherto been excluded, as well as broader social action, to remove sexist bias in education and discrimination against girls in technical courses. But this by itself would be useless if employers were to continue to avoid recruiting women at all. In India, the traditional response to discrimination has been to demand what is called 'reservation'; thus the All-India Trade Union Congress (AITUC) in its 1960 *Report to the Central Wage Board* maintained that the main issue confronting women workers was that of equal opportunities in the matter of recruitment and employment, and since 1966 has been demanding the reservation of 20 per cent of jobs in all industries and services for women.[47] The value of this solution is questionable. In the first place it is not at all clear that reserving 20 per cent of jobs for women really means according them equal opportunities in recruitment and employment; but secondly, it appears that the government opposes even this limited degree of protection for women's employment. According to the Government of India Labour Bureau,

> It is sometimes suggested that one of the remedies for arresting the declining trend in women's employment is to make statutory provision for the reservation of a certain percentage of jobs for women. . . . It is doubtful if Government can by law compel employers to adopt such a course, notwithstanding the other legal obligations the employers have to comply with wherever women are employed. Even if Government were to have the power, legal and constitutional, to give such a directive to employers, it would neither be desirable nor practicable for Government to insist that women should continue to be employed on processes which, though originally they were being looked after by women, had been modernised and rationalised.[48]

The alternative suggested by the Labour Bureau is 'to secure the acceptance and effective implementation of the principle of non-discrimination, a principle embodied in the Indian Constitution and also in ILO Convention No. 111 concerning Discrimination in respect of Employment and Occupation, which the Government of India have already ratified'.[49]

This seems to be an ideal solution until one tries to work out what it will mean in practice. If an employer claims he cannot employ women because he has no space to provide them with separate toilets or a crèche for their children, does this constitute discrimination? If an employer claims he cannot employ women because they are restricted from doing night work and he has to run a three-shift system in order to meet competitive pressures, does this constitute discrimination? Even the ILO is vague on this point. Their Workers' Education Manual on Fighting Discrimination in Employment and Occupation says that

> discrimination against women in employment does not always occur because there is prejudice against them, but sometimes because their employment may create more problems and greater expense for the employer. . . . The obligation to grant maternity leave [and] the need for organising additional welfare facilities are considerations which may induce an employer to employ male instead of female labour. To overcome discrimination which is influenced by such factors it is necessary to tackle the causes out of which it arises.[50]

What are these causes? Foremost among them are the protective laws introduced in order to enable women workers to perform their domestic role adequately – the ban on night work, maternity benefit, crèches and so forth. Where these are enforced, they make women more expensive and less flexible than men, and therefore less attractive to employers, so one way of removing the cause of discrimination would be to abolish protective laws. Yet this legislation was introduced in the first place on the initiative of the ILO; to 'tackle the causes' of discrimination against women by abolishing protective legislation would be in flat contradiction to other ILO conventions.

A closer look at protective legislation shows that it discriminates not so much against women as against employers who employ women. The work done by women in the home ensures that workers can come to their jobs day after day, and also ensures the renewal of the labour force from generation to generation. All employers benefit from this work; why should some of them pay more for it? From their own point of view, it makes sense to put themselves outside the category of those who are discriminated against by refusing to employ women. Clearly, it will be impossible to increase women's employment in the organised sector while discriminating against those who employ them. One solution which has been proposed is that maternity benefits should be funded by a contributory scheme like the ESIS, and presumably this system could be extended to crèches too. Employers' contributions would then be in proportion to the total number of workers they employ, both men and women, and it would not be more expensive to employ women.

If such a scheme could be run efficiently, it would solve part of the problem but not the whole of it. The ban on night work and women's reluctance to work overtime and accept heavier workloads would still make them less attractive employees than men in a period of rapid automation and management demands for flexibility. A more radical solution was discussed by a meeting of women unionists in Bombay in 1983. They did not object to the allowance being made for housework and childcare: they felt this to be necessary. The problem, however, was that work in the home was seen as being solely the responsibility of women, and no allowance was made for men to participate in it. Thus a man was not given leave at the time of his child's birth, or in exceptional cases given just one or a few days' leave; not given the option of bringing his child to a workplace crèche or claiming a crèche allowance; expected to come to work at any time of the day or night, and to work overtime on demand; and so on. Of course men assented to this view of themselves, and this was part of the problem. But until men had the same rights and facilities as women and actually used them, women would continue to be at a disadvantage in the labour market. Equalising the position would involve union demands such as paternity leave, crèche facilities for the children of male workers, drastically shortening the working day of both men and women so as to leave sufficient time and energy for housework and childcare, moving towards the restriction of night work for men, and so on. First and foremost it would involve demanding time off for union meetings and reorganising union work so that people with responsibility for work in the home could also participate fully in the work of the union. Putting forward these demands and making them work would require a campaign not only within the unions but also outside them.

All this seems very far off in India at the moment. Yet it is possible to formulate demands which are not unrealistic but which begin to question the assumption that men have no role in housework and childcare – for example, shortening the statutory maximum working week from forty-eight to forty hours, giving much higher shift allowances and even shorter hours for shiftworkers, fully paid paternity leave of at least two weeks, sufficient time off to allow most union activities to take place during working hours, and so forth. A demand for the right of male workers to bring their children to a workplace crèche would be much more difficult to attain, yet raising it and discussing it has a value in itself to the extent that it results in a rethinking of something which is too often taken for granted not only by men but even by women – namely, that the ultimate responsibility for childcare falls on the mother. In the absence of social security and a situation of high unemployment it seems to make sense to demand a living wage which is adequate to support not only children but also elderly, sick or unemployed adult relatives, both male and female; yet trade unions need to question the justice of a system which assumes, firstly, that the dependents of a wage-earner will include a woman or women whose domestic work can adequately be remunerated through a wage which is paid to someone else; and secondly that anyone who is unable to earn and has no relatives capable of or willing to support him or her can justifiably be left to beg or starve. Trade unions in other countries, including some developing countries, fought for and have been able to obtain social security benefits, and there is no reason why unions in India should accept that a 'living wage' can ever be an adequate substitute.

CONCLUSION

To conclude, then. Trade unions in India have fought for the right of women to remain in employment after marriage, and for facilities such as maternity benefits and workplace crèches which will enable them to do so; they have also fought for equal pay for the same work carried out in the same workplace. Yet the end result of these struggles is that women are being pushed out of better-paid jobs and into low-paid jobs in the unorganised sector or unwaged work in the home. Why is this? The reason seems to be that unions have not attacked other aspects of the gender division of labour. They have not opposed job segregation which relegates women to labour-intensive jobs likely to disappear with automation; they have accepted the existence of an unorganised sector where workers are deprived of the rights enjoyed by workers in the organised sector and do the same work for a fraction of the pay; above all, they have not questioned the assumption that men will take primary responsibility for earning, women will take primary responsibility for unwaged work in the home, and the latter will be economically dependent on the former.

Unless women organise and press the trade-union movement to oppose the gender division of labour in *all* its aspects, it is likely that not only women workers but all workers will continue to suffer the consequences, and the possibilities inherent in the entry of women into the labour force of manufacturing industry will not be fully realised.

NOTES

1   I would like to thank friends and colleagues in the Union Research Group and the trade unions who have contributed to the research in Bombay, and the Institute of Development Studies, Sussex, for a Visiting Fellowship which enabled me to extend the research and write it up.

2   Government of India, Ministry of Labour and Employment, *Women in Employment* (Labour Bureau Pamphlet Series 8, 1964), p.1.

3   Padmini Sengupta, *Women Workers of India* (Asia Publishing House, Bombay, 1960), p.237.

4   Isa Baud, *Women's Labor in the Indian Textile Industry* (Tilburg Institute of Development Research, Research Project IRIS report no. 23, 1983), pp.67, 79.

5   S. Anandalakshmy, 'The female role in craft families', Paper presented at the 10th International Congress of Anthropological and Ethnological Sciences, New Delhi, 1978.

6   Cf. K.N. Subramanian, *Wages in India* (Tata McGraw-Hill, New Delhi, 1977), p.37.

7   Nirmala Banerjee, 'Women and industrialisation in developing countries', Occasional Paper no.71, Centre for Studies in Social Sciences, Calcutta, 1985 p.34.

8   Nirmala Banerjee, 'Women's work and discrimination', Paper presented at Bogota Conference, Columbia, 1984, Table 10.

9   Cf. Union Research Group, *Bulletin of Trade Union Research and Information*, 6-7 (Jan.–April 1985).

10 Banerjee, 'Women and industrialisation in developing countries', p.35.

11 M.D. Morris, *The Emergence of an Industrial Labor Force in India*, (University of California Press, Berkeley and Los Angeles 1965), p.67.

12 Banerjee, Women and Industrialisation, p.36.

13 Subramanian, *Wages in India*, p.93.

14 Mira Savara, *Changing Trends in Women's Employment* (Himalaya Publishing House, Bombay, 1986) p.85.

15 Ibid., p.86.

16 Subramanian, *Wages in India*, p.92.

17 Sengupta, *Women Workers of India*, pp.44-5.

18 Subramanian, *Wages in India*, p.788.

19 'Working class women and working class families in Bombay', *Economic and Political Weekly* (22 July 1978), p.1172.

20 D.T. Lakdawala, H. Joshi and V. Joshi, cited in Joshi, Heather and Vijay, 1976, *Surplus Labour and the City – Study of Bombay* (Oxford University Press, Delhi), p.105.

21 Hilary Standing, 'Gender, employment and family: the changing context of women's employment in Calcutta', Paper presented at University of London Institute of Commonwealth Studies, 1986, pp.6-7.

22   Amrita Chhachhi, 'The experience of retrenchment – women textile workers in India', mimeo, n.d.

23   Sengupta, *Women Workers of India* p.67; Mark Holmstrom, *Industry and Inequality – the Social Anthropology of Indian Labour* (Cambridge University Press, Cambridge, 1984), p.50.

24   Savara, *Changing Trends in Women's Employment*, pp.38-45.

25   Morris, *Emergence of an Industrial Labor Force*, p.103.

26   Ibid., pp.67, 105-6.

27   Ibid., pp. 180-1.

28   S.D. Punekar, *Social Insurance for Industrial Workers in India* (Oxford University Press, Indian Branch, 1950), p.33.

29   Ibid., pp.34, 37.

30   See GOI, Ministry of Labour and Employment, *Women in Employment*, p.9.

31   Morris, *Emergence of an Industrial Labor Force,* p.66 and App.II.

32   Sengupta, *Women Workers in India*, p.133.

33   Ibid., p.136.

34   Ibid., p.139.

35   Punekar, *Social Insurance*, p.46.

36   GOI, Ministry of Labour and Employment, *Women in Employment*, p.6.

37   Naila Kabeer, *Women's Employment in the Newly Industrialising Countries*, Report prepared for IDRC, IDS, Sussex, 1987, pp.57, 241.

38   GOI, Ministry of Labour and Employment, *Women in Employment*, pp.7-8.

39   Union Research Group, *Bulletin of Trade Union Research and Information*, 4, Feb. 1984.

40   Ibid.

41   Baud, *Women's Labor*, pp.31, 43, 73.

42   Ibid., pp.32, 35, 76, 87.

43   Ibid., p.60.

44   Banerjee, 'Women's work and discrimination', p.6.

45   Kabeer, *Women's Employment*, p.78.

46   Cf. Rohini P.H., Sujata S.V. and Neelam C., *My Life is One Long Struggle* (Pratishabd, Belgaum, 1984), pp.9-11, 118.

47   Savara, *Changing Trends in Women's Employment*, p.80.

48   GOI, Ministry of Labour and Employment, *Women in Employment*, p.36.

49   Ibid., p.36.

50   International Labour Office, *Fighting Discrimination in Employment and Occupation* (A Workers' Education Manual), (ILO, Geneva, 1986), pp.93-4.

GENDER AND THE POLITICS OF PRODUCTION IN INDIA[1]

Sallie Westwood

It's very hard for us. . . . Ladies in India don't go to the factory; they are at home, they work in the house, but they have some help from one another and they have time to relax as well. We ladies here we don't have any time to ourselves. We work at the factory all day and at home all night.

Pritty

Work, work, it's always the same in England. In Uganda we had servants to do the washing and cleaning and ladies didn't work.

Usha

The comments by Pritty and Usha were ones that I often heard during my year in a hosiery factory in the East Midlands.[2] Despite the long history of Indian women's involvement in manufacturing and heavy industry in India, Indian women in Britain had imbibed a very powerful myth – that Indian women in India are 'at home'. Indian women in the factory I studied contrasted their lives with those of women on another continent, using the contrast to foreground the ways in which work in all its forms invaded their lives in Britain, and although the language of 'ladies' was used, with its middle-class connotations, it was generalised to include all Indian women. Usha and Pritty were part of a large multi-racial workforce in which the gender division of labour produced low-paid women's work in stitching and the completion of garments for the High Street, while men (mostly white men) monopolised the highly paid, skilled work in knitting. For the Indian women factory work was a novel experience and not one that they wished their daughters to repeat. Nevertheless, their entry into social production and the world of wages did not generate quiescence. Instead, positioned as class subjects through paid work and against the racism of the factory and British society, Indian women demonstrated a strong sense of their identities as 'workers', entering into the struggles on the shopfloor, joining and being active in the union and presenting themselves as militant women with a clear sense of their rights as workers, an understanding of exploitation and their position in the production process. Very often it was Indian women who were most resistant to unfair targets and management power. This resistance was set within the context of a powerful and fiercely oppositional shopfloor culture. Yet, as workers themselves, Indian women still held to a view of Indian women in India as 'non-workers'. It is a contradictory understanding, and it is this contradiction which is explored in the pages that follow; Indian women are seen always as women tied to an ideological construction of the home as a private space in which 'work' does not take place, not as classed subject, working in both the productive and reproductive spheres. However, the myth of the Indian woman at home is itself a production, an ideological one constituted materially by the state through government reports and legislation, by labour markets and the labour process and maintained by union organisations and practices. The analysis that follows draws upon existing work on India and upon research material that is part of a larger project on the labour processes, and ideologies surrounding the gender division of labour, in a variety of working contexts in India. The research was concentrated in Ahmedabad in Gujarat, Western India.[3]

THE POLITICS OF PRODUCTION

Burawoy, writing of the politics of production, notes: 'theories of underdevelopment have failed to examine the labour process or its relationship to the state as mediated by the political apparatuses of production'.[4] His own work on the periphery countries concentrates on the Zambian mines, and more generally his work has emphasised the class character of the politics surrounding production. The issues of gendered relations and the complexities of relations in production in India require a multi-layered account which focuses attention upon both the formal and informal sectors of employment while much of the debate and discussion, from Braverman and Burawoy onwards, has focused on the capitalist labour process.[5] Unfortunately, there is a dearth of information on the labour process in manufacturing in India and less on the informal sector.

Nevertheless, the issues raised by the labour process debates in relation to the politics of the labour process can be separated out and addressed in the Indian context. These issues raise the ways in which gender and class, as two interlocking systems, have their material expression in the labour process through the forms of the division of labour and the forms of subordination. Clearly, issues concerned with managerial strategies in the formal sector are equally relevant because the formal and informal sectors are interlinked and the relationship between time, effort and rewards, and thereby the levels of exploitation of labour, are crucial. Similarly, issues of control both over the labour process and the products of labour and the ways in which skill and expertise are defined are all part of production processes. The politics of production is formed by these issues constituting them as areas of struggle, of contested terrain, where workers individually and collectively resist management imperatives, try to define the rate for the job, measure their effort, try to define what will be skilled work and who will exercise control over entry into skilled work. This politics has its expression both in formal organisations such as trade unions and in the types of shopfloor cultures and work cultures that have been studied in Britain and elsewhere.[6] To provide a gendered account of this politics is to look beyond the figures and the myths about women workers in India and to make problematic some of the taken-for-granted assumptions about waged work and work in the informal sector. However, it is the case, as Nirmala Banerjee reminds us: 'Women workers have always formed a separate category in the labour market, concentrated in certain specific occupations and under particular types of organisations and working conditions'.[7] Women enter any labour market under conditions set by their roles in reproduction. In this chapter the analysis of the politics of production concentrates initially upon the formal sector, using the textiles industry as the context for the discussion, and moving in the latter part of the chapter to the informal sector and the attempts by women to forge a new politics of production through a collective response in a sector noted for its fragmentation.

INDIA: SOME STATISTICS

Contrary to popular images of India as a land of sitars, yogis and peasant production, India is the world's tenth industrial nation, with a large indigenous capitalist sector. From the 1981 Census data we learn of a total population of 665.3 million, of whom 507.6 million are located in rural India and 157.7 million are in the urban world. Men constitute 260.1 million and women 247.6 million in the rural areas, and 83.9 million men and 73.8 million women are urban.[8] In relation to the working lives of this population the 1981 Census distinguished between 'main workers', those who had worked for more than 183 days of paid work, and 'marginal workers', who had worked fewer days. Table 14.1 below demonstrates the patterns within these definitions.

Official statistics always present difficulties, and the definitions of work and main-sector employment have changed with each Indian

TABLE 14.1

Main workers (*millions*)			Rural	Urban
Total:		222.5	176.4	46.1
	m.	177.5	136.8	40.7
	f.	45.0	39.6	5.4
Marginal workers (*millions*)				
Total:		22.1	20.9	1.2
	m.	3.5	3.1	0.4
	f.	18.6	17.8	0.8
Percentage of main workers				
Total:		33.4	34.8	29.2
	m.	51.6	52.6	48.5
	f.	14.0	16.0	7.3

Source: Census of India, 1981

census. However, it is suggested that women's employment in the main or formal sector has risen between 1971 and 1981 from 11.87 % to 14.00%.[9] The statistics point to the continuity in women's involvement in main-sector employment, but, equally, they demonstrate the importance of the informal sector for women as so-called 'marginal workers' – the language of marginality speaks volumes for the way women are positioned in official discourses. Women dominate this sector especially in the urban areas, and this is not discussed when work participation rates are quoted. The overall rate is 33.44%, with 51.23% for men and 14.44% for women.[10] Although the work of women within the informal sector forms part of the discussion in this chapter, initially I want to concentrate on formal-sector employment and the working lives of women in the textile industry in Gujarat and Bombay.

GUJARAT AND THE MANCHESTER OF INDIA

Gujarat is a fast-expanding industrial state in the process of diversifying its industries and moving from its pre-eminence in textiles – hence the title 'Manchester of India' – into chemicals and pharmaceuticals. Gujarat has a population of 23.5 millions with 10.6 million

291

people in the urban areas.[11] There has been a growth in the urban population of 43.5% between 1971 and 1981.[12] Ahmedabad, famous for its mills and textiles, has a population of 2,545,000. It is estimated that 19 of every 1,000 people in the state are engaged in factory employment.[13] Outside Ahmedabad there is a growing new industrial sector with large and small factories making everything from small components to television sets. But it was initially the textile industry that interested me and women's roles within this, which are discussed more generally in Rohini Banaji's paper in this volume. It is a sister industry to the fast-declining hosiery industry, equally in decline, with severe consequences for women's work. There used to be sixty-five textile mills in Ahmedabad employing 150,000 workers, but few now remain, and since 1982 fourteen mills have closed and 40,000 workers have been laid off.[14] However, the retrenchment of women workers started much earlier, just as in the coal, jute and textiles industries generally. As the figures show, in 1911 women workers in textiles constituted 18.6% of the workforce, in 1935 they were 11%, in 1971, 3.0 and in 1981, 3.4%. In 1981 there were only 5,120 women workers in a workforce of 151,499.[15]

Ahmedabad mills had a division of labour worked through in relation to castes and gender. Women worked in spinning, winding and reeling areas and not in weaving or with the large machinery. Many were from the weaving castes but they were introduced into the mills by their mothers and they used their mother's names as a surname until 1955 when the mills insisted that they use their fathers or husbands names.[16] As Renana Jhabvala's study, *Closing Doors*, shows, after 1920 crèches were provided at some of the larger mills, but with the fall-off in women workers these soon fell into disuse. The crèches grew out of the demands of the Textile Labour Association (TLA) (Majoor Mahajan) founded in 1920. Women workers were especially loyal and active in the TLA, and one woman commented that 'The TLA is like our mother'. It had, in fact, a strong welfare bias and was very important in organising the textile workers and in the later campaigns organised by Gandhi.

Yet it was the same TLA that did nothing to halt the expulsion of women workers from the industry. In the twenties and thirties there was a massive crisis in textiles due to the Japanese textile mills. The indigenous owners, faced with a profits squeeze, reorganised the labour process, brought in new machinery and rationalised labour, while in 1933 the great Depression hit. In 1935 the TLA were party to an agreement on rationalisation which nominated married women as the first group of workers to be made redundant – and they went. It is, of course, a familiar story. What is interesting in terms of the invisibility of women as paid workers is the fact that women were ejected from industry at a time when the state, through official surveys like the family budget survey, constructed the family as a nuclear family with mother at the centre.[17] This ideological construction came with a powerful domestic and familial ideology that glorified the role of women in the home as wives and mothers and denied women their roles in production as workers. Men were viewed as providers and as breadwinners. The role of the state in constructing ideologies of this kind, that had clear resonances with both colonial ideologies and extant cultural forms, generated a climate in which it was easy to push women out of the mills. In fact, this vision contradicts customary law and its recognition of the joint family. Equally, the introduction of the notion of the family wage has clear resonances with union struggles in the metropolitan core. As elsewhere, the account took no cognisance of women as sole earners – one Bombay study estimated that 40% of women textile workers were widows.[18] Instead, the secretary of the TLA made a public speech asking women to go home and to look after their families; in this he separated care from cash and the net results were the further impoverishment of some of the poorest mill workers and their families.

Equally pernicious was the way in which male workers were pressured to stop their wives working at a time when new forms of technology had transformed spinning through the use of large machinery designated unfit for women – or women were unfit to use this machinery due to its complexities. Women resisted where they could, but without backing from the TLA it was an impossible struggle. They kept their jobs for a while, but so many pressures forced them out. In her interviews with retrenched mill workers Renana Jhabvala reports the ways in which the women emphasised maternity benefits as the cause of their redundancy.[19] (Maternity benefits were introduced in 1929 under the Maternity Benefit Act, and they became part of the State Insurance Scheme in 1955 which passed into the 1961 central scheme.) This points to the importance of the ideological battle waged against women as workers because the union and the male workers were of the opinion that motherhood and paid work must be separated; the one belongs in the factory, the other in the home. During my own research I met many of these women now trying to eke out a living in the informal sector through the resuscitation of their traditional skills as weavers with state support for the handloom industry. We will return to them later in the chapter.

BOMBAY: WOMEN AND TEXTILES

The militancy of textiles workers is well known, including the resistance of women workers. Women used the *gherrao* (a common form of protest expressing opposition to power and authority by encircling an individual and using language and physical presence to intimidate them) to shame and embarrass both management and union officials. In a 1962 article, Ralph C. James links the decline in women's participation in the industry to a strategy of exclusion by the powerful employers.[20] They used arguments ranging from the sanctity of women and their place in the home to the hardships caused to men by women's employment, but the real reason was the militancy of the women workers. James, in fact, refers to the 'aggression' of women workers. Despite their militancy, however, women were excluded and management was able to reassert power and authority. James, commenting on the women workers, notes, 'They strenuously resist such efforts, frequently by militant displays and threats of violence'.[21] James looked at government accounts of strikes and found that women had fought and won on their own, in some textile mills, more often than male workers and that they had done this by the use of careful strategies and tactics. For example, in one mill the women captured a top management official, locked him up, used a dagger to intimidate him and made their demands. Their grievances were heard and dealt with after his release. Union officials, in several cases, were also *gherraoed*, spat on, called names and generally harassed. Usually the female leaders were operating at the informal level, but they promoted and obtained group solidarity among the women and prompted collective action of a very successful kind. Such was the success that both employers and unions had much to gain by their removal. As one writer commented, 'their resourcefulness in the art of self protection is considerable'.[22] There can be no doubting the importance that women workers attached to their jobs and their solidarity. Given this, the response from the TLA in Ahmedabad is hardly surprising.

The contradictions that surround women in paid employment, so sympathetically portrayed in the films of Satijat Ray and Shyam Benegal, are also to be seen in the reports for the Government of India Labour Bureau where, in the fifties, a report entitled 'The economic and social status of women workers in India' pointed to 'the creation of a new class of persons among women', and a 'raising of social status', but these new persons were also characterised by 'Delinquency, domestic discord and broken families' – much as was said in the fifties in Britain when working mothers were socially constructed as a source of all manner of social problems (see Jephcott for an examination of this in Britain).[23] The Labour Bureau report underlines the fact that women who contribute to the family income have a strong sense of their importance in their families and communities and that they do not regard themselves as inferior to men – an arena ignored by James.

The discourses employed by the state are examined by Radha Kumar in her discussion of women in the Bombay cotton textile industry, 1919-39.[24] In a fascinating reading of government reports,

Kumar discusses the ways in which an opposition was set up between the working-class family and factory production in the lives of women through the idealisation of woman as mother. 'For, while idealogues talked of women's lack of commitment to wage work, labelling it supplementary, and philanthropists glorified "motherhood", the industry retrenched women in large numbers.'[25] It is clear from her account that the issue of maternity benefits was a vital one, as suggested by the mill workers, and that women in Ahmedabad claimed more maternity benefit than those in Bombay – not surprising given the large percentage of widows in the Bombay industry. However, a benefit supposedly to assist working mothers was turned, ultimately, against women generally. Although women fiercely resisted retrenchment, not only economics but also ideologies were ranged against them because, as the women in Britain suggested, 'Ladies don't work in the factories.'

In fact, the attempt to look at gender and the politics of production in an Indian context moves one beyond the factory gate. There have been studies of factory workers like Holmstrom's work and Kelman's famous 1923 study, *Labour in India*, which included women workers. More recently the work done by Alice Thorner and Jyoti Ranadive, Hilary Standing and Rohini P.H. in this volume, for example, has illuminated the processes of waged work in women's lives.[26] Although these latter works are not studies of life in factories, they raise some important points, especially about the relationship between production and reproduction.

Holmstrom's study suggests that female factory workers 'are very often the wives or unmarried daughters of men working in the same or other factories'.[27] Despite this familial pattern, however, in terms of the politics of access to factory work it is the men, through the unions, who have negotiated the ability to inherit jobs from fathers to sons. Equally, the claim to equal pay for equal work in the factories proves, on examination, to be false; earnings of all men and all women show a 57% gap and Holmstrom records that data from Bombay found a 27% gap in earnings.[28] Women are poorly organised through the trade-union movement: in 1974 women made up only 6.2% of trade unionists, an issue explored by Rohini P.H. in this volume. 'In factories there is equal pay for equal work, but in India as elsewhere women's skills are rated separately and paid less.[29]

It is clearly important to concentrate upon the articulation between production and reproduction in the lives of urban women and how this articulation generates a sector of the labour force as subordinated labour. Women's roles in the home help to define them as non-workers, and thereby they are subjected to levels of super-exploitation through employers looking for a cheap and flexible workforce increasingly in the capital export zones, especially in Bombay where women workers are used in garment export companies and electronics as unskilled labour and paid accordingly. The research reported by Alice Thorner and Jyoti Ranadive underlines the complexities of urban working class households and the crucial role that women have in both reproduction and production. While employment opportunities for men in Bombay may place them in the formal sector women are concentrated in the informal sector especially with the demise of women in the textile industry.[30] Rohini P.H.'s chapter in this volume amplifies the discussion by demonstrating the reproduction of a familiar pattern: women workers being retrenched from the textiles industry in the new industries of chemicals and pharmaceuticals where there is also an important shift, for women workers, out of formal sector employment and into informal sector employment.

In Hilary Standing's study of women workers in Calcutta the power relations of the household are opened up and questions concerning the relationship between economic power in production and domestic power are unravelled.[31] This study looked at women across employment sectors, at middle-class and working-class women and their families, and examined gender inequalities in access to education, labour markets and household resources. The picture is a complex one in which outcomes cannot be 'read off', and it cannot be assumed that paid employment for women necessarily raises their status in the domestic unit, nor their access to power and property.[32]

Most women work in the informal, or unorganised, sector. The 1980 statistics show that 60.4% of rural women workers and 44.2% of urban women workers are 'self-employed'.[33] It is to the self-employed that I now turn.

THE INFORMAL SECTOR

There can be no account of the politics of production in India without reference to the informal sector where most women work and generate income.[34] This is a vast and often invisible sector which is statistically under-represented. The 1981 Census of India estimated that there were 8.8 million workers involved in household industry, and the labour statistics suggest that there are 2.2 million bidi workers alone (those who make cigarettes by hand).[35] It is now acknowledged that the informal sector is fragmented, differentiated and unorganised with urban and rural variants but that it is not outside the formal sector. Indeed, the informal sector is crucially bound to the capitalist sector through relations of exploitation where capital can find a cheap and disorganised workforce. As Papola comments: 'Despite the widespread use of the two-way classification of urban economic organisations, it is also well recognised that the distinction is not always analytically clear, nor is it operationally usable for all purposes'.[36] Rather, the designation of the informal sector tends to be the negative of the formal sector. However, it is useful to present a profile of this sector bearing in mind the difficulties.

The ILO in 1972 characterised the informal sector in the following way:

1   Ease of entry;
2   Reliance on indigenous resources;
3   Family ownership of enterprises;
4   Small-scale operations;
5   Labour-intensive, using adaptive technologies;
6   The skills used were acquired outside schooling;
7   It is an irregular and competitive market.[37]

It is also useful to differentiate between petty commodity producers, some of whom will be using 'traditional' skills and crafts methods, and those who are dependent workers in commodity production, sometimes called outworkers or home workers. Vast numbers of women, men and children work in this sector, and for many in India it encompasses their whole working lives. Papola's study of Ahmedabad did not address the issue of women workers, but he concluded:'47% of the workers in Ahmedabad city are found engaged in economic activities in the informal sector: 25% of them in small establishments; 14% as independent workers and 7% as casual workers working for households'.[38] The study also estimated that this sector generated 28% of the GDP produced in the city.[39]

Yet it has too often been assumed that this is a sector of production without the politics of production, without organisation, resistance or struggle. Nirmala Banerjee in her study of Calcutta comments, for example,

> workers in the organized sector can bargain effectively with their employers while other workers in the country cannot. The bargaining strength of the former may be due to their superior skills, though generally it is greatly reinforced by the political militancy of their trade unions. Other workers are not capable of building up such bargaining strength and therefore continue to work under deplorable working conditions.[40]

While the 'deplorable working conditions' are not in doubt, some attempts at bargaining have been made and women have often been in the forefront of organising in this sector. Locked out of formal-sector employment and the union structure, women have generated alternative forms of organisation. One of the most successful of these is SEWA (Self-Employed Women's Association) based in Ahmedabad but with branches in other parts of the country. It was set up in 1972 and now has a membership of 22,739.[41] Other organisations, like the Working Women's Forum, followed in 1978 – it has

297

a membership of 3,000. There are a growing number of these organisations, but I want to concentrate on SEWA, with whom I spent time in 1986.

Although attention in the literature has focused on the economics of this sector, politics and ideologies are inseparable from economics and SEWA has met this with its recognition of the rights of self-employed workers that, they argue, should be akin to trade-union rights based on collective organisation. The emphasis is not surprising given SEWA's home originally within the TLA (until 1981) and the fact that many of the organisers, especially the leader of SEWA, Ela Bhatt, had their roots in the TLA. The crucial and first issue for SEWA is visibility – how to make the millions of self-employed women workers count as workers. SEWA has consistently avoided designations such as 'the informal sector' and concentrates instead upon the language of the self-employed and the fact that as workers they can act collectively. This designation offers dignity as well as rights to women (and men) in the informal sector, and it emphasises that women are workers; contrary to the view that uses their invisibility as a means to emphasise home and family women as daughter, wives and mothers but not as workers. This becomes especially important when so many women workers are actually located in home-based production, the coming together of reproductive and productive relations in one arena.

Renana Jhabvala divides the self-employed sector into two parts. The first group consists of piece-rate workers, who work with materials supplied by contractors who are the employers, and goods are returned to them.[42] They are very poorly paid, as the Maria Mies study of lace-makers discovered, and Jennifer Sebstad's study of workers in Ahmedabad confirmed, as did my own work.[43] These workers include unknown numbers of children. Sebstad's data show that home-based piece-rate workers earned 130 rupees per month compared with 250 rupees for vendors and 170 rupees for labourers.[44] Workers are employed by large and small employers using a putting-out system for parts of production at home. The company stores materials and finished products and may or may not use contractors. There are also small employers who come from the same community as the workers.

Home workers are not governed by most legislation, except for bidi workers. Employers have a 'flexible' workforce which can be rejected with changes in production or new developments; for example, when the shell-less cotton pod was introduced into Gujarat, 30,000 workers who formally shelled the cotton pods lost their jobs, and when cement manufacturers started to use plastic and new bags the bag stitchers lost their jobs.[45] Not only is this workforce flexible but also it uses the home as a site of production and provides machinery within the home. Workers are many but isolated, in competition for work and exploited by employers and contractors. Women are especially vulnerable through the ideologies that surround them and construct them as home-based wives and mothers (Mies's study is a classic statement on the levels of exploitation of home-based workers). Similarly, Martha Roldan's account of outworking in Mexico concludes that, although outworking may aid confidence, gains to women in terms of independence and autonomy are few because home-working does not change the materiality of women's subordination – rather, it fuels this by augmenting domestic ideologies.[46]

The politics of production, are therefore, crucially bound up with ideological struggles alongside the focus on organising isolated workers and generating collective struggles, but it is a perilous path, as SEWA and others have discovered. Women who are organised to fight for better rates may find that they have been bypassed by employers, that their work goes elsewhere, and in conditions of extreme poverty this is a much-repeated pattern. The early attempts to organise women in Ahmedabad had this result, and it has been repeated more recently with Muslim women who work in the ready-made garment industry. Currently, they sew saree petticoats – a difficult task, and one for which they received as little as 7 rupees a dozen, and from this 7 rupees the women calculated that cotton and oil for the machines accounted for 2 rupees.[47] Some of the women were also paying for their machines. Most of the women tried to sew one dozen a day, but this usually meant a joint effort by mothers and daughters. Only by sewing all hours could one woman make 200 rupees a month. The petticoats sell at 15–20 rupees. The women organised to try to raise the price for the job and found it had gone elsewhere. Despite the recent caste and communal violence in Ahmedabad, when the houses of many of these women were destroyed, they were not deterred and remained together. SEWA provided sewing machines for some of the women and helped them pick up work from other sources.

There are important gender issues here where the ideologies of women's work may be brought into play – lace-making, like the making of saree petticoats, is such a case, and Maria Mies's work underlines the ways in which patriarchal assumptions encourage the exploitation of women.[48] The ideologies of home work suggest that it is not as arduous as 'real' work outside the home. The lace-makers were divided and dependent upon brokers between themselves and the multi-nationals. The levels of super-exploitation detailed by the study have a special twist because the lace was made for women's clothes in the west. In one small example are contained all the relations of colonial and gender exploitation historically and currently.

Home-working ties domestic labour and paid work together spatially and in terms of effort. There are ways in which organisations can intervene to control the rate for the job, and organise the distribution and collection of materials through a co-operative. The politics of this form of production is generating strength on the ground, struggling to achieve organisations that are recognised, but, as I have suggested, these struggles are fraught with difficulties. Supplies of materials may be monopolised, a problem that SEWA encountered, and the collection and organisation of distribution is a difficult task when there are extant networks used by retail outlets. It is a circle that has to be broken into, but the early years require not just organisational support but also material support to carry the project through. SEWA organised quilt-makers in Ahmedabad and continues to do so. These are women who sew washed and cleaned rags into quilts for the poorest sections of the population. It is unpleasant, badly paid work, done by many of the Muslim women in the old city. But, although the women are organised for the distribution and collection of materials into a co-operative the co-operative does not break even; so what next? It was this debate that was in process during my time in Ahmedabad.

The second group of self-employed workers are petty commodity producers who use capital and raw materials to produce at home. Many produce handicrafts, and the nature of the work and the labour processes are highly variable but for all there is a need for capital, materials and the inputs of time and effort which produce commodities for specific markets.[49] Attempts have been made to generate credit for the small producers known as the weaker sections. Jana Everett and Mira Savara have provided an account of lending and its effect on women in Bombay.[50] Nationalised banks have provided loans but they find it difficult to collect and recognise that an intermediary is most successful. SEWA has operated a very successful women's bank, lending and collecting from women, but women do not necessarily benefit greatly, as Everett and Savara suggest. The income of the women increases only slightly and they remain below the poverty line, but they also have to pay off their debts and deal with family expenses. Women's loans seem to be smaller than men's. Instead, there has been a movement towards co-operatives; in this way organisational power can be used and competition among small producers can be minimised.

Co-operatives of small, poor producers are, however, beset with problems. Many of the goods that are made are made for the poor, who have a low level of consumption, which means that the circulation of income is small and income generation for households and producers is difficult. There are few ways in which to boost production. Guaranteed markets and price supports have assisted khadi and handloom weavers in the past, but producers need markets and space. It is a politics of production located with small-scale producers disadvantaged in large markets without capital, ways of upgrading their machinery or skills, and without marketing expertise.

UNIONS TO CO-OPERATIVES: CONTRADICTIONS

SEWA has had a particularly interesting experience in relation to the attempt to organise women into a union of self-employed, emphasising initially the SEWA bank and other facilities that link SEWA to its history in the TLA and the welfarism of Indian trade unions. Of late, apart from the success of the SEWA bank as a means through which women could save, it has been involved in loans to producers and vendors, who also form a major part of the informal sector. But the Bank of India still complains that SEWA has too many savers and not enough borrowers, and many of the women use the bank and loans for domestic matters like weddings rather than in pursuit of entrepreneurial goals.

Faced with this knowledge and with their previous experience of the isolation of many home producers, SEWA set up a series of co-operatives with managers employed by SEWA. One of the earliest was the block printing co-operative made up of women from the Chhipa community, a group of Muslim women who worked as hand-block printers, printing cloth using wooden blocks and vegetable dyes as their families would have done before the advent of screen printing. Most of the men now work in screen-printing shops or factories, while the women knowledgeable in the 'traditional' skills set about trying to use them to eke out a living. SEWA provided wages throughout the year (on a scale of 100 rupees during training to 300 rupees per month for the experienced workers), a space in which to work, training and added design consultants. But by 1986 the co-operative, although busy and productive, was not generating a profit and a debate began with the Chhipa women on how to manage the growing debts. One suggestion was to move to a piece-rate system which would control productivity but which meant that the women would be laid off during the rains (this is a time when block-printing cannot take place and previously the women had been paid for two months in which production was stopped). Co-operative or not, self-managed or not, the women responded in the same way that workers throughout the world have done in relation to layoffs and the assertion of managerial control: they resisted them fiercely, set about organising amongst themselves and took on SEWA as workers, using the principles for which SEWA was itself set up. The women refused to accept a move from secure, steady wages to a piece-rate system which they saw as an attempt to exercise greater control over their work. Debates followed on the level of production and time-keeping. In response to complaints about punctuality the women pointed out that, unlike their manager, they had no help in the house. They were, it seemed, acutely aware of the class divide between themselves and the manager. SEWA was

301

in the middle of a management–workers struggle.

The second example is also telling. SEWA had organised a cleaners co-operative with women (originally paper pickers) who were trained to clean some of the educational institutions in Ahmedabad. SEWA had generated a good price for the job on the basis of 4–5 hours' work a day and managed the co-operative overseeing the work and distributing wages. But a local union started to talk to the women cleaners, while the educational institutions complained about the standard of cleaning. The outcome was that the cleaners' co-operative members entered into negotiations with the other union and wanted to leave SEWA on the promise of higher wages. SEWA members had learned some trade-union principles early on and they held fast to them.

The final example of the difficulties brings us back to the weavers made redundant from the mills who had, of course, an industrial background and a familiarity with the TLA. There are government subsidies for the handloom industry, and SEWA encouraged this group of very lively women to take up weaving again, using the old frame looms or even pit looms which are enormous and take up the length of a small house. The women did this and joined together in a co-operative. Immediately, under the principle of self-management, they voted to raise the price for the job – a pay increase for themselves. Despite the self-management and the label of 'co-operative' the women applied their old bargaining skills to the new situation. Equally, they tried to bargain against a piece-rate system, which offered 10 rupees per day if the supply of work was maintained, and for guaranteed monthly wages like the block printers. They were also quite clear that there was no money to be made out of handloom weaving and that they needed mechanised machinery in order to improve the speed and quality of their work, but the government subsidies were for handloom work. As workers they were subject to problems over supply and outlets and space in which to work, and the co-operative struggled to come together with a young designer who was full of ideas, but who recognised that making shawls for the poor was not going to generate a profit and her remit was to take the co-operative into profit.

These are cautionary tales for anyone who imagines that co-operatives are the answer for small producers. SEWA is one of the most able and committed organisations and yet it was faced with hostile economic conditions within a sector of the market that could not sustain the level of income generation necessary for the profitable survival of the co-operatives. So they are subsidised, and workers will not easily relinquish wages for a brave new world of enterprise. The women demonstrate, instead, the collective principles for which SEWA struggles and a very high level of worker solidarity, echoing the mill workers of earlier times.

STRUGGLES OVER SKILL

The issue of skill and the way in which the gender division of labour constructs men's and women's work in relation to skill have been struggled over by women workers globally.[51] Among the textile workers of Bombay and Ahmedabad women lost out to a patriarchal definition of skill, which suggested that as unskilled workers they could not acquire the skills necessary for new technologies in the mills. The women themselves dispute this, but for the weavers who returned to their handlooms there was an added element. They saw in the definitions of waged work that had been used against them all the vagaries of the capitalist sector, and told me that at least with their weaving skills they had something which could not be made redundant at the whim of employers. It was not surprising, therefore, that they tried to trade this with the SEWA co-operative. They still saw a bargain that had to be struck between their skills and the price for the job. The women objected to the piece rate that they were offered and wanted a secure wage like the block printers, but SEWA had learnt important lessons from their experience with the block printers and no longer set up the co-operatives on this basis.

Women's work incorporates skills which are also familiarly cast as 'natural' – located with small hands and nimble fingers and the attributes associated with domestic skills. The potters I worked with always referred to the skills with which women rolled the clay in this way. They suggested that it was a task that only women could do because it was the same as rolling *rotis* and it required those skills.[52] Similarly, stitching work done at home the world over is often defended because women can sew 'naturally', so why not for cash as well as for their families.

The difficulties that the SEWA co-operatives had are repeated elsewhere, and relate to the level of skill in the handicrafts industry of which their co-operatives were a part. How was it possible to upgrade the skills that the women had so that products could move into the more lucrative luxury markets? This was not an easy task, as SEWA and other co-operatives have discovered. The quality of products has to be very high, and women are often using skills that they have acquired along the way in the families of which they are a part, or, because of their position in the family, they will have been locked out of certain skills – a daughter takes her skills to another family on marriage, a point often raised by the block printers who had not received the same level of education and skills training within their families as their brothers. Similarly, in some trades women are simply locked out. Tailors, for example, expect their wives and daughters to do hand-stitching for which they are prepared by nature, it is said, but not cutting or tailoring *per se*, which is viewed as men's work.

303

This has meant that in the new, ready-made garment industry women are doing home-stitching but not cutting, nor are they in the factories. Instead, they do the least skilled work, of sewing side seams. This was especially cruel in those communities where the women had a long history of embroidery work, like the Mochis (shoemakers), who have moved out of shoemaking and into the ready-made garment sector in a big way in Ahmedabad. In my research it was clear that one of the reasons for this shift was ease of access into this sector. The men I interviewed were clear that women in their families could sew and were, therefore, a readily available and skilled workforce for making up garments. They now have little time for the beautiful embroidery for which they were once well known.

In this example, and there are many more, women's skills become part of the economic strategies of men. I did not meet women running export garment firms nor ready-made garment companies, but I did meet many who stitched for such companies which were often run by husbands, brothers or other relatives. These entrepreneurs also had a rationale for the women who worked at home, as one man commented: 'Formerly Mochi women never worked outside the home well, they still stay at home but they do some stitching as well. So, they make some money but the situation does not change.' The ideologies in play are those we have seen in relation to the textile workers, the lace-makers and throughout the official and commonsense accounts of women as workers. Women cannot be workers; their place is in the home – a convenient fiction for the thousands of invisible hands at sewing machines throughout India.[53]

CONCLUSION

The stories told in this chapter point to the difficulties inherent in sustaining co-operatives of small producers. To point to the difficulties is not to undermine the work of SEWA but to highlight its success in generating and reproducing a collective consciousness among women workers. It demonstrates the power of the idea 'we stand on our feet', a notion redolent of the power relations of women's lives inside and outside the home. The factories I studied in Ahmedabad's new industrial sector, large and small, showed no signs of a similar collective strength from women workers because workers, male and female, were not invited to air their views, and were not consulted or offered any control over the production processes of which they were a part. Management exercised control. Similarly, women working in the crafts sector in family-based production units were rarely consulted and invited to participate in decisions affecting production. It is clear from SEWA's experience that self-managing co-operatives in the informal sector do not magically manage themselves. The situation is a deeply contradictory one, fashioned in part by external constraints, but SEWA has not run away from the contradictions but tries, instead, to work with them and through them, looking to both the empowerment of women through income generation and power in the workplace, and the market imperatives for high productivity and efficiency. It is an immensely difficult task.

The foregoing discussion also points to the vitality of the politics of production in the informal sector, especially among women who struggle to organise against opposition from both the private and public spheres. Husbands may object to their wives' involvement in women's organisations and their moves out from the domestic sphere. Equally, men monopolise the distribution chains, with important consequences for women. One example of this was the case of vendors in Ahmedabad. Women selling fruits and vegetables in small quantities around the main market in Ahmedabad are at the end of the distribution chain, while men control the space and goods in both the wholesale and main markets. The women were constantly harassed by the police and other traders until SEWA fought a legal battle to secure their rights to access to public space and thereby to trade and to generate income. This legal battle was a crucial part of the politics of production in the informal sector, and demonstrates the ways in which gender and class relations are articulated in the informal sector as much as the formal sector. As Zubeida, a women who sews quilts, commented: 'Now I am standing on my own I feel better because I am not dependent upon my husband or the merchant and I get protection from SEWA all the time.'

For the women with whom I began this chapter, Pritty and Usha, the issues addressed here are of more than passing interest. The factory I studied and where they work has suffered major cutbacks, and workers, like their counterparts in India, have been made redundant. Both working-class women and men are increasingly pushed into the growing informal/self-employed sector in Britain, but the outcomes tend to be gender-specific. Whereas men, especially British men of South Asian descent, made redundant from the hosiery industry, have tried to buy hosiery machinery or to raise capital to start ready-made garment firms, women have been pushed back into homesewing and other forms of outwork.

However, some of the South Asian women have articulated very specific demands for an outworkers' centre in their locality to organise the distribution and collection of work, to set the rate for the job and to provide a public space (with a crèche) in which women can work. It is a collective response and one for which funds are being sought in Leicester through the Leicester Outwork Campaign.[54] It is also an active response to their situation as workers in the most exploited sector of the economy where both racism and sexism combine to subordinate South Asian women as workers in Britain. But, despite the level of economic activity among Indian women in India or in Britain, the importance of home-based production as a site for their work will allow the myths about Indian women as non-workers to persist. The ideological battles for visibility will continue, not least because, as is clear from the women's lives portrayed in this chapter, women themselves demonstrate a high level of workers' consciousness and a political will to be recognised as workers.

NOTES AND REFERENCES

1   This chapter would not have been possible without the generosity of the women whose lives appear here and without the help and support that I received from SEWA. I am deeply grateful to everyone involved with the research, and especially to Ela Bhatt and Renana Jhabvala. I owe special thanks to Ali Rattansi for his comments upon an earlier draft of this chapter and to Haleh Afshar for editorial support.

2   See S. Westwood (1984) *All Day Every Day: Factory and Family in the Making of Women's Lives* (Pluto Press, London; University of Illinois Press, Chicago).

3   See S. Westwood (forthcoming) 'Gendered relations: caste, class and the labour process in India'.

4   M. Burawoy (1985) *The Politics of Production* (Verso, London), p.210.

5   H. Braverman (1974) *Labor and Monopoly Capital: The Degradation of Work in the Twentieth Century* (Monthly Review Press, New York); M. Burawoy (1979) *Manufacturing Consent: Changes in the Labour Process under Monopoly Capitalism* (University of Chicago Press, Chicago); and for a review of the debates, see P. Thompson (1983) *The Nature of Work: an Introduction to Debates on the Labour Process* (Macmillan, London).

6   See Burawoy, *Manufacturing Consent*; Westwood, 'Gendered Relations'; T. Lupton (1963) *On the Shopfloor* (Pergamon, Oxford); A. Pollert (1981) *Girls, Wives, Factory Lives* (Macmillan, London).

7   N. Banerjee (1985) *Women Workers in the Unorganised Sector* (Sangam, Delhi), p.25.

8   Census of India, 1981.

9   *Statistical Outline of India* (1984), Tata Statistical Services Ltd, Bombay, p.40.

10   Ibid.

11   *Statistical Outline of India* (1984), p.32.

12   Ibid., p.45.

13   Ibid., p.7.

14   R. Jhabvala (1985) *Closing Doors: Study on the Decline of Women Workers in the Textile Mills of Ahmedabad* (SETU Centre for Social Knowledge and Action, Ahmedabad), p.5.

15   Jhabvala, *Closing Doors*, p.27.

16   Ibid.

17   See R. Kumar (1983) 'Family and factory: women in the Bombay cotton textile industry, 1919-1939', *The Indian Economic and Social History Review*, 20(1):81-110.

18   Kumar, 'Family and Factory':88.

19   Jhabvala, *Closing Doors*, pp.26-37.

20   R.C. James (1962) 'Discrimination against women in Bombay textiles', *Industrial and Labor Relations Review*,15(2):209-34.

21   Ibid., p.211.

22   Ibid., p.213.

23   Government of India (1956) *The Economic and Social Status of Women Workers in India* (Delhi); and see P. Jephcott (1962) *Married Women Working* (Allen & Unwin:London).

24   Kumar, 'Family and Factory'.

25   Ibid., p.110.

26   M. Holmstrom (1984) *Industry and Inequality: the Social Anthropology of Indian Labour* (Cambridge University Press, Cambridge); J.H. Kelman (1923) *Labour in India: Study of the Conditions of Indian Women in Modern Industry* (Allen & Unwin, London); Thorner, A. and Ranadive, J. (1985) 'Household as a first stage in a study of urban working-class women', *Economic and Political Weekly*, Vol. XIX No 17. ppWS9-13. H. Standing (1985) 'Resources, wages, and power: the impact of women's employment on the urban Bengali household', in H. Afshar (ed.), *Women, Work and Ideology in the Third World* (Tavistock, London), pp.223-57.

27   Holmstrom, *Industry and Inequality*, pp.227-8.

28   Ibid., p.229.

29   Ibid., p.227.

30   Thorner and Ranadive (1985) *op cit*.

31   Standing, 'Resources, wages and power'.

32   Ibid.

33   Census of India, 1981.

34   For the debate on the informal sector see J.K. Hart (1973) 'Informal income opportunities and urban employment in Ghana', *Journal of Modern African Studies*, 11:61-89; J. Weeks (1975) 'Policies for expanding employment in the informal sector of developing economies', *International Labour Review* (Jan.:1-17); R. Bromley and C. Gerry (eds) (1979), *Casual Work and Poverty in Third World Cities* (Wiley, London); J. Harris (1986) 'The working poor and the labour aristocracy in a South Indian City: descriptive and analytical account', *Modern Asian Studies*, 20(2):231-83.

35   Census of India, 1981.

36   T.S. Papola (1981) *The Urban Informal Sector in a Developing Economy* (Vikas, Delhi).

37   ILO (1972) *Employment, Incomes and Equality: Strategy for Increasing Productive Employment in Kenya* (ILO, Geneva).

38   Papola, *The Urban Informal Sector in a Developing Economy*, p.113.
39   Ibid., p.114.
40   Banerjee, (1983), op.cit., p.6.
41   *Annual Activities Report of SEWA*, Ahmedabad, 1984, p.4. SEWA members pay an annual union subscription of 5 rupees.
42   R. Jhabvala (n.d.) *We, the Self Employed* (SEWA, Ahmedabad).
43   M. Mies (1982) *The Lace Makers of Narsapur: Indian Housewives Produce for the World Market* (Zed Press, London); J. Sebstad (1982) *Struggle and Development among Self-employed Women: Report on the Self-Employed Women's Association, Ahmedabad, India* (Agency for International Development, Washington, DC).
44   Sebstad, *Struggle and Development*, passim.
45   See Jhabvala, *Closing Doors*.
46   M. Roldan (1985) 'Industrial outworking: struggles for the reproduction of working class families and gender subordination', in N. Redclift and E. Minigione (eds), *Beyond Employment, Household, Gender and Subsistence* (Blackwell, Oxford).
47   At 1986 rates, 17 rupees=£1.
48   Mies, *The Lace Makers of Narsapur*.
49   On the handicrafts industry in North India in relation to women, see A. Weston (1987), 'Women and handicraft production in North India', in H. Afshar (ed.), *Women, State and Ideology: Studies from Africa and Asia* (Macmillan, London), pp.173-85.
50   J. Everett and M. Savara (1985) 'Institutional credit as a strategy towards self-reliance for petty commodity producers in India' [in this volume.]
51   See S. Mitter (1986) *Common Fate, Common Bond: Women in the Global Economy* (Pluto Press, London).
52   *Rotis* are flat, unleavened bread.
53   This does not mean that women are not entrepreneurs in Gujarat. There are certainly cases, and some famous examples, of women's business acumen, like Liljat Papad, the makers of papadums for a world market.
54   The Leicester Outwork Campaign organises and advises outworkers in Leicester and campaigns for a better legal and economic status for outworkers generally.

SELECTED BIBLIOGRAPHY

Afshar, H. (ed.) (1987) *Women, State and Ideology* (Macmillan, London).

Afshar, H and Agarwal, B. (eds) (1989) *Women, Poverty and Ideology in Asia* (Macmillan, London).

Agarwal, R.B.L. (1982) 'Concessional finance, do weaker sections benefit?' *Economic Times* (Bombay), 10 Nov. and 16 Aug. 1981.

Agarwal, Bina (1985) 'Women and technological change in agriculture: the Asian and African experience', in Iftikar Ahmed (ed.), *Technology and Rural Women: Conceptual and Empirical Issues* (George Allen and Unwin, London).

Allovla, M. (1987) *The Colonial Harem* (Manchester).

Abu-Lughod, L. (1988) *Veiled Sentiments* (Berkeley, CA).

Angel, A. and Macintosh, F. (1987) *The Tiger's Milk: Women in Nicaragua* (Virago, London).

Anthias, F. and Yuval Davis, N. (eds) (1989) *Women, Nation-State* (Macmillan, London).

Azari, F. (1983) *Women in Iran, the Conflict with Fundamentalist Islam* (London).

Barker, D. and Allen, S. (eds) (1976) *Dependence and Exploitation in Work and Marriage* (London).

Bayat-Phillip, Mongol (1978) 'Women and revolution in Iran', in Lois Beck and Nikki Keddie (eds), *Women in the Muslim World* (Cambridge, MA, Harvard University Press).

Beneria, L. (1981) 'Conceptualising the labor force: the underestimation of women's economic activities', pp.10–28 in N. Nelson (ed.), *African Women in the Development Process* (Frank Cass, London).

Beneria, Lourdes and Sen Gita (1981) 'Accumulation, reproduction and women's role in economic development: Boserup revisited', *Signs Journal of Women in Culture and Society*: 279–98.

Bennoune, M. (1988) *The Making of Contemporary Algeria 1930–1967* (Cambridge).

Boserup, E. (1970) *Women's Role in Economic Development* (London).

Bratton, M. (1986) 'Farmer organizations and food production in Zimbabwe', *World Development,* 14(3):367–84.

Bravdel, F. (1984) *Civilisation and Capitalism*, (London).

Breman, Jan (1976) 'A dualistic labour system? a critique of the informal sector concept', *Economic and Political Weekly*, 27 Nov., 4 and 11 Dec., 1870–6, 1905–8.

Bromley, Ray (1978) 'Introduction – the urban informal sector: why is it worth discussing?' *World Development*, 6 (9–10):1033–9.

Bryant, C. (ed.) (1988) *Poverty, Policy and Food Security in Southern Africa* (Boulder, CO, Lynne Riener Publishers; London, Mansell Publishing Ltd).

Bukh, J. (1979) *The Village Woman in Ghana* (Uppsala).

Buvinic, M. (1986) 'Projects for women in the Third World: explaining their misbehaviour', *World Development*, 14(5):653–64.

Chanock, M. (1985) *Law, Custom and Social Order: the Colonial Experience in Malawi and Zambia*, African Studies series 45 (Cambridge, Cambridge University Press).

Chaptis, W. and Enloe, C. (eds) (1983) *Of Common Cloth* (Amsterdam).

Cheater, A. (1981) 'Women and their participation in commercial agricultural production: the case of medium-scale freehold in Zimbabwe', *Development and Change*, 12: 349–77.

Chipande, G.H.R. (1987) 'Innovation adoption among female-headed households: the case of Malawi', *Development and Change*, 18: 315–27.

CIIR (1987) *Right to Survive – Human Rights in Nicaragua* (Catholic Institute for International Relations, London).

Clark, B.A. (1975) 'The work done by rural women in Malawi', *Eastern African Journal of Rural Development*, 8 (1–2):80–91.

Cleaver, Henry (1972) 'The contradictions of the Green Revolution', *Monthly Review*, 24(2).

Cleveland, D.A. and Soleri, D. (1987) 'Household gardens as a development strategy', *Human Organization*, 46 (3):259–70.

Cloud, K. (1985) 'Women's productivity in agricultural households: How can we think about it? What do we know?' pp.11–35 in J. Monson and M. Kalb (eds), *Women as Food Producers in Developing Countries*, (Berkeley, UCLA African Studies Center African Studies Association/OEF International).

Crehan, K. (1983) 'Women and development in North Western Zambia: from producer to housewife', *Review of African Political Economy*, 27/28: 51–66.

Cutrufelli, Maria (1983) *Women of Africa* (Zed Press, London).

Davidoff, L. and Hall, C. (1987) *Family Fortunes* (London).

De Groot, J. (1989) 'Sex and race in the nineteenth century, the construction of language and image', in S. Mendus and J. Rendall (eds), *Sexuality and Subordination*, (London).

Deighton, J., Horsley, R., Stewart, S. and Cain, C. (1983) *Sweet Ramparts: Women in Revolutionary Nicaragua* (War on Want, London).

De Lamont, S. (1980) *The Sociology of Women* (London).

Dixon, R. (1978) *Rural Women at Work, Strategies for Development in South India* (Baltimore).

Dixon, R.B. (1982) 'Women in agriculture: counting the labor force in developing countries', *Population and Development Review*, 8 (3): 539–66.

Due, J.M. and Summary, R. (1982) 'Contrasts to women and development in Africa', *The Journal of Modern African Studies*, 20(1): 155–66.

Due, J.M. and White, M. (1986) 'Constraints between joint and female-headed farm households in Zambia', *Eastern African Economic Review*, 2(1):94–8.

Dupre, M.T., Hussmans, R. and Mehran, F. (1987) 'The concept and boundary of economic activity for the measurement of the economically active population', *Bulletin of Labour Statistics 1987–3*:ix-xviii.

Edward, A.C. (1953) *The Persian Carpet* (London).

Engleber, L.E., Sabry, J.H., and Beckerson, S.A. (1987) 'Production activities, food supply and nutritional status in Malawi', *The Journal of Modern African Studies*, 25(1):139–47.

Everett, Jana and Savara, Mira (1984) 'Bank loans to lower class women in Bombay: problems and prospects', *Economic and Political Weekly*, 19:M113–M119.

Everett, Jana and Savara, Mira (1984) 'Bank loans to the poor: do women benefit?' *Signs Journal of Women in Culture and Society*, 10(2).

Feldman, R. (1983) 'Women's groups and women's subordination: an analysis of policies towards rural women in Kenya', *Review of African Political Economy*, 27/28:67–85 (publ.1984).

Fieldhouse, D. (1965) *The Colonial Empires* (London).

Friedl, E. (1989) *Women of Deh-Koh* (London).

Gerry, Chris (1979) 'Small scale manufacturing and repairs in Dakar: a survey of market relations within the urban economy', in Ray Bromley and Chris Gerry (eds), *Casual Work and Poverty in Third World Cities* (John Wiley, New York) pp.229–50.

Godelin, M. (1977) *Perspectives in Marxist Anthropology* (Cambridge).

Government of Malaysia (1986) *Fifth Malaysia Plan 1986–1990* (Government Printers, Kuala Lumpur).

Graham-Brown, S. (1986) *Palestinians and Their Society* (London).

Guyer, J.I. and Peters, P.E. (1987) 'Introduction' (to special issue on 'Conceptualizing the Household'), *Development and Change*, 18(1):197–214.

Haller, J. (1971) *Outcasts from Evolution* (Urbana, IL).

Harris, H. (1983) 'War and reconstruction: women in Nicaragua', in O. Harris (ed.), *Latin American Women* (Minority Rights Group, London).

Harris, H. (1984) 'Women in struggle: Nicaragua', in *Third World Quarterly*, 5(4):899–908.

Harris, John (1982) 'Character of an urban economy: small scale production and labour markets in Coimbatore', *Economic and Political Weekly*, 5 and 12 June:945–54, 993–1002.

Hart, Gillian (1987) 'The mechanisation of Malaysian rice production: will petty producers survive?', Working paper (World Employment Programme Research, International Labour Office, Geneva).

Henn, J.K. (1983) 'Feeding the cities and feeding the peasants: what role for Africa's women farmers?', *World Development*, 11(12):1043–55.

Hirschmann, D. and Vaughan, M. (1983) 'Food production and income generation in a matrilineal society: rural women in Zomba, Malawi', *Journal of Southern African Studies*, 10(1):86–99.

Hirschmann, D. and Vaughan, M. (1984) *Women Farmers of Malawi: Food Production in the Zomba District of Malawi* (Berkeley, University of California, Institute of International Studies).

Hobsbawm, E. (1975) *The Age of Capital* (London).

Hoffman, E. (1987) 'Issues concerning a possible revision of the International Classification of Status in Employment (ICSE)', *Bulletin of Labour Statistics 1987–4*:ix-xv.

Hofkin, N. and Bay, E. (eds) (1975) *Women in Africa* (Stanford, CA).

Hourani, A. (1961) *Arabic Thought in the Liberal Age* (Oxford).

House, William J. (1984) 'Nairobi's informal sector: dynamic entrepreneurs or surplus labour?' *Economic Development and Cultural Change*, 32:277–302.

International Labour Office (1972) *Employment Incomes and Equality* (ILO, Geneva).

International Labour Office (1987) *Yearbook of Labour Statistics 1987*, 47th edn (ILO, Geneva).

International Rice Research Institute (1985) *Women and Rice Farming* (Philippines).

Issavi, C. (1971) *Economic History of Iran 1800–1914* (Chicago).

Izzard, W. (1985) 'Migrants and mothers: case-studies from Botswana', *Journal of Southern African Studies*, 11(2):258–80.

Jacobs, S. (1983) 'Women and land resettlement in Zimbabwe', *Review of African Political Economy*, 27/28 33–50 (publ.1984).

Jain, Devaki (1975) *From Dissociation to Rehabilitation: Women in a Developing Economy* (ICSSR, New Delhi).

Jain, Devaki (1980) *Women's Quest for Power* (Vikas, Bombay).

Jhabvala, Renana (1984) 'Neither a complete success nor a total failure: report of a SEWA campaign to organise bidi workers', *Manushi*, 22:18–22.

Kada, Ryohei and Kada, Yukiki (1985) 'The changing role of women in Japanese agriculture: the impact of new rice technology on women's employment', in *Women in Rice Farming* (International Rice Research Institute, Philippines).

Kandiyoti, D. (1987) 'Emancipated but unliberated', *Feminist Studies*.

Kiernan, V. (1972) *The Lords of Human Kind* (London).

Kitching, G. (1980) *Class and Economic Change in Kenya* (London).

Kitching, G. (1982) *Development and Under Development in Historical Perspective* (London).

Kydd, J. and Christiansen, R. (1982) 'Structural change in Malawi since independence: consequences of a development strategy based on large-scale agriculture', *World Development*, 10(5):355–75.

Levi-Strauss, C. (1969) *The Elementary Structures of Kinship* (London).

Lewis, J. (1980) *The Politics of Motherhood* (London).

Lipsky, Michael (1980) *Street-Level Bureaucracy: Dilemmas of the Individual in Public Services* (Russel Sage Foundation, New York).

Little, P.D. and Horowitz, M.M. (1987) 'Subsistence crops *are* cash crops: some comments with illustrations from Eastern Africa', *Human Organization*, 46(3):254–58.

Lorimer, D. (1978) *Colour, Class and the Victorians* (London).

McMillian, J. (1981) *Housewife or Harlot* (New York).

Millman, M. and Kanter, R. (eds) (1975) *Another Voice* (New York).

Mitchell, T. (1988) *Colonising Egypt* (Cambridge).

Molyneux, M. (1981) 'Socialist societies old and new: towards women's emancipation', *Feminist Review*, 8:1–34.

Molyneux, M. (1984) 'Mobilization without emancipation: women's interests, state and revolution in Nicaragua', in *Critical Social Policy* (Summer): 59–75.

Molyneux, M. (1986) 'Women' chapter in T. Walker (ed.), *Nicaragua: the First Five Years* (Praeger Publications, New York).

Moore, H. and Vaughan, M. (1987) 'Cutting down trees: women, nutrition and agricultural change in the Northern Province of Zambia, 1920–1986', *African Affairs*, 86 (345):523–40.

Moser, Caroline O.N. (1978) 'Informal sector or petty commodity production: dualism or dependence in urban development', *World Development*, 6:1041–64.

Muntemba, S. (1982) 'Women as food producers and suppliers in the twentieth century', *Development Dialogue*, 1–2:29–50.

Nash, J. (ed.) (1983) *Women and Men in the International Division of Labour* (New York).

Nelson, Nici (1979) 'How women and men get by: the sexual division of labour in the informal sector of a Nairobi squatter settlement', in Ray Bromley and Chris Gerry (eds), *Casual Work and Poverty in Third World Cities* (John Wiley, New York), pp.283–302.

Neshat, G. (ed.) (1983) *Women and Revolution in Iran* (Boulder, CO).

Ng, Cecilia (1985) 'Gender and the division of labour: a case study', in Hing Ai Yun and R. Talib (eds), *Women and Employment in Malaysia* (Kuala Lumpur).

Ng, Cecilia (1987) 'Agricultural modernization and gender differentiation in a rural Malay community, 1983–1987', in Cecilia Ng (ed.), *Technology and Gender* (Universiti Pertania, Malaysia, Serdang).

Nicaragua Health Fund (1987) *Briefing Notes on Health in Nicaragua* (London).

Nicaragua Health Fund/Nicaragua Solidarity Campaign (1987) *Bulletin 2* (Feb.), 'No more angels' (article on midwives); *Bulletin 3*, 'Women and Health', p.8; *Bulletin 4* (Sept.), 'A Good Day's Work' (article on vaccination), pp.6–7; *Bulletin 5* (Nov.), 'Thought for food' (article on nutrition), pp.4–5.

Nicaragua Health Fund/Nicaragua Solidarity Campaign (1988) *Bulletin 8* (June), 'Health reports from Nicaragua', pp.4–5; *Bulletin 9* (Sept), 'Letter from Esteli' (article on problems in health service), pp.4–5.

Nicaragua Solidarity Campaign (1987) *Women's Network Newsletter 2*, including articles on Women's Office, AMNLAE, AMNLAE Legal Office and proposals for new constitution (London).

Nicaragua Solidarity Campaign (1988) *Women's Network Newsletter 4*, article on the new divorce law, p.1 (London).

Okali, C. (1983) *Cocoa and Kinship in Ghana* (London).

Oomen, M.A. (1980) *Banks in the Service of Weaker Sections* (New Delhi, Oxford and IBH Publishing Co.)

Osuala, J.D.C. (1987) 'Extending appropriate technology to rural African women', *Women's Studies International Forum*, 10(5):481–7.

Palmer, I. (1985) *The Impact of Agrarian Reform on Women* (Kumarian Press, West Hartford, CT).

Papola, T.S. (1980) 'Informal sector: Concept and policy', *Economic and Political Weekly*, 15 (3 May):817–24.

313

Peters, P. (1983) 'Gender, developmental cycles and historical process: a critique of recent research on women in Botswana', *Journal of Southern African Studies*, 10(1):100–22.

Peters, P. (1984) 'Women in Botswana', *Journal of Southern African Studies*, 11(1):150–3.

Purvis, B.M. (1985) 'Family nutrition and women's activities in rural Africa', *Food and Nutrition*, 11(2):28–36.

Ramirez-Horton, S. (1982) 'The role of women in the Nicaraguan revolution', in T.W. Walker (ed.), *Nicaragua in Revolution* (Praeger Publications, New York).

Randall, M. (1981) *Sandino's Daughters* (Zed Press, London).

Randall, M. (1984) *Risking a Somersault in the Air* (Solidarity Publications, San Francisco).

Regan, Carol (1985) 'Kasravi's views on the role of women', in A. Fathi (ed.), *Women and the Family in Iran* (E.J. Brill, Leiden).

Rendall, J. (1985) *Origins of Modern Feminism* (London).

Robertson, C. (1987) 'Developing economic awareness: changing perspectives in studies of African women, 1976–1985', *Feminist Studies*, 13(1):97–135.

Robertson, C. and Klein, M. (eds) (1983) *Women and Slavery in Africa* (Wisconsin).

Rodenburg, Janet (1983) *Women and Padi Farming: Sociological Study of a Village in the Kemubu Scheme* (University of Amsterdam).

Rogers, B. (1980) *The Domestication of Women* (Tavistock, London).

Rooper, A. (1987) *Fragile Victory: a Nicaraguan Community at War* (Weidenfeld and Nicolson, London).

Rosset, P. and Vandermeer, J. (1983) *The Nicaraguan Reader: Documents of a Revolution under Fire* (Grove Press, New York).

Said, E. (1978) *Orientalism* (London).

Sansarian, E. (1981) *The Women's Rights Movement in Iran* (New York).

Savane, M-A. (1981) 'Women and rural development in Africa', in International Labour Office, *Women in Rural Development: Critical Issues* (ILO, Geneva).

Savara, Mira (1981) 'Organising the Annapurna', *Bulletin of the Institute for Development Studies*, 12(3) (July):48–53.

Schumacher, Ilsa, Sebstad, J., and Buvinic, M. (1980) *Limits to Productivity: Improving Women's Access to Technology and Credit* (International Center for Research on Women, Washington DC).

Schweinitz, K. (1983) *The Rise and Fall of British India* (London).

Scott, J. *et al.* (1984) *Households and the World Economy* (London).

Scudder, T. and Colson, E. (1982) 'From welfare to development: a conceptual framework in the analysis of dislocated people', in A. Hansen and A. Oliver-Smith (eds), *Involuntary Migration and Resettlement: the Problem and Responses of Dislocated People* (Westview Press, Boulder, CO).

Sebstad, Jennefer (198–) *Struggle and Development among Self-employed Women: a Report on the Self-Employed Women's Association Ahmedabad, India* (United States Agency for International Development Office of Urban Development, Washington, DC).

Seers, D. (ed.) (1981) *Dependency Theory: a Critical re-assessment* (London).

Shaarwi, H. (1986) *Harem Years* (London).

Shuster, Morgan (1968) *The Strangling of Persia* (New York).

Sibanda, B.M.C. (1986) 'Impacts of agricultural microprojects on rural development: lessons from two projects in the Zambezi Valley', *Land Use Policy*, 3(4):311–29.

Smith, B. (1981) *Ladies of the Leisure Class* (Princeton, NJ).

Smith, T. (1981) *The Pattern of Imperialism* (Cambridge).

Steegmuller, F. (1984) *Flaubert in Egypt: a Sensibility on Tour* (London).

Stokes, E. (1978) *The Peasant and the Raj*, (London).

Sugiyama, Y. (1987) 'Maintaining a life of subsistence in the Bemba Village', *Africa Study Monographs*, Supplementary issue 6, pp.15–32.

Sundar, Pushpa (1983) 'Women's employment and organization modes', *Economic and Political Weekly*, 18 (26 Nov.):M171–M176.

Swantz, M. (1985) *Women in Development, a Creative Role Denied* (London).

Tabari, A. and Yeganeh, N. (compilers) (1982) *In the Shadow of Islam* (Zed Press, London).

Tucker, J. (1987) *Women in Nineteenth Century Egypt* (Cambridge).

United Nations, Department of International and Economic Affairs (1987) *Demographic Yearbook 1985*, 37th issue (United Nations, New York).

Walker, T.W. (ed.) (1985) *Nicaragua: the First Five Years* (Praeger Publications, New York).

Walker, T.W. (1986) *Nicaragua: Land of Sandino*, 2nd ed. revised and updated (Westview Press, New York).

Wallerstein, I. (1974) *The Modern World System* (London).

Weeks, John (1975) 'Policies for expanding employment in the informal urban sector of developing economies', *International Labour Review*, 91(1) (Jan.):1–13.

White, Ben (1985) 'Women and the modernization of rice agriculture: some general issues and a Javanese case study', in *Women and Rice Farming* (International Rice Research Institute, Philippines).

White, D. (1985) *Aren't I a Woman?* (New York).

Wright, M.C. (1957) *The Last Stand of Chinese Conservatism* (Stanford, CA).

Young, K., Wolhowitz, C. and McCallogh, R. (eds) (1981) *Of Marriage and the Market*, Conference of Socialist Economist (CSE), London.

Youssef, N. (1974) *Women and Work in Developing Societies* (Berkeley, University of California).

NOTES ON CONTRIBUTORS

Haleh Afshar was born and brought up in Iran and educated in York and Cambridge. She teaches politics and women's studies at the University of York. She worked as a civil servant and a journalist in Iran before the revolution and remains actively involved in Iranian politics. Her research interests are centred on Islam and Iran. She has also been working with Muslim women in West Yorkshire. She is a founder member of the Development Studies Association's Women and Development study group and is its Joint Convenor, as well as a member of the Council of the British Society for Middle Eastern Studies. She has edited *Iran, a Revolution in Turmoil* (1985, reprinted 1989), *Women, Work and Ideology* (1985), *Women, State and Ideology* (1987) and, with Bina Agarwal, *Women, Poverty and Ideology in Asia* (1990).

Bina Agarwal is Professor at the Institute of Economic Growth in Delhi. She was educated at the Universities of Cambridge and Delhi. She has been a Visiting Fellow at the Institute of Development Studies, and a Research Fellow at the Science Policy Research Unit, both at the University of Sussex. She is currently the Bunting Fellow at the Bunting Institute, Harvard University. Bina Agarwal has written extensively on rural development, technological change in agriculture, the fuelwood and environmental crisis and the position of women in India and other Third World countries. She is the author of *Mechanization in India: an Analytical Study based on the Punjab* (1983) and *Cold Hearths and Barren Slopes: the Woodfuel Crisis in the Third World* (1986), the editor of *Structures of Patriarchy, State Community and Household in Modernising Asia* (1988), and with Haleh Afshar *Women, Poverty and Ideology in Asia* (1990).

Anne Akeroyd is a Lecturer at the Department of Sociology, Centre for Women's Studies and Centre for Southern African Studies at the University of York. Her current main interests are in the anthropology of gender, women in southern Africa, the ethics of social research and its implication for information technology for research practice. Her recent publications have been, in the areas of research, ethics of social research and the implications of data protection laws for social research methods. She is Chairperson of the Subcommittee on Ethics for the Association of Social Anthropologists of the Commonwealth, a member of the councils of the Royal Anthropological Society and of the African Studies Association of the UK and of the Standing Committee on Library Materials on Africa.

Delia Davin teaches at the Department of East Asian Studies, University of Leeds. She taught in Beijing from 1963 to 1965 and worked as a translator there from 1975 to 1976. She has written extensively on women and the family in China and her publications include *Women-Work: Women and the Party in Revolutionary China* (1976, reprinted 1978) and is the co-editor of *Chinese Lives: an Oral History of Contemporary China* (1988, reprinted 1989).

Carolyne Dennis taught and did research for seventeen years in Cameroon and Nigeria rural industrialisation, the labour market for women, and the provision of health and planning systems. She is now a Lecturer at the Project Planning Centre at the University of Bradford and is doing research on the labour market for women in West Yorkshire and a study of the institutional context within which Third World planners take decisions. Carolyne Dennis is the joint convenor of the Development Studies Association's Women and Development Study Group.

Jana Everett is an Associate Professor of Political Science at the University of Colorado at Denver. She has written widely on women, development and social change, and her publications include *Women and Social Change in India*. Jana Everett and Mira Savara are currently writing a book about their three years' study on 'Women and organisation in the informal sector – a study of five occupations in Bombay city'.

Joanna de Groot was born in 1947. She went to secondary school in London and was an undergraduate and graduate student at Oxford University. Since 1974 she has taught history, and since 1984 women's studies at York University. She has a long-standing interest in the Middle East and India, and has had periods of work, travel and research in Iran. Her doctoral dissertation was on regional socio-economic development and its political consequences in south-east Iran between *c.* 1850 and 1914. She is currently completing a book on the social history of religious politics in Iran, *c.* 1870-1980. Her other main sphere of interest is in feminism and women's studies, and she has written on relations between ideological and material aspects of women's situation. She has recently completed an article-length study of the interactive development of racial and sexual ideology in nineteenth century western Europe. Her teaching interests include women's history, imperialism and racism, the role of theory and ideology in historical/social enquiry, developments in Marxist and feminist thought, and the role of women in socialist labour movements.

Le Thi Nham Tuyet is Professor of Ethnology, currently Visiting Fellow at the Southeast Asia Programme, Cornell University. She is a member of the Academic Council of Research Centre on Women of the Vietnam Committee for Social Sciences. She is the Vice-Director of the Ministry of Higher Education and Secondary Vocation Training's Research Programme on Women in Higher Education. In addition to research on the history,

317

culture sociology and ideology of Vietnamese women and family, Le Thi Nham Tuyet's research interests include the ethnological studies of the Viet people, the Kinh majority population, with special reference to the historical evolution of traditional culture and ideology.

Leena Mehendale gained her M.Sc. in Physics in 1972 from the University of Patna. She joined the Indian Administrative Service in 1974 and has since then worked in the State of Maharashtra in various government posts, such as Collector and Chief Executive Officer in the districts and as deputy and joint secretary in the Departments of Education, Agriculture and Industry.

Cecilia Ng Choon Sim was educated at Swarthmore College, Pennsylvania (BA), Harvard University (N.Ed.), and the University of Kuala Lumpur (Ph.D.). She is Senior Lecturer and the Co-ordinator of the Women's Studies Unit at the Centre for Extension and Continuing Education, Pertanian University Serdang, Malaysia. Cecilia Ng is also a committee member of the Malaysian Social Science Association, the Acting Secretary of the Federation of Family Planning Associations of Malaysia, Secretary of the Institute of Social Analysis, Adviser to the Catholic Students' Society and a member of the Steering Committee and South-east Asia Representative on the Asian Women Research Action Network, and a member of Women's Development collective and the Malaysian Support Group of the Singapore ISA Detainees.

Rohini P.H. was born in Sri-Lanka in 1948 and spent the early part of her life there. Her education was completed in Britain, where she obtained a degree in Psychology and Physiology at Oxford University. She married an Indian and came with him in 1979 to Bombay, where her home has been ever since. She has coordinated research projects on 'Working class women and working class families in Bombay' and 'Women, work organisation and struggle' and helped to set up the 'Forum against Oppression of Women' and The Women Centre. Her work in the Union Research Group has brought her into close contact with women workers and unionists. She has two children and is the co-author of *My Life is One long Struggle: Women, Work, Organisation and Struggle*, (Belgium, 1984) and *Beyond Multinationals Management Policy and Bargaining Relationships in International Companies* (forthcoming).

Mira Savara is a research consultant, freelance researcher, journalist and activist. She obtained her Ph.D. from the University of Bombay. She is currently writing on a variety of issues including health and reproduction, prostitution and sexuality, credit and development and her publications include *Changing Trends in Women's Employment – a Case Study of Textile Industry in Bombay*. She co-ordinates Shakti, a non-profit-making women's research and resource centre, and is currently co-authoring a book with Jana Everett.

Mary Stead was educated at Oxford. She received her BA in Geography in 1970, an MA from Liverpool in Latin American Studies in 1982 and an MA from Bradford in Women Studies in 1984. Mary Stead works as a supply teacher in Sheffield. She is an active member of Latin American Solidarity Groups working with Nicaragua and El Salvador. She has also been on several visits to Nicaragua, both as a researcher and an interpreter for Nicaraguan women's groups. Mary Stead spent six months in Nicaragua on a research project on women working in the tobacco industry in Esteli, northern Nicaragua, and was active in the 'twinning' between Sheffield and Esteli.

Sallie Westwood teaches at Leicester University, Department of Adult Education. Her doctoral work, for Cambridge University, was on class formation in Ghana, and recently her research has been in urban India and in Britain with the Gujarati populations. She is currently working on health issues. Sallie Westwood is the author of *All Day Every Day, Factory and Family in the Making of Women's Lives*, 1985, and the joint editor of *Enterprising Women, Ethnicity, Economy and Gender Relations*, 1982.

INDEX

Index